SPANISH

for

LAW ENFORCEMENT

PATRICIA RUSH

Ventura College

PATRICIA HOUSTON

Pima Community College

ROBERT CAMARILLO

Professor of Criminal Justice, Emeritus
Ventura College

GILBERTO SERRANO

Assistant Professor of Spanish and French
Columbus State Community College

PEARSON

Prentice
Hall

UPPER SADDLE RIVER, NEW JERSEY 07458

Library of Congress Cataloging-in-Publication Data

Rush, Patricia, 1948–
    Spanish for law enforcement / Patricia Rush, Patricia Houston.
        p. cm—(Spanish at work series)
    Includes bibliographical references and index.
    ISBN 0-13-140133-5 (alk. paper)
    1. Spanish language—Conversation and phrase books (for police)
    I. Houston, Patricia, 1948– II. Title. III. Series.

PC4120.P64R87 2004
468.3'421'0243632—dc22   2004019643

SENIOR ACQUISITIONS EDITOR: *Bob Hemmer*
EDITORIAL ASSISTANT: *Pete Ramsey*
SR. DIRECTOR OF MARKET DEVELOPMENT: *Kristine Suárez*
DIRECTOR OF EDITORIAL DEVELOPMENT *Julia Caballero*
PRODUCTION SUPERVISION: *Nancy Stevenson*
COMPOSITION/FULL-SERVICE PROJECT MGMT: *Katie Ostler & Sandy Reinhard, Black Dot Group*
ASST. DIRECTOR OF PRODUCTION: *Mary Rottino*
SUPPLEMENTS EDITOR: *Meriel Martinez Moctezuma*
MEDIA EDITOR: *Samantha Alducin*
MEDIA PRODUCTION MANAGER: *Roberto Fernandez*
PREPRESS AND MANUFACTURING MANAGER: *Brian Mackey*
PREPRESS AND MANUFACTURING ASSISTANT MANAGER: *Mary Ann Gloriande*
INTERIOR DESIGN: *Javier Amador-Peña*
LINE ART COORDINATOR: *Maria Piper*
ILLUSTRATOR: *Steve Mannion*
EXECUTIVE MARKETING MANAGER: *Eileen B. Moran*
PUBLISHER: *Phil Miller*

Photo Acknowledgments appear on p. XV, which constitute a continuation of the copyright page.

© 2005 by Pearson Education, Inc.
Upper Saddle River, NJ 07458

Printed in the United States of America

ISBN 0-13-140133-5

Pearson Education LTD., *London*
Pearson Education Australia PTY, Limited, *Sydney*
Pearson Education Singapore, Pte. Ltd.
Pearson Education North Asia Ltd., *Hong Kong*
Pearson Education Canada, Ltd., *Toronto*
Pearson Educación de México, S.A. de C.V.
Pearson Education—Japan, *Tokyo*
Pearson Education Malaysia, Pte. Ltd.
Pearson Education, *Upper Saddle River*, New Jersey

Las Patricias ofrecen la serie Spanish at Work *a los que se dedican a hacer lo mejor posible en su trabajo por medio de usar el español para alcanzar a todos.*

A mi Tocaya: Salud, dinero y amor...

Para comenzar 1

¡Por aquí, por favor!

Los saludos y
 las despedidas 3

El abecedario/el alfabeto 4

Lección 1 16

En la ciudad

Módulo 1

- El vecindario 17
- Telling time: *La hora* 20
- ¿Cómo es? 22
- Describing yourself and others:
  Ser + *adjetivos* 25

Lección 2 45

En la carretera

Módulo 1

- En la calle 46
- Naming and describing: *Más sobre los adjetivos* 49
- El tráfico y las infracciones 52
- Talking about present activities:
  Los verbos que terminan en **-ar** 55

Lección 3 74

En mi barrio

Módulo 1

- La vigilancia 75
- Activities in progress: *El presente progresivo* 78
- La vida familiar y la vida loca 80
- Ways of being: **Ser** vs. **estar** 82

Los números 0–100 5

El calendario:
* Los días de la semana 8

* Los meses del año 10
* La fecha 11

Los pronombres
personales 12

Expresiones de cortesía 13

Módulo 2

* Los testigos 27
* Describing things:
  Los artículos 30
* ¿Quiénes son? 33
* Asking for information:
  Las preguntas 35

Síntesis

* A escuchar 41
* A conversar 41
* A leer 42
* A escribir 42

Algo más

* Ventana cultural:
  Los apellidos
  hispanos 43
* A buscar 44
* A conocer:
  Apodos comunes 44

Módulo 2

* ¿Multa o advertencia? 57
* Talking about present activities:
  Los verbos que terminan en
  -er, -ir 60
* ¡Está borracha! 62
* Physical conditions: *Expresiones*
  *con **tener** y **estar*** 65

Síntesis

* A escuchar 70
* A conversar 71
* A leer 71
* A escribir 71

Algo más

* Ventana cultural:
  Los amigos no dejan que
  sus amigos manejen
  borrachos 72
* A buscar 73
* A conocer: MADD llega a
  la comunidad latina 73

Módulo 2

* La guerra de pandillas 85
* Telling what you are going to
  do: *El verbo **ir** y el futuro*
  inmediato 88
* Soplón 89
* More activities in the present:
  Verbos irregulares en el
  presente 92

Síntesis

* A escuchar 96
* A conversar 96
* A leer 97
* A escribir 98

Algo más

* Ventana cultural:
  Graffiti 98
* A buscar 99
* A conocer: Leroy D. Baca,
  Sheriff, Los Angeles
  County 100

Lección 4 101

La drogas

Módulo 1

- La conexión   102
- Indicating relationships:
  Los adjetivos posesivos   105
- La compra   107
- Describing daily activities:
  *Los verbos con cambios de
  raíz*   110

Lección 5 126

¡Emergencia!

Módulo 1

- Una llamada al 911   127
- Making requests: *Los mandatos
  formales*   130
- La escena del accidente   132
- Los mandatos irregulares/con
  cambios ortográficos/con
  pronombres de objeto
  indirecto   135

Lección 6 152

Repaso I

Lección 1: En la ciudad   153
- La hora
- **Ser** + adjetivos
- Los artículos
- Las preguntas

Lección 2: En la carretera   156
- Más sobre los adjetivos
- Los verbos que terminan en
  -ar
- Los verbos que terminan en **-er,
  -ir**

Módulo 2

- Están arrestados
  112

- Comparing and contrasting:
  Los comparativos   114

- Las prioridades   117

- Comparing and contrasting:
  Los superlativos   120

Síntesis

- A escuchar   123

- A conversar   123

- A leer   124

- A escribir   124

Algo más

- Ventana cultural: Spanglish
  —is it a language?   124

- A buscar   125

- A conocer: Enrique
  Camarena   125

Módulo 2

- Los desastres   137

- Expressing negative ideas:
  *Las expresiones afirmativas y
  negativas* 140

- Un incendio   142

- Más sobre las expresiones
  negativas   144

Síntesis

- A escuchar   148

- A conversar   148

- A leer   149

- A escribir   149

Algo más

- Ventana cultural: La imagen
  de la policía   150

- A buscar   151

- A conocer:
  Rich Gonzales   151

- Expresiones con **tener** y
  estar

Lección 3: En mi barrio   158

- El presente progresivo

- **Ser** y **estar**

- El verbo **ir** y el futuro
  inmediato

- Verbos irregulares en el
  presente

Lección 4: Las drogas   160

- Los adjetivos posesivos

- Los verbos con
  cambios de raíz

- Los comparativos

- Los superlativos

*Lección 5:
¡Emergencia!*   163

- Los mandatos
  formales

- Los mandatos
  irregulares/con
  cambios ortográficos/
  con pronombres de
  objeto indirecto

- Las expresiones afirmativas
  y negativas

- Más sobre las expresiones
  negativas

Lección 7 *166*   La policía y la
comunidad—unidas

Módulo 1

- ¡Cooperamos!   167

- Expressing generalizations,
  expectations and passive
  voice: **Se** impersonal   170

- ¡Acaban de robar mi auto!   171

- The recent past: **Acabar de** +
  infinitivo   174

Lección 8 *191*   La violencia doméstica

Módulo 1

- Me golpea, me viola, me
  amenaza. . . pero me ama   192

- Describing daily routines: Los
  verbos reflexivos   194

- Nos apoyamos   196

- More on reflexive verbs: Los verbos
  recíprocos   198

Lección 9 *215*   Delitos

Módulo 1

- Pregunte a la policía   216

- Expressing hope or desire:
  Introducción breve al subjuntivo
  219

- La prostitución   221

- Giving advice or suggestions:
  More on the subjunctive
  (Más sobre el subjuntivo)   224

Módulo 2

- Me gusta este barrio   176
- Expressing likes and dislikes: **Gustar**   178
- El botín   180
- Numbers: *De cien a millones; los números ordinales*   183

Síntesis

- A escuchar   187
- A conversar   188
- A leer   188
- A escribir   188

Algo más

- Ventana cultural: El machismo   189
- A buscar   190
- A conocer: Tnte. Margarita Moris Rivera   190

Módulo 2

- El abuso de ancianos   200
- Expressing knowledge and familiarity: **Saber** y **conocer**   203
- Me acosa   205
- Receiving the action of a verb: *El objeto directo*   207

Síntesis

- A escuchar   211
- A conversar   211
- A leer   212
- A escribir   212

Algo más

- Ventana cultural: La diversidad entre hispanoamericanos   213
- A buscar   214
- A conocer: Carlos Álvarez, Director de la Policía de Miami-Dade   214

Módulo 2

- Los juegos de azar   226
- Giving recommendations: *El subjuntivo con expresiones impersonales*   229
- Delitos de fraude: *La identidad falsa*   230
- Expressing emotion and doubt: *El subjuntivo con expresiones de emoción y duda*   233

Síntesis

- A escuchar   237
- A conversar   237
- A leer   238
- A escribir   238

Algo más

- Ventana cultural: El poder del crimen organizado—los cárteles   239
- A buscar   239
- A conocer: Manuel Covarrubias   239

Módulo 1

- La escena del crimen 241
- Discussing past activities: *Introducción al pretérito* 244
- La investigación 246
- More on the preterite: *Verbos irregulares* 248

Lección 10 240   *El crimen*

Módulo 1

- Pederastas sexuales 265
- Describing past situations: *El imperfecto* 267
- ¡Capturado! 269
- More on the imperfect: *Estados mentales, físicos y más* 271

Lección 11 264   *Tragedias*

Lección 12 286   *Repaso II*

Lección 7: La policía y la comunidad—¡unidas! 287
- **Se** impersonal
- **Acabar de** + infinitivo
- **Gustar**
- De cien a millones; los números ordinales

Lección 8: La violencia doméstica 289
- Los verbos reflexivos
- Los verbos recíprocos

Módulo 2

- El defensor público   250
- Relating past activities: *Verbos en **-ir** con cambios en el pretérito*   252
- El fiscal   254
- More past activities: *Usos del pretérito*   257

Síntesis

- A escuchar   260
- A conversar   260
- A leer   261
- A escribir   262

Algo más

- Ventana cultural: El poder de los latinos   262
- A buscar   263
- A conocer: Richard T. García   263

Módulo 2

- La violación por acompañante: *¡El date-rape!*   273
- Narrating in the past: *El pretérito y el imperfecto*   275
- ¡Quería suicidarse!   277
- Contrasting past tenses: *El pretérito y el imperfecto*   279

Síntesis

- A escuchar   282
- A conversar   283
- A leer   283
- A escribir   284

Algo más

- Ventana cultural: La mordida   284
- A buscar   284
- A conocer: Anthony M. Chapa   285

- **Saber** and **conocer**
- El objeto directo

Lección 9: Delitos   292

- Introducción breve al subjuntivo
- Más sobre el subjuntivo
- El subjuntivo con expresiones impersonales
- El subjuntivo con expresiones de emoción y duda

Lección 10: El crimen   294

- Introducción al pretérito
- Verbos irregulares
- Verbos en **-ir** con cambios en el pretérito
- Usos del pretérito

Lección 11: Tragedias   296

- El imperfecto
- Estados mentales, físicos y más
- El pretérito y el imperfecto
- El pretérito y el imperfecto

Preface

Purpose

One of the fastest-growing markets for Spanish-language instruction throughout the country is the field of occupational or vocational courses, either for contract training within organizations or for general student access as a regularly scheduled class. This series of materials, *Spanish at Work,* is designed to allow colleges to create and deliver pragmatic, "real-world" language and culture training programs so that students can master "need-to-know" language. It is designed for students without previous Spanish study, at the beginning level, but it also works well to reinforce background knowledge already in place for intermediate level students. *Spanish for Law Enforcement* is the fourth of this series, following *Spanish for Health Care, Spanish for Business* and *Spanish for School Personnel.* Students, whether professionals already working in the field or career/goal-oriented students in an occupational training program, are presented key vocabulary in a comprehensible-input format, focusing on easily mastered core expressions. Art, realia, photographs, and brief dialogues reinforce needed terms, supported by concise grammar explanations. In class, students will practice communicative survival using key vocabulary essential to each context to enable them to utilize their Spanish in the real world at work.

Highlights of the Program

Spanish for Law Enforcement has ten chapters plus a brief preliminary lesson and two review chapters. Each lesson has two modules, each with a vocabulary segment and a grammar segment using the context-appropriate vocabulary. The lessons end with the vocabulary list and synthesis activities combining listening, speaking, reading, and writing. All exercises move from mechanical to production-oriented, following the logical progression of language acquisition. The final section, *Algo más,* features a culturally informative reading and sends the student out to the real world to look for material tied to the theme of the chapter.

Organization of the Text

- **Vocabulary presentation:** Each of the two modules presents key vocabulary by means of art, realia, photographs, and brief dialogues. The inclusion of two separate spreads in each module allows for manageable amounts of easily-mastered, core expressions pertinent to each occupational area.

* **¡OJO!** The need for street vocabulary in the area of Law Enforcement has compelled us to include slang often considered inappropriate for the formal classroom, yet essential in the real-world environment.

* **Grammar approach:** Grammar practice is embedded automatically in context, not called out as mastery exercises. In class, students will focus on communicative survival using basic vocabulary essential to the topic to enable them to utilize their Spanish in the real world of their job environment. Concise grammar explanations, two per module, are presented in "chunks."

* **Vocabulary summary:** Each module's vocabulary is listed by function—nouns, verbs, adjectives, and other expressions. The glossary at the end of the book lists the lesson in which the item was introduced, intended as a convenient reference, especially for preview/review.

* *Síntesis:* Skills and topics are interwoven at the end of each chapter into a series of skill-building and skill-chaining activities that bring together the chapter vocabulary, structures and cultural content. In recognition of the increased interest in Applied Spanish courses across the country, each of the ten regular lessons concludes with a task-based module in which students use Spanish in a realistic, applied way. Modules focus on a variety of fields where students may be likely to seek their future or current careers. Art, articles, and other documents emphasize the usefulness and vitality of Spanish in today's world.

   A escuchar develops students' ability to understand spoken Spanish in a variety of authentic contexts.

   A conversar includes open-ended speaking activities based on naturally-occurring discourse situations. Students learn to express and discuss their own needs and interests.

   A leer introduces basic readings for students to become independent readers, able to understand the general meaning of a text as well as to come away with an understanding of specific information from it.

   A escribir provides activities in which students learn to compose messages and memos, paragraphs, and publicity announcements.

* *Algo más:* This section focuses on contemporary cultural issues related to the chapter theme. The **Ventana cultural** reading exposes the student to key information. A broad variety of contemporary topics is featured, appropriate to the lesson's context. *A buscar,* immediately following, then guides students to gather information to enhance their own connection to this topic. *A conocer* introduces students to prominent Hispanics succeeding in the occupational field and to in-depth cultural close-ups related to education.

Components

* Text

* Audio CD with available tapescript, including listening segments, dialogues, and vocabulary lists

* Instructor's Resource Manual, including tests

* Interactive, text-specific Website, including tests and links

For the student

Welcome! *Spanish at Work* has been designed for YOU to use in your daily work situation, improving your ability to interact with your colleagues and the general public. You'll find a user-friendly text, combining appropriate vocabulary and concise grammar explanations combined with realia from today's world to lead you into the real world of *Spanish for Law Enforcement*. We want you to be able to react to your daily job environment, meeting your needs with hands-on language and giving you enough to survive in the law enforcement area without loading you down with translation exercises. Our real-life context is intended to transfer directly to your daily "need-to-know" activities. We encourage you to jump right in and join us.

Acknowledgments

First, *gracias* to all who have helped us to bring **Spanish for Law Enforcement** into existence. While it is clear that core language courses continue to be the foundation of our profession, the demand for pragmatic, rapid-acquisition courses is exploding. We want to acknowledge our colleagues and our students who have shown us beyond a doubt the unquestionable need for this series. Their insight, support, and collaboration have been a powerful force in the creation of these texts.

We are grateful to the members of the Spanish teaching community for their invaluable comments and suggestions on everything from the sequence of material to the final versions of the lessons. Gilberto Serrano, Bob Camarillo, and Rebecca Ogden advised us from our initial brainstorm list on, providing valuable input based on their extensive background in law enforcement. We also thank our reviewers José Alentado, David & Collette Dees, Luis Latoja, Marsh Mawhirter, David Diego Rodríguez, Tommy Sickels, Neil Tiller, and Yvonne Unnold.

Our Prentice Hall partners enabled the vision to become reality and we are grateful. We offer special thanks to Phil Miller, Publisher; Bob Hemmer, Senior Acquisitions Editor; Pete Ramsey, Editorial Assistant; and Eileen Moran, Marketing Manager. Our appreciation extends to Katie Ostler, Editorial Project Manager at PreMediaONE, a Black Dot Group Company.

Our developmental editor, Mariam Rohlfing, deserves more thanks than we can ever say. Her vision, language skill, organization, and attention to detail keep us focused on our task— she should be listed as a co-author!

We appreciate the expert input provided by Bob Camarillo and Gilberto Serrano who read our manuscript to be sure we provided accurate information.

We owe *besos y abrazos* to our families and friends for enduring our long hours, especially to Bud and Bob. An occasional dialogue is based on reality, so if you recognize yourself in any situation, we hope you like your portrait!

Credits

Page 43: Patrick Osio/The Connection; San Diego Metropolitan; **page 54:** Patricia Rush; **page 64:** Patricia Rush; **page 99:** Patricia Houston; **page 134:** Patricia Houston; **page 139:** American Red Cross of Ventura County, printing by Farmers Insurance; **page 143:** Patricia Rush; **page 151:** http://www.9news.com/latino/gonzales_rich.htm; **page 169:** NCPC (National Crime Prevention Council) 1000 Connecticut Avenue, NW, 13th Floor, Washington, DC 20036; **page 173:** LoJack en Puerto Rico www.lojackpr.com; **page 182:** Courtesy 88-Crime, Tucson, AZ; **page 198:** Reprinted with the permission of the Arizona Criminal Justice Commission; **page 202:** California Attorney General's Office; Inclusion of this material in no way represents an endorsement of this textbook; **page 212:** Reprinted with the permission of the Arizona Criminal Justice Commission; **page 213:** Reprinted with the permission of the Arizona Criminal Justice Commission; **page 218:** The National Center for Missing and Exploited Children: www.missingkids.com; **page 256:** Patricia Rush

¡Por aquí, por favor!

Los saludos y las despedidas

El abecedario/el alfabeto

Los números 0–100

El calendario:
- los días de la semana
- los meses del año
- la fecha

Los pronombres personales

Expresiones de cortesía

¡Bienvenidos!

Buenos días, if you are reading this in the morning.

Buenas tardes, if you are reading this in the afternoon.

Buenas noches, if you are reading this after dark.

As a professional working in one of the many areas of law enforcement, you have recognized the growing need for basic Spanish on the job. This book will help you build a language bridge to your Spanish-speaking community members. Be aware that, because this text is geared to the use of Spanish in the workplace, we will emphasize language that reflects formal, professional relationships more than personal and familiar ones, unless we are focusing on children. The formality or informality of address is an extremely important aspect of the Spanish language and the variety of cultures it represents.

In this preliminary chapter, we will show you such basic—and critical—Spanish points as:

* Greetings, courtesies, and amenities,
* Pronunciation and listening strategies,
* Using *cog*nates (words that you can re*cog*nize from one language to the other),
* The important cultural courtesies implied in polite or formal address and informal address,
* And enough about days, months, and numbers so that you can *immediately* begin to work with identification, provide telephone numbers and addresses, make appointments, and offer other basic information.

In addition, we will offer you some strategies to take the stress out of learning a new language and to make your study time efficient, productive—and even fun! The key to your success will be your willingness to practice and speak out loud without worrying about feeling silly and making mistakes. Mistakes are a very normal and natural part of learning a language. The more mistakes you allow yourself to make, the faster you will learn.

Ready? ¿Listos? ¡Vamos!

Los saludos y las despedidas

OFICIAL:	Buenas tardes. Soy el agente Álcaraz. ¿Cómo se llama usted?
SEÑOR:	Me llamo Pablo Fernández.
OFICIAL:	Mucho gusto, señor Fernández.
SEÑOR:	Igualmente.

POLICÍA:	Buenos días, señora. Soy Alejandro Ramírez, un oficial de la policía municipal. A sus órdenes.
MADRE:	Mucho gusto. Soy Claudia Móntez, madre de Cecilia y Marco.
POLICÍA:	Es un placer.

LA OFICIAL:	Hola, Alejandro. ¿Cómo estás hoy?
EL OFICIAL:	Regular. ¿Y tú, Ángela?
LA OFICIAL:	Muy bien, gracias. Nos vemos.
EL OFICIAL:	Hasta luego.

* Use **Buenos días** usually before noon to say *Good morning,* before lunchtime in some regions; **Buenas tardes** until dark to say *Good afternoon;* and **Buenas noches** after dark to say *Good evening* or *Goodnight.*

* Both **usted** and **tú** mean *you.* In professional settings, especially, it is important to show respect by using **usted**, unless addressing very close friends or children. Children show respect to adults by using the **usted** form.

* **Yo soy** followed by a name means *I am.* **Me llamo** followed by a name means *My name is ...* (literally: *I call myself...*) Both are proper in making introductions.

* **Mucho gusto** *(it's a pleasure)* and **igualmente** *(likewise)* are courtesies, usually accompanied by the gesture of a handshake.

Para practicar

La reunión de la asociación de vecinos.   You are a community police officer at your first meeting with a new Neighborhood Watch group. You don't know anyone yet, but you are determined to meet as many of the neighbors as you can! Lift your imaginary punch glass or Perrier in the air and walk around the room, meeting as many of the neighbors (classmates) as possible. Follow the above dialogues for guidance, and don't forget the three steps:

1. the salutation, depending on the time of day
2. the exchange of names
3. the courtesy replies and handshake

When you sit down again, write down as many of the names as you can remember.

El abecedario/el alfabeto

Spanish forms words around vowel sounds, while English forms them around consonants. Mastering these five sounds will enable you to pronounce nearly any word. The vowel sounds in Spanish are short, precise, and clear, not drawn out as in English.

Las vocales		
A	(ah)	Open your mouth and say "**Ah.**"
E	(eh)	Pet the dog.
I	(ee)	We have another me**e**ting at thr**ee**.
O	(oh)	**Oh,** no, not another meeting!
U	(oo)	**Boo,** scared ya!

¡OJO!

As in English, some letters change pronunciation in certain combinations. Note the following list:

C ca, co, cu, or c preceding consonant sound like (k).
ce, ci sound like (s).

G ga, go, gu, or g preceding consonant sound like (g).
ge, gi sound like the Spanish **j.**

R rolled or trilled when it is the first letter of a word, just like **RR.**

El abecedario

Letra	Nombre		Ejemplo
A	a		agente
B	be		bicicleta
C	ce		crimen/cerveza
D	de		droga
E	e		educación
F	efe		familia
G	ge		garaje, gente
H	hache	*always silent*	hospital
I	i		investigación
J	jota	*like English "h"*	justicia
K	ka		kilo
L	ele		licencia
M	eme		motocicleta
N	ene	*"n" sound*	narcótico
Ñ	eñe	*"ny" sound*	señores
O	o		oficial
P	pe		policía
Q	cu		quince
R	ere, erre		perdón, radio, terror
S	ese		silencio
T	te		teléfono
U	u		uniforme
V	ve (ve chica)	*"b" sound*	velocidad
W	doble ve		el walkie-talkie
X	equis		los rayos X
Y	y griega		yoga
Z	zeta	*"s" sound*	zona

* **Cognados:** As you read down the list of Spanish words on the right of the alphabet list, see how many you can recognize. Cognates are great tools to help you understand spoken and written Spanish.

Para practicar

A. Favor de contestar. Provide the appropriate information.

1. Which letter is always silent?
2. Pronounce the difference between **n** and **ñ**.
3. Which five letters form the basis for Spanish pronunciation?
4. Pronounce the five Spanish vowels.
5. What do you call words that you can recognize in two languages?

B. Entre amigos. Spell your name in Spanish, letter by letter, as a classmate writes it down. Check to see if it is correct. When it is, you write as your classmate spells his/her name. Note that it is extremely rare for Spanish speakers to "spell" words or names, as nearly everything is pronounced exactly as it is written!

MODELO: Jaime
Jota-a-i-eme-e

C. Personas famosas. Continue taking turns spelling out the names of famous people to each other—in Spanish! See how many you can get right.

Los números

Is there anything in our lives that doesn't require numbers? Well, yes, but not that much! By learning a few basic numbers now, you will have the foundation for many services in Spanish. With just a few numbers, you can give and take telephone numbers or messages and work with money. Add a few days and months and you can make appointments. Two or three more words and you are telling time!

Here we go with numbers 1–15! As you read through these, remember to use the five Spanish vowel sounds as a pronunciation guide.

0	cero	4	cuatro	8	ocho	12	doce
1	uno	5	cinco	9	nueve	13	trece
2	dos	6	seis	10	diez	14	catorce
3	tres	7	siete	11	once	15	quince

Para practicar

A. A contar. You are on DUI patrol and are testing a driver's responses. Have "the driver" count the following patterns.

1. Count from 1 to 10 in Spanish.
2. Count from 1 to 10 by 2s (2, 4, 6, etc.).
3. Count backwards from 10 to 1.
4. Count from 1 to 15.
5. Count backwards from 15 to 1.
6. Count by 3s from 1 to 15 (3, 6, 9, etc.).

B. Con un colega. Time for some arithmetic! Now, you can practice some basic addition. One of you will make up a simple arithmetic problem and await a response. Then switch roles—five times.

MODELO: E1: *5 y (and) 5 (cinco y cinco)*
E2: *10 (diez)*

Más números

After 15, numbers in Spanish are formed by addition. For example, 16 is the sum of **diez y seis,** and often it is written just that way. Also common is the one-word alternative for numbers from 16 to 29. There is no one word alternative after 30.

16	diez y seis	o	dieciséis
17	diez y siete	o	diecisiete
18	diez y ocho	o	dieciocho
19	diez y nueve	o	diecinueve
20	veinte		
21	veinte y uno	o	veintiuno
22	veinte y dos	o	veintidós
23	veinte y tres	o	veintitrés
24	veinte y cuatro	o	veinticuatro
25	veinte y cinco	o	veinticinco
26	veinte y seis	o	veintiséis
27	veinte y siete	o	veintisiete
28	veinte y ocho	o	veintiocho
29	veinte y nueve	o	veintinueve
30	treinta		
31	treinta y uno		

When counting things or objects in Spanish, the word **hay** (sounds like "eye," not "hey") can be used to indicate "there is" or "there are." Both questions "is there?" and "are there?" are simply stated with **¿Hay...?** For example:

Hay siete días en una semana.	*There are seven days in a week.*
Hay una víctima aquí.	*There is a victim here.*
¿Hay una víctima por aquí?	*Is there a victim here?*
¿Hay víctimas por aquí?	*Are there victims here?*

Para practicar

A. ¡A contar!   You are helping the victims of a minor car accident. Make sure your victims stay alert by having them count the following number patterns.

1. Count from 11 to 30.
2. Count backwards from 30 to 20.
3. Count from 1 to 30 by 5s.
4. Count from 1 to 30 by 2s.
5. Count the number of people in the room with you right now.

B. ¿Cuántos?   Oops! Another accident victim seems to be dazed. Check to see if the victim is alert and can answer the following questions—in Spanish.

MODELO: E1: *How many hours are there in a day?*
　　　　　　　 E2: *Hay veinticuatro.*

1. How many days are there in a week?
2. How many minutes are there in a half hour?
3. How many days are there in September?
4. How many days are there in February (usually)?
5. How many female students are in your Spanish class?
6. How many male students are in your Spanish class?

¡Y más números!

Learning more numbers may *seem* difficult, but they are really easy.

Los números 40–100

40	cuarenta		70	setenta
41	cuarenta y uno		80	ochenta
42	cuarenta y dos, etc.		90	noventa
50	cincuenta		100	cien
60	sesenta			

Remember, there is no one-word spelling alternative for numbers after 29.

Para practicar

A. ¡A contar! You are speculating with your partner on how many calls you will answer this week. Read the following numbers and your partner will estimate five more.

MODELO: 30

¿Treinta? No, ¡treinta y cinco!

1.	25	**4.**	35	**7.**	77
2.	15	**5.**	27	**8.**	90
3.	41	**6.**	63	**9.**	95

B. ¡Menos! You and your partner are still trying to estimate the number of calls you will answer. One of you will read the original number and the other— an optimist—will estimate five fewer!

MODELO: 100

¿Cien? No, ¡noventa y cinco!

1.	95	**5.**	73	**8.**	24
2.	80	**6.**	34	**9.**	100
3.	66	**7.**	59	**10.**	83
4.	41				

El calendario: Los días de la semana

Hay siete días en la semana:

el lunes	*Monday*	**el viernes**	*Friday*
el martes	*Tuesday*	**el sábado**	*Saturday*
el miércoles	*Wednesday*	**el domingo**	*Sunday*
el jueves	*Thursday*		

- Hispanic calendars often use Monday as the first day of the week.
- To say *on* a day, use **el** or **los**.

No hay clase **el** lunes.	*There is no class on Monday.*
No hay clase **los** lunes.	*There is no class on Mondays.*

- Days of the week are not capitalized in Spanish unless they begin a sentence or stand alone as distinct words.
- To ask what day it is, use **¿Qué día es hoy?**
- To answer, use **Hoy es (martes).**

lunes	martes	miércoles	jueves	viernes	sábado	domingo
1	2	3 Trabajo	4	5	6	7
8	9	10	11	12	13	14
15	16	17	18	19	20	21
22	23	24	25	26	27	28
29	30	31				

Para practicar

A. Los días. You have just received your work schedule for the month. For the next 30 days, you are to report for duty Wednesdays through Sundays. Use this calendar to say if you work—**Trabajo**—or don't work—**No trabajo**—on the following days.

MODELO: el cinco

El cinco es viernes. Trabajo.

1. el quince **3.** el cinco **5.** el diecisiete
2. el veintiuno **4.** el treinta **6.** el seis

B. Números. Here's a list of the days you have to work on the desk. Use the calendar to say and write the numbers of the dates in Spanish.

1. El *tres*, el _____, el _____, el _____ y el _____ son miércoles.

2. El _____, el _____, el _____ y el _____ son sábados.

3. El _____, el _____, el _____ y el _____ son viernes.

4. El _____, el _____, el _____ y el _____ son jueves.

C. En parejas. You and a partner have volunteered to help on an information hotline for an important case. You are responsible for making sure there is coverage next week Monday through Saturday. Decide which one of you will work which days and then make a list of the dates you are on and off. Use a current calendar for help.

MODELO: E1: *No trabajo el lunes.*
E2: *Yo sí trabajo el lunes.*

Los meses del año

Most of the months are cognates. As with days of the week, only use capital letters with the months if they begin a sentence.

Hay doce meses en el año:

enero	*January*	**mayo**	*May*	**septiembre**	*September*
febrero	*February*	**junio**	*June*	**octubre**	*October*
marzo	*March*	**julio**	*July*	**noviembre**	*November*
abril	*April*	**agosto**	*August*	**diciembre**	*December*

Para practicar

A. Los días festivos.   Even a busy police station loves to recognize different holidays. Write what month—or months—you would use the following decorating themes.

1. Santa Claus

2. graduations

3. the Great Pumpkin

4. fireworks and flags

5. New Year's

6. valentines and cupids

B. Fiesta de cumpleaños.   ¡Feliz cumpleaños! Circulate among your classmates and find out who else was born in the same month as you. Get them to sign next to the month. Then, report back to the class how many students you found.

MODELO: *¿Febrero? Firma, por favor. Hay cinco estudiantes con cumpleaños en febrero.*

enero	
febrero	
marzo	
abril	
mayo	
junio	
julio	
agosto	
septiembre	
octubre	
noviembre	
diciembre	

La fecha

To ask what the date is, use: **¿Cuál es la fecha de hoy?** or **¿Qué fecha es hoy?**

Use the following format to answer: **Hoy es** (día), **el** (número) **de** (mes).

Hoy es lunes, el 24 de julio.   *Today is Monday, the 24th of July.*

While ordinal number **primero** is used for the first of the month in many places, some regions will use **uno.** All other dates are given in cardinal numbers.

El primero de enero/el uno de enero   *January 1st*
El dos de enero   *January 2nd*

Para practicar

A. Días feriados.   The Court system you work for has asked you to block the following days on the calendar because all regular offices will be closed. Write a memo to the office workers telling them exactly what days they will have off. Use a current calendar to see what day each date falls on.

MODELO: 1/1

   Sábado, el primero de enero

1.   15/1
2.   12/2
3.   27/3
4.   4/7
5.   2/9
6.   31/10

B. Más cumpleaños.   Find again the people in your class who were born in the same month as you were. Then find out the rest of the date to see if any of them match yours exactly. If no one was born in the same month as you, use a family member's birthday.

MODELO: E1: *¿Cuál es la fecha de su cumpleaños?*
   E2: *El 14 de febrero.*

Los pronombres personales

Use a subject pronoun to tell who or what is doing an action. Subject pronouns can also express the familiarity or formality of relationships. Professional relationships in Spanish-speaking cultures require the courtesy of the formal term of address (**usted** and **ustedes)** to say *you*, while relationships among friends and family use the informal terms of address (**tú** for the singular form and, in Spain, **vosotros/as** for the plural form). In the professional context of law enforcement, our focus will be on using the more formal forms, unless we are focusing on communication with children.

The subject pronouns are:

Singular (one person)		Plural (more than one person)	
yo	*I*	nosotros/as	*we*
tú	*you (informal)*	(vosotros/as)	*you—plural (informal, Spain)*
usted (Ud./Vd.)	*you (formal)*	ustedes (Uds./Vds.)	*you—plural*
él	*he*	ellos	*they*
ella	*she*	ellas	*they (fem.)*

- Use nosotr**as** (*we*) if referring to an all-female group. In Spanish, if the group is all male or mixed male and female, the masculine form is used, in this case, nosotr**os.**
- Use **tú** *(informal),* **usted** *(formal),* or **ustedes** *(plural)* to mean *you* when talking *to* people.
- Use **él** *(he),* **ella** *(she),* **ellos** *(they, all masculine, or mixed),* or **ellas** *(they, feminine)* when talking *about* people.
- Subject pronouns are not necessary in Spanish as the verb form indicates the subject. You will find them used in the early lessons of this book, and then omitted unless included for emphasis or clarity.

Para practicar

A. ¿Recuerda usted? Answer the following questions about subject pronouns.

1. What information does the subject pronoun supply?
2. In a professional relationship, would you be more likely to express the subject *you* with **tú** or **usted?**
3. What subject pronoun would you use to address more than one person as *you* in most regions, whether the relationship is formal or informal?

B. ¿Quiénes?   Which subject pronoun from the list above would you use in the following situations?

MODELO: You are talking about two victims (two possibilities).
ellos or *ellas*

1.   You are talking *about* yourself.
2.   You are talking *to* a commander.
3.   You are talking *about* a colleague's daughter.
4.   You are talking *about* two Community Action Board members (two possibilities).
5.   You are talking *to* two Community Action Board members.
6.   You are talking *about* yourself and a friend.
7.   You are talking *about* the President of the United States.
8.   You are talking *to* a 7-year-old child.

C. ¡Ahora en español!   Change the following subjects to subject pronouns.

MODELO: *Usted y su amigo son inteligentes.*
Ustedes son inteligentes.

1.   *Elena y María son dedicadas.*
2.   *Susana y yo somos secretarios.*
3.   *El capitán y su secretaria son dinámicos.*
4.   *El asistente es perfeccionista.*
5.   *El muchacho es rebelde.*
6.   *Usted y su colega son inteligentes.*

Expresiones de cortesía

Use these expressions of courtesy to help establish good relations with Spanish-speaking clients.

A sus órdenes.	*At your service; may I help you?*
Por favor.	*Please.*
Gracias.	*Thank you.*
De nada.	*You're welcome.*
No hay de qué.	*You're welcome.*
Con permiso.	*Excuse me.*
Perdón, Disculpe.	*Pardon me.*
¿Mande?	*Excuse me?*

* **Con permiso** is primarily used *before* an action—leaving a room, making your way through a crowd, getting up from a table, or interrupting a conversation.
* **Perdón** is usually used *after* the action is complete—if you have accidentally bumped or jostled someone.

Para practicar

A. ¿Qué dice usted?   As a desk sergeant in a busy precinct, you interact with a wide variety of people all day long. Give the expression of courtesy that you would use in each of the following situations.

MODELO: a citizen comes to your desk
A sus órdenes.

1.   A co-worker brings you a home-grown rose.
2.   You ask a new member of the team to fill out papers.
3.   You bump into another colleague behind the crowded desk.
4.   You must interrupt the captain's meeting for an urgent phone call.
5.   A victim thanks you for your time and help.
6.   You have to leave a meeting early to attend to a parent who is waiting.

Vocabulario

Saludos y contestaciones

bien	*well*	**¿Cómo estás?**	*How are you? (familiar)*
bienvenidos	*welcome*		
buenas noches	*good evening, goodnight*	**hola**	*hello, hi*
		mal	*not well*
buenas tardes	*good afternoon*	**más o menos**	*more or less*
buenos días	*good morning*	**regular**	*so-so*
¿Cómo está Ud.?	*How are you? (formal)*		

Presentaciones

¿Cómo se llama Ud.?	*What is your name? (formal)*	**igualmente**	*likewise*
		Me llamo …	*My name is …*
¿Cómo te llamas?	*What is your name? (familiar)*	**mucho gusto**	*pleased/nice to meet you*
es un placer	*it's a pleasure*		

Despedidas

adiós	*good-bye*	**hasta luego**	*see you later*

Expresiones de cortesía

a sus órdenes	*at your service; may I help you?*	**gracias**	*thank you*
		¿Mande?	*Excuse me?*
con permiso	*excuse me*	**no hay de qué**	*you're welcome*
de nada	*you're welcome*	**perdón**	*pardon me*
Disculpe.	*Pardon me.*	**por favor**	*please*

Los pronombres personales

él	*he*	**tú**	*you (familiar)*
ella	*she*	**usted**	*you (formal)*
ellos/as	*they*	**ustedes**	*you (plural)*
nosotros/as	*we*	**yo**	*I*

Los días de la semana

¿Qué día es hoy?	*What day is today?*	**miércoles**	*Wednesday*
		jueves	*Thursday*
domingo	*Sunday*	**viernes**	*Friday*
lunes	*Monday*	**sábado**	*Saturday*
martes	*Tuesday*		

Los meses del año

el calendario	*calendar*	**mayo**	*May*
¿Cuál es la fecha de hoy?	*What's today's date?*	**junio**	*June*
		julio	*July*
¿Qué fecha es hoy?	*What's today's date?*	**agosto**	*August*
		septiembre	*September*
enero	*January*	**octubre**	*October*
febrero	*February*	**noviembre**	*November*
marzo	*March*	**diciembre**	*December*
abril	*April*		

Personas

el/la agente	*the agent*
el/la amigo/a	*friend*
el/la asistente	*assistant*
la madre	*mother*
el/la muchacho/a	*boy/girl*
el/la secretario/a	*secretary*

Otras expresiones

dedicado	*dedicated*
muy	*very*
soy	*I am*

¡OJO! Don't forget to study **los números 0–100** and **el abecedario!**

ℒECCIÓN 1

En la ciudad

Módulo 1
- El vecindario
- Telling time: *La hora*
- ¿Cómo es?
- Describing yourself and others: **Ser** + *adjetivos*

Módulo 2
- Los testigos
- Describing things: *Los artículos*
- ¿Quiénes son?
- Asking for information: *Las preguntas*

Síntesis
- A escuchar
- A conversar
- A leer
- A escribir

Algo más
- Ventana cultural: Los apellidos hispanos
- A buscar
- A conocer: Apodos comunes

Módulo 1

El vecindario

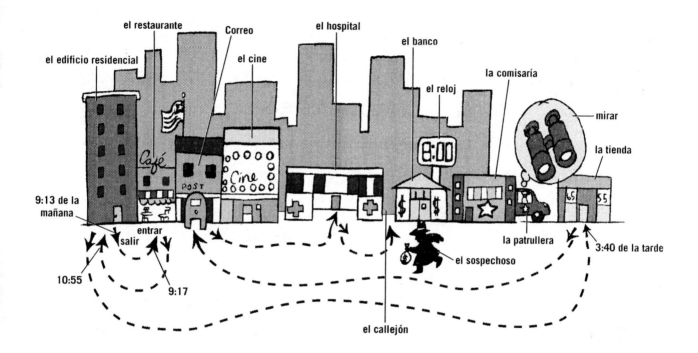

el restaurante   Correo   el hospital   el banco

el edificio residencial   el cine   la comisaría

el reloj   mirar

la tienda

9:13 de la mañana

entrar   salir

10:55   9:17

la patrullera   3:40 de la tarde

el sospechoso

el callejón

A. ¿Cómo se dice?   Look back at the picture and match the words from column **A** with a logical definition from column **B**.

A		**B**
1. el reloj	**a.**	muchas casas o apartamentos
2. el hospital	**b.**	para un sándwich
3. el edificio residencial	**c.**	marca las horas del día
4. el banco	**d.**	para mi dinero $$$
5. el restaurante	**e.**	para servicios médicos
6. la casa de correo	**f.**	para mandar mis comunicaciones

B. Acciones.   Choose the verb that matches the following descriptions.

1. _____ observar   **a.** salir

2. _____ abandonar un edificio; necesita decir "adiós".   **b.** entrar

3. _____ ingresar en un edificio; necesita decir "hola".   **c.** mirar

En la ciudad

Two undercover officers are "tailing" a suspect through the city and taking careful notes about all of his activities and whereabouts during a two-day period. Here is the journal they are keeping for the report.

Informe de observación: | ·

Oficiales: M. Aguilar y R. Kerzner   **Patrullera:** 817

Apellidos del sospechoso: J. López Braun

Dirección del sospechoso: 7033 Avenida Polar, Apto. 223B

Ciudad: Las Vegas   **Estado:** NV

Fechas de observación: 29/6/05-30/6/05

Día 1. el 29 de junio

1. Ahora, son las 8:00 en punto de la mañana. El sargento Aguilar y yo observamos el apartamento del sospechoso. No hay movimiento.

2. Ahora son las 8:43 (son las nueve menos diez y siete). No hay movimiento.

3. A las nueve y trece (9:13), el sospechoso sale del edificio residencial: Las Lomas. Entra en el restaurante, El cafecito, a las nueve y diez y siete. (9:17)

4. A las diez menos cinco (9:55) el sospechoso sale del restaurante y regresa al apartamento.

5. En este momento son las 5:00 de la tarde y no hay movimiento del sospechoso. El sargento y yo regresamos a la comisaría con el reporte de las actividades de hoy. Mañana, a las 8:00 de la mañana, continuamos la observación.

C. ¿Comprende usted?   Give the following information based on the report.

1.   El nombre del sospechoso:
2.   Los nombres de los oficiales:
3.   El sospechoso regresa al apartamento a las:
4.   Los oficiales van a continuar la observación mañana a las:

D. Mi información personal.   Fill out the following form as if you were the suspect.

E. ¿Y usted?   Think of your own schedule. Give days of the week and

---

Información personal

Apellido(s)_____   Nombre _____

Dirección _____   Ciudad _____

Estado _____   Teléfono _____

---

approximate times that you might be in these places. If you are not likely to be there—**lie** and tell us anyway!

MODELO: el café:
            el café: lunes y martes a las ocho de la mañana

1.   en la casa o departamento (apartamento)
2.   en el trabajo
3.   en el banco
4.   en la jefatura (comisaría)

Estructuras   *Telling time: La hora*

* To ask *What time is it?* use **¿Qué hora es?**
* Answer with: **Es la...** when saying one o'clock, or **Son las...**+ the hour for all other hours.

    Es la una.   *It's one o'clock.*   **Son las** dos.   *It's two o'clock.*

* To tell how many minutes past the hour it is, add **y** + the number of minutes.

    Son las tres **y diez.**   *It's 3:10.*   Es la una **y cinco.**   *It's 1:05.*

* To tell how many minutes before the hour it is, use the next hour **menos** the number of minutes.

    Son las **tres menos cinco.**   *It's 2:55.*   Es la **una menos veinte.**   *It's 12:40.*

* For the half hour, use **y media** or **treinta.**

    Son las tres **y media.** *or* Son las tres **y treinta.**   *It's 3:30.*

* For quarter hours, **cuarto** and **quince** are interchangeable.

    Son las tres menos **cuarto.** *or* Son las tres menos **quince.**   *It's a quarter to three (2:45).*

* Other useful time-telling phrases are: **en punto** for *on the dot* or *sharp;* **de la mañana** for A.M., **de la tarde** for P.M. until dark, and **de la noche** for P.M. after dark. Use **el mediodía** for noon and **la medianoche** for midnight.

La reunión es a las diez **en punto.**	*The meeting is at ten o'clock sharp.*
Son las cuatro **de la tarde.**	*It's four P.M.*
Es **el mediodía.**	*It's noon.*

* To tell the time *at* which an event will take place, use **a las** or **a la** + the hour.

¿A qué hora es la observación?	*At what time is the observation?*
La observación es **a las once.**	*The observation is at eleven.*
El sospechoso sale **a las tres y media.**	*The suspect leaves (goes out) at three thirty.*

Para practicar

A. ¿Qué hora es?   Tell what time it is now, according to the following digital clocks. If there is more than one correct way to express the time in Spanish, provide both ways.

MODELO: 6:30 A.M.

> *Son las seis y media de la mañana. Son las seis y treinta de la mañana.*

1.	7:00 A.M.	**3.**	8:55 P.M.	**5.**	6:15	**7.**	1:20
2.	2:20 P.M.	**4.**	12:00 A.M.	**6.**	10:30	**8.**	12:35

B. Citas.   You are a possible witness to a crime and the police want to talk to you. Your schedule is busy, but you do have a few free moments during the day. Read the available appointment times **(citas)** as listed below to the officers.

MODELO: 4:30 P.M.

> *Hay una cita a las cuatro y media de la tarde.*

1.	10:15 A.M.	**5.**	9:00 A.M. sharp
2.	2:40 P.M.	**6.**	9:15 A.M.
3.	1:10 P.M.	**7.**	12:30 P.M.
4.	5:45 P.M.	**8.**	5:10 P.M.

C. ¿A qué hora?   You are a police officer who has found the appointment calendar of an important suspect wanted for questioning. Tell at what time the suspect will be in the following places.

MODELO: Comer en el Café Luna Azul

> *Al mediodía.* or *A las doce.*

1.   En el hospital para visitar a Fred
2.   En casa con la televisión
3.   En el consultorio del dentista
4.   En el Café Luna Azul
5.   En el Teatro San Ramón
6.   En el gimnasio
7.   En una consulta con el abogado
8.   En el restaurante La Fuente

Citas		
6		
7	7:00	Ejercicio en el gimnasio
8	8:10	Visitar a Fred en el hospital
	8:45	Conferencia con el abogado (the lawyer)
9		
10		
11		
12	12:00	Café Luna Azul con los amigos
1	1:15	Cita con el dentista
2	2:25	Reunión de empleados en la oficina
3		
4	4:55	Consulta telefónica con el abogado
5		
6		
7	7:35	Teatro San Ramón con los Menéndez
8		
9		
10	10:00	Reservación en el Restaurante La Fuente
11	11:30	Las noticias del día—televisión
12		

Módulo I

¿Cómo es?

A. ¿Cómo se dice? Complete the following with information from the drawing.

1. Para mirar, necesito los _____.

2. Para tocar el piano uso los _____.

3. Para caminar *(walk)* uso las _____ y los _____.

4. Para hablar *(talk)* y escuchar *(listen)* necesito la _____ y las

_____.

B. Descripciones. Find a word that describes key physical characteristics of these famous people.

1. Shaquille O'Neal **3.** Arnold Schwartzenegger

2. Danny De Vito **4.** Calista Flockhart

¿Cómo es?

Agents Aguilar and Kerzner have brought several witnesses back to the police station to try to get a clear description of the suspect. Are all the witnesses describing the same person?

ENTREVISTA I

OFICIAL AGUILAR: Señorita González, ¿puede describir a la persona del banco?

SEÑORITA GONZÁLEZ: Claro que sí. Es muy alto con pelo largo y negro y una cicatriz grande en la cara.

OFICIAL AGUILAR: ¿Es todo?

SEÑORITA GONZÁLEZ: Sí. Es todo.

ENTREVISTA II

OFICIAL KERZNER: Señor González, ¿Puede describir a la persona que observó?

SEÑORITA GONZÁLEZ: Persona, ¡no! Las *dos* personas. El hombre es muy bajo y calvo con un tatuaje en la mano. La mujer es alta y bonita con pelo rizado y corto. Los dos son fuertes.

ENTREVISTA III

SARGENTO: Usted es la víctima del crimen. ¿Puede describir al hombre?

VÍCTIMA: ¡Hombre! No es hombre. ¡Es mujer! Y es peligrosa.

SARGENTO: ¿Mujer? ¿Es posible?

VÍCTIMA: Sí, es posible. Yo soy muy buena observadora.

C. ¿Comprende usted? Answer the following questions with **Sí** or **No.** If the statement is incorrect, provide the correct information.

1. La señora González describe al sospechoso como alto y pelón (calvo).
2. La señora González afirma que hay dos sospechosos.
3. El señor González describe el tatuaje.
4. La víctima describe al sospechoso como mujer.

¡OJO!

The metric system is commonly used to describe height (**metros** and **centímetros**) and weight (**kilogramos**) in Spanish. Each meter is approximately 3 feet. A suspect described as **"dos metros"** would be approximately 6 feet tall. A **kilogram,** often shortened to **kilo,** is 2.2 pounds. A person weighing **60 kilos** would be approximately 132 pounds.

¡Imaginación!

azul

rojo

blanco

color café

verde

amarillo

gris

D. De colores. All descriptions of people are more complete if you can identify colors for hair, eyes, skin, and clothing. Study these basic colors associated with the following objects, then look at some ways to apply them to identify the characteristics of the famous people listed below. Add any other characteristics previously learned in the chapter.

Etnicidad:	Ojos:	Pelo:
Blanco	ojos azules	pelo negro
Negro	ojos color café	pelo castaño (moreno)
Latino	ojos negros	pelirrojo
Indio	ojos verdes	pelo canoso (color gris)
Asiático		pelo rubio (güero) (color amarillo)

MODELO: Jerónimo

Jerónimo: indio, ojos negros

1. Lucille Ball
2. Paul Newman
3. Denzel Washington
4. Yao Ming
5. Salma Hayek
6. You

E. Descripciones. Look at the drawings to the left and describe 1. ethnicity, 2. body type, and 3. hair type.

Estructuras   *Describing yourself and others: Ser + adjetivos*

The verb **ser** is one of the Spanish equivalents to the verb *to be* in English. Use **ser** to tell who people are, what they do, where they are from or what they are like. The forms of **ser** are:

ser to be					
yo	**soy**	*I am*	nosotros/as **somos**		*we are*
tú	**eres**	*you are (familiar)*			
usted	**es**	*you are (formal)*	ustedes **son**		*you are (pl)*
él	**es**	*he is*	ellos **son**		*they are (m)*
ella	**es**	*she is*	ellas **son**		*they are (f)*

—¿Quién **es** usted?	*Who are you?*
—Yo **soy** Susana.	*I am Susana.*
—¿**Son** ustedes oficiales?	*Are you police officers?*
—Yo **soy** oficial y ella **es** Comandante.	*I am an officer and she is a commander.*

* To describe what a person or thing is like, use **ser** with an adjective.

—¿Cómo **es** la oficial?	*What is the officer like?*
—Ella **es** simpática.	*She is nice.*
—¿Cómo **es** usted?	*What are you like?*
—Yo **soy** tímido.	*I am timid (shy).*
—El caso **es** difícil.	*The problem is difficult.*

* Many adjectives end in **–o** when describing male characteristics and **–a** when describing female characteristics.

Masculine	Feminine	
tímid**o**	tímid**a**	*shy*
peligros**o**	peligros**a**	*dangerous*
antipátic**o**	antipátic**a**	*unpleasant*
alt**o**	alt**a**	*tall*
baj**o**	baj**a**	*short*
calv**o**	calv**a**	*bald*

* Most adjectives ending in a letter other than **–o** or **–a** use only one form for masculine or feminine.

El oficial es inteligent**e**.	*The (male) agent is intelligent.*
La oficial es inteligent**e**.	*The (female) agent is intelligent.*
La situación es grav**e**.	*The situation is serious.*
El caso es difíci**l**.	*The case is difficult.*

* To pluralize nouns and adjectives ending in **-o, -a,** or **-e,** simply add an **-s.**

  L**a** víctima es interesant**e.**   La**s** víctima**s** son interesante**s.**

* To pluralize nouns and adjectives ending in consonants, add **-es.**

Es observado**r.**	*He is observant.*
Son observado**res.**	*They are observant.*
La víctima es jove**n.**	*The victim is young.*
Las víctimas son jóve**nes.**	*The victims are young.*

* Use **ser** with adjectives to talk about nationality. In Spanish, nationalities are not capitalized, but countries are capitalized.

Yo **soy mexicana.**	*I am Mexican.*
Yo **soy de** México.	*I am from Mexico.*
El sospechoso **es puertorriqueño.**	*The suspect is Puerto Rican.*
El sospechoso **es de** Puerto Rico.	*The suspect is from Puerto Rico.*

* Use **ser** with **de** to tell what something is made of or to whom it belongs.

Las pastillas **son de** azúcar.	*The pills are made of sugar.*
El dinero **es de** la señora Rosa.	*The money is Mrs. Rosa's.*

Para practicar

A. ¿Quiénes?   To whom might the following sentences refer? Insert names of people you know or people who are famous.

MODELO: Es un agente famoso.
> *Elliot Ness es un agente famoso.*

1. Son criminales famosos.   **3.** Es muy peligroso.
2. Es muy inteligente.   **4.** Es alto y atlético.

B. ¿Cómo son?   As a new police recruit, you are always testing your powers of observation. As you observe the following people, use the correct form of the verb **ser** to describe them.

MODELO: (La señora Ramírez) viuda
> *La señora Ramírez es viuda.*

1. (Los niños) altos y guapos   **5.** (La música) suave
2. (La recepcionista) simpática   **6.** (El estudiante) muy serio
3. (Las agentes jóvenes) mexicanas   **7.** (El sofá) de cuero *(leather)*
4. (Nosotros) no tímidos

C. Una fiesta de cóctel. You are undercover at a cocktail party and would like to get to know more about the person next to you. Find out everything you can about this potential suspect: who s/he is, where s/he is from, what profession s/he is, and what s/he is like. Then, switch roles. When you are finished, describe this person to the class.

¿Cómo se llama?	¿De dónde es?	¿Cuál es su profesión?	¿Cómo es?

Módulo 2

Los testigos

A. ¿Cómo se dice? Tell what articles of clothing or equipment are used on the following body parts. More than one article of clothing or piece of equipment is allowed!

MODELO: los ojos:
los lentes

1. la cabeza
2. los pies
3. los brazos y los hombros
4. las piernas

B. ¿Para quién?   Tell if the following items are traditionally associated with men: **los hombres** or women: **las mujeres** or both: **los hombres y las mujeres.**

1. _____ las faldas

2. _____ las corbatas

3. _____ los vestidos

4. _____ los pantalones

5. _____ los zapatos

Los testigos

Our officers are still trying to get a description of the suspects. Now the witnesses are trying to remember—and to describe—their clothing.

ENTREVISTA I

OFICIAL AGUILAR: Señorita González, ¿puede describir la ropa de la persona del banco?

SEÑORITA GONZÁLEZ: ¡Ay, sí! La recuerdo claramente.

OFICIAL AGUILAR: ¿Por qué la recuerda claramente?

SEÑORITA GONZÁLEZ: Porque el hombre es muy guapo y elegante—y rico. Lleva ropa muy fina: un traje negro, una camisa azul y una corbata bonita. ¡Es un señor muy guapo!

ENTREVISTA II

OFICIAL KERZNER: Señor González, ¿puede describir la ropa de las personas que observó?

SEÑOR GONZÁLEZ: El hombre bajo y calvo con el tatuaje lleva pantalones cortos, sandalias—con calcetines—y una sudadera roja. La mujer lleva una falda negra, un suéter amarillo y sandalias de tacón alto. Ah, y medias negras.

ENTREVISTA III

SARGENTO: Y usted, ¿cómo describe la ropa de la sospechosa?

VÍCTIMA: ¿La vieja? El vestido es viejo, negro y largo. Las medias están rotas y por las rodillas. No recuerdo los zapatos. Usa lentes grandes para los ojos y un bastón.

SARGENTO: Y usted dice que es peligrosa. ¿Por qué?

VÍCTIMA: Por el bastón. En las manos de esta mujer, ¡es un arma!

C. ¿Comprende usted?   Fill in the missing information based on the dialogue.

1. La señora González dice que el hombre lleva un _____ negro,

    una _____ azul y una _____ bonita.

2. El señor González describe la ropa del hombre como _____

    cortos y _____ con _____.

3. La mujer con el señor del tatuaje lleva una _____ negra y

    _____ azul.

4. La mujer que describe la víctima es peligrosa porque tiene un

    _____.

D. El artista de la policía.   You are a police artist who has to talk to witnesses and try to capture the "look" of the suspects they describe. Try drawing these possible "perps" according to the witnesses' descriptions.

1. Es una mujer alta y gorda. Tiene los ojos pequeños y la nariz grande. Ah. Y los pies son grandes también. Lleva una falda roja y una chaqueta grande. Tiene una cachucha con la letra Y—tal vez de los Yankees.

2. Es un hombre bajo y fuerte. Tiene los brazos muy musculosos. Tiene una cicatriz en la cara y orejas grandes. El pelo es largo y rizado. Lleva pantalones cortos, una camiseta grande y zapatos de tenis—sin calcetines. Es muy guapo.

E. El testigo y el artista.   One of you is a witness and the other a police artist. The witness will describe the suspect in terms of body size and shape and at least two distinguishing characteristics, hair color, etc., while the artist sketches the description. Check the completed drawing for accuracy and then change roles and do it again!

Estructuras   *Describing things: Los artículos*

You have already seen that all nouns in Spanish have *gender*, meaning they are classified as either masculine or feminine. Words associated with nouns—adjectives and articles—take on the same characteristics as the noun and will match the noun in number and gender.

- There are four ways to express the definite article *the* in Spanish. The one you use depends on the characteristics of the noun that follows it—whether it is masculine or feminine, singular or plural.

The definite article: *The*		
	Singular	**Plural**
Masculine	**el** teléfono	**los** teléfonos
Feminine	**la** casa	**las** casas

- Noun gender has little to do with being male or female, unless the noun refers to a being that has a gender:

el sargento   **los sargentos**
la sargenta   **las sargentas**

- Nouns ending in **–e** generally have the same form for males and females. Only the article will change. It is important to note that in groups of mixed males and females, the masculine form is used.

el agent**e**   *the (male) agent*
la agent**e**   *the (female) agent*
los agentes   *the agents (either all male or mixed male and female)*

- In general, nouns ending in **–a, –ción, –sión, –dad,** and **–tad** are feminine.

la esta**ción**   las esta**ciones**
la ciu**dad**   las ciu**dades**

- Generally, nouns ending in **–o** or **–l** are masculine:

el patruller**o**   **los** patruller**os**
el pape**l**   **los** pape**les**

- There are many exceptions to the general rules of gender. Some of the most common are:

la man**o (f)**   *the hand*
el dí**a (m)**   *the day*
el map**a (m)**   *the map*

* Additional exceptions include words ending in **–ma**. While there are **–ma** words that are feminine: **la mamá** *(the mama)* and **la pluma** *(the pen)*, many **–ma** words are masculine.

el proble**ma**	*the problem*	**el** trau**ma**	*the trauma*
el dra**ma**	*the drama*	**el** idio**ma**	*the language*

To say *a, an,* or *some,* use the form of the indefinite article that matches the noun in number and gender. **Un** and **unos** are masculine indefinite articles and **una** and **unas** are feminine indefinite articles.

un zapato	*a shoe*	**unos** zapa**tos**	*some shoes*
una falda	*a skirt*	**unas** fald**as**	*some skirts*

Para practicar

A. Las partes del cuerpo. Use the correct form of the definite article **(el, la, los,** or **las)** to identify the location of these things associated with the body and its clothing. Be careful!

1. _____ orejas están en _____ cabeza.

2. _____ manos están en _____ brazos.

3. _____ zapatos está en _____ pies.

4. _____ lentes están en _____ ojos.

5. _____ falda está en _____ cuerpo.

6. _____ problema está en _____ nariz.

B. El mundo de la policía: Complete the following thoughts, first with a form of the indefinite article **(un, una, unos,** or **unas)**, and then with the name of an appropriate person, place or thing. When you are finished, compare your responses with those of a classmate.

MODELO: _____ policía famoso es _____.
Un policía famoso es Dick Tracy.

1. _____ programa de televisión de policía es _____.

2. _____ criminal famoso es _____.

3. _____ problema grave para la policía es _____.

4. _____ testigo da _____ descripción del sospechoso.

5. _____ publicación sensacional y famosa sobre el crimen y los criminales

   es _____.

C. En la casa de la víctima.   You and a partner are investigating a crime scene in the home of a victim. In your report, include the following things that you have found using an indefinite article.

MODELO: zapatos viejos
Hay unos zapatos viejos.

Inventario de la casa de la víctima

1. vestidos nuevos

   _____

2. bolsa grande con $20

   _____

3. pantalones de hombre

   _____

4. blusa rota *(torn)*

   _____

5. cachuchas con emblemas de equipos de béisbol

   _____

Módulo 2

¿Quiénes son?

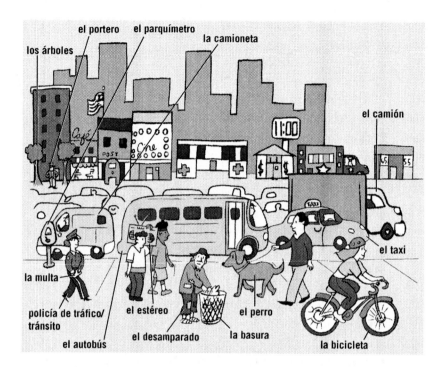

A. ¿Como se dice?   Choose the word from the list below that best fits the definition given:

a. desamparado   **b.** portero   **c.** el árbol   **d.** el perro

1. _____ una persona que vigila la puerta de un edificio residencial

2. _____ una persona pobre que no tiene casa

3. _____ una planta grande

4. _____ un animal doméstico

B. El transporte.   Tell what form of transportation the following refer to:

1. vehículo para una persona: la _____

2. vehículo público para 60 personas: el _____

3. vehículo público para tres o cuatro personas: el _____

4. vehículo enorme para transportar carga *(freight)*: el _____

¿Quiénes son?

It looks like a normal day on the street where the suspect lives, but is it really? Who are those people? What is happening? And when, where, and how will it all happen?

PREGUNTA: **¿Qué** pasa?

RESPUESTA: Es la captura de un sospechoso.

PREGUNTA: **¿Cuándo?**

RESPUESTA: En más o menos **una hora.**

PREGUNTA: **¿Quién** es el sospechoso?

RESPUESTA: Es **Joselito Aguirre**, un criminal peligroso.

PREGUNTA: **¿Por qué** no ven *(see)* las personas a la policía?

RESPUESTA: **Porque** son agentes secretos—no llevan uniforme.

PREGUNTA: **¿Cuántos agentes** hay?

RESPUESTA: Hay **ocho** agentes secretos.

PREGUNTA: **¿Quiénes** son los agentes?

RESPUESTA: Los agentes son **las personas** de la calle: **el portero** del edificio residencial es agente; **la persona** de la bicicleta es agente; **el desamparado** es agente; **los jóvenes** con el estéreo son agentes, y **la señora** y el perro son una unidad canina.

PREGUNTA: Son seis agentes. **¿Dónde** están los otros dos?

RESPUESTA: Los otros dos están **en la camioneta** con las comunicaciones electrónicas.

PREGUNTA: **¿Cómo** es posible?

RESPUESTA: Con entrenamiento *(training)*, dedicación y coordinación—¡todo es posible!

C. ¿Comprende usted? Answer the following questions based on the report you just read.

1. ¿Qué pasa ahorita?
2. ¿Cuándo?
3. ¿Quién es el sospechoso?
4. ¿Por qué no ve a los agentes?

D. Respuestas. They say that for every question there is an answer. Then for every answer there must be a question! Read each of the answers below (*Respuestas*) and then decide which of these question words was used to elicit that response.

a. ¿Cuándo?   **b.** ¿Dónde?   **c.** ¿Por qué?   **d.** ¿Cuántos?   **e.** ¿Quién?   **f.** ¿Qué?

MODELO: Respuesta: El sospechoso **es una persona** que se llama William Smith.
Pregunta: *d.* *¿Quién?*

1.   Respuesta: Los agentes están en **el parque.**

Pregunta: _____ ¿_____?

2.   Respuesta: **A las tres** de la tarde.

Pregunta: _____ ¿_____?

3.   Respuesta: Hay **diez** agentes.

Pregunta: _____ ¿_____?

4.   Respuesta: **Porque** es un criminal peligroso.

Pregunta: _____ ¿_____?

E. Una cita urgente.   A friend of yours calls and all he says is that he needs to see you—urgently. That's all you know. What four **question words** immediately come to your mind? When you have your list, compare it with another student's list.

Estructuras   *Asking for information: Las preguntas*

- To ask a question requiring a yes or no answer, change the intonation of a statement.
- The word *do,* used in English questions, is not translated into Spanish.
- The subject of the sentence usually comes after the verb in a question.

¿Tiene identificación?   *Do you have identification?*
¿Hay algún problema aquí?   *Is there a problem here?*

▪ The Spanish question, **¿verdad?** or **¿no?,** can be added to the end of a statement if your question is just confirming what you believe to be true. It is the equivalent of the English, *"Right?"*

Usted es Marta, ¿verdad?	*You are Marta, right?*
Son parte de la unidad canina, ¿no?	*They are part of the canine unit, correct?*

▪ When your question requires new information to be provided, use the following question words:

¿Quién/es?	*Who?*	**¿Cómo?**	*How?*
¿Qué?	*What?*	**¿Cuánto/a?**	*How much?*
¿Cuál/es?	*Which?*	**¿Cuántos/as?**	*How many?*
¿Dónde?	*Where?*	**¿Por qué?**	*¿Why?*
¿Cuándo?	*When?*		

▪ Some question words have plural forms (**¿Cuál?** and **¿Quién?**) depending on whether the questioner is expecting a singular or plural response.

—**¿Quién es** la señora alta?	*Who is the tall woman?*
—**Es Mónica,** una agente.	*She is Monica, an agent.*
—**¿Quiénes son** las señoras altas?	*Who are the tall women?*
—**Son Mónica y Elena,** unas agentes.	*They are Monica and Elena, some agents.*

▪ **¿Cuánto?** meaning *how much,* can become feminine (**¿Cuánta?**), depending on the gender of the noun that follows.

¿Cuánt**o** diner**o** hay?	*How much money is there?*
¿Cuánt**a** informa**ción** hay?	*How much information is there?*

▪ **¿Cuántos?** meaning *how many,* can also become feminine (**¿Cuántas?**), depending on the gender of the noun that follows.

¿Cuánt**os** sospechos**os** hay?	*How many suspects are there?*
¿Cuánt**as** víctim**as** hay?	*How many victims are there?*

▪ Use **¿Cuál?** or **¿Cuáles?** to indicate a selection—or selections—from a group. It may also replace **¿Qué?** when asking for specific or personal information, rather than general definitions.

¿Qué es un teléfono?	*What is a telephone?*
¿Cuál es su número de teléfono?	*What is your telephone number?*

Para practicar

A. Una invitación. *You and your partner have received information that there is illegal activity at a new club in your neighborhood. When a friend receives an invitation to the official grand opening, you decide to go to "check out the action." Read the invitation and then answer the questions that follow.*

> ¡Roberto Ornelas y Mariana López
> celebran la apertura (opening) de su
> nuevo club social "El Desvelado"!
> La fiesta es el quince de septiembre, desde las ocho de la
> tarde hasta la medianoche, en el Club, Calle 10 número 12.
> Favor de confirmar su presencia en el número
> de teléfono: 630-2115 antes del diez de septiembre.

1. ¿Quiénes dan la fiesta?
2. ¿Qué celebran?
3. ¿Cuándo es la celebración?
4. ¿Cuántas horas dura *(lasts)* la celebración?
5. ¿Dónde es la celebración?

B. ¡Jeopardy! The following statements are logical answers to specific questions. Give the logical question that would precede each answer listed below.

MODELO: Son las ocho de la noche.
¿Qué hora es?

1. La comisaría está en la calle Estonia.

2. La cita con la víctima es a las cinco de la tarde.

3. Yo soy Patricia y ella es Elena.

4. Hay dos víctimas en la casa.

C. El profesor sospechoso. You and your partner think that there is something suspicious about your Spanish class—and your teacher. Together, make up three questions about your Spanish class. Then interrogate other students for the answers.

MODELO: ¿Quién es el profesor/la profesora?

¡OJO!

From time to time you will see verbs followed by a series of letters in parentheses—i.e., **tener (ie)** or **demostrar (ue)**. These are spelling hints that will help you to conjugate the verbs in later chapters.

Vocabulario Módulo 1

Sustantivos

el/la agente	agent	la hora	hour
el apellido	last name	la jefatura	headquarters
el banco	bank	la mano	hand
el brazo	arm	la mañana	morning
la cabeza	head	la medianoche	midnight
el café	coffee, café	el mediodía	noon
la calle	street	la mujer	woman
el callejón	alley	la nariz	nose
la cara	face	el nombre	name
el caso	case	el ojo	eye
la cicatriz	scar	la patrullera	patrol car
el cine	movie theater	el pelo	hair
la cita	appointment, date	la persona	person
la ciudad	city	el peso	weight
la comisaría	police station	el pie	foot
el correo	mail	la pierna	leg
el crimen	crime	el reloj	watch, clock
la dirección	address	el/la sospechoso/a	suspect
el edificio	building	la tarde	afternoon
la entrevista	interview	el tatuaje	tatoo
el estado	state	la tienda	store
la estatura	stature	el trabajo	work
la fecha	date	la víctima	victim
el hombre	man		

Verbos

buscar	to look for	escuchar	to listen (to)
comer	to eat	leer	to read
conocer (zc)	to know, be acquainted with	mirar	to look at, watch
		regresar	to return
conversar	to talk	salir (g)	to leave, go out
entrar	to enter	ser	to be
escribir	to write	tocar	to play (music), to touch

Adjetivos

alto/a	tall	**indio/a**	Indian
amarillo/a	yellow	**joven**	young
antipático/a	unpleasant	**lacio/a**	straight
asiático/a	Asian	**largo/a**	long
azul	blue	**liso/a**	straight
bajo/a	short (height)	**mediano/a**	medium
blanco/a	white	**moreno/a**	brown haired, (or
bonito/a	pretty		brown skinned)
calvo/a	bald	**negro/a**	black
canoso/a	gray haired	**peligroso/a**	dangerous
castaño/a	brown (hair, eyes)	**pelirrojo/a**	red-headed
cojo/a	lame	**pelón/ona**	bald
fuerte	strong	**peludo/a**	hairy
gordo/a	fat	**rizado/a**	curly
grande	big	**rojo/a**	red
gris	gray	**rubio/a**	blond/blonde
guapo/a	handsome	**verde**	green
güero/a	blond	**viejo/a**	old

Otras expresiones

algo	something	**mañana**	tomorrow
claro (que sí/no)	of course (not)	**más**	more
¿Cómo?	How?	**¿Qué?**	What?
de	of, from	**sí**	yes
en punto	on the dot	**todo**	all

Módulo 2

Sustantivos

el/la abogado/a	lawyer	**los calcetines**	socks
el apodo	nickname	**el camión**	truck
el árbol	tree	**la camioneta**	station wagon, van
el autobús	bus	**la camisa**	shirt
el barrio	neighborhood	**la camiseta**	T-shirt
el bastón	cane	**la casa**	house
la basura	trash	**los chonis**	underwear (boxers)
la bicicleta	bicycle	**la corbata**	tie
el bigote	moustache	**el cuerpo**	body
la blusa	blouse	**el dinero**	money
la bolsa	purse, bag	**la edad**	age
las botas	boots	**la emergencia**	emergency
la cachucha	cap	**la estación**	station
la cadena	chain	**el estéreo**	stereo

la falda	skirt	la policía	police department
la fiesta	party	el portero	doorman
la gorra	cap	la puerta	door
el hombro	shoulder	la ropa	clothing
la libra	pound	las sandalias	sandals
los lentes	glasses	el sombrero	hat
las medias	panty hose	la sudadera	sweatshirt
la multa	ticket, fine	el suéter	sweater
el nacimiento	birth	el tacón	heel
la oreja	ear	el testigo	witness
el oro	gold	el tráfico	traffic
los pantalones	pants	el traje	suit
las pantuflas	slippers	el tránsito	traffic
el parquímetro	parking meter	los vaqueros	jeans
el/la perro/a	dog	el vestido	dress
la playera	T-shirt	el zapato	shoe
el/la (mujer) policía	police officer		

Verbos

| llegar | to arrive | recordar (ue) | to remember |
| llevar | to wear, to carry | ver | to see |

Adjetivos

corto/a	short (length)	pobre	poor
desamparado/a	homeless	rico/a	rich
flaco/a	skinny	roto/a	broken, torn
pequeño/a	small		

Otras expresiones

ahora	now	hay	there is, are
ahorita	right now	inmediatamente	immediately
¿Cuál/es?	Which (one/s)?	¿Por qué?	Why?
¿Cuándo?	When?	porque	because
¿Cuánto/a?	How much?	¿Quién/es?	Who?
¿Cuántos/as?	How many?	¿Verdad?	True? Right?
¿Dónde?	Where?		

Síntesis

A escuchar

Hay una persona en mi casa. Listen to the following 911 call and then tell if the following statements are true or false by writing **Sí** o **No** next to each statement. If the answer is **No,** then correct the statement.

1. _____ Hay una mujer en el patio de la casa.

2. _____ La operadora tiene unas preguntas.

3. _____ El intruso es bajo, gordo y calvo.

4. _____ El policía llega en dos horas.

A conversar

In groups of three, take turns being a missing person while the other two group members describe you according to these items. If the information is too personal: lie. Just make sure you lie using good grammar!

MODELO: 1. Nombre:
2. Fecha de nacimiento:
3. Edad actual:
4. Estatura:
5. Peso:
6. Pelo:
7. Características especiales:
8. Ropa:

A leer

Nombre: Marta Aurelia Castellón-Barrientos
Fecha de nacimiento: 08-02-1998
Desapareció: 12-12-2002
Edad Actual (*age at this time*): 7años
Sexo: Femenino
Pelo: negro
Ojos: negros
Estatura: 36" — mediana
Peso: 45 libras (lbs.) gordita
Desapareció de: Miami, Florida
Características especiales: una cicatriz
cerca del ojo, pelo rizado
Ropa (en el momento de la desaparición):
jeans, una camiseta roja y tenis azules.

¿Comprende usted?   Answer the following questions based on the information given above.

1. ¿Quién es la niña desaparecida?
2. ¿Cuándo desapareció?
3. ¿Es joven o vieja?
4. Describa la ropa.
5. ¿Tiene características especiales?

A escribir

With a partner, create a missing person's poster for your Spanish teacher. Make sure to include physical traits, clothing, and any distinguishing characteristics!

Algo más

Ventana cultural: Los apellidos hispanos

THE CONNECTION
BY PATRICK OSIO

It Pays To Know "What's in A Name"

Very few things are as confusing to Americans as the names in Spanish-speaking countries. Since we are a single-last-name society, we become confused when two or more last names are used.

In Mexican culture, males carry for life both the paternal and maternal last name. A woman never loses her paternal last name, but does drop her maternal name at marriage. Here is how it works:

Alberto's paternal name is Rodríguez. Garza is his mother's maiden name, thus Rodríguez Garza. His wife, María Guadalupe, keeps her maiden (paternal) name, Martínez, and adds her husband's paternal name after her maiden name. The "de" (meaning "of") in front of Rodríguez indicates the name was acquired through marriage, thus Martínez de Rodríguez.

Their children's last names will be Rodríguez Martínez. Each succeeding generation of males will add their own mother's last name after Rodríguez. So there are no "juniors" or Roman numerals to distinguish the same first name of future generations. Females born to Alberto and María Guadalupe will, until married, have the Rodríguez Martínez name. On marriage they too will drop their mother's maiden name, and their children will have their maiden name, Rodríguez, for life as their second last name.

Each generation thusly honors and respects the mother, and is able to trace both parents' ancestry. There is a good reason for the name structure, and it has to do with family values, repect and honor for one's mother and ancestry.

Así es

Based on the information in the preceding article, can you determine the names of these newborn Latino babies?

1. The mother is Antonia (Toña) López de Suárez and the father is Gonzalo Suárez Hernández. Baby Antonio's full name will be Antonio

    _____   _____ .

2. Mario Soto Machado is married to Angelina Gómez Pérez. Their daughter Elena's full name is Elena _____ .

¡OJO!

If you need to look up a Latino name in an official directory, be sure to start with the first of the two last names (the paternal surname) to determine alphabetical order. For example, José Antonio López Suárez would be found in the "L" listings: López Suárez, José A. If a hyphen is placed between the two last names, the computer will then alphabetize by father's surname. If in doubt, specifically ask a person for his father's last name.

A buscar

The Internet offers a wealth of information—both linguistic and cultural. Have you looked for Spanish websites? Find information on everything from grammar tutorials to traditions and customs for naming children and researching identities online to tracing missing children in South America. Go to our website for links to some of these things worth researching.

A conocer: Apodos comunes

Common Spanish Nicknames		
MALE	Alberto o Roberto	Beto
	Alejandro	Alex, Alejo, Sandro
	Antonio	Toni, Toño
	Eduardo	Lalo
	Enrique	Quique
	Francisco	Paco, Pancho
	Guillermo	Memo, Guille
	Ignacio	Nacho
	Jesus	Chuy, Chuchi, Chucho
	José	Pepe
	José María	Chema
	Luis	Lucho
	Manuel	Manolo, Meme
	Rafael	Rafa
	Ramón	Moncho
FEMALE	Ana	Anita
	Antonia	Toña, Toni
	Carmen	Menchu, Mamen
	Concepción	Conchita
	Consuelo	Coni
	Dolores	Lola
	Encarnación	Encarna
	Graciela	Chela
	Guadalupe	Lupe (males also)
	Isabel	Chabela, Mabel
	María Amparo	Mariam
	María Elena	Malena
	María Isabel	Maribel
	María Luisa	Marisa, Marilú
	María Teresa	Maritere, Marité, Maite
	Mercedes	Mencha, Merche
	Patricia	Pati
	Rosario	Charo, Chayo
	Teresa	Tere

LECCIÓN 2

En la carretera

Módulo 1
* En la calle
* Naming and describing: *Más sobre los adjetivos*
* El tráfico y las infracciones
* Talking about present activities: *Los verbos que terminan en –ar*

Módulo 2
* ¿Multa o advertencia?
* Talking about present activities: *Los verbos que terminan en –er, –ir*
* ¡Está borracha!
* Physical conditions: *Expresiones con **tener** y **estar***

Síntesis
* A escuchar
* A conversar
* A leer
* A escribir

Algo más
* Ventana cultural: Los amigos no dejan que sus amigos manejen borrachos
* A buscar
* A conocer: MADD llega a la comunidad latina

Módulo I

En la calle

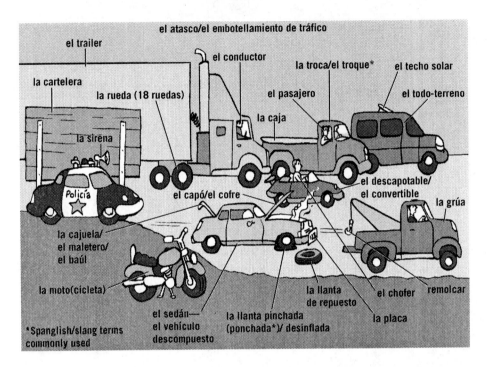

el atasco/el embotellamiento de tráfico

el trailer

la cartelera

la rueda (18 ruedas)

la sirena

Policía

el conductor

la troca/el troque*

el techo solar

el pasajero

el todo-terreno

la caja

el descapotable/
el convertible

la grúa

el capó/el cofre

la cajuela/
el maletero/
el baúl

la moto(cicleta)

la llanta
de repuesto

el chofer

remolcar

el sedán—
el vehículo
descompuesto

la llanta pinchada
(ponchada*)/ desinflada

la placa

*Spanglish/slang terms
commonly used

A. ¿Cómo se dice? Identify the following vehicles named on the chart.

1. la grúa

2. la rueda

3. la troca

4. el todo terreno

5. carro de policín

B. A identificar.   Name the vehicle or the car part most often associated with the following. If there is more than one, name them all.

1. Aquí está el motor.
2. Aquí están los pasajeros y el conductor.
3. Aquí están las llantas de repuesto y otras herramientas *(tools)*.
4. Aquí están las llantas.

Problemas en la carretera

Two Highway Patrolmen have just received a call on the radio about a situation on the highway.

RADIO: Hay reportes de problemas serios en la Carretera 19 en el kilómetro 83.

POLICÍA: Estamos en camino. Hay un terrible atasco de tráfico con muchos camiones comerciales. Es difícil ver. ¿Hay algún accidente?

RADIO: No. Hay un nuevo reporte de un vehículo descompuesto en la carretera. Es un todo-terreno blanco y negro, marca Ford, modelo Bronco. El chofer es un señor viejo y su pasajera es una mujer discapacitada *(disabled)*.

POLICÍA: ¿Hay víctimas que necesitan atención médica?

RADIO: No hay problemas médicos. Sólo hay problemas de tráfico por la curiosidad de las personas.

POLICÍA: Aquí está la grúa. Pero un buen samaritano ya *(already)* instaló la llanta de repuesto.

C. ¿Comprende usted?   See how much of the dialogue you understand by answering the following questions.

1. ¿Dónde hay reportes de problemas serios?
2. Describa el auto descompuesto.
3. ¿Cómo es el chofer?
4. ¿Por qué hay atasco de tráfico?
5. ¿Quién pone la llanta de repuesto?

D. Mi licencia de manejar. You're applying for your driver's license. Fill out the following form.

	Solicitud de Licencia de Manejar, Tarjeta de Identidad, o Cambio de Nombre
DMV Una Agencia de Servicio Público	

NÚMERO DE SEGURO SOCIAL ___ - __ - ____

¿Desea inscribirse para votar?	☐ Sí. Por favor, complete el formulario adjunto. ☐ No. No complete el formulario.
Solicitud de Licencia de Manejar	☐ A -Vehículos combinados y remolques con más de 10,000 libras ☐ B -Vehículos sencillos de 26,001 libras o más ☐ C -Clase básica ☐ D -Vehículos que transporten materiales peligrosos ☐ M1 -Motocicletas de dos ruedas de 150 cc o más ☐ M2 -Motocicletas de dos ruedas de 149 cc o menos
Solicitud de Tarjeta de Identidad	Anote el número de la tarjeta de identidad, si la tiene _____ Se vence en _____
Información, Nombre y Dirección de todos los solicitantes	Nombre completo_____ Dirección _____ Apellidos_____ Ciudad_____ Sufijo (JR, SR)_____ Estado_____
Información Personal	Sexo___ Color del cabello_____ Color de ojos _____ Estatura ___ Peso____ Fecha de nacimiento____ (Día) _____ (Mes) _____ (Año)
Declaración de Perjurio	Certifico bajo pena de perjurio conforme a las leyes del Estado de California, que lo anterior es verdadero y correcto.
Firma del solicitante	_____ _____ _____ Fecha Firma Teléfono (día)

E. ¡Siempre los viernes! In your town there are always traffic jams on certain days at certain hours. Think of a typical traffic situation in your area and call the highway patrol tip line on your cell phone to warn others of the problem. Your classmate will be the operator **(el/la operador/a)** who asks the following questions. Answer them with the details of your traffic situation. Then switch roles. You may need some additional vocabulary:

la autopista	*freeway*	la avenida	*avenue*	el bulevar	*boulevard*
la calle	*street*	el camino	*road*	la carretera	*highway*
el carril	*lane*	Ceda el paso	*Yield*	la cuota/ el peaje	*toll*
el desvío	*detour*	la entrada	*entry on-ramp*	el ferrocarril	*railroad*
la gasolinera	*gas station*	la iglesia	*church*	el parque	*park*
el paseo	*drive*	el peligro	*danger*	la salida	*exit, off-ramp*

MODELO: El/La operador/a: *9-1-1. ¿Por qué llama usted?*

Usted: *Hay un accidente serio.*

El/La operador/a: *¿Dónde?*

Usted: *En la carretera 66, en la salida Los Osos.*

El/La operador/a: *¿Los vehículos están en el carril derecho* (right)*?*

Usted: ...

El/La operador/a: *¿Qué necesitan?*

Usted: ...

Estructuras   Naming and describing: Más sobre los adjetivos

* Some of the most useful adjectives in a police setting define physical characteristics of people or things. Because the adjective becomes part of the identity of the noun it describes, it assumes the same characteristics as its noun: masculine, feminine, singular or plural. If you are unsure if a noun is masculine or feminine, you can often tell by looking at the article. Remember: If the adjective ends in a letter other than **-o** or **-a,** it becomes plural or singular, but not masculine or feminine.

Colors:

blanco/a	*white*	**el** coche **blanco**	*the white car*
negro/a	*black*	**las** llant**as negras**	*the black tires*
rojo/a	*red*	**la** camionet**a roja**	*the red van*
amarillo/a	*yellow*	**el** autobús escolar **amarillo**	*the yellow schoolbus*
verde	*green*	**la** troc**a verde**	*the green pickup*
azul	*blue*	**los** uniformes **azules**	*the blue uniforms*

Conditions:

descompuesto/a	*broken*	**el** auto **descompuesto**	*the broken (disabled) car*
discapacitado/a	*disabled (people)*	**los** señores **discapacitados**	*the disabled men*
limpio/a	*clean*	**la** camionet**a limpia**	*the clean van*
nuevo/a	*new*	**el** auto **nuevo**	*the new car*
peligroso/a	*dangerous*	**la** situac**ión peligrosa**	*the dangerous situation*
serio/a	*serious*	**el** proble**ma serio**	*the serious problem*
sucio/a	*dirty*	**las** troc**as sucias**	*the dirty pickups*
viejo/a	*old*	**la** moto(clet**a) vieja**	*the old motorcycle*

Other:

grande	large	**los** camiones **grandes**	*the large semis*
chico/a	small	**el** carr**o chico**	*the small car*

Note: **pequeño/a** is another common way of saying *small*.

* When **grande** is placed before the noun, the meaning changes from *large* to *great,* and the ending **–de** is omitted in the singular.

un gran	*a great*	**unos grandes**	*some great*
policía	*policeman*	policías	*policemen*
una gran	*a great*	**unas grandes**	*some great*
sargenta	*sergeant*	sargentas	*sergeants*

* **Bueno** and **malo** are adjectives meaning *good* and *bad*. When placed after the noun they modify, they become masculine, feminine, singular, or plural.

bueno/a	*good*	**el** auto buen**o**	*the good car*
malo/a	*bad*	**las** notici**as** mal**as**	*the bad news*

* When **bueno** or **malo** is placed before a masculine singular noun, omit the **-o.**

un bue**n** samaritan**o**	*a good samaritan*
unos buen**os** samaritan**os**	*some good samaritans*
un ma**l** cas**o**	*a bad case*
unos mal**os** cas**os**	*some bad cases*

Para practicar

A. Asociaciones. What color(s) do you associate with the following items? Rewrite the phrase to include the description. Don't forget to change the verb, if necessary.

MODELO: los camiones del servicio postal
Los camiones del servicio postal son blancos, rojos y azules.

1. la sangre *(blood)* rojo
2. las bananas amarillos
3. las llantas negro
4. los uniformes de las enfermeras blanco, o azul
5. las plantas en el parque verde
6. el autobús escolar amarillo
7. las patrulleras de su ciudad negro, blanco, azul colores deferentes
8. el océano azul

B. Más sobre los vehículos. Do you know your vehicle models? Look at the following models and tell what type(s) of vehicle it is likely to be. Can you also identify the brand name—**la marca**—and whether it is a new model **(modelo nuevo)**, an old model **(modelo viejo)** or a classic **(clásico)**? Now add one adjective to describe it. If you get stuck, move on and then later, see if any of your classmates can help.

MODELO: Murano

Murano es un todo-terreno de Nissan. Es un modelo nuevo. Es moderno.

1. Mustang
2. Yugo
3. SLK 320 Roadster
4. Avalanche
5. Sequoia
6. MACK
7. Harley Davidson
8. Edsel

C. ¿Bueno o malo? Make sure the following adjectives match their nouns and then tell a classmate if situations or conditions are good news **(buenas noticias)** or bad news **(malas noticias)**. Then, with a classmate, make up your own and ask another team.

MODELO: situación/violento

la situación violenta: malas noticias

1. accidente/serio
2. llantas/desinflado
3. problemas/peligroso
4. samaritanos/simpático
5. víctima/herido *(wounded)*
6. atasco/severo
7. ambulancia/rápido
8. criminal/nervioso

Módulo I

El tráfico y las infracciones

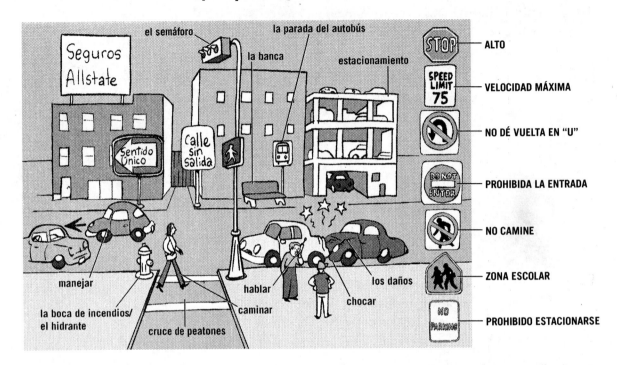

A. ¿Cómo se dice? See if you can match the following traffic control items in column **A** with a logical phrase in column **B**.

A	**B**
1. el semáforo	**a.** una persona que camina por la calle
2. boca de incendios	**b.** luz roja, verde, o amarilla
3. sentido único	**c.** el tráfico no tiene dos direcciones
4. calle sin salida	**d.** para el uso de los bomberos *(firemen)*
5. el peatón	**e.** un camino que solamente tiene entrada

B. ¿Infracción o legal? Indicate if the following situations constitute an infraction **(I)** or a legal maneuver **(L)**.

MODELO: chocar con un peatón

_____I_____ *Chocar con un peatón es una infracción.*

1. _____ no parar en la luz verde

2. _____ estacionar el carro en una boca de incendios

3. _____ manejar a 50 mph *(millas por hora)* en una zona escolar

4. _____ dejar *(leave)* el auto en un "estacionamiento"

5. _____ estacionar en una parada de autobús

La multa de tráfico

Officers Early and Rivers are waiting at a red light when a speeding car comes from around the corner and hits another car. Officer Early checks on the victim while Officer Rivers talks to the driver who caused the problem.

OFICIAL EARLY:	Are you all right?
VÍCTIMA:	Perdone, oficial, pero yo no **hablo** inglés. Sólo **hablo** español.
OFICIAL EARLY:	Ah. Entonces, ¿está usted bien?
VÍCTIMA:	Sí, yo creo que sí. ¿Cómo está mi carro? ¿Hay muchos daños?
OFICIAL EARLY:	Los daños del carro son mínimos. Un momento por favor... (**Escucha** su radio.)
VÍCTIMA:	Sí, claro, entonces **espero** en el carro y **llamo** por teléfono a mi esposa.
OFICIAL RIVERS:	¿Usted siempre **maneja** a alta velocidad en la ciudad?
RESPONSABLE:	No, oficial, normalmente yo no **manejo** rápidamente. Es que **regreso** al trabajo después de **visitar** a un amigo en el hospital y no quiero **llegar** tarde.
OFICIAL RIVERS:	Su licencia, el registro (la registración) del carro y su seguro, por favor. (El oficial **examina** los papeles y **observa** al responsable.)
RESPONSABLE:	Por favor, **necesito** regresar al trabajo.
OFICIAL RIVERS:	Paciencia. Primero mi colega y yo **necesitamos ayudar** a la víctima y **preparar** los reportes del accidente. Entonces, **hablamos** de la multa.

C. Identificación. For each statement, indicate to whom the statement refers: Oficial Early **(E)**; La víctima **(V)**; Oficial Rivers **(R)**; o El responsable **(R)**.

1. _____ Maneja muy rápidamente.

2. _____ Llama a su esposa.

3. _____ Habla con la víctima.

4. _____ Habla con el responsable.

5. _____ Causa el accidente.

D. Una multa de advertencia. Uh-oh. You've been issued a warning ticket due to an equipment violation, but it's in Spanish and you're not sure for which problem you were ticketed. Study the car parts and unscramble the words to find out!

el (espejo) retrovisor

la bocina

el asiento delantero

el parabrisas

el volante

el asiento de atrás

el limpiaparabrisas

los faros

la luz direccional/
los intermitentes

los cambios/las marchas

el parachoques

los frenos

el cinturón de seguridad

el guardafango

MODELO: *Multa de advertencia: Su/s _____ no funciona/n o No hay _____.*

1. _____ C I B O A N

2. _____ P M R I L B A P S A I A R I A

3. _____ L C N R D I U C Z I L A O E

4. _____ G R U D S C N T R Ó I A E E D U N I D

5. _____ E V O E I S P R T J R E R O S O

6. _____ R O S A F

7. _____ S F N O E R

8. _____ C P A H O R Q S E A U

Estructuras
Talking about present activities: Los verbos que terminan en -ar

* An infinitive is the basic form of the verb that is not yet matched to fit a specific person or subject. In English, an infinitive always starts with *to: to play, to speak, to run.*

* In Spanish, infinitives are single words that end in **-ar, -er** or **-ir.**

  habl**ar**   *to speak*   com**er**   *to eat*   viv**ir**   *to live*

* The stem is the portion of the verb that tells the action and the ending tells who or what the subject is.

  hablo   *I speak*   **habl** is the stem   and   **o** tells that the subject is **yo.**

* In order to indicate the different subjects of a verb, use different endings. This is called *conjugating a verb.* To conjugate **-ar** verbs, drop the final **-ar** and add these endings:

hablar (to talk or speak)			
yo hab**lo**	*I speak*	**nosotros/as** habl**amos**	*we speak*
tú hab**las**	*you (familiar) speak*		
usted hab**la**	*you speak*	**ustedes** hab**lan**	*you (all) speak*
él/ella hab**la**	*he/she speaks*	**ellos/ellas** hab**lan**	*they speak*

* Some additional **-ar** verbs that follow this pattern are:

ayudar	*to help*	**llegar**	*to arrive*
buscar	*to look for*	**limpiar**	*to clean*
cambiar	*to change*	**llamar**	*to call*
caminar	*to walk*	**mirar**	*to look at/to watch*
contestar	*to answer*	**necesitar**	*to need*
descansar	*to rest*	**observar**	*to observe*
escuchar	*to listen*	**preparar**	*to prepare*
esperar	*to wait/to hope*	**regresar**	*to return*
estudiar	*to study*	**tocar**	*to touch*
examinar	*to examine*	**tomar**	*to take*
fumar	*to smoke*	**trabajar**	*to work*

When the subject of the verb is clear from the ending and the context, the subject pronoun may be omitted.

(Yo) hablo con el oficial.   *I speak with the officer.*

¡OJO!

In a sentence where two verbs come together, the first verb is conjugated and the second verb stays in the infinitive form.

Necesito **ver** al policía.   *I need to see the policeman.*

Voy a **llamar** al trabajo.   *I am going to call my work.*

Para practicar

A. ¿Quién habla?   Tell the subject pronoun or pronouns that would match the following verbs.

MODELO: Observa al sospechoso.
Él, ella or *usted observa al sospechoso.*

1. Mir**amos** el accidente.
2. Tom**o** fotos del accidente.
3. Necesit**an** más información.
4. Escuch**a** el radio.
5. Manej**an** a una velocidad excesiva.
6. Examin**amos** los daños.
7. Busc**o** evidencia.
8. Prepar**as** los reportes.

B. El accidente.   Fill in the blanks with the correct form of the given verb to find out just how accidents happen.

1. En este momento, yo _____ (manejar) mi todo-terreno nuevo.

2. Yo _____ (escuchar) el excelente sistema estereofónico.

3. Briiiiing, Briiiiing.... Alguien *(someone)* _____ (llamar) por teléfono.

4. Yo _____ (buscar) el teléfono. ¡Ajá! Aquí está, y _____ (contestar): "Bueno".

5. Es mi amigo Paco. Nosotros _____ (estudiar) juntos en la universidad.

6. Yo _____ (tomar) un poco de mi café mientras *(while)* nosotros _____ (conversar).

7. En un momento, el semáforo _____ (cambiar) de verde a rojo y un peatón _____ (cruzar) la calle.

8. Yo _____ (usar) los frenos y la bocina.

9. El peatón _____ (escapar). ¡Gracias a Dios!

10. Pero mi nuevo todo-terreno _____ (chocar) con otro carro. ¡Daños! ¡Multas! ¡Ay de mí!

C. Las distracciones.   Using the list of **-ar** verbs learned in this chapter, can you come up with a list of five common activities that keep drivers from concentrating? First, give the infinitive and then tell if you are guilty of doing the same thing.

MODELO: Hablar por teléfono y manejar.
Sí, yo hablo por teléfono y manejo.

Módulo 2

¿Multa o advertencia?

A. ¿Cómo se dice?   Study the illustration and tell which of the new words each of the following statements describes.

1. Resultado de una infracción de tráfico en la que el chofer paga dinero o va a juicio
2. Resultado de una infracción de tráfico en la que el chofer no paga nada
3. Manejar a 70 millas por hora en una zona escolar
4. Protección financiera para los gastos *(expenses)* de un accidente de tráfico

B. Acciones. Can you guess which of the following verbs is described by each of these statements?

| escribir | ver | beber | comer |

1. Absorber información por medio de los ojos
2. Introducir comida por medio de la boca
3. Tomar líquidos
4. Transmitir información por medio de pluma y papel

Infracciones menores

*It's after midnight—on a school night!—and Officers Jennings and Castro observe a car full of teenagers driving erratically down a main street. Reasons for stop: speeding, violating curfew **(el toque de queda)**, and possible DUI. Lights! Siren! Action!*

ALICIA: ¿Hay algún problema, oficial?

OFICIAL CASTRO: Sí. Hay varios. ¿Cómo se llama usted? Necesito **ver** su licencia, su registro y su seguro, por favor.

ALICIA: Me llamo Alicia Pérez. Aquí tiene mis documentos. No **comprendo** por qué estamos detenidos.

OFICIAL: ¿Dónde **viven** ustedes?

ALICIA: **Vivimos** a unos dos kilómetros de aquí—somos residentes de Lakeview.

OFICIAL: ¿Qué **hacen** ustedes aquí a estas horas? Hay toque de queda a las 11.

ALICIA: Mañana hay examen de historia. Nosotros siempre estudiamos así. Yo manejo el carro, Alejandro **lee** el libro y Gregorio **escribe** las notas. Entonces, todos **discutimos** la materia y así **comprendemos** la historia. Cuando estudiamos en el carro, siempre **recibimos** "A" en los exámenes.

OFICIAL: ¿Qué **beben** ustedes? Es ilegal tener bebidas alcohólicas en el carro.

ALICIA: Yo **bebo** agua, y Marco, Alejandro y Gregorio **beben** café. No hay bebidas alcohólicas. **¿Recibimos** una multa?

OFICIAL: ¡Si **cometen** una infracción, **sufren** las consecuencias! Pero si regresan inmediatamente a casa, sólo **escribo** una advertencia y no una multa.

¡OJO!

For nearly all distances, weights, and measures, the metric system is the most commonly used. A kilometer is roughly ⅗ of a mile.

C. ¿Comprende usted?   Answer the following questions with information from the dialogue.

1.   ¿Por qué están detenidos Alicia y sus amigos?
2.   ¿Dónde viven ellos?
3.   ¿Por qué están en el carro los amigos?
4.   ¿Recibe Alicia una multa?

D. Más infracciones.   Tell which of the following traffic violations is being cited by placing the letter of the infraction next to a logical definition.

a.   exceso de velocidad   *speeding*
b.   abandonar el sitio de un accidente   *abandon the site of an accident*
c.   manejar bajo la influencia de alcohol/drogas   *DUI*
d.   infracción de semáforo o señal   *failure to obey a traffic signal or sign*
e.   infracción de estacionamiento   *parking violation*
f.   cambio de carril peligroso   *dangerous lane change*

1.   _____ 50 millas (80 kilómetros) en una zona escolar

2.   _____ beber mucha cerveza y manejar

3.   _____ proceder con una luz roja

4.   _____ causar un accidente y continuar manejando

5.   _____ manejar agresivamente, cambiando de carril con frecuencia

E. Mandatos.   The following commands might be useful in a low risk traffic stop. Study the commands and then match the command with the appropriate situation.

¡Baje del carro!   **¡Suba al carro!**   **¡Apague el motor!**   **¡Pare el carro!**

What would you say if you wanted the driver to:

1.   stop the car?
2.   get out of the car?
3.   get into the car?
4.   turn off the engine?

Estructuras   *Talking about present activities: Los verbos que terminan en -er, -ir*

- Verbs ending in **-er** and **-ir** follow a pattern very similar to the **-ar** ending verbs.
- Use the same endings for both **-er** and **-ir** verbs for all subjects except **nosotros/as.**

	comer *to eat*	**vivir** *to live*
yo	com**o**	viv**o**
tú	com**es**	viv**es**
él, ella, usted	com**e**	viv**e**
nosotros/as	com**emos**	viv**imos**
ellos, ellas, ustedes	com**en**	viv**en**

- Additional regular **-er** and **-ir** verbs that will be useful include:

-er		**-ir**	
beber	*to drink*	**decidir**	*to decide*
correr	*to run*	**discutir**	*to argue*
comprender	*to understand*	**existir**	*to exist*
creer	*to believe*	**insistir (en)**	*to insist*
temer	*to be afraid*	**recibir**	*to receive*
ver	*to see* (yo **veo)**	**sufrir**	*to suffer*

Para practicar

A. ¿Comer o beber?   Law Enforcement personnel are always there to help when help is needed! Please be kind enough to help one of our authors who is confused and in need of guidance. Tell if the following people would eat or drink these items.

MODELO: el hombre/una pizza
El hombre come una pizza.

1. los niños en el parque/un sándwich
2. los futbolistas/Gatorade
3. Yo/cerveza
4. Juan y Lucía/ unos tacos y enchiladas
5. mis amigos y yo/Pepsi
6. los oficiales de policía/café

B. Actividades en el parque.   You are on foot patrol today in a busy park. By choosing the correct form of the verb in parentheses, describe some of the activities going on there.

1.   Dos señores en una banca ————————— (leer) el periódico.

2.   El estudiante ————————— (escribir) sus notas.

3.   Dos señoras ————————— (beber) café.

4.   Un señor ————————— (vender) globos *(balloons)*.

5.   Unos atletas ————————— (correr) por el parque.

6.   Mi compañero y yo ————————— (ver) todo lo que pasa en el parque.

7.   Unos niños ————————— (comer) sándwiches en un picnic.

C. Entre amigos.   On a sheet of paper, write the following headings:

La casa   El restaurante   El carro

With a classmate, brainstorm as many activity verbs as possible for each place. Next, from your list of verbs, write sentences telling what people are doing in those places.

MODELO: El restaurante
comer. Unos policías comen donuts.

Módulo 2

¡Está borracha!

A. Nuevas expresiones. Can you match these physical conditions with a logical description that follows? Next, provide the name of a product that would help.

MODELO: tener sueño:
Necesita una siesta. Sealy Posturepedic

1. _____ tener hambre
2. _____ tener sed
3. _____ estar borracho
4. _____ tener frío

a. Necesita agua y otros líquidos.

b. Está en Alaska en diciembre.

c. Necesita alimentos y nutrición.

d. Tomar cinco cervezas, una botella de champaña y varios martinis.

B. ¿Legal o ilegal?   You are on a DUI task force, stopping cars randomly to check for infractions. Indicate if the following things, that might be found in a car, are legal **(L)** or illegal **(I)**.

1. _____ cerveza en la cajuela

2. _____ un martini en la mano del chofer

3. _____ una hamburguesa y una Coca Cola

4. _____ marihuana

¿Toma usted bebidas alcohólicas?

It's after three A.M and Officers Cisneros y Sullivan have just stopped a major celebrity singing star for driving erratically and in the wrong direction on a one-way street. At first look, all visible signs point to DUI. Will a closer look confirm that initial impression?

ESTRELLA:	*(slurred)* ¡Ay, oficial! **Estoy perdida.** Necesito direcciones.
OFICIAL CISNEROS:	¿Adónde va?
ESTRELLA:	A McDonald's. **Tengo mucha** hambre.
OFICIAL CISNEROS:	McDonald's **está cerrado.** *(Sees beverage)* ¿Qué toma usted?
ESTRELLA:	*(laughing)* Un poquito de cerveza. También **tengo sed.**
OFICIAL:	¿Cuántas cervezas ha tomado?
ESTRELLA:	Solamente dos. Pero también aquí **tengo** unas margaritas. ¿Quieres? ¿No? Oficial, no **estoy borracha**... ¡no, no, no! Es que **estoy muy cansada** después de mucho trabajo. **Tengo sueño** *(she yawns)*. Quiero regresar a mi casa ahora.
OFICIAL:	Por favor, señora, salga del coche.
ESTRELLA:	¡Ay, no! Es diciembre y **tengo frío. Tengo** un concierto mañana y no quiero estar enferma.
OFICIAL:	Baje del coche, por favor. Necesita una prueba de aliento para alcohol.
ESTRELLA:	*(crying)* Oficial, no, por favor, **tengo miedo** de la publicidad negativa.

C. ¿Comprende usted?   Answer the following questions based on the dialogue.

1.   ¿Por qué está detenido el coche de la estrella?
2.   ¿Qué necesita ella?
3.   ¿Qué toma ella?
4.   ¿Por qué no quiere ella bajar del coche?
5.   ¿Qué necesita hacer el oficial?

SI TOMA
NO MANEJE

D. ¿Maneja bajo la influencia del alcohol?   These questions are useful in determining sobriety **(sobriedad)**. Write the number of the question that matches the appropriate answer.

1.   ¿Toma usted medicina?   *Do you take medicine?*
2.   ¿Está enfermo?   *Are you ill?*
3.   ¿Hay drogas en el vehículo?   *Are there drugs in the vehicle?*
4.   ¿Cuántas bebidas alcohólicas tomó?   *How much alcohol have you consumed?*
5.   ¿Tiene armas?   *Do you have weapons?*

a.   _____ Sí, tengo muchos problemas de estómago.

b.   _____ Hay un poquito de marihuana en la cajuela.

c.   _____ No tengo pistolas.

d.   _____ Tomé una o dos cervezas. No mucho.

e.   _____ Sí, tomo Vicodin para el dolor de espalda.

E. Mandatos.   These commands will be helpful in a DUI stop. Study them, and then write the letter of the command that matches the appropriate situation.

a. Venga aquí, por favor.   *Come over here, please.*
b. Quítese los lentes, por favor.   *Please take off your glasses.*
c. Mire la punta de mi pluma.   *Look at the point of my pen.*
d. Camine en línea recta.   *Walk in a straight line.*

1. _____

3. _____

2. _____

4. _____

Estructuras   *Physical conditions: Expresiones con tener y estar*

- **Estar** *(to be)* and **tener** *(to have)* are two very useful verbs to describe certain temporary physical conditions.
- Use **estar** with an *adjective* to indicate *variable* physical or emotional circumstances. (Like **ser,** the English equivalent is *to be.* Remember that **ser** is used to describe long term or identifying characteristics, while **estar** is used to indicate that a characteristic is more subject to change and circumstance.) Use these forms of **estar:**

estar	to be				
yo	**estoy**	*I am*	**nosotros/as**	**estamos**	*we are*
tú	**estás**	*you are*			
Ud./él/ella	**está**	*you are, s/he is*	**ustedes/ellos/ellas**	**están**	*you/they are*

—¿Cómo **están** ustedes?   *How are you?*
—**Estamos** enfermos.   *We are ill.*

The following descriptive words are commonly used with **estar** to describe how people are feeling:

aburrido/a	*bored*	**nervioso/a**	*nervous*
borracho/a	*drunk*	**ocupado/a**	*busy*
cansado/a	*tired*	**perdido/a**	*lost*
confundido/a	*confused*	**preocupado/a**	*worried*
contento/a	*happy/content*	**triste**	*sad*
intoxicado/a	*intoxicated*	**bien**	*well*
lastimado/a	*hurt*	**mal**	*bad*

La estrella está preocupada por la publicidad.	*The star is worried about the press.*
La víctima está muy cansada.	*The victim is very tired.*

▪ Also, use **estar** to indicate where someone or something is located.

El vehículo **está en** la Calle 2.	*The vehicle is on Second Street.*
La marihuana **está en** la cajuela.	*The marihuana is in the trunk.*

▪ The verb **tener** usually means *to have*. Use these forms:

tener: to have					
yo	tengo	*I have*	nosotros/as	tenemos	*we have*
tú	tienes	*you have*			
Ud./él/ella	tiene	*you have/s/he has*	Uds./ellos/ellas	tienen	*you/they have*

Yo **tengo** un problema médico.	*I have a medical problem.*
El sospechoso **tiene** armas.	*The suspect has weapons.*

▪ Used in the following idiomatic phrases with nouns, the English equivalent of **tener** is also *to be*. *Very* is expressed using **mucho (calor, frío, miedo, sueño)** or **mucha (hambre, sed, prisa, razón).**

tener... años	*to be ... years old*	**tener prisa**	*to be in a hurry*
tener calor	*to be hot*	**tener razón**	*to be right*
tener cuidado	*to be careful*	**tener sed**	*to be thirsty*
tener frío	*to be cold*	**tener sueño**	*to be sleepy*
tener hambre	*to be hungry*	**tener que +**	
tener miedo	*to be afraid*	*infinitive*	*to have to*

Para practicar

A. ¿Cómo están?   Use the correct form of **estar** to describe how the following people feel. Make sure the adjective matches the subject in gender and number.

MODELO: (Los policías) (aburrido) mientras esperan la acción.
Los policías están aburridos mientras esperan la acción.

1.   (Los padres) (preocupado) porque su adolescente tiene marihuana.
2.   (La mamá) (contento) con el resultado del examen médico.
3.   (Las víctimas) (confundido) después del accidente.
4.   (Todos nosotros) (nervioso) antes de una prueba de aliento para alcohol.
5.   En una emergencia, (la policía) (ocupado).

B. ¿Qué tienen?   It is very late at night at the DUI checkpoint and there is not too much action. Use one of the **tener** phrases to give logical information about the following situations.

MODELO: Es diciembre y la temperatura es de 23° F. Necesito un suéter. Yo...
Yo tengo frío.

1.   Son las tres de la mañana y los oficiales están cansados. Ellos...
2.   En la calle, dos testigos y yo observamos un asalto horrible. Nosotros...
3.   Un oficial toma mucha agua. Él...
4.   Yo como dos donuts más. Yo...
5.   El señor borracho dice que 2 +2 = 5. Él no...
6.   El paramédico maneja rápidamente al sitio del accidente. El...

C. En la clase de español.   Make a list of five things you are feeling right now in your Spanish class. Then, look around and see if you can guess who else might be feeling the same way.

MODELO: Yo tengo hambre; yo estoy contento.
Helen y Robert también tienen hambre.
El/La profesor/a está contento/a.

Vocabulario Módulo I

Sustantivos

el asiento	seat	la infracción	violation
el atasco	jam (traffic)	el intermitente	turn signal
la banca	bench	la licencia	license
el baúl	trunk	el limpiaparabrisas	windshield wiper
la boca de incendios	fire hydrant	la llanta	tire
la bocina	horn	la llanta de repuesto	spare tire
el bombero	firefighter	la luz	light
la caja	bed (of truck), box	el maletero	trunk
la cajuela	trunk	la marca	brand, make
el cambio	change	la marcha	gear
el capó	hood	la moto(cicleta)	motorcycle
la carretera	highway	el parabrisas	windshield
la cartelera	billboard	el parachoques	bumper
el chofer	driver	la parada	stop (bus)
el cinturón de		el parque	park
seguridad	seatbelt	el/la pasajero/a	passenger
el cofre	hood	el/la peatón/ona	pedestrian
el/la colega	colleague	el peligro	danger
el/la conductor/a	driver	la placa	badge, license
el cruce	crossing		plate
el daño	damage	la rueda	wheel
el descapotable	convertible	la salida	exit
el embotellamiento	bottleneck	el seguro	insurance
el (espejo) retrovisor	rearview mirror	el semáforo	stoplight
el/la esposo/a	husband, wife	la sirena	siren
el estacionamiento	parking	el techo	roof, ceiling
el faro	headlight	el todo-terreno	SUV
los frenos	brakes	la troca/el troque★	truck
la grúa	tow truck	la velocidad	speed
el guardafango	fender	el volante	steering wheel
la herramienta	tool		

Verbos

caminar	to walk	hablar	to talk, speak
chocar	to crash	instalar	to install
contestar	to answer	limpiar	to clean
creer	to believe	llamar	to call
escapar	to escape	manejar	to drive
esperar	to wait for,	necesitar	to need
	to hope	observar	to observe
examinar	to examine	preparar	to prepare
fumar	to smoke	visitar	to visit

Adjetivos

chico/a	*small*	pinchado/a	
delantero/a	*front*	(ponchado/a★)	*punctured*
descompuesto/a	*broken down*	solar	*sun*
desinflado/a	*uninflated, flat*	sucio/a	*dirty*
discapacitado/a	*disabled*	violento/a	*violent*
herido/a	*wounded*		

Otras expresiones

alto	*stop*	dar vuelta	*to turn around*
aquí	*here*	sentido único	*one way*
atrás	*back*	sólo	*only*

Módulo 2

Sustantivos

la advertencia	*warning*	la estrella	*star*
el agua (f.)	*water*	el exceso	*excess*
el alcohol	*alcohol*	el frío	*cold*
el aliento	*breath*	el hambre (f.)	*hunger*
el/la amigo/a	*friend*	la indicación	*direction*
el año	*year*	la línea	*line*
el asalto	*assault*	el miedo	*fear*
la ayuda	*help*	la muerte	*death*
la boca	*mouth*	el papel	*paper*
el camino	*road*	el periódico	*newspaper*
el carril	*lane*	la pluma	*pen*
la cerveza	*beer*	la prisa	*hurry*
el choque	*crash*	el problema	*problem*
el coche	*car*	la razón	*reason*
la consecuencia	*consequence*	el registro	*registration*
el documento	*document*	la sed	*thirst*
la droga	*drug*	el sueño	*sleep, dream*
la escuela	*school*	el tiquete★	*ticket*

Verbos

beber	*to drink*	insistir (en)	*to insist (on)*
comer	*to eat*	ir	*to go*
cometer	*to commit*	recibir	*to receive*
conducir (zc)	*to drive*	sufrir	*to suffer*
correr	*to run*	temer	*to fear*
decidir	*to decide*	tomar	*to take, drink*
discutir	*to argue*	vender	*to sell*
estar	*to be*	vivir	*to live*
hacer	*to do, make*		

Adjetivos

aburrido/a	bored	lastimado/a	injured
borracho/a	drunk	menor	younger
cansado/a	tired	ocupado/a	busy
cerrado/a	closed	perdido/a	lost
confundido/a	confused	preocupado/a	worried
contento/a	content, happy	recto/a	straight
detenido/a	stopped	serio/a	serious
ebrio/a	drunk	sobrio/a	sober
enfermo/a	sick	triste	sad
intoxicado/a	intoxicated		

Otras expresiones

¿Adónde?	Where to?	Es que...	It's just that...
allí	there	Pare el carro.	Stop the car.
Apague el motor.	Stop the motor.	pero	but
Baje del carro.	Get out of the car.	Quítese...	Remove...
		siempre	always
darse prisa	to hurry up	solamente	only
demasiado	too much	Suba al carro.	Get in the car.
derecho	straight	también	too, also
después	after	un poquito	a little bit
en este momento	at this moment	Venga.	Come.

★denotes slang

Síntesis

A escuchar

Necesito ayuda. Listen to the following 911 call and then tell if the following statements are true or false by writing **Sí** o **No** next to each statement. If the answer is **No,** correct the statement.

1. _____ Hay un accidente pero no es serio.

2. _____ Hay tres personas que están lastimadas.

3. _____ El señor viejo está borracho.

4. _____ La señora necesita esperar para hablar con la policía.

A conversar

You and your partner are on DUI checkpoint duty. Using the commands you learned earlier in this chapter, create a series of five requests that you would use to talk to a suspected drunk driver.

MODELO: *Apague el motor, por favor.*

A leer

> ### Si usted recibe una citación por una infracción de tráfico civil, usted tiene tres opciones:
>
> **Opción 1: Escuela de tráfico**
> Usted puede optar a esta opción si:
> - Recibe una infracción civil en movimiento;
> - Durante los previos 24 meses usted no ha asistido a una escuela de tráfico en Arizona;
> - Su infracción no ha causado daños a personas.
>
> **Opción 2: Pagar la multa por correo** *(mail)*
> Usted puede elegir esta opción si admite su responsabilidad por la infracción.
> - Complete la información del pago en este formulario.
> - Determine la cantidad de la multa.
> - Escriba un cheque y envíelo a la Corte de Menlo.
>
> **Opción 3: Disputar la infracción**
> - Con esta opción, usted tiene la oportunidad de disputar la citación en una audiencia *(hearing)* con un juez *(judge)*.
> - Si elige esta opción, no tiene el privilegio de ir a la escuela de tráfico.
> - Escriba el número de la citación y conteste las preguntas en el formulario.

¿Comprende usted? Answer the following questions based on the information given above.

1. ¿Cuántas opciones hay para la persona que recibe una citación civil?
2. ¿Qué opción elige para tomar una clase de manejar?
3. Si la persona quiere disputar la citación, ¿qué opción elige?
4. ¿Por qué necesita una persona tener una audiencia con un juez?

A escribir

Today you and your partner are teaching the Defensive Driving class. Make a poster of the most common moving violations you would discuss with the class. Then make a poster of a vehicle showing the most common mechanical defects that result in citations.

Algo más

Ventana cultural: Los amigos no dejan que sus amigos manejen borrachos

1 LLEVA A TU AMIGO A SU CASA

Si estás dando una fiesta y uno de tus amigos bebió demasiado, no debe manejar. Para asegurarte de que llegue a su casa seguro, tú lo puedes llevar si no has estado bebiendo. O escoge a alguien de antemano que esté sobrio para que sea el conductor designado.

2 INVITA A TU AMIGO A DORMIR EN TU CASA

Invitar a un amigo o huésped a que se quede a dormir en tu casa es una buena manera de evitar que maneje borracho. Tu no tendrás que manejar y tu amigo no tendrá que regresar al día siguiente a buscar su auto. El alcohol afecta tu visión, reflejos y coordinación.

3 LLAMA A UN TAXI PARA TU AMIGO

Si no puedes llevar a tu amigo a su casa, llama a un taxi para que lo lleve. Deberías pagar el viaje por adelantado. De esa manera le demonstrarás que verdaderamente eres un buen amigo. Así, le evitarás que sea arrestado, multado o más problemas.

CONDUCTORES BORRACHOS MATAN CERCA DE 18,000 PERSONAS AL AÑO

AMIGOS NO DEJAN QUE LOS AMIGOS MANEJEN BORRACHOS

U.S. Department of Transportation
National Highway Traffic Safety Administration

Línea de información de NHTSA 1-888-327-4236 www.nhtsa.dot.gov/multicultural

NHTSA
People Saving People
www.nhtsa.dot.gov

A buscar

The National Highway Traffic Safety Administration has embarked on a variety of campaigns—in Spanish—to reach the growing Latino community. Go to their website: www.nhtsa.gov and enter "Spanish" in the internal search engine. You may want to print some of the materials out as handy references!

A conocer: MADD llega a la comunidad latina

Mothers Against Drunk Driving (MADD) anuncia un nuevo sitio en Internet en español. El sitio trae noticias sobre conducir ebrio, información y servicios al público de habla hispana: www.madd.org/spanish o "MADD en español" en www.madd.org. Los visitantes de Internet pueden obtener valiosa información en español con el mensaje de MADD de salvar vidas.

En la communidad latina, los choques de vehículos son la principal causa de muerte de latinos hasta la edad de 24 años, y la segunda causa principal de muerte para la edades de 25 a 44. Además, el número de latinos que conducen por las noches se ha incrementado y la cantidad de consumo de alcohol ha aumentado. En el año 2000, 16,653 personas murieron en accidentes de tráfico relacionados con el alcohol en Estados Unidos, el primer aumento de esta cifra en cinco años. También, más de 640,000 personas sufren daños en choques relacionados con el alcohol cada año, más de una persona por minuto.

MADD es una organización no lucrativa con aproximadamente 600 afiliadas en Estados Unidos. La misión de MADD es detener la conducción en estado ebrio, apoyar a las víctimas de este violento crimen y prevenir el consumo de bebidas por parte de los menores de edad. La visión de MADD es reflejar el rostro de América y tratar de llevar a cabo activamente su misión entre todas las razas y comunidades étnicas. Para obtener más información, visite www.madd.org o llame al 1-800-GET-MADD.

LECCIÓN 3

En mi barrio

Módulo 1
- La vigilancia
- Activities in progress: *El presente progresivo*
- La vida familiar y la vida loca
- Ways of being: **Ser** *vs.* **estar**

Módulo 2
- La guerra de pandillas
- Telling what you are going to do: *El verbo* **ir** *y el futuro inmediato*
- Soplón
- More activities in the present: *Verbos irregulares en el presente*

Síntesis
- A escuchar
- A conversar
- A leer
- A escribir

Algo más
- Ventana cultural: Graffiti
- A buscar
- A conocer: Leroy D. Baca, Sheriff, Los Angeles County

Módulo I

La vigilancia

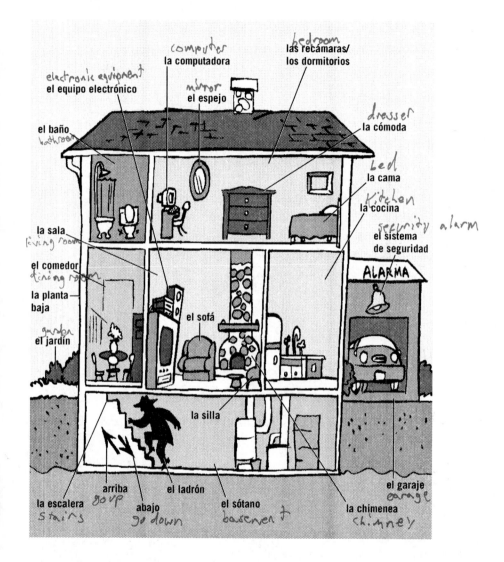

Handwritten annotations on diagram:
- computer — la computadora
- bedroom — las recámaras/ los dormitorios
- electronic equipment — el equipo electrónico
- mirror — el espejo
- dresser — la cómoda
- el baño — bathroom
- bed — la cama
- kitchen — la cocina
- security alarm — el sistema de seguridad
- la sala — living room
- el comedor — dining room
- la planta baja
- garden — el jardín
- el sofá
- ALARMA
- la silla
- la escalera — stairs
- arriba — go up
- abajo — go down
- el ladrón
- el sótano — basement
- el garaje — garage
- la chimenea — chimney

A. ¿Cómo se dice?   Tell what part of a house you might associate with the following activities.

1. Tiene hambre o sed.   **3.** Mira la televisión.
2. Tiene sueño.   **4.** Usa el auto.

B. Cosas.   Tell in which part of the house you would be likely to find the following items:

1. el refrigerador   **4.** las joyas *(jewelry)*
2. el sofá   **5.** una mesa y ocho sillas
3. el champú

La vigilancia

There have been so many burglaries in an Eastside neighborhood that the local police have teamed up with a security company to monitor houses that are likely to be targeted. Watch as Officer Rosales in the van helps a supervisor to test the system by following two officers' paths through the home—by video camera.

OFICIAL ROSALES:	Allí está Luis. **Está entrando** en la cocina por la puerta de atrás. Ahora **está caminando** a la sala y **está mirando** el equipo electrónico.
SUPERVISOR:	¿Dónde está Margarita?
OFICIAL ROSALES:	No la veo. **Estoy vigilando** todos los monitores de la casa, y ella no está. Un momento: hay movimiento en el patio. Creo que es Margarita. **Está buscando** algo en el jardín. No la veo bien.
SUPERVISOR:	Y, ¿dónde está Luis en este momento?
OFICIAL ROSALES:	**Luis está subiendo** la escalera para las recámaras. Un momento. Margarita está escondida *(hidden)* en el baño.
SUPERVISOR:	Pues, entonces, ¿quién es la figura en el jardín?
OFICIAL ROSALES:	¡Dios mío! Yo creo que es un verdadero ladrón que en este momento **está entrando** en el sótano por la ventana.

C. ¿Comprende usted?   Use **Sí** or **No** to tell if the following information is correct. If it is incorrect, make any necessary changes.

1. _No_ El oficial Rosales es un ladrón.

2. _No_ Primero, Luis entra por la ventana del sótano.

3. S: ~~Es~~ Al principio *(at first)*, Margarita está en el baño, invisible a la cámara.

4. _No_ Margarita entra en el sótano.

5. No ~~Sí~~ En realidad, hay un ladrón.

D. ¿Dónde está?   Use the following phrases with the verb **estar** to describe physical placement of people or objects:

cerca de	*close to*	**detrás de**	*behind*
lejos de	*far from*	**encima de**	*above*
al lado de	*next to*	**enfrente de**	*in front of* or *facing*
entre	*between*	**hasta**	*until*

Explain where the following things are using a form of **estar** + one of the adverbs of location. Then compare your answers with a classmate's. They may be different!

MODELO: la cartera *(the wallet)*
La cartera está debajo del auto.

1. la zapatería
2. la pastelería
3. el almácen
4. la camioneta verde
5. el restaurante

E. Mandatos. Use the following basic commands to give someone walking or driving directions:

Siga derecho.	*Go straight ahead.*
Doble a la izquierda.	*Turn left.*
Doble a la derecha.	*Turn right.*
Suba la escalera.	*Go upstairs.*
Baje la escalera.	*Go downstairs.*
Vaya a...	*Go to...*

Using the house plan at the beginning of this chapter, tell your partner how to get to the following places from the back yard.

MODELO: el dormitorio con la computadora
Vaya a la cocina, suba la escalera y doble a la izquierda.

1. la cocina   3. el baño
2. el garaje   4. la sala

Estructuras

Activities in progress:
El presente progresivo

* To tell what someone is in the process of doing at a specific moment, use the present progressive.

En este momento estoy hablando con la víctima. — *I am speaking to the victim right now.*

* The present progressive is formed by a combination of the verb **estar** and the present participle *(-ing form)* of the verb expressing the action in progress.
* To form the present participle of **-ar** verbs, take off the **-ar** ending and add **-ando.**

hablar > habl + ando = hablando — *speaking*
preparar > prepar + ando = preparando — *preparing*

* To form the present participle of most **-er** and **-ir** verbs, take off the **-er** or **-ir** ending and add **-iendo.**

comer > com + iendo = comiendo — *eating*
vivir > viv + iendo = viviendo — *living*

* To form the present progressive tense, use a conjugated form of **estar** to indicate the person doing the action, and then the present participle.

Estoy comiendo. — *I am eating.*
Estamos esperando. — *We are waiting.*
Están escribiendo. — *They are writing.*

* The following verbs have irregular present participles:

dormir *(to sleep)* **durmiendo** **morir** *(to die)* **muriendo**

* **Spelling rule:** Any time an unaccented **-i** falls between two vowels, it automatically changes to **-y.**

leer *(to read)* > le + iendo > leyendo — **Estoy leyendo.** — *I am reading.*

traer *(to bring)* > tra + iendo > trayendo — **Está trayendo el agua.** — *He is bringing the water.*

Para practicar

A. Actividades.   By changing the following verbs to the present progressive tense, you will be able to tell what your colleagues are doing right now.

MODELO: El agente Sánchez examina la evidencia.
El agente Sánchez está examinando la evidencia.

1.   Los oficiales *investigan* el crimen.
2.   El sargento y yo *leemos* el reporte.
3.   El detective *estudia* la escena del crimen.
4.   Un técnico *prepara* los monitores de vigilancia.
5.   Unos agentes *descansan* en el patio y *comen* un sándwich.
6.   Nosotros *esperamos* a los testigos en la sala.
7.   Los investigadores *buscan* más evidencia.

B. La agenda.   Tell what you are probably doing at the following times.

MODELO: Son las ocho de la mañana y ...
Son las ocho de la mañana y estoy tomando café.

1.   Es mediodía y ...
2.   Son las nueve de la noche y ...
3.   Son las seis de la mañana y ...
4.   Son las seis de la tarde y...
5.   Es medianoche y...
6.   Son las tres y media de la tarde y ...

C. Mis compañeros de clase.   Look around the room and describe ten things that your classmates or teacher are doing now.

MODELO: *Laura está escribiendo su tarea.*

Módulo I

La vida familiar y la vida loca

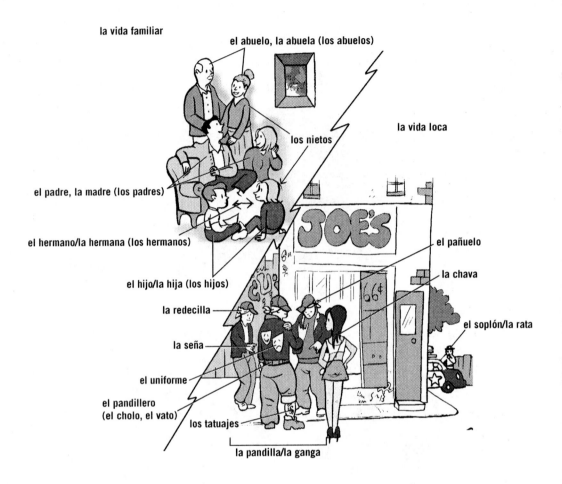

la vida familiar

el abuelo, la abuela (los abuelos)

la vida loca

los nietos

el padre, la madre (los padres)

el hermano/la hermana (los hermanos)

el pañuelo

la chava

el hijo/la hija (los hijos)

el soplón/la rata

la redecilla

la seña

el uniforme

el pandillero
(el cholo, el vato)

los tatuajes

la pandilla/la ganga

¡OJO!

This chapter introduces street slang, often needed in police situations. Its purpose is to present the learner with real-life language as used in gang and drug situations.

A. ¿Cómo se dice?   From **la vida familiar,** find a word that matches the following descriptions of relationships.

1.   La mamá de mi mamá es mi _____.

2.   El hijo de mi hijo es mi _____.

3.   Mi _____ es el hijo de mi abuelo.

4.   El otro hijo de mis padres es mi _____.

5.   Mi madre y mi padre son _____.

B. En la calle. Give the word from the drawing **la vida loca** that describes the following situations. Check the drawing if you need help.

1. Un "club" de jóvenes que defiende su territorio—a veces con violencia— es una _____.

2. Dos palabras informales que describen a los miembros de una pandilla son

_____ y _____.

3. Los saludos que los miembros de la pandilla dan con las manos son las

_____.

4. La _____ significa la vida de un miembro de una pandilla.

La hermana del vato

Officer Rosales has caught the criminal entering the basement of the house under surveillance. As it turns out, the "perp" is a young woman who is very, very scared. But is it the police she is afraid of?

OFICIAL ROSALES: ¿Quién **es** usted y por qué **está** entrando en esta casa?

JOVEN: **Soy** Mariana Carrillo Armenta. No **estoy** entrando en esta casa.

OFICIAL: ¿De dónde **es** usted? Enséñeme su identificación.

JOVEN: **Soy** de Nicaragua.

OFICIAL: ¿Por qué **está** aquí?

JOVEN: *(silencio)*

OFICIAL: Mariana, tiene que hablarme. ¿Por qué **está** aquí?

JOVEN: **Estoy** buscando a mi hermano.

OFICIAL: ¿Por qué busca a su hermano aquí?

JOVEN: *(crying)* No **soy** soplona. No quiero hablar.

OFICIAL: Mariana, **es** evidente que usted **está** muy preocupada. ¿Su hermano **está** en peligro?

JOVEN: Sí, señor. Mucho peligro. Él **es** miembro de la pandilla "Los Cholos" y la pandilla rival, "Círculo 13" **está** cerca. Ellos **son** violentos.

OFICIAL: ¿Dónde **está** su hermano ahora?

JOVEN: No sé. No **está** aquí...Tengo miedo.

C. ¿Comprende usted? Answer the following questions with information from the dialogue.

1. ¿Quién es la joven que investiga el oficial Rosales?
2. ¿Por qué está aquí?
3. ¿Dónde está su hermano?
4. ¿Por qué está nerviosa Mariana?
5. ¿Cómo son los miembros de la pandilla "Círculo 13"?

D. La familia moderna. Besides learning the members of the traditional family, it is very important to learn to identify the members of the modern family. Study these modern family relationships, and then identify the relationships described below.

ex–esposo o ex–esposa	*ex-husband or ex-wife*
el padrastro	*stepfather*
la madrastra	*stepmother*
el hijastro	*stepson*
la hijastra	*stepdaughter*
el hermanastro	*stepbrother*
la hermanastra	*stepsister*
medio–hermano/a	*half brother/sister*

1. El hijo de mi nueva esposa es mi _____.

2. Mi _____ y yo tenemos la misma madre pero padres diferentes.

3. Mi _____ es la hija de la nueva esposa de mi padre.

4. Mi _____ es el nuevo esposo de mi madre.

5. Antes del divorcio, Elena era mi esposa. Ahora es mi _____.

E. Mandatos. Circulate around the room and give five students you meet one of the above commands. Then, let that student give you a command. See if you and your classmates can carry out the orders. Be patient—it's tricky!

Enséñeme...	**sus manos.**	*Show me...*	*your hands.*
	su identificación.		*your identification.*
	sus documentos.		*your documents.*
Describa...	**al sospechoso.**	*Describe...*	*the suspect.*
	a su hermano, el auto.		*your brother, the car.*
Hábleme.		*Talk to me* or *Speak to me.*	
Dígame.		*Tell me.*	

MODELO: E1: **Describa** al profesor:
E2: *Es alto, calvo e inteligente.*

Estructuras   *Ways of being: Ser y estar*

* You have already seen that in Spanish, the English verb *to be* has two equivalents: **ser** and **estar.** Each of these Spanish verbs has its own meanings and usage. They are not interchangeable.

Use **estar** to indicate:

* where something or someone is located

El policía **está** en la calle Broadway.	*The policeman is on Broadway.*
La pistola **está** en la mano.	*The gun is in his hand.*

* physical or mental conditions

El padre **está** enfermo hoy.	*The father is sick today.*
Yo **estoy** nerviosa esperando al policía.	*I am nervous waiting for the police.*

* circumstances or variable conditions indicating a change from the normal condition

La víctima **está** herida.	*The victim is wounded.*
Los ojos de la víctima **están** cerrados.	*The victim's eyes are closed.*

* an action in progress with a present participle

La niña **está llorando**.	*The girl is crying.*
Está entrando por la ventana.	*She is entering through the window.*

Ser is used to:

* identify people or things

Yo **soy** policía.	*I am a police officer.*
El hermano **es** pandillero.	*The brother is a gang member.*

* tell what someone or something is like, including personality and physical traits

¿Cómo **son** los miembros de la pandilla?	*What are the gang members like?*
Mi hermano **es** fuerte y simpático.	*My brother is strong and nice.*

* tell where someone or something is from

La señora **es de** México.	*The woman is from Mexico.*
La pandilla **es del** Barrio Nuevo.	*The gang is from Barrio Nuevo.*

* to whom something belongs or what it is made of

El grafiti **es de** la pandilla.	*The tagging belongs to the gang.*
El tatuaje **es de** tinta casera.	*The tattoos are made of homemade ink.*

* to indicate the time and place of an event

La cita con el soplón **es** a las diez.	*The appointment with the informant is at ten.*
La cita **es** en la calle 19.	*The appointment is on 19th Street.*

Para practicar

A. ¿Cómo son?   As a surveillance officer, you are always observing people. Describe what the following people or things are like by finding a logical description from the choices in column **B** and joining them with **ser** to the items in column **A**. Be sure to make the adjectives match.

MODELO: Los pandilleros/violento
Los pandilleros **son** *violentos.*

	A		**B**
c **1.**	El vato que no habla inglés	**a.**	muy alto
d **2.**	Los tatuajes del pandillero	**b.**	alcohólico
a **3.**	El jugador de básquetbol	**c.**	de Colombia
e **4.**	El policía veterano	**d.**	artístico
b **5.**	El chofer borracho *(drunk driver)*	**e.**	dedicado

B. ¿Cómo están?   Now guess what the following people are feeling in these situations. You may want to review the phrases with **estar** at the end of Lección 2!

MODELO: Yo, en un examen de español.
Estoy nervioso/a.

1.   El pandillero que completa un grafiti artístico
2.   Una madre que no sabe dónde está su hijo a la una de la mañana
3.   Los abuelos durante una celebración familiar
4.   Dos amigos que se saludan con señas

C. En la calle.   You are hard at work on the streets on a busy night. Use the proper form of **ser** or **estar** to describe what is happening out there. Be sure to match the adjectives to the subjects!

MODELO: Mi colega *(partner)* y yo/cansados
Mi colega y yo estamos cansados.

1.   El padre del pandillero/preocupado
2.   Los padres de la bebé en el accidente/joven
3.   La víctima del asalto/María Espinoza
4.   La familia grande/de México y no habla inglés
5.   Esta pistola/del sospechoso
6.   La puerta de la casa de la víctima/abierto

Módulo 2

La guerra de pandillas

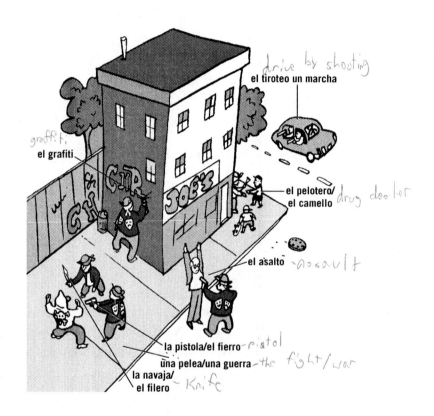

drive by shooting
el tiroteo un marcha

graffiti
el grafiti

**el pelotero/
el camello** *drug dealer*

el asalto *assault*

la pistola/el fierro *pistol*
una pelea/una guerra *the fight/war*
**la navaja/
el filero** *Knife*

A. ¿Cómo se dice?   Using the drawing above and your memory of previous vocabulary, match one of these words with the most appropriate definition.

a. soplón   **b.** tiroteo en marcha   **c.** hermano   **d.** jefe   **e.** chavos

1. _____ b _____ El uso de armas de fuego por la ventana de un auto en movimiento

2. _____ e _____ Los amigos y asociados de la misma pandilla o barrio

3. _____ a _____ Una persona que secretamente da información a la policía

4. _____ c _____ Un miembro de mi familia—el otro hijo de mis padres

5. _____ D _____ El líder de una pandilla

¡OJO!

Placa has a wide variety of street meanings: sometimes used for police, graffiti with gang identification marks, sometimes used for marihuana, sometimes used just for identification.

B. Armas y crímenes.   Match a word below with a logical definition.

a. grafiti   **b.** pistola   **c.** asalto   **d.** guerra

1. ___d___ un conflicto entre dos grupos de rivales

2. ___b___ un arma de fuego

3. ___c___ cuando una persona inocente es la víctima de un robo o una pelea

4. ___a___ expresión artística o informativa de una pandilla

La guerra

*Mariana's brother, Chato and his best friend **(su carnal)** Diablo are both leaders in their neighborhood gang, **Los Cholos.** They are at war with members of **El Círculo 13** who have challenged their turf by overwriting the Cholos' "tag" of identity **(la placa)** with their own and setting up their own drug dealers. Mariana is right to be worried about her brother. This is the conversation she overhears.*

CHATO: (greeting Diablo) Hola, Ese. ¿Qué onda?

DIABLO: Aquí no más. Oye, ¿tienes la plata *(money)*?

CHATO: Sí. ¿Adónde vamos?

DIABLO: Ahora yo voy por el fierro que tiene el Gordo. Entonces, tú y yo, 'mano, vamos a buscar al chingao★ pelotero que les vende el polvo de ángel y la mota a mi vieja y a mis hermanitas. ¿Estás conmigo?

CHATO: Simón. Aquí tengo la navaja bien afilada. ¿Qué vamos a hacer?

DIABLO: Primero, corremos el barrio hasta verlo. Si está muy visible, hacemos un tiroteo en marcha. Si no, vamos a necesitar las navajas.

C. ¿Comprende usted?   Indicate whether the following statements are **Cierto (C)** or **Falso (F).** If it is false, correct it.

1. _____ Chato y Diablo son rivales.

2. _____ Chato tiene la plata (el dinero) para comprar una pistola.

3. _____ Van a buscar al narcotraficante que vende drogas a su familia.

4. _____ No necesitan armas—sólo van a hablar.

★In street pronunciation, the "d" in "ado" endings is frequently not heard; thus terms such as "chingado," "embollado" and "arrebatado" sound like "chingao," "embollao," and "arrebatao."

D. ¿Amigo o enemigo?   The following two lists contain "terms of endearment" in street slang used for friends and for enemies. Study each list and then decide if the term refers to a **"carnal" (C)** or to a **"rival" (R).**

Términos para amigos:

camarada	*homie* -comrade
carnal	*best friend or brother* ~Mexican
chavo/a	*boyfriend or girlfriend of a gang member*
compa	*short for* **compadre**—*good friend* –close friends
cuate	*close friend (twin)*
ese	*dude*
'mano	*short for brother* **(hermano)**
vato	*dude*
viejo/a	*the spouse, parent, or "significant other" of a member*

Términos para los enemigos:

bote	*jail*
cabrón	*bastard*
chingón/ona	*bastard or bitch*
chulo	*pimp*
chuntaros	*illegal Mexican (very derogatory)*
culero	*asshole*
hijo de puta	*son of a bitch*
jota	*gay, lesbian*
juda	*police (from Judas, traitor)*
maricón	*faggot*
mayate	*black (very derogatory)*
migra	*INS*
mojado	*wetback (highly insulting)*
pendejo	*jerk (highly insulting)*
perros	*cops (dogs)*
pinche placas	*damn cops*
puta	*whore*
puto	*homosexual*
rata/ratón	*snitch*
Sancho	*wife's boyfriend*

I. _____ carnal   **4.** _____ ese

2. _____ puto   **5.** _____ vieja

3. _____ maricón

Estructuras   *Telling what you are going to do:*
El verbo ir y el futuro inmediato

* Use these forms of the verb **ir** to indicate where someone is going.

ir (to go)			
yo	voy	nosotros/as	vamos
tú	vas		
él, ella, Ud.	va	ustedes, ellos/as	van

—¿**Va** Ud. a la casa?   *—Are you going home?*
—No, **voy** a la casa de mi chava.   *—No, I am going to my girlfriend's.*

* A simple way to indicate what is going to happen in the future is to use
ir a + an infinitive.

—¿**Van Uds. a buscar** al sospechoso?   *—Are you both going to look for the suspect?*

—No, **vamos a hablar** con su hermana.   *—No, we are going to talk to his sister.*

—¿El Chato **va a tener** la plata?   *—Is Chato going to have the money?*

—Sí, **va a tener** el dinero pronto.   *—Yes, he is going to have the money soon.*

Para practicar

A. ¿Dónde?   Tell where these people have to go in order to do what they
need to do.

MODELO: Yo tengo hambre. Quiero comer.
              Yo voy a un restaurante.

1. El policía necesita trabajar. (a la comisaría)
2. Los drogadictos necesitan comprar crack. (al pelotero)
3. Nosotros necesitamos dormir. (al dormitorio)
4. Yo necesito ver a un amigo herido *(wounded)*. (al hospital)
5. Usted y yo necesitamos hablar. (a mi casa)

B. ¿Qué van a hacer?   Here's the situation. Tell what can be done to help.

MODELO: Nosotros tenemos un examen de español.
(Nosotros) vamos a estudiar.

I.   Ustedes tienen hambre.
2.   Los policías están cansados después de trabajar ocho horas.
3.   Un rival insulta a la chava del carnal.
4.   El policía necesita un soplón.
5.   Estoy en el auto y veo un asalto terrible.
6.   El prisionero tiene sed.

C. ¿Y usted?   Pick three places that you will go to today and tell three things you will do in each place. Compare answers with a classmate.

MODELO: Voy a mi casa.
Voy a estudiar español, voy a mirar la televisión y voy a comer.

Soplón

A. La memoria.   Use your memory and the information from the drawing to match each word in the list with its most logical definition.

a. la seguridad   **b.** el detector de metales
c. la entrada   **d.** la salida

I.   _____ ingreso en un edificio

2.   _____ egreso de un edificio

3.   _____ máquina para buscar armas de metal escondidas

4.   _____ el grupo de iniciativas para la protección de las personas

B. Acciones. Find a verb from the drawing that matches the description below.

1. tener información sobre algo _____

2. recibir información por las orejas *(ears)* _____

3. abandonar un sitio para ir a otro _____

4. situar una cosa en otro lugar _____

5. transportar una cosa de un lugar a otro _____

La soplona

Mariana does not want to be a "soplón," but she does not want to lose her brother to street violence either. She is afraid enough to call Officer Rosales for help.

MARIANA: Oficial Rosales, si mi hermano y el Diablo **saben** que estoy hablando con usted, me van a matar. Pero en este momento, ellos **salen** a buscar a "Vicious", el jefe de la pandilla "Círculo 13" y **traen** armas. Hablan de un tiroteo en marcha. Tengo miedo.

OFICIAL: **Hace** bien en llamarme, Mariana. **¿Conoce** a "Vicious"? ¿Sabe dónde radica *(hangs out)*?

MARIANA: Sí, **conozco** a Vicious. Él **pone** muchas drogas en manos de los chicos de la escuela primaria. Yo siempre **oigo** de los chavos que es muy malo. No **sé** exactamente dónde radica, pero me **parece** que normalmente está cerca de la Escuela Menlo en la Calle 13.

OFICIAL ROSALES: Gracias, Mariana. Yo **salgo** inmediatamente para la escuela. Y, no se preocupe. Su hermano no va a **saber** que usted y yo hablamos.

C. ¿Comprende usted? Try to answer the following questions based on the dialogue.

1. ¿Por qué llama Mariana al oficial Rosales?
2. ¿Qué va a pasar si su hermano sabe que ella habla con la policía?
3. ¿Cómo es el jefe de "Círculo 13"?
4. ¿Dónde radica Vicious?

D. Más armas. The following is a short list of street weapons. Study the list and then identify each one described in the following sentences.

a.	**la ametralladora**	*machine gun*
b.	**el machete**	*a machete / large, curved sword blade*
c.	**el cuerno del chivo**	*AK-47*
d.	**la bala**	*the bullet*
e.	**el balazo**	*the bullet shot or wound*
f.	**el disparo**	*the shot*

1. Dos armas automáticas son la _____ y el _____.

2. Una arma que se usa para cortar las plantas—y a las personas—es el

_____.

3. Una _____ es la munición que se dispara de una pistola.

E. Mandatos. Study these **mandatos** that are useful when you must stop a potentially violent situation, then choose the most appropriate one for each situation described below.

Abra su chaqueta.	*Open your jacket!*
Entrelace los dedos.	*Put your hands together!*
Levántese.	*Get up.*
¡Manos arriba!	*Hands up!*
¡No se mueva!	*Don't move!*
Ponga las manos...	*Put your hands on...*
en la cabeza.	*your head.*
en la pared.	*the wall.*
en el carro.	*the car.*
detrás de la espalda.	*behind your back.*
¡Salga!	*Get out!*
Siéntese.	*Sit down.*
¡Silencio!	*Be quiet / Shut up!*
¡Suelte la pistola!	*Drop the pistol!*
... **la navaja!**	*... the knife!*
¡Suéltelo!	*Drop it! (unnamed)*
¡Venga aquí!	*Come here!*

1. _____ The suspect is sitting in a car.

2. _____ The suspect is holding a knife.

3. _____ You are trying to handcuff the suspect.

4. _____ The suspect is using Spanish street slang to communicate with his "carnal."

Estructuras   *More activities in the present: Verbos irregulares en el presente*

⁕ In the present indicative tense, the following verbs are conjugated as regular **-er** and **-ir** verbs in all forms except the **yo** form.

hacer	*(to make or do)*	**hago,**	haces, hace, hacemos, hacen
poner	*(to put or place)*	**pongo,**	pones, pone, ponemos, ponen
salir	*(to go out, to leave, to appear suddenly as in a rash)*	**salgo,**	sales, sale, salimos, salen
traer	*(to bring)*	**traigo,**	traes, trae, traemos, traen
saber	*(to know—information, how to)*	**sé,**	sabes, sabe, sabemos, saben

⁕ The verb **oír** *(to hear)* follows a different pattern:

oigo, oyes, **oy**e, **oí**mos, **oy**en

⁕ Verbs ending in **-cer** and **-cir** add the letter **z** before the **c** in the **yo** form only.

parecer *(to seem)*	pare**zco**, pareces, parece, parecemos, parecen
conocer *(to be acquainted with, to personally know people or places)*	cono**zco**, conoces, concoce, conocemos, conocen
traducir *(to translate)*	tradu**zco**, traduces, traduce, traducimos, traducen
producir *(to produce)*	produ**zco**, produces, produce, producimos, producen
conducir *(to drive)*	condu**zco**, conduces, conduce, conducimos, conducen

⁕ **Ways of knowing: saber vs. conocer**

Both **saber** and **conocer** have equivalents in English: *to know.*

⁕ Use **saber** to indicate that someone knows facts, information, or when followed by an infinitive, how to do something.

Yo **sé** el número de teléfono del pelotero.	*I know the dealer's phone number.*
El pelotero **sabe** vender drogas.	*The dealer knows how to sell drugs.*

⁕ Use **conocer** to indicate that somebody is personally familiar with a person or place.

Yo **conozco** al jefe de la pandilla.	*I know the gang leader personally.*
Yo no **conozco** este barrio.	*I am not familiar with this neighborhood.*

Para practicar

A. En la clase de la escuela secundaria. As you observe this high school class, tell what the students are doing. Then, tell if you ever do the same things.

MODELO: Antonio trae drogas a la escuela.
    Yo no traigo drogas.

1. Manuela es muy inteligente. *Sabe* todas las respuestas.
2. Aristeo *sale* de la clase para fumar en el baño.
3. Corina *hace* planes para comprar mota.
4. Marco *pone* los pies en la silla.
5. Carolina *oye* música Hip Hop en su Walkman.
6. Gregorio *hace* mucho ruido para distraer *(distract)* a la maestra.
7. Ana *trae* Fritos para comer en la clase.
8. Elena *hace* muchas notas y dibujos *(doodles)*.

B. El vato. You have just arrested a gang member for threatening violence. Tell if you or your suspect does the following things:

MODELO: Traer un cuerno del chivo.
    El sospechoso trae un cuerno del chivo.

1. Oír información de un soplón
2. Poner esposas *(handcuffs)* en las manos
3. Conducir el patrullero
4. Traer mota y polvo de ángel en los pantalones
5. Saber recitar el Aviso Miranda *(the Miranda Warning)*

C. Estudiantes de la vida loca. You and your classmate are trainees with the Gang Prevention Task Force. Each of you must give three points of information that you know about gangs and then each of you must tell if you have any personal familiarity with them.

MODELO: *Yo sé que hay pandillas en el Barrio Hollywood.*
    Yo no conozco el Barrio Hollywood.

Vocabulario Módulo I

Sustantivos

el/la abuelo/a	*grandparent*	**la chimenea**	*fireplace*
el baño	*bathroom*	**el/la cholo/a★**	*person of mixed*
el/la bebé	*baby*		*race*
la cama	*bed*	**la cocina**	*kitchen*
la cámara	*camera*	**el comedor**	*dining room*
el/la chavo/a★	*boy/girlfriend of*	**la cómoda**	*dresser*
	gang member	**el/la compañero/a**	*companion*

la computadora	computer	la madre	mother
el divorcio	divorce	el/la miembro	member
el dormitorio	bedroom	el/la nieto/a	grandchild
el equipo electrónico	electronic equipment (home theater)	el padrastro	stepfather
		el padre	father
la escalera	stairs	la pandilla	gang
la escena	scene	el pañuelo	handkerchief
el espejo	mirror	la planta baja	ground floor
la evidencia	evidence	la rata★	stool pigeon
la figura	figure	la recámara	bedroom
la ganga★	gang	la sala	living room
el garaje	garage	la seña	sign, signal
el/la hermanastro/a	stepbrother/sister	la silla	chair
el/la hermano/a	brother/sister	el sistema de seguridad	security system
el/la hijastro/a	stepchild	el/la soplón/soplona	whistle blower
el/la hijo/a	son/daughter	el sótano	basement
la identificación	identification	el uniforme	uniform
el jardín	garden, yard	el vato★	homeboy
la joya	jewel	la ventana	window
el/la jugador/a	player	la vida	life
el/la ladrón/ona	thief	la vigilancia	surveillance
la madrastra	stepmother		

Verbos

dormir (ue)	to sleep	morir (ue)	to die
enseñar	to show, teach	subir	to go up, climb
llorar	to cry		

Adjetivos

abierto/a	open	invisible	invisible
escondido/a	hidden	loco/a	crazy
familiar	family related	verdadero/a	true

Otras expresiones

a la derecha	to the right	Doble...	Turn...
a la izquierda	to the left	en realidad	in reality
abajo	down	encima de	on top of, above
al lado de	next to	enfrente de	in front of
arriba	up, above	entonces	then
cerca de	near	entre	between
debajo de	under	Hábleme.	Talk to me.
Describa...	Describe...	lejos de	far from
detrás de	in back of	pues	well
Dígame.	Tell me.	Siga derecho.	Straight ahead.
¡Dios mío!	My God!	Vaya a...	Go to...

Módulo 2

Sustantivos

el abrazo	hug	la guerra	war
la amenaza	threat	el/la jefe/a	boss, chief
la ametralladora	machine gun	la lana★	money (wool)
el arma de fuego (f.)	firearm	el machete	big knife
el auto(móvil)	automobile	el/la maestro/a	teacher
la bala	bullet	la mota★	marihuana
el balazo	bullet shot	el narcotraficante	drug trafficker
el camello★	drug dealer	la navaja★	switchblade
la cosa	thing	el/la pandillero/a	gang member
el/la criminal	criminal	la pared	wall
el cuerno del chivo★	AK-47	la pelea	fight
el detector de metales	metal detector	el pelotero★	drug dealer
el desafío	challenge	la pistola	pistol
el disparo	shot	la plata★	money (silver)
el/la drogadicto/a	drug addict	el polvo de ángel	angel dust
el/la enemigo/a	enemy	la pregunta	question
la entrada	entry	el/la prisionero/a	prisoner
la espalda	back	el/la rival	rival
las esposas	handcuffs	el ruido	noise
el fierro★	gun	la seguridad	security
el/la fugitivo/a	fugitive	el territorio	territory
el grafiti	graffiti	el tiroteo en marcha	drive-by shooting
		el/la vendedor/a	salesperson

Verbos

atacar	to attack	poner (g)	to put, place
cortar	to cut	producir (zc)	to produce
defender (ie)	to defend	radicar★	to hang out
entender (ie)	to understand	recomendar (ie)	to recommend
insultar	to insult	saber	to know
matar	to kill	terminar	to end, finish
oír (ig) (y)	to hear	traducir (zc)	to translate
parecer (zc)	to seem	traer (ig)	to bring

Adjetivos

afilado/a	sharpened	querido/a	dear
encubierto/a	undercover	secreto/a	secret

Otras expresiones

a veces	at times	Oye.	Hey.
Chale.★	Nope.	Ponga…	Put…
ese★	dude	primero	first
mientras	while	pronto	soon

★Additional slang terms are on p. 91. More commands are on pp. 81, 86, 96.

¿Qué hubo?★	*What happened?*	**Silencio.**	*Be quiet.*
		Simón.★	*Sure.*
¿Qué onda?★	*What's up?*	**Suelte...**	*Drop...*
quizás	*maybe*	**todavía**	*yet, still*

★ denotes slang

Síntesis

A escuchar

¿Qué es eso? Listen to the following definitions in Spanish and then circle the letter of the word that best describes what you have heard.

1. **a.** un desfile *(parade)* de policía
   b. un tiroteo en marcha
   c. armas de fuego
2. **a.** una pandilla
   b. un vato
   c. un soplón
3. **a.** una chava
   b. la mota
   c. un soplón
4. **a.** armas
   b. animales domésticos
   c. miembros de la policía

A conversar

In groups of four, brainstorm things your community is doing to fight gang violence and drug use among young people.

A leer

The following letter poses a very common question about gangs and gang members. Read the question, then read the answer from an ex-gang member, and test your comprehension by stating whether the following statements are **Cierto (C)** or **Falso (F)**.

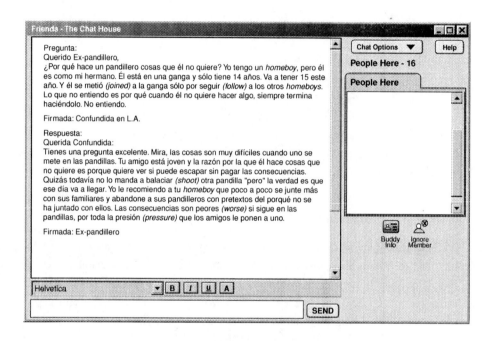

Friends - The Chat House

Pregunta:
Querido Ex-pandillero,
¿Por qué hace un pandillero cosas que él no quiere? Yo tengo un *homeboy*, pero él es como mi hermano. Él está en una ganga y sólo tiene 14 años. Va a tener 15 este año. Y él se metió *(joined)* a la ganga sólo por seguir *(follow)* a los otros *homeboys*. Lo que no entiendo es por qué cuando él no quiere hacer algo, siempre termina haciéndolo. No entiendo.

Firmada: Confundida en L.A.

Respuesta:
Querida Confundida:
Tienes una pregunta excelente. Mira, las cosas son muy difíciles cuando uno se mete en las pandillas. Tu amigo está joven y la razón por la que él hace cosas que no quiere es porque quiere ver si puede escapar sin pagar las consecuencias. Quizás todavía no lo manda a balaciar *(shoot)* otra pandilla "pero" la verdad es que ese día va a llegar. Yo le recomiendo a tu *homeboy* que poco a poco se junte más con sus familiares y abandone a sus pandilleros con pretextos del porqué no se ha juntado con ellos. Las consecuencias son peores *(worse)* si sigue en las pandillas, por toda la presión *(pressure)* que los amigos le ponen a uno.

Firmada: Ex-pandillero

1. _____ A veces el "homeboy" de Confundida hace cosas contra su voluntad *(against his will)*.

2. _____ El "homeboy" se metió a la pandilla para tener acceso a las drogas.

3. _____ El ex-pandillero dice que un día es evidente que el "homeboy" va a tener que usar armas contra una pandilla rival.

4. _____ El ex-pandillero recomienda que el "homeboy" pase más tiempo con los pandilleros de ganga.

A escribir

Using the "present progressive" verb form (**estar** + ing), write a list of at least five activities being done locally to curb gang activities and drug use.

MODELO: *La policía está organizando grupos de padres y maestros.*

Algo más

Ventana cultural: Graffiti

It is common to hear graffiti among rival gangs referred to as "the newspaper of the streets." Graffiti, known also as **"tags"** or **"grafitis"** or **"etiquetas,"** or **"placas,"** is rarely random art for art's sake to beautify a downtown area. Graffiti is a language with structure and syntax. And if you can learn to understand it, you just may understand the threats and challenges of street warfare. Graffiti is usually composed of the following elements:

Names (Los nombres): The name of the gang or its abbreviated symbol.

Nicknames (Los apodos): Nicknames are a normal part of everyday Latino culture, often describing physical characteristics of the person. In gang culture, nicknames are the key to identity. In the dialogues in this chapter, two of the more common **"apodos"** were used: **El Cholo** and **El Diablo.** Often the nicknames of the gang members will appear in a vertical line within graffiti to demonstrate the hierarchy of their leadership.

Turf (El territorio): The turf that the gang is claiming is often represented by the name of the gang: **Círculo 13** o **Barrio Hollywood.** Sometimes the turf is identified by street boundaries.

Threats and **challenges (Amenazas y Desafíos):** Gang signs that appear in another gang's territory are direct threats of impending war. Also, a group's **placa** in its own territory that has been crossed out, broken or erased—**borrada**—will also be taken as an invitation to war.

1. V: Varrio or Barrio, meaning neighborhood or group/gang.
2. SS: Double S means South Side, the geographical sector of this particular Barrio. (WS might mean West Side, etc.)
3. CH is the abbreviation of the actual gang or barrio identification. In this case, "CH" = Chula Heights.
4. R: "Rifa" is a declaration of superiority. It stands for "rules" or "controls."
5. 13: The number 13 stands for allegiance to Southern California. The number 14 is an indicator of allegiance to Northern California.

Reading graffiti is not always easy. But it is literally a window on the world—
or, at least the barrio—for gangs.

En mis propias palabras.   As a member of law enforcement, you often see
placas on the streets. Next time you pass one, copy down the "tag" and see if
you can interpret it according to the previous explanation. It may not be easy!

A buscar

The Web is full of invaluable information about street gangs in both English
and Spanish. For additional information on gang language, go to the following
URL: www.csun.edu/~hcchs006/12.html.

A conocer: Leroy D. Baca, Sheriff, Los Angeles County

Leroy D. Baca, Sheriff, Los Angeles County

El sheriff del condado de Los Ángeles es un latino, importante si consideramos el número de hispanos en el sur de California. Aquí presentamos una breve biografía de él.

Los Angeles County Sheriff Leroy D. Baca was born in East Los Angeles in 1942. He graduated from Benjamin Franklin High School in 1960. He worked a variety of jobs to support himself while attending East Los Angeles College, and entered the United States Marine Corps Reserves in 1964.

Sheriff Baca began his public service career in 1965 as a Deputy Sheriff Trainee, working through the early portion of his career in custody, recruitment, on patrol on the streets of East Los Angeles, and as staff instructor at the Sheriff's Academy. In 1981 he was appointed to Captain and selected to command Norwalk Station; subsequent promotions to Commander and Chief followed.

Believing strongly in education, Sheriff Baca continued his studies, and in 1993 he graduated from the University of Southern California with a Doctorate of Public Administration. In 1998, he was sworn in as Los Angeles County's 30th Sheriff, having been elected by the citizens of Los Angeles County. Sheriff Baca commands the largest Sheriff's Department in the world and supervises more than 13,000 sworn and civilian personnel. Sheriff Baca strongly believes in the concept of mentoring. He has provided leadership, management, and direction to thousands of deputy sheriffs and police officers throughout his career.

LECCIÓN 4

Las drogas

Módulo I
- La conexión
- Indicating relationships: *Los adjetivos posesivos*
- La compra
- Describing daily activities: *Los verbos con cambios de raíz*

Módulo 2
- Están arrestados
- Comparing and contrasting: *Los comparativos*
- Las prioridades
- Comparing and contrasting: *Los superlativos*

Síntesis
- A escuchar
- A conversar
- A leer
- A escribir

Algo más
- Ventana cultural: Spanglish—is it a language?
- A buscar
- A conocer: Enrique Camarena

Módulo I

La conexión

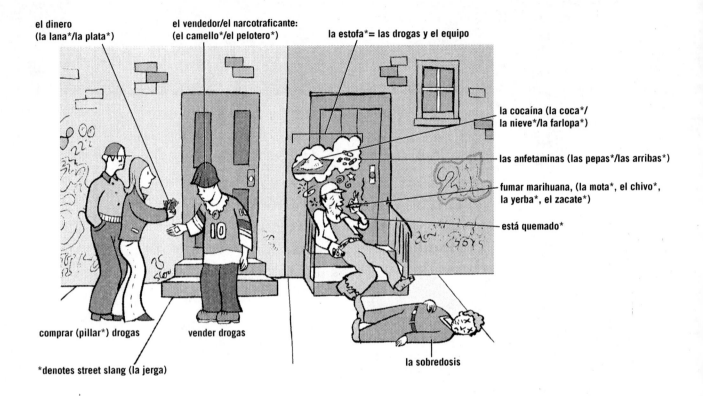

el dinero
(la lana*/la plata*)

el vendedor/el narcotraficante:
(el camello*/el pelotero*)

la estofa*= las drogas y el equipo

la cocaína (la coca*/
la nieve*/la farlopa*)

las anfetaminas (las pepas*/las arribas*)

fumar marihuana, (la mota*, el chivo*,
la yerba*, el zacate*)

está quemado*

comprar (pillar*) drogas

vender drogas

la sobredosis

*denotes street slang (la jerga)

A. La jerga. There is a great deal of slang used on the streets. Give the more standard word that describes the following drug terms.

1. la lana, la plata: el _____

2. la mota, el chivo, la yerba: la _____

3. la coca, la nieve, la farlopa: la _____

4. el camello, el pelotero: el _____

5. la estofa: las _____ y el _____

B. Acciones. See if you can match the words in column **A** with close equivalents in column **B**.

	A		**B**
1.	_b_ comprar	**a.**	sentir *(to feel)* los efectos de las drogas
2.	_c_ fumar	**b.**	dar dinero y recibir un producto
3.	_d_ vender	**c.**	inhalar el humo de los cigarros o drogas
4.	_a_ estar quemado	**d.**	recibir dinero y dar un producto

La compra

Some days there's a drug deal going down on nearly every street corner. Lots of "lana" and lots of "coca" changing hands. The agents can't stop it all, but they can come close!

EL CAMELLO:	Bienvenido a nuestro barrio, amigos. ¿Buscan algo para escapar de la rutina?
EL DROGADICTO:	Mi compa, el Loco, dice que aquí venden de todo. ¿Qué tienes?
EL CAMELLO:	¡Uno de tus compas ya está quemado! Yo, personalmente, no vendo nada. Pero tengo mis conexiones. ¿Qué quieren pillar?
EL DROGADICTO:	Mis chavos y yo queremos nieve. Colombiana. La pura. Las muchachas prefieren unas pepas.
EL CAMELLO:	Quiero ver tu plata.
EL DROGADICTO:	*(flashes money)* Aquí está. Y si me haces buen precio, hay mucho más dinero y negocio *(business)* para ti—y tu jefe. Pero necesito hablar con el jefe.
EL CAMELLO:	Esperen ustedes aquí. Voy por su "estofa" y por el hombre.

C. ¿Comprende usted? Indicate whether these statements are **Cierto (C)** or **Falso (F).** If the information is false, correct it.

1. _____ El camello compra las drogas.

2. _____ El camello tiene las drogas allí.

3. _____ Los chavos quieren nieve.

4. _____ Las muchachas quieren mota.

5. _____ El camello necesita ver primero la lana.

D. Más términos de drogas. **El pito** *(whistle)* is a slang word for "joint," **la grifa** for "dope," **las mujeres** refers to kilos of cocaine, and **la negra, la goma** are both street slang for black tar heroin. The following terms are also prevalent on the streets. Can you figure out their English equivalents? If you don't recognize them immediately, try sounding them out.

Las drogas:

1. los diablos rojos _____
2. el hachis (costo, chocolate, kif) _____
3. la cucaracha _____
4. el hero (caballo, fango, manteca) _____
5. el ácido (tripi, sello) _____
6. el crack, el pan _____

Otras palabras:

7. bosteado _____
8. el cúquer _____
9. la jeringa (chuta) _____
10. juquiado _____

1. red devils **2.** hashish **3.** roach **4.** heroin **5.** acid/LSD **6.** crack **7.** busted **8.** the cooker
9. syringe **10.** "hooked" on drugs

E. Charades. Study the drug terms in the previous activity and in the dialogue. Then with a partner, take turns acting out the following terms and seeing if the other can guess the word—in Spanish, of course!

1. jeringa
2. cucaracha
3. pepas
4. cúquer
5. bosteado
6. quemado

Estructuras   *Indicating relationships:*
Los adjetivos posesivos

* Possessive adjectives describe relationships among people and their belongings.

Los adjetivos posesivos

	Singular			Plural	
yo	**mi/s**	*my*	nosotros	**nuestro/a/os/as**	*our*
tú	**tu/s**	*your, (familiar)*			
usted	**su/s**	*your, (formal)*	ustedes	**su/s**	*your*
él	**su/s**	*his*	ellos	**su/s**	*their*
ella	**su/s**	*her*	ellas	**su/s**	*their*

* Possessive adjectives agree in number with the noun that *follows* them. Only **nuestro/a** has additional forms for masculine and feminine.

Mi amig**o** es policía.	*My friend is a policeman.*
Mis amig**os** son policías.	*My friends are policemen.*
Nuestra famili**a** vive en el barrio.	*Our family lives in the barrio.*

* Since **su/s** can mean *his, her, your, their* or *its,* the form **de + él, ella, usted, ellos, ellas** or **ustedes** is frequently substituted to ensure clarity. The accented **él** meaning *he* does not contract to **del**. Only **de + el** (unaccented meaning *the*) has that ability.

sus amigos	=	los amigos **de él**	*his friends*
		los amigos **de ella**	*her friends*
		los amigos de **Ud./Uds.**	*your friends*
		los amigos de **ellos/ellas**	*their friends*

Los amigos **de ella** están en casa.	*Her friends are at home.*
Los amigos **de él** están en la calle.	*His friends are out on the street.*

* Note that there is **no** apostrophe *s* ('s) in Spanish to show possession. Use the **definite article + noun + de** to show possession.

la familia de María	*María's family*
los amigos de Julio	*Julio's friends*

* To find out to whom something belongs, ask **¿De quién es...?**

—**¿De quién es la pistola?**	*Whose gun is this?*
—**Es la pistola del sargento.**	*It's the sergeant's gun.*

Para practicar

A. Mi familia.   Do you remember the members of the family? Tell which of my relatives are described here.

MODELO: El otro hijo de mis padres
Mi hermano

1. Los hermanos de mi padre   _____

2. Los padres de mi madre   _____

3. Las hijas de mi madre con otro padre   _____

4. La madre de mi padre   _____

B. Posesión.   Give the correct form of the possessive adjectives **mi/s, tu/s, su/s, nuestro/a/as/os.**

MODELO: Yo tengo una abuela. _____ abuela vive aquí.
Mi abuela vive aquí.

1. Usted tiene drogas. _Sus_____ drogas no son de la farmacia.

2. Ustedes tienen drogas. _Sus_____ drogas no están aquí.

3. Ella tiene un hermano. ___Su_____ hermano está en la cárcel *(jail)*.

4. Nosotros tenemos un problema. _Nuestro_____ problema es serio.

5. Ellos tienen problemas con la policía. ___Sus_____ problemas no son serios.

6. Ella tiene un problema. ___Su_____ problema es difícil de resolver.

7. Yo tengo tres problemas. _Mis_____ problemas son fáciles.

C. La entrevista.   Pair up with somebody in the class that you don't know and ask the following questions in order to get to know him/her better. Then present your new friend to the class.

MODELO: E1: ¿Dónde está su casa?
E2: Mi casa está en la Avenida Moraga.
E1: Es mi nuevo amigo, Brian. Su casa está en la Avenida Moraga.

Preguntas para la entrevista:

1. ¿Cuál es su nombre?
2. ¿Dónde está su casa?
3. ¿Su familia es grande?
4. ¿Tiene esposa/o? ¿Tiene hijos? ¿Cómo se llama/n?
5. ¿Cuáles son sus programas de televisión favoritos?

Módulo I

La compra

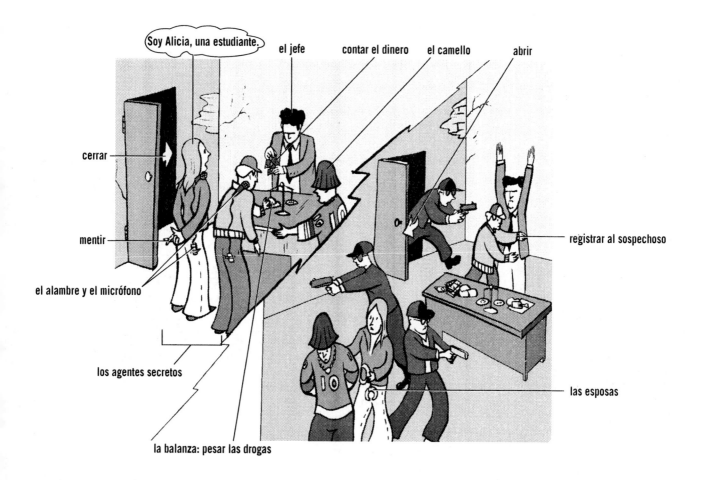

Soy Alicia, una estudiante.

el jefe — contar el dinero — el camello — abrir

cerrar

mentir

el alambre y el micrófono

los agentes secretos

la balanza: pesar las drogas

registrar al sospechoso

las esposas

A. ¿Cómo se dice?   Insert the correct vocabulary word in each of the following sentences.

1. Un agente encubierto *(undercover)* es un _____

_____ .

2. Una manera secreta de escuchar las conversaciones remotas es un

_____ y un _____ .

3. Una máquina que pesa onzas o kilos es un _____ .

4. Un joven que va a la escuela es un _____ .

B. Acciones.   See if you can match the actions in Column **A** with the verbs in Column **B**.

	A		**B**
1.	Enumerar: uno, dos, tres, cuatro...	**a.**	medir *(measure)*
2.	La regla *(ruler)* es para _____ centímetros y pulgadas *(inches)*.	**b.**	mentir
3.	Comunicar información falsa	**c.**	contar
4.	Buscar objetos escondidos *(hidden)* en una persona	**d.**	registrar

La compra

Success! The two undercover agents have piqued the "Jefe's" curiosity and they are invited in to chat about bigger and better deals.

EL CAMELLO: Pasen. El jefe quiere hablar con ustedes.

EL AGENTE: Excelente. Nosotros queremos hablar con él.

JEFE: Ustedes tienen un propósito de negocio, ¿eh?

LA AGENTE: Sí, pero primero preferimos ver la calidad del producto que compramos.

EL JEFE: Y yo prefiero primero contar su dinero. Entonces podemos hablar del futuro. Aquí tienen su mercancía. Y aquí tengo mi dinero. *(They trade).*

EL AGENTE: *(Recibe las drogas)* ¡Alto! ¡Soy policía! Ustedes están arrestados. Jefe, primero voy a registrarlo. ¿Tiene algún arma o algo afilado *(sharp)* que pueda lastimarme?

C. ¿Comprende usted?   Answer the questions based on the dialogue.

1.   ¿Quién quiere hablar con los jóvenes?

2.   En realidad, ¿qué son los jóvenes?

3.   Antes de hablar del futuro, ¿qué quiere hacer el jefe?

4.   ¿Cuándo anuncia el agente que es policía?

5.   ¿Qué busca el agente en el jefe?

D. El arresto.   The following phrases are most important in an arrest situation. Study them, then match the phrase with a picture below.

a.	¡Silencio! ¡Está arrestado!	*Be quiet! You are under arrest!*
b.	Soy policía. Aquí está mi placa.	*I am the police. Here is my badge.*
c.	Voy a registrarlo.	*I am going to search you.*
d.	¿Tiene armas o algo afilado?	*Do you have any weapons or anything sharp?*
e.	¿Tiene drogas?	*Do you have any drugs?*
f.	Voy a ponerle esposas/Voy a esposarlo.	*I am going to handcuff you.*

1. _____
2. _____
3. _____
4. _____
5. _____
6. _____

👥 **E. Mandatos.**   Study the following action commands and then, with a partner, take turns acting them out and guessing the action. Keep repeating and taking turns until the commands are very familiar. There were additional commands in Lesson 3 to add to your practice.

a.	¡No se mueva!	*Don't move!*
b.	¡Siéntese!	*Sit down!*
c.	¡Levántese!	*Stand up!*
d.	¡Ponga las manos en la mesa!	*Put your hands on the table!*
e.	¡Manos arriba!	*Hands up!*

Estructuras   *Describing daily activities: Los verbos con cambios de raíz*

* You have already seen an example of a verb that has a spelling change in the stem (main part of the verb) as well as in the endings:

tener > tengo, tienes, tiene, tenemos, tienen

Venir *(to come)* works the same way:

venir > vengo, viene, viene, venimos, vienen

Note that **nosotros/as** is the *only* form that is based on the spelling of the infinitive. That is what all stem-changing verbs have in common:

* When stem-changing verbs are conjugated, the stressed **e** will become **ie** or **i,** and the stressed **o** will become **ue** in all forms *except* **nosotros.**

	recomendar (ie) to recommend	poder (ue) to be able	pedir (i) to ask for
yo	recomiendo	puedo	pido
tú	recomiendas	puedes	pides
él, ella, usted	recomienda	puede	pide
nosotros/as	recomendamos	podemos	pedimos
ellos, ellas, ustedes	recomiendan	pueden	piden

* More stem-changing verbs are:

e > ie	**o > ue**	**e > i**
cerrar *to close*	**acostar(se)** *to go to bed*	**decir** *to say/tell*
comenzar *to begin*	**almorzar** *to eat lunch*	**despedirse** *to say goodbye*
entender *to understand*	**contar** *to count*	**elegir** *to opt/elect*
mentir *to lie*	**costar** *to cost*	**medir** *to measure*
pensar *to think*	**dormir** *to sleep*	**repetir** *to repeat*
perder *to lose*	**encontrar** *to meet*	**seguir★** *to follow*
preferir *to prefer*	**recordar** *to remember*	**★(yo sigo)**
querer *to want*	**volver** *to return*	**servir** *to serve*

* The verb **jugar** *(to play)* is the only **u > ue** verb in Spanish.

juego, juegas, juega, jugamos, juegan

* The verb **decir (i)** *(to tell or say)* has an additional spelling change in the **yo** form:

    digo, dices, dice, decimos, dicen

¡Recuerde! Stem-changing verbs, **e > ie, e > i,** and **o > ue,** change in all forms except **nosotros/as.**

Para practicar

A. ¡Yo también! Break time. You are on break from your training session and you overhear two colleagues discussing how they handle things. Tell if you do the same things.

MODELO: Nosotros almorzamos en la patrullera mientras trabajamos.
Yo almuerzo en la cafetería.

1. Nosotros volvemos tarde al trabajo después del almuerzo.
2. Nosotros queremos ayudar a las víctimas.
3. Nosotros pensamos mucho en las soluciones.
4. Nosotros dormimos en la patrullera.
5. Nosotros repetimos la Declaración Miranda con frecuencia.
6. Nosotros mentimos mucho a los sospechosos.
7. Nosotros servimos el almuerzo a los camellos.

B. ¿Quién? Tell if you, a police officer **(Yo)**, your suspect **(El sospechoso)**, or both **(Nosotros)** would do the following things in the course of a day.

MODELO: empezar un registro a un camello
Yo empiezo un registro a un camello.

1. _____ dormir en la cárcel *(jail)*

2. _____ almorzar en la patrullera

3. _____ volver a la comisaría todos los días

4. _____ mentir a la policía

5. _____ pesar las drogas

6. _____ pedir apoyo *(backup)* de otros agentes

7. _____ servir una orden de búsqueda *(search warrant)*

8. _____ pedir un abogado *(lawyer)*

C. Con un amigo. You and your partner never know what will come up on the job and what you are going to have to do. In groups of twos or threes, brainstorm as many activities as you can for each of the following verbs.

empezar   pedir   servir   medir   contar

MODELO: **empezar**
Empezamos un registro.
Empezamos una investigación.

Módulo 2

Están arrestados

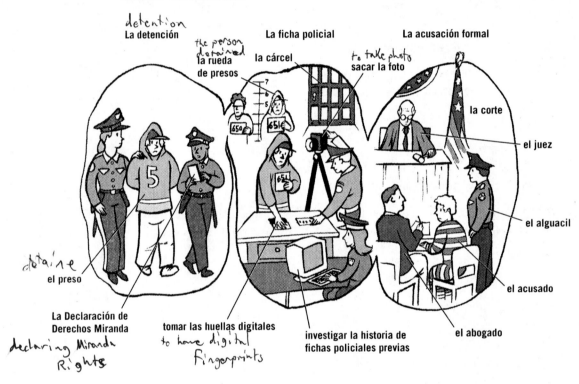

detention
La detención

the person detained **la rueda de presos**

La ficha policial

la cárcel

to take photo **sacar la foto**

La acusación formal

la corte

el juez

el alguacil

detaine **el preso**

La Declaración de Derechos Miranda
Declaring Miranda Rights

tomar las huellas digitales
to have digital fingerprints

investigar la historia de fichas policiales previas

el acusado

el abogado

A. ¿Cómo se dice? Can you identify the following descriptions with a single word or phrase from the drawing?

1. Aviso *(warning)* contra la auto-incriminación
2. Las marcas individuales de las manos de una persona
3. El proceso de abrir un caso policial con la información personal de un acusado
4. La historia de acusaciones previas de un acusado
5. El proceso en que un testigo identifica a un acusado entre *(among)* un grupo de cinco o seis personas

B. Gente del sistema. See if you can match the people in column **A** with their roles in legal proceedings in column **B**.

A   **B**

1. el juez   _____ la persona que defiende al "criminal"

2. el alguacil   _____ la persona encargada de la corte; toma las
                                  decisiones

3. el abogado   _____ el preso

4. el acusado   _____ la persona que organiza la operación de la corte;
                                  ayuda al juez

La Declaración de Derechos Miranda

Usted queda acusado de _____. Antes de
hacerle preguntas, le voy a leer sus derechos:

1. Usted tiene el derecho de mantener silencio.

2. Todo lo que diga puede ser usado en contra de usted
   en una corte legal.

3. Tiene el derecho de consultar a un abogado y de tener
   a su abogado presente durante la interrogación.

4. Si no puede pagar los servicios de un abogado, uno le
   será asignado gratis para que le represente antes y
   durante la interrogación.

5. Usted tiene el derecho de terminar la interrogación en
   cualquier momento.

— Memorize

C. ¿Comprende usted? Clearly, we all understand the Miranda Warning, but are we sure we understand it *in Spanish?* Match the following lines from Miranda in Spanish with their English equivalents.

a. Tiene el derecho de mantener silencio.

b. Tiene el derecho de terminar la interrogación en cualquier momento.

c. Si no puede pagar los servicios de un abogado, uno le será asignado gratis.

d. Todo lo que diga puede ser usado en contra de usted en una corte legal.

1. _____ Anything you say can be used against you in a court of law.

2. _____ You have the right to terminate the questioning at any time.

3. _____ You have the right to remain silent.

4. _____ If you cannot afford the services of a lawyer, one will be
         appointed to represent you, free of charge.

¡OJO!

There is no uniform Miranda Warning. You will see many variations on its exact wording. Practice reading and pronouncing this one out loud until you are comfortable with it.

D. Infracciones. Study the following list of criminal activities and then look at the following pairs of words to determine which is the more serious "crime" and which is less serious.

Clases de infracciones

falta *misdemeanor*
delito *felony (non-violent)*
crimen *felony (violent)*

Más infracciones

asalto *assault*
homicidio *murder*
hurto menor *petit (petty) larceny*
hurto mayor *grand larceny*
ratería *shoplifting/street theft*
violación sexual *rape*

[Handwritten notes: V | S — asesinar | asesinato "to hit" "golpear, y tonar"; secuestrar | secuestro; perder | perdida; asaltar | asalto; sobornar — bribe; pedir/secate — ransom; pagar; tiroteo → disparar; (en marcha); incendiar | incendio premeditado]

MODELO: vandalismo/violación sexual
La violación sexual es una infracción más seria que el vandalismo.
El vandalismo es menos serio que la violación sexual.

1. el hurto menor/el hurto mayor
2. el homicidio culposo *(pre-meditated)*/el homicidio calificado *(manslaughter)*
3. la violación sexual/el hurto menor
4. una falta/un crimen

Estructuras — Comparing and contrasting: Los comparativos

▪ For comparisons of inequality (more than/less than), use **más...que** or **menos...que** with an adjective or adverb.

El hurto mayor es **más** serio **que** el hurto menor. — *Grand larceny is more serious than petit larceny.*

El hurto menor es **menos** serio **que** el hurto mayor. — *Petit larceny is less serious than grand larceny.*

En español, un crimen es **más** violento **que** un delito. — *A "crimen" is a more violent felony than a "delito" in Spanish.*

* For comparisons of equality (the same as) use **tan ... como** with adjectives and adverbs, and **tanto/a/os/as ... como** with nouns.

El ADN es **tan** importante **como** las huellas digitales.	*DNA is as important as fingerprints.*
La violación sexual es **tan** prevalente **como** el asalto.	*Rape is as prevalent as assault.*
En Menlo, hay **tantos** delitos **como** aquí.	*In Menlo, there are as many felonies as here.*
La heroína vale **tanto** dinero **como** un coche nuevo.	*The heroin is worth as much as a new car.*

* **Más, menos** and **tanto como** can all be used with verbs to compare actions.

Trabajamos **más** ahora.	*We work more now.*
Él trabaja **menos** estos días.	*He works less these days.*
El abogado trabaja **tanto como** siempre.	*The lawyer works as much as always.*

* Use the following irregular comparisons to say *better, worse, older,* or *younger.*

Esta cárcel es **mejor que** la cárcel vieja.	*This jail is better than the old one.*
La prisión es **peor que la** cárcel.	*The prison is worse than the jail.*
El camello es **mayor que** el jefe.	*The dealer is older than the boss.*
El jefe es **menor que** el camello.	*The boss is younger than the dealer.*

* To say *more than* or *less than* with numbers, use **más de** or **menos de.**

Hay **más de 100** kilos aquí.	*There are more than 100 kilos here.*
Hay **menos de cinco** sospechosos para la rueda de presos.	*There are fewer than five suspects for the lineup.*

Para practicar

A. ¿Es serio?   Use **más que** or **menos que** to tell which one of the following pairs of infractions is more serious or less serious. If they are equally serious, use **tan** or **tanto como** to make your statement. Don't forget to make sure that the adjectives match the nouns in gender and number!

MODELO: posesión de un gramo de coca/posesión de un kilo de coca
La posesión de un kilo de coca es más seria que la posesión de un gramo.
La posesión de un gramo de coca es menos seria que la posesión de un kilo.

1.   escribir grafiti/vender narcóticos ilegales
2.   el homicidio/el asalto
3.   la violación sexual/el vandalismo
4.   el robo de un auto/el robo de un sándwich
5.   una infracción de estacionamiento/una infracción de exceso de velocidad

B. En su opinión.   Tell if you think there is more evidence of the following criminal activities in the following places, or equal in each.

MODELO: 1. cultivo de cocaína   Estados Unidos/Colombia
Hay más cultivo de cocaína en Colombia que en Estados Unidos
2. homicidios   Los Ángeles/New York
Hay tantos homicidios en Los Ángeles como en New York.

1.   hurtos mayores   una ciudad grande/un pueblo pequeño
2.   grafiti   Chicago/Miami
3.   ratería   Walmart/Target
4.   homicidios   Metropolis/Pleasantville
5.   crímenes sexuales   un barrio de prostitutas/un barrio residencial

C. El círculo de crimen.   In groups of four, state a crime statistic using a comparison. Each group member should offer one equal and one unequal comparison. See if you can go around the circle at least twice.

MODELO: *Hay más robos de Cadillac Escalades que de Ford Mustangs.*
Hay tantas pandillas en Chicago como en Miami.

Módulo 2

Las prioridades

A. ¿Cómo se dice?   Choose the words from the drawing—or from previous drawings—that identify the following crimes or emergencies.

1.   el robo de una persona para pedir dinero como rescate *(ransom)*

_____

2.   incendiar un edificio deliberadamente _____

3.   una guerra de pistolas o ametralladoras _____

4.   un asalto sexual _____

B. Descripciones.   Choose the word that best describes the following priorities for police.

a.   peligroso   **b.**   urgente
c.   menos importante   **d.**   importante pero no urgente

1.   _____ unos adolescentes con pistolas en una escuela

2.   _____ un accidente de tráfico con fatalidades

3.   _____ un robo en una casa elegante

4.   _____ un gato perdido

Los operadores de 911

*The Emergency Dispatchers **(Los operadores de 911)** in our city cannot keep up with the number of calls coming in tonight: everything from a lost cat to a gang shootout to arson. How do they establish their priorities? After it is over, a local news reporter wants to know!*

REPORTERO: Parece que ésta es la noche más difícil del año.

OPERADOR: Así es. No sé por qué. Normalmente Halloween es una noche difícil, el 4 de julio es una noche más difícil y el Año Nuevo es la noche más difícil del año. Pero esta noche es dificilísima y no sabemos por qué.

REPORTERO: Durante una noche así con tantas llamadas de toda clase, ¿cómo establecen ustedes las prioridades para responder?

OPERADOR: Tenemos un orden de urgencia establecido.
Prioridad 3: Urgente: una llamada que recibe atención cuando haya personal disponible
Prioridad 2: Más urgente: llamada que requiere atención pronto
Prioridad 1: La más urgente: la llamada de emergencia que requiere atención inmediata

REPORTERO: ¿Puede darnos un ejemplo?

OPERADOR: Bueno, esta noche por ejemplo, había tres llamadas simultáneas: 1. un reporte de una pelea entre pandillas; 2. un robo en una casa; y 3. un tiroteo en la calle.
3. El robo en la casa es una situación seria.
2. La pelea entre pandillas es una situación más seria.
1. El tiroteo en la calle es la situación más seria de todas. Es la mayor prioridad.

REPORTERO: ¡Es increíble! ¡Ustedes tienen el trabajo más intenso del mundo!

C. ¿Comprende usted? Tell if the following statements are **Cierto (C)** or **Falso (F).** If false, make the needed corrections.

1. _____ Normalmente Halloween es más difícil que el Año Nuevo.

2. _____ El operador comprende por qué esta noche es tan difícil.

3. _____ No hay prioridades establecidas.

4. _____ Un tiroteo se considera más peligroso que un robo en una casa.

5. _____ El reportero cree que el trabajo del operador es el más fácil del mundo.

D. La evidencia más importante. Depending on the type of crime, the most important type of evidence varies. Try to match the most important evidence to the crimes below.

a. las huellas digitales
b. el ADN *(DNA)*
c. los informantes y soplones
d. los testigos

1. En el caso de una violación sexual, la evidencia de _____ es la más importante.

2. En la identificación de un participante en un asalto, el testimonio de _____ es la evidencia más importante.

3. En la prevención de un crimen, la información de _____ es la más crítica.

4. En un robo, a veces las marcas dejadas por las manos o _____ son la evidencia más importante.

E. Mandatos. When a report of an emergency is made, sometimes it is difficult to understand what the caller is saying. Use these commands to get better information and then use them in the contexts below:

a. **Cálmese.** *Calm down.*
b. **Hable despacio.** *Speak slowly.*
c. **Describa el problema.** *Describe the problem.*
d. **Manténgase en la línea.** *Stay on the line.*
e. **No cuelgue el teléfono**. *Don't hang up the phone.*

What would you tell the person...

1. _____ who is speaking so fast you cannot understand the problem?

2. _____ who is too upset to speak?

3. _____ who has not told you yet what has happened?

4. _____ y _____ whom you need to stay with you on the phone? (two possibilities)

Estructuras   *Comparing and contrasting: Los superlativos*

* Use a superlative to express *the most* or *the least* when comparing more than two things.
* The superlative in Spanish uses the definite article (**el, la, los, las**) with the comparative form of the adjective.

Adjetivo: Los Cholos son una pandilla **peligrosa.**   *The Cholos is a dangerous gang.*

Comparativo: M-13 es **más peligrosa.**   *M-13 is more dangerous.*

Superlativo: Barrio B **es la más peligrosa.**   *Barrio B is the most dangerous.*

* Adjectives that have irregular forms in the comparative use the same forms in the superlative, with the addition of the definite article.

bueno > mejor   viejo > mayor
malo > peor   joven > menor

Adjetivo:	Una falta es **mala.**	*A misdemeanor is bad.*
Comparativo:	Un delito es **peor.**	*A felony is worse.*
Superlativo:	Un crimen violento es **el peor de** todos.	*A violent felony is worst of all.*

* Another way to give an adjective a superlative meaning of *extremely* or *very* is to add one of the forms (**-o, -os, -a, -as**) of the suffix **–ísimo/a** to the adjective. If the adjective ends in a vowel, drop the final vowel and then add the correct form of **-ísimo.**

Una pistola es peligros**a.**   *A gun is dangerous.*
Una ametralladora es peligros**ísima**.   *A machine gun is extremely dangerous.*

* If the adjective ends in a consonant, add the suffix directly to the stem.

La prevención del uso de drogas es dificil**ísima.**   *Prevention of drug use is extremely difficult.*

Para practicar

A. Asociaciones.   Write down the names of the people, things, or places you associate with these descriptions and then compare your answers with a classmate.

1. el programa de policía más popular de la televisión
2. el criminal más famoso del mundo
3. el crimen más peligroso de esta época
4. el policía más famoso de la historia
5. la droga ilegal más adictiva
6. la droga más popular entre adolescentes

B. Extremísimo. "Anything you can do, I can do better." You and your partner are having a discussion about personal traits and police issues. For every statement that your friend makes, use an **-ísimo/a** adjective to show that you and yours are even more so!

MODELO: E1: Estoy cansado.

E2: Yo estoy cansadísimo/a.

1. Soy inteligente.
2. Soy un/a policía excelente.
3. Tengo un problema difícil.
4. Tengo una entrevista con un soplón importante.
5. Voy a detener a un sospechoso peligroso.
6. Mis superiores están contentos con mi trabajo.

C. En pareja. You and your partner are working in dispatch to determine which calls will get first response. As you look at each of these groups of three, put them into priority order according to the adjective given.

MODELO: serio: un accidente de bicicleta
un accidente de automóvil
un accidente de avión *(airplane)*

El accidente de bicicleta es serio.
El accidente de auto es más serio.
El accidente de avión es el más serio.

1. Urgente: el robo en una casa
la violación sexual
el tiroteo en la calle
2. Fácil: acompañar a un acusado a la cárcel
escribir los reportes del día
investigar un homicidio
3. Interesante: investigar un robo
investigar un homicidio
investigar la violencia doméstica
4. Grave: la víctima estable
la víctima en condición seria
la víctima en condición crítica

Vocabulario Módulo 1

Sustantivos

		el chivo★	*marihuana*
el alambre	*wire*	**la coca**★	*cocaine*
las arribas★	*uppers*	**la estofa**★	*stash*
la balanza	*scale*	**el/la estudiante**	*student*
la calidad	*quality*	**la farlopa**★	*cocaine*
la cárcel	*jail*	**el humo**	*smoke*

SPANISH FOR LAW ENFORCEMENT

la jerga	slang	el precio	price
la lana★	money (wool)	el/la preso/a	prisoner
la mercancía	merchandise	el propósito	proposition
la mota★	marihuana	la rutina	routine
el negocio	business	el/la sargento	sergeant
la nieve★	cocaine (snow)	la sobredosis	overdose
las pepas★	uppers	la yerba★	marihuana
la plata★	money (silver)		(grass)

Verbos

abrir	to open	pedir (i)	to ask for, order
almorzar (ue)	to have lunch	pensar (ie)	to think, plan
anunciar	to announce	perder (ie)	to lose
cerrar (ie)	to close	pesar	to weigh
comprar	to buy	pillar★	to score (drugs)
contar (ue)	to count	poder (ue)	to be able, can
decir (i) (g)	to say, tell	querer (ie)	to want
empezar (ie)	to begin	registrar	to search
jugar (ue)	to play	repetir (i)	to repeat
medir (i)	to measure	servir (i)	to serve
mentir (ie)	to lie	tener (ie) (g)	to have
pasar	to pass, spend	venir (ie) (g)	to come
	(time)	volver (ue)	to return

Adjetivos

mi	my	su	his, her, your,
nuestro/a	our		their
quemado/a★	burned, wasted	tu	your (familiar)

Otras expresiones

nada	nothing	ya	already

Módulo 2

Sustantivos

el/la acusado/a	accused	el homicidio	murder
el alguacil	sheriff, bailiff	la huella digital	fingerprint
la corte	court	el hurto	larceny, burglary
el cuidado	care	el incendio	fire
el delito	crime, felony	la ratería	shoplifting, theft
el ejemplo	example	el robo	robbery
la falta	misdemeanor	el secuestro	kidnapping
la ficha policial	police record	el tiroteo	shooting
la foto(grafía)	photograph	la violación sexual	rape
el/la gato/a	cat		

Verbos

arrestar	*to arrest*	**sacar**	*to take (out)*
dejar	*to leave (behind)*		

Adjetivos

disponible	*available*	**peor**	*worse*
gratis	*free (of charge)*	**premeditado/a**	*premeditated*
mayor	*older, greater*	**previo/a**	*previous*
mejor	*better*		

Otras expresiones

como	*as*	**tan**	*as*
en contra de	*against*	**tanto/a**	*as much*
menos	*less*	**tantos/as**	*as many*
que	*that, than*		

Síntesis

A escuchar

Las drogas ilegales.   Listen to the following dialogue between a drug dealer and a customer, then indicate whether the following statements are **Cierto (C)** or **Falso (F)** based on what you hear.

1. _____ El camello quiere comprar drogas.

2. _____ El drogadicto busca la mota y la heroína.

3. _____ El camello quiere vender coca también.

4. _____ Las drogas cuestan $50.

5. _____ El amigo no necesita más drogas.

A conversar

They say that there are no good or bad drugs—only abused drugs. DMX and OxyContin, for example, are two of the latest drugs to leap from the pharmacy shelves to the "dangerous drug" list for use by people of all ages and lifestyles. In groups of four, discuss the "hottest" drugs in your area and who might be using them. Mention any famous names that have been connected with that drug and, finally, any street names connected with the drug—in English or in Spanish.

MODELO: *OxyContin. Es una droga tan intensa como la heroína. Es popular en los clubes entre los adolescentes y las personas mayores. Rush Limbaugh admite su adicción a OxyContin. Otros nombres son: Poor Man's Heroin, OC's, y Oxies.*

A leer

The following words are examples of English words with Spanish pronunciation, a characteristic of borrowing common in Spanglish. Read them aloud to see if you can guess what they're supposed to say.

¿Comprende usted?   Pick five Spanglish terms from the above list and give their correct English and Spanish equivalents.

MODELO: *Librería is bookstore, not library, which is* **biblioteca.**

A escribir

Now it's your turn—create five terms that you think would fit well with the pattern of Spanglish.

MODELO: *¿Dónde está mi bíper?*

Algo más

Ventana cultural

Spanglish—is it a language?

There are two basic components of Spanglish—a "language" being spoken more and more on the streets of the United States, usually by second or third generation children of immigrant parents. The approaches are switching and borrowing. Switching you'll hear while in line at the supermarket, when a sentence has pieces in Spanish and in English: *¿Por qué no vamos al show tonight?*

Borrowing makes new words by pronouncing an English word "Spanish style"—have you gone to a baseball game and heard terms such as *jonrón, pícher, cácher?* What are you planning to eat for your *lonche—es hora de lonchar?* Maybe you received a *tíquite* from *el cherife? ¡Ay, qué estrés!* Sometimes this idiom is actually not understandable if you only speak English or Spanish; it's so mixed it's literally neither language.

The mother of a student in trouble for having fireworks on a high school campus in California told the dean, *"Los chuteó en la yarda".* And someone in Miami with a chest cold entered a drug store requesting *Bicbaporru* = Vick's VapoRub. Of course, you must *parquear su carro* and clean your carpet with the *bacuncliner.*

En mis propias palabras. What is your opinion of/experience with Spanglish?

A buscar

Whether you approve of Spanglish or not, it's clearly here to stay. Pick up a copy of <u>Latina</u> magazine and see how they mix language codes in their articles: *Love your **curvas!*** This website has a Spanglish dictionary—check it out! http://www.members.tripod.com/~nelson_g/spanglish.html

A conocer: Enrique Camarena

Enrique Camarena, agente secreto contra el narcotráfico, fue asesinado (was killed) en 1985. Su fama como luchador en la guerra contra las drogas ilegales es legendaria—recibió el Premio administrativo de honor de la DEA después de su muerte—el premio más alto de la agencia.

Enrique Camarena joined the United States Marine Corps in 1972, at the age of 24. After having served as a police investigator and fireman, he joined the DEA, working in Calexico, Fresno, and Guadalajara.

His work in breaking up drug trafficking bands was successful, but one of the groups he was attempting to infiltrate recognized him as an undercover agent. He was kidnapped and shot to death in 1985.

LECCIÓN 5

¡Emergencia!

Módulo I
- Una llamada al 911
- Making requests: *Los mandatos formales*
- La escena del accidente
- Los mandatos irregulares/con cambios ortográficos/con pronombres de objeto indirecto

Módulo 2
- Los desastres
- Expressing negative ideas: *Las expresiones afirmativas y negativas*
- Un incendio
- Más sobre las expresiones negativas

Síntesis
- A escuchar
- A conversar
- A leer
- A escribir

Algo más
- Ventana cultural: La imagen de la policía
- A buscar
- A conocer: Rich Gonzales

Módulo 1

Una llamada al 911

Un accidente con una víctima

- la ambulancia
- la resucitación cardiopulmonar (RCP)
- despachar una ambulancia
- mover
- la operadora de 911
- no respirar
- la camilla
- la cobija
- los paramédicos
- el muerto
- la sangre
- la fractura

A. ¿Cómo se dice? Choose the correct Spanish word that fits each of the following definitions.

1. Persona que contesta el teléfono en una emergencia _____

2. Medio de transporte para el hospital _____

3. Fluido vital perdido con una herida _____

4. Acción de inhalar y exhalar el aire _____

5. Una mesa portátil *(portable)* para transportar al paciente a la ambulancia _____

B. ¡Hay un accidente!   Complete the following statements with the correct verb.

1. Cuando hay un accidente, es importante _____*llamar*_____ al 911 inmediatamente.

2. El operador del 911 necesita _____*despachar*_____ una ambulancia rápidamente al accidente.

3. Para mantener la temperatura, es buena idea _____*poner*_____ una cobija sobre la víctima.

4. Si hay una fractura en el hueso *(bone)*, es difícil _____*mover*_____ la pierna.

¡Auxilio! ¡Emergencia!

Sarita Suárez, 11, has just been in a hit and run accident (atropellar y huir) *that has seriously injured her and left one person dead. A witness, Juanita Gutiérrez, is calling 911. Here's the conversation.*

OPERADORA: 911. ¿Cuál es la emergencia?

JUANITA: Hay un accidente muy serio en la calle 7ª con la 36. Hay dos víctimas—una niña herida y otra persona—un hombre—creo que está muerto. Por favor, **mande** una ambulancia rápidamente.

OPERADORA: ¿Está respirando el hombre? ¿Está consciente?

JUANITA: El hombre no está respirando, ni está consciente. La niña, está llorando por su mamá. ¿Qué hago?

OPERADORA: Primero, **mantenga** la calma. Voy a despachar la ambulancia inmediatamente. ¿Hay otras personas allí con ustedes?

JUANITA: Sí, hay dos. Un señor que está moviendo a la pobrecita fuera de la calle y otro que está con el hombre. ¿Busco identificación y llamo a las familias?

OPERADORA: ¡No **mueva** a la muchacha! No **busque** la identificación y no **toque** nada. Nosotros podemos notificar a las familias inmediatas.

JUANITA: Señorita, hay mucha sangre. Parece que hay una herida profunda en la cara, cerca del ojo. No puedo verla bien.

OPERADORA: **Pare** la hemorragia con un poco de presión, pero **tenga** mucho cuidado si no puede ver la herida.

JUANITA: La niña está gritando que tiene mucho dolor. ¡Por favor! **Díga**les a los paramédicos que **vengan** lo más rápido posible.

OPERADORA: **Espere** con la niña. El personal de emergencia está en camino.

C. ¿Comprende Ud.?   Answer the following based on the dialogue.

1. ¿Quién llama al 911?

2. ¿Dónde ocurrió el accidente?

3. ¿Qué problemas tiene la niña? ¿El hombre?

4. ¿Cuáles son tres acciones que la operadora dice que NO haga?:

    a. No _____.

    b. No _____.

    c. No _____.

5. ¿Qué está en camino?

D. ¡Socorro! ¡Auxilio!   You've just happened on the scene of a terrible accident. You must organize the first aid assistance from other passersby until professional help arrives. Place these commands in order of importance.

Verifique si la persona respira.	No mueva a la niña.
Pregunte si hay médico aquí.	Busque un teléfono.
Llame al 911.	Espere con la víctima.

E. Cómo buscar asistencia médica de inmediato.   After reading the following article, make up six questions a dispatcher might ask a caller to 911. Compare your questions with those of a partner.

Cómo buscar asistencia médica de inmediato

Los primeros auxilios y la RCP (resucitación cardiopulmonar) salvan vidas. Mientras una persona está proporcionando cuidados de emergencia a un enfermo o herido, otra debe ir en busca de asistencia médica.

Marque el 911 o el número para emergencias que corresponda a su zona. Esté preparado para responder a preguntas y dar información importante; a saber:

La dirección del lugar de la emergencia, incluyendo el cruce de calles, el piso, el número de la habitación y el número de teléfono de donde llama.

Lo que sucedió. Tenga el mayor número de datos posibles respecto al accidente, las heridas sufridas o la enfermedad.

El número de personas que necesitan ayuda. ¿Hay alguien con hemorragia, inconsciente o sin pulsaciones? ¿Qué tipo de primeros auxilios se le están dando? Tome nota de cualquier instrucción que le den.

No sea el primero en colgar. Asegúrese de haber dado toda la información necesaria. Espere a que cuelgue primero la persona que atendió su llamada de emergencia.

MODELO: *¿Cuántas personas necesitan ayuda?*

F. Un accidente. Your partner and you will each make up the details of an emergency based on the following information. One of you will call 911 to request help and the other will be the dispatcher asking the questions you formulated in exercise E. After finishing the scenario, switch roles.

> *Información:*
>
> *accidente de tráfico*
>
> *2 víctimas—un adulto y un niño*
>
> *mucha sangre*
>
> *uno no está consciente*

Estructuras

Making requests: Introducción a los mandatos formales

Culturally, the formal command may be one of the most important grammatical structures you will learn. By using this form with all individuals you would address with **usted,** you will show courtesy and respect as you tell or order them to do something. To form the command, drop the final **–o** of the **yo** form of the verb in the present tense (the **yo** form will give you the necessary spelling changes) and add these endings:

For **–ar** verbs, add **–e**:

hablar	habl**o**	⇒	**¡Hable** más despacio, por favor!
llamar	llam**o**	⇒	**¡Llame** al 911 inmediatamente!

For **–er** and **–ir** verbs, add **–a**:

cubrir	cubr**o**	⇒	**¡Cubra** la herida con una toalla!
mover	m**ue**vo	⇒	¡No **mueva** a su esposa!

(Note: for the **ustedes** form of the command, add an **–n**).

venir	**vengo**	⇒	**¡Vengan** directamente aquí!

Para practicar

A. Preguntas urgentes. You are a 911 operator and have to answer the caller's questions. For each question the caller asks, respond with the appropriate command.

MODELO: ¿Hablo con el policía?
Sí, hable con el policía.

1. ¿Vengo al hospital después?
2. ¿Pongo una toalla húmeda en la herida?
3. ¿Escribo un reporte?
4. ¿Espero con la víctima?
5. ¿Salgo a la calle?
6. ¿Tomo el pulso de la víctima?
7. ¿Pido una ambulancia?
8. ¿Muevo a la víctima?

B. Una madre desesperada. You have just received an emergency phone call from a panicky mother. Use the following cues to tell her what to do:

MODELO: Hablar despacio
¡Hable despacio!

1. Esperar mis instrucciones
2. Escuchar al paramédico
3. Pedir una ambulancia
4. No respirar rápidamente
5. Poner presión en la herida
6. Cubrir la herida
7. Escribir este número de teléfono
8. No comer nada
9. No llorar
10. Tener paciencia

C. Consejos. You are on security duty at the hospital when a distressed family comes into the emergency room. Use formal commands to tell the ones who...

MODELO: no hablan claramente (*don't speak clearly*)
Hablen claramente. (Speak clearly.)

1. no contestan las preguntas
2. no recuerdan los detalles del accidente
3. no dicen la verdad
4. están muy nerviosos
5. pelean (*fight*) con otros miembros de la familia
6. lloran mucho
7. no comprenden que la situación es grave
8. escriben grafiti en las paredes

Módulo I

La escena del accidente

A. ¿Cómo se dice?   Choose the correct Spanish word that fits each of the following definitions.

1. Personas expertas en apagar incendios y hacer rescates   _____

2. El transporte de los bomberos   _____

3. Un profesional de la medicina que no es médico   _____

4. Una clase de mesa portátil donde descansa el paciente
   durante su transporte en ambulancia   _____

5. Un grupo de personas con curiosidad que observan
   las emergencias   _____

B. ¿Qué hace?   Complete the following statements with the correct verb.

1. _bomberos_____ es liberar *(free)* a una persona de una situación
   peligrosa.

2. Los bomberos usan agua y químicos para _apagar_____ un incendio.

3. El policía tiene que _desivar_____ el tráfico para evitar *(avoid)*
   accidentes adicionales.

4. Si los espectadores de un incidente causan más problemas, la policía tiene
   que _controlar_____ a la muchedumbre.

Primeros auxilios

Controlling an accident scene takes teamwork: victim rescue, traffic flow changes, hazardous conditions, crowd control, accident investigation and evidence gathering each require specialized expertise. The following conversations might seem familiar!

EL POLICÍA Y EL CONTROL DEL TRÁFICO:

CHOFER: *(Al policía que dirige el tráfico)* ¿Cuál es el problema, oficial?

POLICÍA: Hay un accidente serio. El camino está cerrado a todos menos a los vehículos de emergencia. Hay un desvío. **Salga** aquí y **vaya** usted por este camino. Entonces, **siga** los letreros que dicen: "Desviación".

LOS BOMBEROS Y EL EQUIPO DE RESCATE:

VÍCTIMA EN

EL CARRO: **¡Ayúdenme!** ¡Por favor! Me duele la pierna. Tengo miedo.

BOMBERO: **Esté** tranquila, señora. No **tenga** miedo. Vamos a liberarla en este momento. Yo sé que tiene dolor y el personal médico está aquí para ayudar. *(A los paramédicos)* Jorge, Sandra, **traigan** la camilla y **empiecen** los primeros auxilios.

LOS PARAMÉDICOS Y LOS PRIMEROS AUXILIOS:

PARAMÉDICO: Señora, no se **mueva**. Vamos a inmovilizar la pierna que posiblemente esté fracturada. **Dígame** si hay dolor en otra parte del cuerpo. *(Toca el brazo.)*

SEÑORA: ¡Ay, por favor! No me **toquen** allí. *(Ella llora.)*

PARAMÉDICO: No **llore**. **Deme** la otra mano y yo tomo el pulso—con mucho cuidado.

LA POLICÍA QUE CONTROLA A LA MUCHEDUMBRE Y BUSCA EVIDENCIA:

LA POLICÍA: *(A las personas curiosas que miran)* Señoras y señores, por favor, **quédense** detrás de las barricadas o **regresen** a sus casas y vehículos. Esta es una escena de investigación. *(A dos otros policías)* **Busquen** evidencia, **saquen** las fotos y **midan** las marcas de las llantas, por favor. La muchedumbre ya está bajo control.

C. ¿Comprende usted? Decide whether the following statements refer to **La policía (P), La víctima (V), Los bomberos (B),** or **Los paramédicos (PM)**.

1. _____ Le duele la pierna.

2. _____ Pide cooperación a la muchedumbre.

3. _____ Controla el tráfico.

4. _____ Va a tomar el pulso.

5. _____ Libera a la víctima del auto.

D. ¿A qué agencia llamo? You are working dispatch for 911 and answer the following calls. It's up to you to decide which emergency service—or services—to send and note them at the end of each statement.

I. Una víctima necesita resucitación cardiopulmonar porque su respiración se paró *(stopped)*.
2. Hay un robo en la casa vecina.
3. Mi primo no puede caminar porque tiene dolor de cuello como resultado del accidente.
4. Hay humo *(smoke)* y llamas *(flames)* en la cocina de mi casa.
5. Hay un tiroteo en marcha aquí. Hay heridos.

E. ¿Llamar al 911 o no? Many calls come into an emergency operator that are not life-threatening. In groups of four, discuss the following situations, decide whether or not it may be an emergency, and tell the caller what to do next.

MODELO: *Llamada:* *No sé donde está mi gato.*
Operador/a: *No es una emergencia. Camine por la calle y llámelo por su nombre.*

I. Mi amigo tiene dolor en el pecho.
2. Hay un accidente de una bicicleta y un carro.
3. Hay un incendio en una casa abandonada.
4. Mi coche no tiene gasolina.
5. Los estudiantes de la casa de al lado tienen su estéreo muy alto.
6. Un hombre entra en mi casa por una ventana.
7. Alguien está disparando una pistola en la calle.
8. Mi compañero de cuarto tomó muchas pastillas para dormir.
9. Tomamos mucha tequila y anfetaminas y mi amigo no se despierta *(wake up)*.

Estructuras

Los mandatos irregulares/con cambios ortográficos/con pronombres de objeto indirecto

The following verbs have irregular **Ud.** command forms:

ser	$\Rightarrow$	sea(n)
estar	$\Rightarrow$	esté(n)
ir	$\Rightarrow$	vaya(n)
saber	$\Rightarrow$	sepa(n)
dar	$\Rightarrow$	dé/den

In order to preserve the original pronunciation of the verb, formal commands for verbs ending in **-car, -gar,** and **-zar** have the following spelling changes:

bus**car**	$\Rightarrow$	bus**que**	**Busquen** evidencia cerca de aquí.
entre**gar**	$\Rightarrow$	entre**gue**	**Entregue** el reporte del accidente al agente de seguros.
empe**zar**	$\Rightarrow$	emp**iece**	**Empiecen** los primeros auxilios ahora.

Don't forget the steps to forming a command:

1. go to the **yo** form
2. take off the **-o**
3. add the opposite ending.

Commands and Indirect Object Pronouns

Use the pronouns **me** to mean *me, for me,* or *to me* and **nos** to mean *us, to us,* or *for us.* These pronouns are attached to the *end* of a command if it is affirmative—a "yes" command. When adding a pronoun to the end of affirmative commands of two or more syllables, be sure to place an accent mark above the stressed vowel in order to preserve the original pronunciation. If the command is negative, put the pronoun in front of the verb.

¡Explíque**me** el problema!	*Explain the problem to **me**.*
¡**No me** explique el problema!	*Don't explain the problem to **me**.*
¡Díga**nos** la verdad!	*Tell **us** the truth.*
¡No **nos** diga ninguna mentira!	*Don't tell **us** a single lie.*

Use the pronoun **le** to mean *to* or *for you, him,* or *her* and **les** to mean *to* or *for you (plural)* or *them.* Put it before negative commands and after affirmative ones. You may clarify any ambiguity by adding **a** + the person's name.

¡Pída**les** información a los testigos!	*Ask the witnesses for information.*
¡Háble**les** a los padres de la víctima!	*Talk to the victim's parents.*
¡No **les** hable a los padres de la víctima!	*Don't talk to the victim's parents.*

Para practicar

A. ¡Los teléfonos otra vez!   You are back on phone duty and must respond to the following statements or questions with polite commands. ¡Tenga Ud. cuidado!

MODELO: Paciente: ¡Estoy nervioso!
Ud: *¡Esté tranquilo!*

1. ¿Busco al policía?
2. ¿Voy por ayuda?
3. ¿Doy mi nombre?
4. ¿Empiezo la resucitación cardiopulmonar?
5. ¿Vuelvo al hospital?
6. ¡Tengo miedo!
7. ¿Pago la ambulancia?
8. ¿Inmovilizo la pierna?
9. ¿Le toco la herida con las manos sucias?
10. ¿Les explico el problema ahora?

B. Un accidente.   You are the first on the scene of a car accident. Many people want to help. Use the following list of verbs to give appropriate commands to the bystanders—add any words necessary to complete the thought.

MODELO: Buscar....
Busque un teléfono.

1.	Llamar...	6.	Hablar...
2.	Poner...	7.	Esperar...
3.	Ir...	8.	Preguntar...
4.	Cubrir...	9.	Dar...
5.	Venir...	10.	Estar...

C. Con un amigo. Role-play the following situations with a friend. One of you will be an operator on duty and the other will call about the emergencies listed below. The operator will give three suggestions to the caller. Do two situations and change roles for the next two.

MODELO: Una señora llama porque hay un accidente serio en la calle donde vive.

E1: *Hay un accidente serio en mi calle.*

E2: *1. Dígame la dirección.*

   2. Espere con las víctimas.

   3. No mueva a las víctimas.

1. Un señor llama porque tiene información sobre un robo.

2. Una madre llama porque hay drogadictos en el parque donde están los niños.

3. El director de una escuela llama porque un estudiante tiene una pistola.

4. Un testigo de un accidente de "atropellar y huir" llama.

Módulo 2

Los desastres

A. ¿Cómo se dice? Choose the correct Spanish word to complete the following ideas:

a. alguien   **b.** nadie   **c.** ¡Socorro!   **d.** tirador   **e.** herida

1. _____ Una lesión en el cuerpo que requiere atención médica

2. _____ Una persona que usa una pistola u otra arma

3. _____ Una persona no identificada

4. _____ La ausencia completa de personas

5. _____ Una palabra que indica que una persona necesita ayuda inmediata

B. Acciones. Complete the following statements with the correct verb as indicated in the drawing.

1. ___llorar___ es indicar mucha emoción con gotas de agua que salen de los ojos.

2. ___tirador___ es usar una pistola.

3. ___gritar___ es la acción de hablar en voz **MUY ALTA.**

4. ___esconder___ es el intento de hacerse invisible frente a un peligro.

5. ___nada___ es el acto de vaciar *(empty)* un edificio.

Los niños con armas

A 911 operator receives a chilling call from a terrified middle school student hiding in the boys' locker room at her school.

SARITA: Estoy en el baño del gimnasio. **Alguien** tiene una pistola y está disparando en el gimnasio.

OPERADORA: ¿Hay peligro inmediato en el baño?

SARITA: No. No pasa **nada** aquí.

OPERADORA: ¿Quién es el tirador?

SARITA: No lo sé, pero creo que es estudiante aquí.

OPERADORA: ¿Dónde está ahora?

SARITA: No sé dónde está **tampoco.** Yo no veo **nada** porque estoy escondida en el baño. Pero hay muchos gritos en el pasillo cerca de aquí. Yo creo que **algo** está pasando al otro lado de la puerta del gimnasio. ¡Socorro! ¡Por favor!

OPERADORA: ¿Hay **alguien** más allí?

SARITA: No, no hay **nadie** aquí ahora. Yo estoy sola. ¡O, no! La puerta del baño se está abriendo; **alguien** entra aquí. ¡Ay Dios! Es mi amigo, Daniel. ¡Está herido! ¡En el hombro!

OPERADORA: No hagan **nada.** La policía y los paramédicos están localizando al tirador y evacuando a los otros estudiantes. Esperen ustedes allí y **alguien** va a ir en unos momentos. Quédense en la línea conmigo.

C. ¿Comprende usted? Read the following sentences based on the dialogue and decide whether each is **Cierto (C)** or **Falso (F).** If you find incorrect information, correct it.

1. __C__ Alguien en la escuela está tirando una pistola.

2. __F__ Sarita está con muchos estudiantes que tienen miedo.

3. __F__ Sarita puede identificar al tirador.

4. __C__ Un amigo herido entra en el baño.

5. <u>C</u> Los paramédicos están evacuando el edificio.

6. <u>F</u> Sarita debe salir del baño.

D. ¿Eso pasa? Tell whether you or someone you know does the activities listed always or never. Use the words in the box in your answers.

alguien	nadie	siempre	nunca *(never)*	algunas veces *(sometimes)*

1. Trae armas al trabajo o a la escuela.

2. Va en patrullera a la escuela todos los días.

3. Habla español en la casa.

4. Se esconde en el baño del gimnasio.

5. Grita "¡Socorro!" si no hay peligro.

E. ¡Un terremoto! Not all emergencies are man-made. Read the instructions from the Red Cross on how to survive an earthquake. Have you ever experienced one? Decide which suggestions you followed or would follow in such a circumstance. Compare your choices with a classmate.

MODELO: *Es importante no usar el teléfono, excepto para una emergencia real.*

CRUZ ROJA AMERICANA
LISTA DE SUPERVIVENCIA PARA TERREMOTOS Y DESASTRES

Durante un terremoto:

1. Si usted está adentro, colóquese debajo de una mesa o escritorio. Tenga cuidado de las cosas que caen y de los objetos que vuelan por el aire. Permanezca lejos de las ventanas.
2. Si usted está afuera, muévase a un área amplia, lejos de edificios, árboles, postes de luz, paredes de ladrillo o de bloques y otros objetos que puedan caer.
3. Si usted está en un automóvil, pare y permanezca en él hasta que la sacudida pase. Evite parar debajo o cerca de árboles y cables de la luz o bajo pasos a desnivel *(overpasses)*.
4. Si usted está en un edificio alto, colóquese debajo de un escritorio. No use el ascensor para salir—use las escaleras.
5. Si usted está en un almacén, busque protección debajo de una mesa o de cualquier objeto pesado. Evite pararse debajo de cualquier cosa que pueda caer.

Después de un terremoto:

1. Use zapatos fuertes para evitar heridas al caminar sobre vidrios y deshechos.
2. Busque heridos y dé primeros auxilios.
3. Protéjase contra posibles incendios y sus peligros:
   • Si huele a gas o sospecha un escape, cierre la válvula principal, abra las ventanas y salga de la casa.

• Si sospecha escapes de agua, cierre la llave principal.
• Si sospecha de daños en el sistema de electricidad, cierre el circuito principal o retire los fusibles.

4. Prenda el radio y escuche las instrucciones.
5. No toque los cables caídos de la luz.
6. Haga limpieza de todo material potencialmente peligroso.
7. Inspeccione las tuberías antes de usar los baños.
8. Chequee la casa por daños en el techo, chimenea, etc.
9. No use el teléfono, excepto para una emergencia real.
10. Esté preparado para temblores recurrentes.
11. Abra los armarios cuidadosamente.
12. Coopere con las autoridades de seguridad pública.

Si usted tiene que evacuar:

1. Ponga en sitio visible un mensaje haciendo saber el lugar donde usted puede ser localizado.
2. Lleve con usted lo siguiente:
   • medicina y equipo de primeros auxilios
   • linterna, radio y baterías
   • papeles importantes y dinero
   • comida, sacos para dormir, cobijas y ropa extra

Estructuras   *Expressing negative ideas:*
Las expresiones afirmativas y negativas

- In Spanish, sentences are made negative by placing either **no** or a negative expression *before* the verb. The following affirmative expressions must be changed to their negative equivalents if one part of the sentence is negative:

alguien	*somebody*	**nadie**	*nobody*
algo	*something*	**nada**	*nothing*
también	*also*	**tampoco**	*neither*
siempre	*always*	**nunca**	*never*

—¿Ve Ud. **algo** peligroso en el gimnasio?	*Do you see anything dangerous in the gym?*
—**No** veo **nada** peligroso.	*I don't see anything dangerous.*
—¿Ve **algo** en baño?	*Do you see anything in the bathroom?*
—No, **no** veo **nada** allí **tampoco.**	*No, I don't see anything there either.*
—¿Hay **alguien** escondido en el baño?	*Is there anyone hiding in the bathroom?*
—**No** hay **nadie** allí.	*There is no one is there.*

Para practicar

A. Siempre, a veces, nunca...   Tell how often you do the following:

MODELO: Responder a accidentes en la calle
A veces respondo a accidentes en la calle.

1. Ir al hospital con una víctima
2. Pedir una ambulancia para ir a la escuela
3. Dar primeros auxilios a las víctimas de un accidente
4. Arrestar a estudiantes de la escuela secundaria *(high school)*
5. Llamar al 911
6. Evacuar un edificio por peligros

B. Las quejas. Every community has someone who just loves to complain—even when there really is nothing to complain about. Lucky you! You get to respond to these complaints.

MODELO: —**Nunca** responde la policía cuando necesito algo.
—*Siempre respondemos cuando necesita algo.*

1. *Nunca* hay *nadie* para contestar mis preguntas. ~~Ter~~ *Siempre hay alguien para contestar mis preguntas*
2. Los agentes *siempre* son antipáticos. *Los agentes nunca son antipaticos*
3. *Alguien siempre* me amenaza *(threaten).* *Nadie nunca te amanza*
4. *Siempre* hay ladrones en mi garaje. *Nunca hay ladrones es le garaje*
5. *También* hay narcotraficantes en la casa vecina.
6. *Alguien* necesita vigilar mi casa 24 horas al día. *Nadie necesita vigilar mi casa 24 al día*
7. Hay *algo* peligroso en mi carro.
8. *Nadie* comprende el peligro.

C. Siempre o nunca... With a partner, create a list of five commands for things that people should always do to help victims of accidents or violence and five things that they should never do.

MODELO: *Siempre llame al 911.*
Nunca mueva a la víctima.

Módulo 2

Un incendio

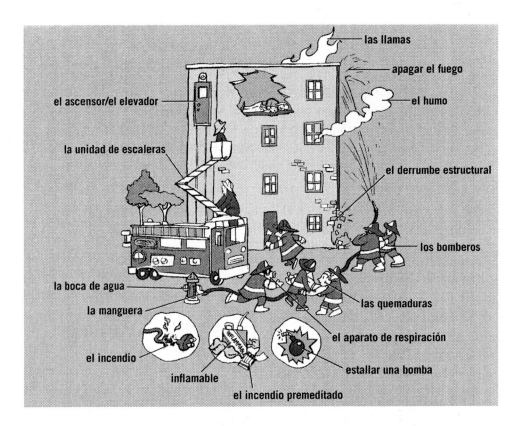

A. ¿Cómo se dice?   Choose the correct Spanish word to complete the following:

1. Dos indicaciones de un incendio son el _____ y las

_____.

2. El aparato que transporta el agua de la boca al incendio es una

_____.

3. Un incendio que no es accidental sino intencional es un incendio

_____.

4. Éstas son útiles para llegar a pisos altos sin usar un ascensor:

_____.

5. Una persona que combate los incendios es un _____.

B. Acciones.   Complete these statements with the most logical verb.

1.   El trabajo de un bombero es _____ un fuego o incendio.

2.   Los bomberos entran en un edificio en llamas para _____ a
las víctimas.

3.   La acción que produce una explosión es _____.

4.   La acción de sacar a las víctimas del peligro es _____.

El rescate

*Here we go again! Yet another fire alarm has been reported from the apartment
building on Maple and Stone. While this building is famous for false alarms*
(alarmas falsas), *the fire department can take no chances. Oh, no! This
time it's real. But, is it accident or arson?*

BOMBERO: *(Por radio al comandante)* Estamos en el primer piso y
no vemos ni escuchamos a **nadie.** Hay humo, pero
no hay llamas aquí. Parece que estos residentes están
evacuados. Hay olor de gasolina. Subimos al segundo
piso.

COMANDANTE: El conserje *(superintendent)* del edificio está aquí
conmigo y dice que **algunos** residentes todavía están
dentro del edificio.

BOMBERO: Nosotros no vemos a **ningún** residente hasta ahora,
ni **ninguna** víctima. Estamos en el tercer piso.
Tampoco hay **nadie** en el ascensor. Hay más humo
aquí y algunas llamas. Pero por el momento no
encontramos a **ninguna** persona.

COMANDANTE: Es un edificio viejo. Estén alertas a **alguna** señal de derrumbe
estructural. ¿Me oyen?

BOMBERO :   Oímos perfectamente. *(Con calma)* Comandante, en el cuarto
piso, apartamento de frente, hay una señora y un bebé
inconscientes en el dormitorio. No hay escape por la puerta
donde entramos. Necesitamos inmediatamente la unidad de
escaleras a la ventana principal.
Miau… miau…
¡Ay, gatito! Vamos a rescatarte, también.

C. ¿Comprende usted?   Answer the following questions based on the dialogue.

1.   ¿Con quién habla el bombero?
2.   ¿Cuántas personas hay en el segundo piso?
3.   ¿Qué problema potencial indica el comandante con el edificio viejo?
4.   ¿Cómo están la madre y la bebé?
5.   ¿Hay alguna indicación de un incendio premeditado?

D. Una manifestación.   A small demonstration is beginning to get out of hand and the police have been called to disperse the crowd. You and your partner arrive. Act out a dialogue, including lines you might hear from the demonstrators. You may need some additional vocabulary.

el derecho	*right*	la baliza, luz de emergencia	*flare*
detenido/a	*arrested*	el/la puerco/a, el/la cerdo/a, el/la cochino/a	*pig*
¡Cállese!	*Shut up!*	el permiso	*permit, permission*
el cono	*traffic cone*	el/la desamparado/a	*homeless*
el odio	*hate*	la huelga	*strike*
cancelado/a	*cancelled*	quedar disuelto	*to be dissolved*
¡Váyanse!	*Go away!*	el megáfono	*bullhorn*

MODELO: Policía: *Necesitan irse del área.*
Manifestante: *¡Cochinos!*

Estructuras   *Más sobre las expresiones negativas*

* **Alguno** and **ninguno** are usually used before a noun and must agree in number and gender with the noun they describe. **Ningún/ninguno/a** literally means *not even one.* To indicate "there aren't any..." both the noun and **ningún/ninguno/a** become singular.

Hay algun**os** herid**os.**   *There are some injured persons.*
No hay ning**ún** herid**o.**   *There are no injured people.*
                              (There's not even one injured person.)

* **Algún** and **ningún** are used before masculine singular nouns. **Ninguno/a** is not used in the plural unless no singular form of the noun exists: (i.e., **pantalones, tijeras** *(scissors)*).

Algunos residentes están en el edificio.	*Some residents are in the building.*
No hay **ningún residente** aquí.	*There are no residents here. (not even one)*
Hay **algunas señales** de derrumbe estructural.	*There are some signs of a collapse.*
No hay **ninguna señal** de derrumbe.	*There isn't a single sign of a collapse.*
Necesito **unas tijeras.**	*I need some scissors.*
No hay **ningunas tijeras.**	*There aren't any scissors.*

Para practicar

A. ¿Tiene Ud...?   Tell whether or not you personally have any of the following:

MODELO: alguna quemadura...
No tengo ninguna quemadura.

1. algunos aparatos de respiración
2. algunas escaleras
3. algún amigo en el hospital
4. algunas víctimas que no hablan inglés
5. algo importante que hacer mañana
6. algunos materiales inflamables

B. En el edificio quemado.   Change the italicized words to describe the opposite situation.

MODELO: Hay *algunas* indicaciones de incendio premeditado.
No hay ninguna indicación de incendio premeditado.

1. Yo *siempre* voy a un incendio sin aparato de respiración.
2. Hay *algunos criminales* que cometen incendios premeditados, por el dinero del seguro.
3. *Algunas víctimas* gritan "¡Socorro!"
4. *Nunca* rescatamos a las víctimas.
5. Los bomberos tienen *algunas mangueras* para apagar el fuego.
6. *Nunca* hay *nada* que puedan hacer los bomberos en un incendio menor.
7. No veo a *ninguna víctima* aquí. (¡OJO!)
8. Necesito *unas tijeras* para cortar los pantalones.

C. Durante el rescate. You are on the radio with your Commander during a rescue from a burning building. The pressure is on and there is no time to lose. The Commander will ask you if you see the first five items while on your way to perform your heroic rescues, and you will answer in the affirmative or in the negative according to the indication. Switch roles every few items.

MODELO: señales de derrumbe estructural/ no
Comandante: *¿Ve algunas señales de derrumbe estructural?*
Bombero/a: *No, no veo ninguna señal de derrumbe estructural.*

1. niños/sí
2. llamas/sí
3. gatos/no
4. personas en el ascensor/no
5. indicaciones de incendio premeditado/no

6. víctimas/no
7. bomberos/sí
8. materiales inflamables/sí
9. problemas eléctricos/no
10. animales/sí

Vocabulario Módulo I

Sustantivos

la ambulancia	*ambulance*	**el/la paramédico**	*paramedic*
la barricada	*barricade*	**la pastilla**	*pill*
la bomba	*fire truck*	**el pecho**	*chest*
la camilla	*stretcher*	**el piso**	*floor*
la cobija	*blanket*	**el/la pobrecito/a**	*poor thing*
el cuello	*neck*	**la presión**	*pressure*
el dolor	*pain*	**los primeros**	
la fractura	*fracture*	**auxilios**	*first aid*
la habitación	*room*	**el pulso**	*pulse*
la hemorragia	*hemorrhage*	**el rescate**	*rescue*
la herida	*wound*	**la resucitación**	
el hospital	*hospital*	**cardiopulmonar**	*CPR*
el hueso	*bone*	**la sangre**	*blood*
el letrero	*sign*	**la temperatura**	*temperature*
la lluvia	*rain*	**la toalla**	*towel*
la muchedumbre	*crowd*	**el viento**	*wind*
la nieve	*snow*		

Verbos

colgar (ue)	*to hang up*	**marcar**	*to dial*
cubrir	*to cover*	**mover (ue)**	*to move*
deber	*to ought to, should*	**rescatar**	*to rescue*
		respirar	*to breathe*
despachar	*to dispatch*	**salvar**	*to save*
entregar	*to hand over*		

Adjetivos

consciente	*conscious*	**muerto/a**	*dead*
desesperado/a	*desperate*	**profundo/a**	*deep*

Módulo 2

Sustantivos

el aire	*air*	**la llama**	*flame*
el aparato	*apparatus*	**la llave**	*key*
el armario	*wardrobe*	**la manguera**	*hose*
el ascensor	*elevator*	**el mensaje**	*message*
la ausencia	*absence*	**la mesa**	*table*
la biblioteca	*library*	**los muebles**	*furniture*
la bomba	*bomb*	**el olor**	*smell*
el cuarto	*room*	**el pánico**	*panic*
el derrumbe	*collapse*	**el pasillo**	*hall*
el desastre	*disaster*	**la queja**	*complaint*
el elevador	*elevator*	**la quemadura**	*burn*
el escritorio	*desk*	**la respiración**	*breathing*
la esquina	*corner*	**la supervivencia**	*survival*
el fuego	*fire*	**el terremoto**	*earthquake*
la gasolina	*gasoline*	**la tierra**	*earth*
el gimnasio	*gym*	**el tirador**	*shooter*
el ladrillo	*brick*	**el vidrio**	*glass*
la limpieza	*cleaning*	**la voz**	*voice*

Verbos

agacharse	*to crouch down*	**gritar**	*to shout*
apagar	*to put out*	**oler (ue)**	*to smell*
caer (ig)	*to fall*	**prender**	*to turn on*
demoler (ue)	*to demolish*	**proteger**	*to protect*
escoger	*to choose*	**sacudir**	*to shake*
esconder	*to hide*	**sospechar**	*to suspect*
estallar	*to explode*	**sujetarse**	*to hold on to something*
estremecer	*to tremble*		
evacuar	*to evacuate*	**volar (ue)**	*to fly*
evitar	*to avoid*		

Adjetivos

inflamable	*flammable*	**útil**	*useful*
próximo/a	*next*		

Otras expresiones

acá	*here*	**frente a**	*facing*
adentro	*inside*	**nadie**	*nobody*
afuera	*outside*	**ningún/una/a**	*none*
alguien	*somebody*	**nunca**	*never*
algún/uno/a	*some*	**¡Socorro!**	*Help!*
contra	*against*	**tampoco**	*neither*
dentro de	*within*		

Síntesis

A escuchar

The receptionist at Hudson Middle School receives an alarming call during fifth period of finals week. Listen to the call and answer the following questions:

1. ¿Quién contesta el teléfono?
2. ¿Por qué tienen que evacuar la escuela?
3. ¿Cómo se llaman las personas que llama?
4. ¿Cómo sabe la recepcionista que llaman Marco Antonio y Daniel?

A conversar

Disasters! At any given moment there is a disaster being reported in some part of the world. In groups of four, look through the following lists of disasters—both natural and man-made—and tell: 1. if the disaster is natural **(desastre natural),** accidental **(accidental),** or deliberate **(premeditado);** 2. what possible consequences might arise; and 3. create your own list of emergency responders needed to help. Add any additional information you might have.

MODELO: tornado

   1. Es un desastre natural.

   2. Consecuencias: muchos heridos, edificios derrumbados, robos

   3. Expertos: Paramédicos, policía, bomberos, oficiales del gobierno

1. incendio premeditado
2. derrame químico *(chemical spill)*
3. huracán
4. bioterrorismo

A leer

LOS PELIGROS DE UN TERREMOTO

En un terremoto, el movimiento de la tierra en sí raramente es la causa directa de muertos y heridos. La mayoría de las víctimas se debe a la caída de diversidad de escombros *(rubble)*, pues los temblores pueden sacudir, dañar o demoler edificios y otras estructuras. Los terremotos también pueden causar derrumbes, al igual que generar maremotos (olas sísmicas) que pueden causar graves daños.

Los accidentes personales comúnmente son causados por:

1. Derrumbes parciales de edificios: caída de chimeneas, ladrillos, cornisas, paredes, cielos rasos, avisos luminosos, etc.
2. Caída de vidrios rotos de ventanas, que especialmente cuando vienen de edificios altos, son peligrosos.
3. Caída de bibliotecas, muebles y otros objetos colocados en partes altas.
4. Incendios causados por chimeneas rotas, tuberías de gas en malas condiciones, cables de la luz expuestos a cortocircuitos. El peligro puede ser más grave por falta de agua a causa de daños en las tuberías principales.
5. Cables de la luz y de líneas de teléfono caídos.
6. Desórdenes provocados por el pánico.

¿Comprende usted? Prepare a list of five causes of accidents following an earthquake.

Use your own words to explain; don't just copy from the reading selection. Does the actual earthquake usually cause death or injury?

MODELO: *1. El vidrio (glass) de ventanas rotas puede causar heridas.*

A escribir

List three common reasons for law enforcement officials to go to schools, either for educational presentations or for problems. Compare your list with others in your group.

MODELO: *1. Charlas de DARE, el programa contra el uso de drogas.*

Algo más

In Latino communities, mistrust of any law enforcement agent can often be related to previous associations of police with oppressive military regimes in countries of origin. Language barriers, coupled with a general reluctance to interact with public safety officials, can lead to serious delays in disaster situations. Public safety agencies are teaming up with community service groups in many communities to provide disaster management outreach before, during, and after an emergency situation. The American Red Cross is even targeting children to help parents be prepared in case of disasters. Here is one of the children's safety pages from the American Red Cross.

Laberinto

En tu hogar, y con tu familia, debes practicar dos maneras de salir de cada habitación. Al igual que tu plan de escape de incendios, hay dos maneras de salir de este laberinto. ¿Podrías encontrarlas? También recuerda los siguientes consejos de seguridad para hacer un simulacro de incendios en tu hogar.

- Arrastrarte para evitar el humo y el calor.
- Toca las puertas con la parte posterior de la mano antes de abrirlas.
- No abras la puerta si se siente caliente—usa la segunda salida.
- Sal rápidamente.
- Reúnete con tu familia afuera y después llama para pedir ayuda.
- Escribe el número de teléfono de emergencia aquí_____.

Escape Maze

At home, you should practice two ways out of every room with your family. Just like your escape plan, there are two ways out of this maze. Can you find them? Also, remember these safety tips for your home fire escape drill:

- Crawl low to avoid smoke and heat.
- Feel doors with the back of your hand before opening them.
- Do not open the door if it feels hot—use your second exit.
- Get out fast.
- Meet outside and then call for help.
- Fill in your emergency number here

_____

En mis propias palabras. Have you experienced a situation in which a language barrier existed while trying to resolve an emergency situation? Explain.

A buscar

There are many sites that focus on school violence. Go to the website for this book and check out a few of them—there may be useful information for you!

A conocer: Rich Gonzales

Rich Gonzales era (was) *bombero en Denver por 30 años, incluyendo 13 años como jefe. Por su herencia latina, reconoce la importancia de la familia y un sentido de comunidad. En sus propias palabras, "Mi casa es su casa".*

Rich Gonzales is a Denver native who graduated from North High and Regis University. He served as a Denver firefighter for nearly 30 years including 13 years as Fire Chief. During his tenure as Chief, Gonzales oversaw a $69 million annual budget and 1,000 employees. As part of his commitment to the communities he served, he encouraged fire stations to help Denver neighborhoods complete various projects such as playgrounds and basketball courts.

Gonzales, who also has a master's degree in public administration, now heads up corporate campaigns for Mile High United Way. He oversees workplace fundraising and donor relations.

He believes that community issues that need immediate attention are: quality child care, preparing children to succeed in school, emergency assistance (i.e., the homeless), programs that give people the tools for self-reliance and success, and protecting everyone from violence.

He credits his Latino heritage for his family orientation, developed sense of community, and the proposition that the accommodation of the whole is more important than that of the individual. Gonzales therefore feels an obligation to help those with less, and he shows compassion and tolerance for all people.

LECCIÓN 6

Repaso I

Lección 1: En la ciudad
- La hora
- **Ser** + adjetivos
- Las artículos
- Las preguntas

Lección 2: En la carretera
- Más sobre los adjetivos
- Los verbos que terminan en **–ar**
- Los verbos que terminan en **–er, –ir**
- Expresiones con **tener** y **estar**

Lección 3: En mi barrio
- El presente progresivo
- **Ser** y **estar**
- El verbo **ir** y el futuro inmediato
- Verbos irregulares en el presente

Lección 4: Las drogas
- Los adjetivos posesivos
- Los verbos con cambios de raíz
- Los comparativos
- Los superlativos

Lección 5: ¡Emergencia!
- Los mandatos formales
- Los mandatos irregulares/con cambios ortográficos/con pronombres de objeto indirecto
- Las expresiones afirmativas y negativas
- Más sobre las expresiones negativas

Lección 1

En la ciudad

Módulo 1

A. El reporte.   Part of your job is to report on the suspects you are observing. Indicate the "question" for which the following answers would be given.

MODELO: el 27 de enero de 2005
            La fecha:

1.   153 Calle Concordia   **4.**   Soto López
2.   Las Vegas   **5.**   Nevada
3.   Armando

B. E.T.A.   It is very important to maintain radio contact with the dispatchers to let them know your estimated times of arrival at the different crime scenes. As you check in with them by radio, tell them what time it is now and then at what time you will arrive (always 15 minutes later).

MODELO: 10:05 A.M.
            Son las diez y cinco de la mañana. Llegamos (we arrive) a las diez y veinte.

1.   1:05 P.M.   **4.**   12 noon
2.   6:15 P.M.   **5.**   8:30 A.M.
3.   7:00 A.M. on the dot   **6.**   9:55 P.M.

C. Descripciones.   Here are some of the observations the witnesses you are interviewing make about the crime scene and the suspects. Use the verb **ser** to link the subjects and verbs, and don't forget to match nouns and adjectives!

MODELO: El auto/moderno
            El auto es moderno.

1.   Las víctimas/viejo   **5.**   La ropa/interesante
2.   La sospechosa/bonito   **6.**   Las blusas/rojo
3.   Los criminales/eficiente   **7.**   El sistema telefónico/complicado
4.   El sospechoso/guapo   **8.**   El pelo/largo

D. Problemas, problemas. You are interviewing many witnesses to a recent crime. The line of people who want to talk to you is out the door! Speed up the process by completing the witness information for two witnesses at a time and interview two classmates to fill in the form. Remember: They don't have to tell the truth—just use good grammar!

Apellido(s)_____ Nombre _____	Apellido(s)_____ Nombre _____
Dirección _____	Dirección _____
Ciudad _____ Estado _____ Código postal_____	Ciudad _____ Estado _____ Código postal_____
Teléfono_____	Teléfono_____
Fecha _____	Fecha _____

Módulo 2

A. Un testigo sin memoria. You are interviewing an older witness who has keen powers of observation, but he sometimes forgets his words. Read the descriptions and supply the missing terms.

MODELO: la parte del cuerpo que usamos para mirar y observar...
¡Ah! Los ojos.

1. la parte del cuerpo que usamos para respirar *(breathe)*...
2. la parte del cuerpo donde tengo los lentes...
3. la parte del cuerpo donde tengo los zapatos...
4. la parte del cuerpo que usamos para hablar...
5. la(s) parte(s) del cuerpo que usamos para caminar...

B. Muchas preguntas. Sherlock Holmes often knew the answers even before he knew the questions! Test your own deductive powers by giving questions that would have been asked to elicit these answers.

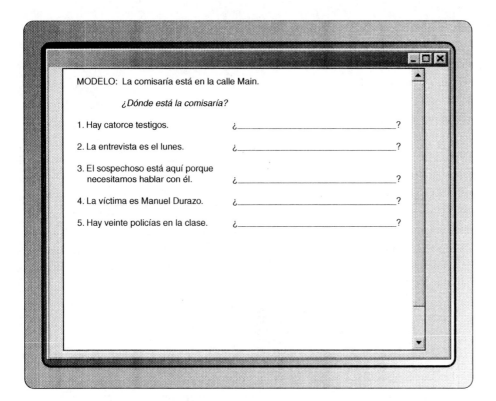

MODELO: La comisaría está en la calle Main.

¿Dónde está la comisaría?

1. Hay catorce testigos. ¿_____?

2. La entrevista es el lunes. ¿_____?

3. El sospechoso está aquí porque
   necesitamos hablar con él. ¿_____?

4. La víctima es Manuel Durazo. ¿_____?

5. Hay veinte policías en la clase. ¿_____?

C. Direcciones. While you are on street patrol, a series of visitors stop by to ask you where they might find the following things or people. Use your best Spanish to tell them—some things may be found in more than one place.

MODELO: un sandwich
En el café

1. un portero   **4.** una película con Salma Hayek
2. mucho dinero   **5.** el comandante de la policía
3. servicios médicos

D. Las relaciones humanas. Maintaining good relationships with witnesses is often a key to their cooperation. Tell what question you would have asked to get the following answers from the people you are interviewing.

MODELO: Hoy estoy bien, gracias.
¿Cómo está usted hoy?

1. Me llamo Mario Andaloro.
2. Trabajo en el hospital.
3. Tengo tres hijos.
4. Hablo dos idiomas: inglés y español.
5. El sospechoso es alto con pelo corto y rizado.
6. Estoy aquí porque es mi obligación cívica.

Lección 2

En la carretera

Módulo I

A. En la calle. Can you identify these traffic terms by their description?

1. Un vehículo de transporte con 18 ruedas _____

2. Muchos vehículos en la calle que no pueden moverse _____

3. Una colisión entre dos vehículos _____

4. Un camión especial para ayudar los vehículos descompuestos

_____

B. ¿Qué es? A confused student driver is trying to learn all of this traffic terminology. Please match the word with a likely definition.

1. semáforo   **a.** sanción por cometer una infracción
2. estacionamiento   **b.** luz roja, verde o amarilla
3. peatón   **c.** el auto está aquí cuando no está en uso
4. multa   **d.** una persona que camina por la calle
5. parada   **e.** aquí las personas esperan al autobús

C. Optimismo. If only the world worked exactly the way we think it should! Write the adjective that you usually associate with the following nouns. Then, compare your list with a classmate's to see if you think alike.

MODELO: el teniente *(lieutenant)*
       E1: El teniente es excelente.
       E2: El teniente es serio.

1. el samaritano   **4.** el dinero
2. las llantas   **5.** el semi
3. el autobús escolar   **6.** yo

D. La división del trabajo. You have been sent by the police station to be sure that everyone at the scene of the accident is doing his or her job. Look at the following list of tasks and tell who does each one using the job categories below.

El policía, el responsable, la víctima, los paramédicos, el señor con la grúa, el operador de 911, los testigos

MODELO: contestar el teléfono
       El operador de 911 contesta el teléfono.

1. hablar con el responsable
2. causar el accidente
3. manejar muy rápidamente
4. preparar los reportes del accidente
5. dar atención médica a la víctima
6. explicar sus observaciones
7. poner una multa al responsable
8. retirar el vehículo descompuesto

Módulo 2

A. ¿Dónde? Can you match the following motor vehicle terms with a definition?

1. seguro
2. multa
3. escuela de tráfico
4. el registro

a. documento para verificar posesión de un vehículo
b. clases para mejorar la manera de manejar
c. protección financiera para los gastos de un accidente
d. sanción por una infracción de tráfico

B. ¿Está borracho? You suspect a driver of being impaired while operating a motor vehicle. With a partner, brainstorm a list of questions and commands you will need in order to determine how serious the situation is. When you are finished writing as many as you can remember, compare your list with that of another team.

MODELO: E1: *¿Está enfermo?*
E2: *Apague el motor.*

C. ¿Qué hacen? For each subject and verb pair, write a complete sentence with a logical ending.

MODELO: Los agentes/escribir
Los agentes escriben multas y reportes.

1. Los oficiales/comer
2. El operador de 911/recibir
3. El chofer responsable/discutir
4. Cuando tenemos mucha sed/beber
5. La víctima de un accidente/sufrir
6. El testigo/ver

D. Expresiones. Explain how the following people feel by using a **tener** expression.

MODELO: Los agentes están en Alaska en diciembre.
Tienen frío.

1. Los investigadores necesitan alimentos y nutrición.
2. El policía pone el aire acondicionado en la patrullera.
3. ¡Ay! ¡Una persona entra en mi casa!
4. La sospechosa necesita agua.

Lección 3

En mi barrio

Módulo I

A. Identificación.   Can you complete each line with a logical vocabulary word related to house and neighborhood?

1. El lugar de la casa para el auto. _____

2. Voy aquí cuando tengo sueño. _____

3. Aquí voy cuando tengo hambre o sed. _____

4. Debajo de la casa está el _____.

5. El sofá normalmente está en el _____.

B. La familia.   Can you define the following family members—in Spanish? Follow the form for your answers.

MODELO: abuela
           La abuela es la mamá de mi mamá.

1. el tío   **3.** los nietos
2. la hermana   **4.** los padres

C. Modelo de conducta.   It's after-hours and you are staying late to take care of paperwork and other odds and ends at the station. One of your most devoted trainees has volunteered to help you. Your student officer is particularly curious and wants to know exactly what you are doing at every moment. Answer all of the following questions with a logical response and the present progressive tense.

MODELO: ¿Qué lee usted?
           Estoy leyendo los boletines del departamento.

1. ¿Qué escribe? **3.** ¿Qué prepara?
2. ¿Qué mira?   **4.** ¿Por qué duerme?

D. Centro de información.   As the spokesperson for the police department, you are often called on to give information and briefings about incidents in the city. Use the correct form of **ser** or **estar** to complete the following sentences.

MODELO: El incidente... en la calle Main.
           El incidente está en la calle Main.

1. Los pandilleros... del Barrio 9.

2. Una persona... herida.

3. El comandante Cabrera... experto en Justicia Penal Juvenil.

4. Los investigadores... muy cansados después de investigar un homicidio toda la noche.

5. Los pandilleros... violentos.

6. El grafiti... de la pandilla Los Cholos.

Módulo 2

A. Con la prensa.   As public relations officer for the city, you often do press briefings. Today, there are members of the press who don't understand some of the vocabulary you are using. Supply the proper term for the words they define.

MODELO: El líder de una pandilla
  el jefe

1. Una persona que secretamente da información a la policía

2. El uso de armas de fuego por la ventana de un auto en movimiento

3. Un conflicto violento entre dos pandillas rivales

4. Expresión artística e información pública de una pandilla

B. ¿Para qué sirven?   Can you explain—in Spanish, of course—what you would need the following for?

MODELO: una puerta
  Necesito una puerta para entrar y salir.

1. un detector de metales   **3.** una pistola

2. un soplón   **4.** una bala

C. ¿Qué va a hacer?   Tell where the following people are going or what they are going to do to remedy the following situations.

MODELO: La víctima es un niño. El policía...
  El policía va a llamar a sus padres.

1. Veo un asalto en la calle. Yo...

2. Los adictos necesitan crack. Ellos...

3. No tengo plata. Yo...

4. Usted está muy cansado. Usted ...

5. Ustedes tienen hambre. Ustedes...

6. Soy un agente secreto y necesito información. Yo...

D. ¿Quién o quiénes?   You are undercover doing surveillance during a period of gang warfare. Tell if you **(yo=el/la policía)**, the gang members **(los pandilleros)**, or all of us **(nosotros)** do the following things.

MODELO: oír conversaciones electrónicamente
Yo oigo las conversaciones electrónicamente.

1. _____ conducir el auto al tiroteo en marcha

2. _____ hacer planes para la guerra

3. _____ traer ametralladoras

4. _____ conocer a los jefes de las pandillas

5. _____ poner las armas en el carro

6. _____ saber donde radican los rivales

Lección 4

Las drogas

Módulo 1

A. Traducción, por favor.   Your knowledge of street Spanish has made you invaluable on the job. Help another officer understand what the suspects are talking about by matching the "street term" on the left with the "official" term on the right.

En la calle...

1.   Necesito lana.

2.   Las chavas quieren nieve.

3.   Mis compas están quemados.

4.   El camello es un cabrón.

5.   ¿Dónde está la cucaracha?

En la comisaría...

a.   Busco la marihuana. _____

b.   El narcotraficante es malo. _____

c.   Las mujeres desean cocaína. _____

d.   Quiero ganar dinero. _____

e.   Estos señores no están sobrios. _____

B. Identificación. Can you define in your own words (in Spanish, of course!) these terms related to illegal drugs?

MODELO: el pelotero
Es un camello—una persona que vende drogas.

1. la estofa   **4.** la mota
2. la plata   **5.** la jeringa
3. la farlopa   **6.** el equipo

C. Posesión. Use the appropriate form of the possessive adjectives **mi(s),** **tu(s), su(s),** or **nuestro/a/os/as** to describe the relationships that follow.

MODELO: Tengo un tío que es policía.
Mi tío es policía.

1. Ustedes tienen una operación secreta.   _____ operación es secreta.

2. Nosotros tenemos agentes
excelentes.   _____ agentes son excelentes.

3. Elena tiene varios narcóticos.   _____ narcóticos son para
vender.

4. Tú tienes amigos quemados.   _____ amigos están quemados.

5. Ellos tienen una bandera mexicana.   _____ bandera es mexicana.

D. Personas diferentes. You and your friend Eduardo are just the opposite of the two other undercover officers, Juan and Lucía. Explain how by finishing the following sentences.

MODELO: dormir mucho en la patrullera.
*Eduardo y yo no dormimos mucho en la patrullera. Juan y Lucía duer-
men mucho.*

1. preferir los días sin acción
2. pensar mucho antes de sacar las armas
3. siempre perder la evidencia
4. almorzar en la patrullera
5. empezar el día temprano
6. pedir colaboración a los soplones
7. querer ser agentes excelentes
8. decir siempre la verdad a los sospechosos

Módulo 2

A. Las relaciones con la comunidad. Law enforcement officials are expected to offer many services to the members of the community in which they work. Read the following scenarios and indicate whether the officer is offering better than average service **M (Mejor)** or worse than average service **P (Peor)**.

MODELO: Padre: Tengo una pregunta.

____P____ *Oficial: Estoy ocupado. No tengo tiempo.*

1. Madre: Oficial, creo que mi hijo es miembro de una pandilla. No sé qué hacer.

_____ Oficial: Es un problema difícil. Si Ud. quiere, yo puedo hablar con su hijo.

2. Padre: Mi hijo tiene muchos problemas con las drogas. Quiero pedir una intervención penal.

_____ Oficial: ¡Ja, ja, ja!

3. Estudiante: Los pandilleros mayores siempre me asaltan e intentan venderme drogas. Tengo miedo.

_____ Oficial: Pues, simplemente "Diga ¡No!"

4. Chavas: Creo que mis camaradas están planeando un tiroteo en marcha contra otra pandilla. No quiero ser soplón, pero no quiero ver violencia.

_____ Oficial: Es bueno que me hables. ¿Dónde podemos ir para hablar? Nosotros podemos ayudar.

B. El comandante que no recuerda nada. Your aging commander is having one of his forgetful spells again. Help him by supplying the word he is trying to describe.

MODELO: Comandante: la persona que defiende y representa a los acusados en la corte
Usted: *El abogado*

1. Un crimen en que una persona es asesinada *(murdered)*
2. Una infracción que sólo tiene consecuencias menores
3. Un crimen muchas veces conectado con la pornografía
4. Los símbolos que los pandilleros pintan en edificios, trenes, y puentes *(bridges)*

C. En mi jurisdicción. In my precinct, there are two very competitive officers—one is Sargento Vargas, and the other is Sargento Santana. They are constantly comparing records. Using the following list, make at least three comparative statements of equality **(tan/tanto... como)** and three statements of inequality **(más... que, menos... que).**

MODELO: El Sargento Vargas habla tres idiomas. La Sargento Santana habla dos idiomas.

El Sargento Vargas habla más idiomas que la Sargento Santana.

Sargento Vargas	**Sargento Santana**
34 detenciones	34 detenciones
muy inteligente	no muy inteligente
perezoso	trabajadora
tiene 2 soplones buenos	tiene 4 soplones buenos
tiene 5 comendaciones	tiene 5 comendaciones
es muy fuerte	es muy fuerte
es un buen agente	es muy buena agente

D. El o la mejor sargento. Using the chart above, draw two conclusions about the best and worst sergeants in the precinct. Then write a sentence with **–ísimo/a/os/as** to explain.

MODELO: *La Sargento Santana es la mejor sargento de la jurisdición.*
Es buenísima.

Lección 5

¡Emergencia!

Módulo I

A. El comandante olvidadizo. Your forgetful boss is having trouble remembering the word he needs to use. Please help him out by supplying the word he is trying to describe.

MODELO: el vehículo de emergencia que transporta a las víctimas al hospital
¿La ambulancia?

1. una persona que ya no tiene vida
2. el fluido vital que se pierde por una hemorragia
3. el resultado de un accidente en el que un hueso *(bone)* está roto
4. la actividad vital de inhalar y exhalar el aire
5. una mesa con ruedas para transportar a una víctima en la ambulancia

B. ¿Condición peligrosa o auxilio? Which of the following items do you associate more with **peligro (P)** and which do you associate with **auxilio** *(help)* **(A)?**

1. _____ los bomberos

4. _____ la muchedumbre fuera de control

2. _____ la nieve en la calle

5. _____ el desvío de tráfico

3. _____ el incendio

6. _____ los primeros auxilios

C. Los consejos. As a dispatch operator, you frequently tell callers what they should be doing. Use a formal command to tell each caller what he or she ought to be doing.

MODELO: esperar a la ambulancia
Espere a la ambulancia.

1. tomar precauciones
2. tener cuidado con la víctima
3. no llorar

4. escribir información personal
5. venir al hospital inmediatamente
6. salir de la casa inmediatamente

D. ¡Cuidado! Each of these callers thinks he knows just how to take charge of the emergency at hand. Read each of the following actions and then use a formal command to tell them to do it or not to do it.

MODELO: Muevo a la víctima fuera de la calle.
¡No mueva a la víctima!

1. Busco la identificación de la víctima.
2. Empiezo RCP *(CPR)*.
3. Apago el incendio.

4. Voy al hospital en la ambulancia.
5. Pido los servicios de un médico.
6. Pago la ambulancia.

Módulo 2

A. ¿Hay peligro? The following 911 calls come in from a school. It is up to you to decide if the school is in danger **(Hay peligro)** or not **(No hay peligro)** when these things happen.

MODELO: Hay un intruso con una pistola.
Hay peligro.

1. Alguien accidentalmente rompe una ventana.
2. Hay un simulacro *(drill)* de incendio.
3. Hay un tornado en otra ciudad.
4. Hay un incendio en la cafetería.
5. Un estudiante grita "Socorro".
6. Dos estudiantes se pelean.

B. ¿Cómo se dice?   Disaster vocabulary is critical. Name the word(s) in Spanish described below.

1. El agua para apagar un incendio viene de _____.

2. El camión que los bomberos usan para llegar a un apartamento en el sexto

(6th) piso es _____.

3. Una persona herida en un incendio puede tener _____.

4. Un incendio planeado es _____.

5. Los bomberos llevan una máscara en la cara que se llama _____.

6. ¡BUM! Una explosión—estalló (blew up) una _____.

C. ¡Emergencia!   Read the following list of disasters and emergencies, and tell if someone is responsible **(Alguien)** or no one is responsible **(Nadie)**.

MODELO: Hay un tornado en la ciudad.
             Nadie es responsable.

1. Hay un incendio premeditado.
2. Hay un incendio eléctrico.
3. Hay un tiroteo en marcha.
4. Estallan unas bombas.
5. Hay muchos accidentes a causa de la nieve.
6. Un edificio muy viejo se derrumba.

D. Los bomberos.   You are inside a burning structure and are communicating with the incident commander by radio. Answer all of his questions in the negative.

MODELO: ¿Hay víctimas en el sótano?
             No hay ninguna víctima en el sótano.

1. ¿Alguien grita "socorro" en el edificio?
2. ¿Necesitas algún lente protector?
3. ¿Las víctimas tienen algún problema con la respiración?
4. ¿Notan ustedes alguna indicación de incendio premeditado?
5. ¿Hay alguna señal de derrumbe estructural?

LECCIÓN 7

La policía y la comunidad—unidas

Módulo I

- ¡Cooperamos!
- Expressing generalizations, expectations, and passive voice: *Se impersonal*
- ¡Acaban de robar mi auto!
- The recent past: *Acabar de* + infinitivo

Módulo 2

- Me gusta este barrio
- Expressing likes and dislikes: *Gustar*
- El botín
- Numbers: *De cien a millones; los números ordinales*

Síntesis

- A escuchar
- A conversar
- A leer
- A escribir

Algo más

- Ventana cultural: El machismo
- A buscar
- A conocer: Tnte. Margarita Moris Rivera

Módulo I

¡Cooperamos!

A. ¿Cómo se dice?   Escriba la palabra que corresponda a cada una de las definiciones.

1. Un programa de protección a la comunidad en el que los vecinos y la

policía cooperan es _____.

2. Las personas que tienen casas en la misma calle o edificio son

_____.

3. Una persona sospechosa que no tiene ninguna razón obvia para observar

una casa es un _____.

4. Una emoción de triunfo o satisfacción por un trabajo bien hecho es el

_____.

5. La música que se escucha por todo el vecindario es un ejemplo del

_____.

B. Acciones. Empareje la palabra de la columna **A** con una identificación lógica de la columna **B**.

A		**B**	
1.	_____ un vehículo con dos ruedas	**a.**	el parque
2.	_____ "zapatos" con ruedas	**b.**	la bicicleta
3.	_____ notificación sistemática	**c.**	los faroles
4.	_____ luces que iluminan la calle	**d.**	la cadena telefónica
5.	_____ un lugar público donde los niños pueden jugar	**d.**	los patines

El programa de la Vigilancia vecinal

Unos vecinos del barrio Menlo ya no toleran el crimen y la basura y la falta de respeto en la comunidad. Con la ayuda de la Oficina de "Protección orientada a la comunidad" (Community Policing) de su ciudad, deciden organizar un programa de "Vigilancia en el vecindario" también conocido como "Neighborhood Watch." ¿Es fácil? Claro que no. ¿Vale la pena? Enfáticamente: ¡Sí!

¿Por qué?
Se vigila... se observa... se informa...

1. **Se vigilan las casas** de los vecinos ausentes.

2. **Se notifica a la policía** si hay algo sospechoso.

3. **Se mantiene la limpieza** de los parques.

4. **Se aprenden maneras** de no ser víctimas del crimen.

5. **Se siente orgullo** por su vecindad.

¿Cómo se hace?

1. **Se organiza una reunión** de los vecinos interesados.

2. **Se piden voluntarios.**

3. **Se entrena a los voluntarios** con la ayuda de la patrulla de la vecindad.

4. **Se forman comités** para encargarse de las alertas telefónicas, la limpieza de los parques, la seguridad de los niños.

5. **Se coopera con la policía** para tomar el control de la vecindad.

Estimados vecinos,
¡Es hora de tomar el control de nuestro vecindario!
Están invitados a asistir a una reunión en mi casa, el
20 de octubre, a las 7 de la tarde. ¡Sí se puede!
Carlos Viana

C. ¿Comprende usted?   Conteste las siguientes preguntas según la información del diálogo.

1.   ¿Qué organizan los vecinos?

2.   ¿Por qué organizan este grupo?

3.   ¿Quién ayuda a los vecinos con la organización y el entrenamiento?

4.   Mencione tres actividades del grupo.

D. Más sobre la vigilancia vecinal.   McGruff es el famoso "perro guardián" de la seguridad de las comunidades. Lea el folleto sobre los vecindarios seguros y luego escriba tres o cuatro oraciones como resumen de las sugerencias contenidas en este folleto. Compare su información con la de un compañero.

Tome posición frente al crimen	Únase a un Comité Vecinal de Vigilancia

✔ Organice reuniones regulares para hablar de los temas corrientes: el abuso de drogas, la violencia motivada por el odio racial, el crimen en las escuelas, el cuidado de los niños.

✔ Organice patrullas de vecinos que caminen por las calles o dentro del complejo de apartamentos y alerten a la policía sobre actividades sospechosas.

✔ Coopere con las autoridades para tener cerraduras (candados), alarmas de incendio y otros dispositivos de seguridad en las casas.

✔ Coopere con los grupos de padres y escuelas para organizar un "McGruff House" u otro programa de seguridad para los niños en caso de emergencia.

✔ Publique un boletín con sugerencias para prevenir el crimen.

✔ No se olvide de organizar eventos sociales que ayuden a que los vecinos se conozcan— una fiesta de manzana *(block party)*, cena "potluck", juegos de voleibol o softball, picnics, etc.

Sugerencias para la prevención del crimen:

Consejo Nacional de Prevención del Crimen
1700 K Street, NW, Second Floor
Washington, DC 20006-3817

Estructuras *Expressing generalizations, expectations, and passive voice: Se impersonal*

* Use **se** to state generalizations about what is or is not done. Phrases with **se** are expressed in the following ways in English.

Se habla español en el vecindario. *They speak Spanish in the neighborhood.*
One speaks Spanish in the neighborhood.
Spanish is spoken in the neighborhood.

¿Se tolera la violencia allí? *Does one tolerate violence there?*
Do people tolerate violence there?
Is violence tolerated there?

¿Cómo se dice *How is "Community Policing" said in Spanish?*
"Community Policing" *How do you say "Community Policing" in Spanish?*
en español? *How does one say "Community Policing" in Spanish?*

* With **se,** use the third person form (**él, ella, ellos, ellas, usted, ustedes**) of the verb. It may be singular or plural, depending on the subject. To make it plural, simply add **-n** to the verb.

Se vigila el barrio. *The neighborhood is watched.*
Se vigilan las casas. *The houses are watched.*
Se reporta la actividad sospechosa. *Suspicious activity is reported.*
Se reportan las actividades sospechosas. *Suspicious activities are reported.*

* Use a singular verb with people introduced by the personal **a** and with infinitive verbs used as subjects, even if referring to more than one person or action.

Se puede notificar a la policía. *One can notify the police.*
Se notifica a los vecinos. *You notify the neighbors.*

Para practicar

A. ¿Adónde se va?   Identifique un lugar donde se hacen estas cosas.

MODELO: comprar cerraduras
Se compran candados en Home Depot.

1. plantar flores
2. contratar *(contract)* un servicio de teléfono celular
3. buscar información para prevenir el crimen
4. tirar la basura
5. pedir ayuda durante una emergencia
6. reportar a los merodeadores

B. El extraterrestre.   Usted tiene un visitante de otro planeta que no comprende nuestras costumbres. Explíquele lo que hacemos en este planeta con las siguientes cosas. ¡OJO! Recuerde que puede poner el sujeto antes o después del verbo.

MODELO: el agua

El agua se toma o *Se toma el agua.*

1. las flores   **4.** los sándwiches
2. una pistola   **5.** la música
3. un carro

C. ¿Qué se hace con...?   Escriba una o más oraciones usando **se** para explicar qué se hace con lo siguiente.

MODELO: español

Se habla español. Se lee español. Se escucha español. Se aprende español.

1. los criminales   **4.** la basura
2. las casas de vecinos ausentes   **5.** los voluntarios
3. los merodeadores

Módulo I

¡Acaban de robar mi auto!

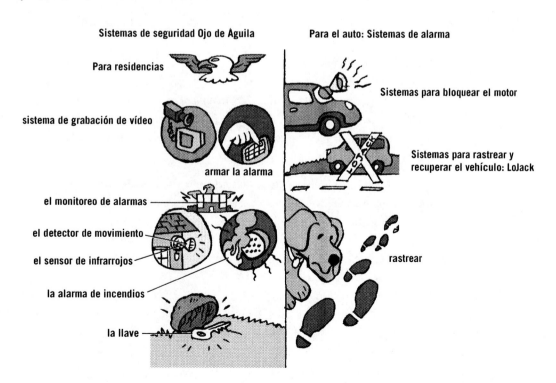

Sistemas de seguridad Ojo de Águila

Para residencias

sistema de grabación de vídeo

armar la alarma

el monitoreo de alarmas

el detector de movimiento

el sensor de infrarrojos

la alarma de incendios

la llave

Para el auto: Sistemas de alarma

Sistemas para bloquear el motor

Sistemas para rastrear y recuperar el vehículo: LoJack

rastrear

A. ¿Cómo se dice?   Escriba la palabra que corresponda a cada una de las definiciones.

1. Un sonido fuerte que indica un problema es una _____.

2. Un pájaro *(bird)* grande, famoso por su excelente visión es el

_____.

3. El aparato que anuncia la presencia de humo o llamas es una

_____.

4. Si una persona quiere grabar *(record)* lo que pasa dentro de su casa durante

su ausencia, debe instalar un sistema de _____.

5. Una luz en el techo de una casa que se ilumina cuando detecta el calor

humano es un _____.

B. Acciones.   Empareje cada acción de la columna **A** con el sinónimo correspondiente de la columna **B**.

	A		**B**
1.	_____ armar	**a.**	impedir la función
2.	_____ rastrear	**b.**	preparar para utilizar
3.	_____ recuperar	**c.**	rescatar una cosa perdida o robada
4.	_____ bloquear	**d.**	determinar—paso a paso—dónde está algo

¡LoJack! ¡Lo tenemos!

Inmediatamente después de la organización de la Vigilancia vecinal de Menlo, los vecinos se ponen en acción para controlar el crimen. Forman amistades y cadenas telefónicas. Instalan nuevos candados y sistemas de seguridad en las casas y autos. Y empiezan a ser los "ojos de águila" de la policía. Lynn, una vecina de Menlo, nota algo sospechoso y llama al agente de su barrio.

LYNN: Agente Andrade, siento molestarlo, pero **acabo de notar** que hay una persona sospechosa observando la casa de mi vecina, Lidia. Probablemente no es nada, pero...

AGENTE: Lynn, usted hace bien en llamar. ¿Qué hace el sospechoso?

LYNN: Nada. Sólo mira la casa de mi vecina desde su carro estacionado al otro lado de la calle.

AGENTE: ¿Su vecina está en casa?

LYNN: No, señor. **Acaba de salir** para el trabajo hace 15 minutos. No hay nadie. Creo que ellos **acaban de instalar** un sistema de seguridad en la casa, pero Lidia no sabe armar la alarma. No la usa.

AGENTE: ¿Puede ver la placa del carro sospechoso?

LYNN: Es FVT-394. Un ...

AGENTE: **Acabamos de recibir** un reporte del dueño de ese vehículo. Es un auto robado con sistema LoJack—que precisamente en este momento **acaba de activarse.** ¡Ajá! Allí está... ¡Lo tenemos!

C. ¿Comprende usted? Conteste las preguntas según la información del diálogo.

1. ¿Por qué llama Lynn al agente?
2. ¿Qué hace el hombre en el carro?
3. ¿Dónde está Lidia?
4. ¿Por qué no usa Lidia el sistema de seguridad?
5. ¿Cómo sabe el agente que es un carro robado?

D. LoJack en Puerto Rico. Después de leer la publicidad de LoJack, escriba dos ventajas de comprar este sistema. Compare sus ideas con las de un compañero.

LO/JACK
PUERTO RICO

Rastreo Policial de Vehículos Robados

Quiénes Somos
Qué es LOJACK
Servicios
Estadísticas
Preguntas y Respuestas
Contáctenos

Proteja su Inversión

Qué es LoJack PUERTO RICO

ACTUALIZACIÓN DE DATOS Aquí

DEALERS AUTORIZADOS

LO JACK

Real Stories

NEWS

Único sistema de rastreo y recuperación de vehículos robados, que opera junto a la Policía de Puerto Rico. LoJack es un transmisor de avanzada tecnología que se oculta en el vehículo. Para mayor seguridad, la ubicación de este dispositivo la desconoce hasta su dueño. Al producirse un robo o asalto, el propietario del vehículo deberá hacer la denuncia a la policía de Puerto Rico y después a la central de LoJack, accesible 24 horas al día, 365 días al año.

Cómo Funciona
1.- Después de reportar el vehículo robado a la policía y a LoJack (1-877- 2 LOJACK, 787-999-JACK) una señal de radio activa el dispositivo LoJack instalado en su vehículo.
2.- El dispositivo LoJack emite una señal únicamente reconocible por los equipos de localización instalados en los vehículos de la policía.
3.- La policía recibe la señal, la decodifica, la identifica y se dirige directamente hasta su carro robado. El tiempo promedio de recuperación es de 2 horas desde que se activa el dispositivo.

¿Precios?
El precio del sistema es $695.00 e incluye instalación. Se efectuará un cargo adicional de $149.00 anual por concepto de servicio. Este cargo incluye una inspección gratuita anual del sistema. Los precios para equipo pesado varían de acuerdo al modelo y uso. Favor de comunicarse con un representante de ventas y servicio o si prefiere puede escribirnos a nuestro e-mail: **info@lojackpr.com**
"LoJack garantiza la recuperación de su vehículo en 24 horas; de no ser así, devolveremos el dinero pagado por la adqusición del sistema."

subir >>

© Copyright 2002 Lojack Puerto Rico

Estructuras   *The recent past: Acabar de + infinitivo*

* To say what you have just done, use the phrase **acabar de** + *infinitive*. Conjugate **acabar** as a regular **–ar** verb.

Yo acabo de hablar con el agente.	*I have just spoken with the policeman.*
El agente acaba de recibir el reporte.	*The officer has just received the report.*
Nosotros acabamos de instalar alarmas.	*We have just installed alarm systems.*
Ellos acaban de salir de su casa.	*They have just left the house.*

* When talking about recently completed acts, you may find it useful to establish how long ago the event took place. Use **hace** + *a period of time* to tell how long ago the action happened.

Acabo de hablar con el agente.	*I have just spoken with the policeman.*
¿Cuándo?	*When?*
Hace diez minutos.	*Ten minutes ago.*

* Additional time phrases to tell how long ago something happened are:

hace dos días	*two days ago*
hace una semana	*a week ago*

* The following time phrases express specific moments in time rather than *ago*. **Hace** is not used with these phrases.

ayer	*yesterday*
anoche	*last night*
anteayer	*the day before yesterday*
la semana pasada	*last week*

Para practicar

A. Las tareas.   El comandante, su jefe, está muy nervioso hoy. Quiere saber cuándo van a hacer las siguientes tareas *(tasks)* usted y sus compañeros de trabajo. Ustedes son muy eficientes. Use **acabar de** para decirle que todo está bajo control.

MODELO: ¿María va a hablar con los testigos?
María acaba de hablar con los testigos.

1. ¿José y Pedro van a salir para el patrullaje del vecindario?
2. ¿Usted va a llamar a las víctimas?
3. ¿Nosotros vamos a preparar una declaración para la prensa *(press release)*?
4. ¿Los acusados van a hablar con sus abogados?
5. ¿Nosotros vamos a recibir los resultados forénsicos?
6. ¿Los agentes van a recuperar el auto robado del gobernador?
7. ¿Ustedes van a arrestar a los narcotraficantes?
8. ¿Los técnicos van a arreglar *(fix)* la computadora?

B. ¿Cuándo? Acaban de suceder *(happen)* los siguientes eventos. Primero explique lo que pasó usando **acabar de** y después indique **cuándo.**

MODELO: yo/ver a los acusados/media hora
  Yo acabo de ver a los acusados.
  ¿Cuándo?
  Hace media hora.

1. Ellos/instalar un sistema de seguridad/dos días
2. Nosotros/comprar los candados/ayer
3. Elena/visitar a la víctima del accidente/anteayer
4. El agente/arrestar al ratero/media hora
5. Los padres del delincuente/llegar/cinco minutos
6. Los ladrones/salir del banco/un cuarto de hora

C. ¿Y usted? Escriba cinco actividades que usted acaba de hacer.

MODELO: *Acabo de tomar un café.*

Módulo 2

Me gusta este barrio

- **llamar por respaldo**
- ¡Salga del carro!
- ¡De rodillas!
- ¡Suéltela!
- ¡Saque las manos!
- ¡Manos en la espalda!
- ¡Manos arriba!
- ¡Despacio—voltéese!
- ¡Tire las llaves acá!
- Separe los pies
- registrar al sospechoso

A. ¿Cómo se dice?   Diga qué mandato se debe usar bajo las siguientes condiciones.

I.	_____ ¡De rodillas!	**a.**	El agente quiere ver los brazos en el aire.
2.	_____ ¡Manos en la espalda!	**b.**	El agente quiere ver la cara del sospechoso.
3.	_____ ¡Voltéese!	**c.**	El agente quiere ponerle esposas al sospechoso.
4.	_____ ¡Suéltela!	**d.**	¡Asuma la "posición de rezar" *(prayer)*!
5.	_____ ¡Manos arriba!	**e.**	El sospechoso tiene un arma.

B. Más. Escriba la palabra o frase apropiada para cada una de las siguientes oraciones.

1. Un policía que posiblemente enfrenta un peligro debe llamar para

_____ .

2. Si un agente sospecha que una persona tiene armas escondidas, debe

_____ .

3. Si el sospechoso _____ las llaves, no puede escapar manejando el vehículo.

4. Si el agente ve una navaja en la mano de un sospechoso, grita:

_____ .

¡Manos en el carro!

El agente Andrade pide respaldo cuando ve al sospechoso en el vehículo robado. El sospechoso no nota nada—tiene la música del radio del carro a todo volumen. ¡Qué sorpresa cuando los agentes tocan a la ventana!

AGENTE: (Toca a la ventana.)

SOSPECHOSO: (No responde—sólo "baila" al ritmo de la música.)

AGENTE: (Toca más fuerte.) ¡Abra la ventana, por favor! ¡Baje la música!

SOSPECHOSO: ¿Por qué? Yo no molesto a nadie. **Me gusta la música** así.

AGENTE: Ajá, **a usted le gusta la música** así. ¿Qué hace usted aquí en esta calle?

SOSPECHOSO: Eh, hombre, **me gusta el barrio.** Pienso comprar una casa aquí.

AGENTE: **¡Le gustan estas casas!** Muy interesante. Y supongo que **a usted le gustan los todo-terrenos** que valen $75.000,00 (setenta y cinco mil dólares), también, ¿no?

SOSPECHOSO: Así es. **¿A usted le gustan mis ruedas?**

AGENTE: A mi colega y a mí **nos gustan mucho.** ¿Tiene el registro?

SOSPECHOSO: ¿Cómo? ¿El registro? Chingado. Es que lo tengo prestado *(borrowed)* de un amigo. (Empieza a arrancar el carro.)

AGENTE: ¡Pare usted! ¡Tire las llaves! ¡Salga del carro! Manos en el carro; separe los pies. Y mire... parece que **a usted le gustan también las pistolas y navajas.** A ver si **le gusta la cárcel.**

C. ¿Comprende usted? Conteste las siguientes preguntas con información del diálogo.

1. ¿Qué hace el sospechoso cuando toca la policía?
2. ¿Por qué tiene la música a todo volumen?
3. ¿Cuál es la razón que da el sospechoso para estar en esta calle?
4. ¿Por qué no tiene el registro?

D. ¡Actores! En un momento de conflicto, es sumamente importante que usted recuerde estos mandatos para controlar la situación. Para practicarlos, uno/a de ustedes es el sospechoso inconforme *(non-compliant)* y el otro es el agente que necesita controlarlo. El agente va a dar cinco de estos mandatos y el sospechoso va a representarlos. Después háganlo al revés cambiando los papeles de sospechoso y agente. Practiquen hasta aprenderlos.

1. Manos arriba. *(Hands up.)*
2. Separe los pies. *(Spread your legs.)*
3. Manos en el carro. *(Hands on the car.)*
4. Suéltela. *(Drop it.)*
5. Baje del carro. *(Get out of the car.)*
6. De rodillas. *(On your knees.)*
7. Tire las llaves. *(Throw out the keys.)*
8. Manos en la espalda. *(Hands behind your back.)*

Estructuras   *Expressing likes and dislikes: Gustar*

* While the most convenient English translations of **me gusta** and **le gusta** are *I like* and *you/he/she likes,* they literally mean *(it) is pleasing to me* and *(it) is pleasing to you/him/her.*
* Use the following forms to tell if people are pleased or displeased by something.

Me gusta escuchar música.	*I like to listen to music.*
Te gusta vivir en esta calle.	*You (familiar) like to live on this street.*
Le gusta manejar un todo terreno.	*You (formal), he, she likes to drive an SUV.*
Nos gusta arrestar a los criminales.	*We like to arrest criminals.*
Les gusta llamar por respaldo.	*You (plural)/they like to call for back-up.*

* If the noun following the verb is plural, or if the verb is followed by a series of items, use **gustan.** If the verb is followed by one infinitive or a series of infinitives, use **gusta.**

Me gusta el todo terreno.	*I like the SUV.*
Me gustan los todo terrenos.	*I like SUVs.*
Me gusta capturar, arrestar e interrogar a los criminales.	*I like to capture, arrest and interrogate criminals.*

* To tell or ask the name of the person who is pleased or displeased by something, use **a** before the name. The use of **a** + *personal pronoun* before **me gusta, le gusta,** etc. is optional and can be used to emphasize the person who is pleased or displeased or clarify any ambiguity.

A Héctor no le gusta el barrio.   *Hector does not like the neighborhood.*

(A mí) me gustan las casas.   *I like the houses.*

(A ti) te gusta bailar en el carro.   *You like to dance in the car.*

(A él/a ella/a usted) le gusta la música.   *He/she/you like the music.*

(A nosotros) nos gustan las ruedas.   *We like the wheels.*

(A ellos/a ellas/a ustedes) les gusta la Vigilancia vecinal.   *He/She/You like Neighborhood Watch.*

Para practicar

A. A usted, ¿qué le gusta más?   Diga usted cuál de estas opciones le gusta más.

MODELO: ¿la patrullera o las motocicletas?
    Me gusta la patrullera or *Me gustan las motocicletas.*

1. una persona de paz o los criminales
2. los ladrones o un miembro de Vigilancia vecinal
3. la música a todo volumen o la música suave
4. el agua o la cerveza
5. los sospechosos o un acusado
6. los robos o los homicidios
7. los drogadictos o los narcotraficantes

B. ¿Le gusta o no le gusta?   Empareje a las siguientes personas con la cosa que les gusta y escriba una oración completa.

MODELO: Elliott Ness/capturar a los criminales
    A Elliot Ness le gusta capturar a los criminales.

1. A George W. Bush/los terroristas
2. A los asesinos/un testigo
3. A un drogadicto/la cocaína
4. A usted/los sospechosos cooperativos
5. Mis amigos y yo/programas de policía en la televisión
6. A un acusado/las esposas

C. El trabajo.   Prepare una lista de tres preguntas y pregúnteles a tres de sus compañeros de trabajo si le(s) gustan o no ciertos aspectos de su oficio y por qué.

MODELO: USTED: *¿Le gusta la patrullera?*
    AMIGO #1:   *Me gusta la patrullera porque me gustan las computadoras a bordo.*

Módulo 2

El botín

el botín de varios robos = $500.000 (quinientos mil dólares o medio millón de dólares)

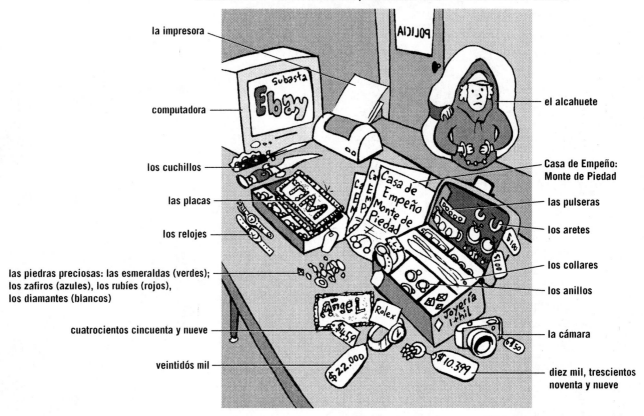

A. ¿Cómo se dice? Escriba la palabra que corresponda a cada una de las definiciones.

1. Las joyas que se ponen en las orejas son _____.

2. Para adornar el brazo y para saber la hora, necesito mi

_____.

3. Una joya que se pone en el dedo y a veces indica el matrimonio es un

_____.

4. Cuatro piedras valiosas son _____, _____,

_____ y _____.

B. ¿Cómo se dice?   Empareje las siguientes palabras nuevas con una definición.

a. impresora   **b.** subasta   **c.** botín   **d.** casa de empeño   **e.** joyería   **f.** alcahuete

1. _____ negocio de préstamos *(loans)* que compra y vende cosas de valor

2. _____ negocio que vende artículos de piedras preciosas y semi-preciosas

3. _____ las cosas de valor que tiene un ladrón después de un robo

4. _____ una venta en que cada comprador ofrece más dinero que los otros compradores

5. _____ parte de una computadora que produce documentos en papel— copias duras

6. _____ persona que compra propiedad robada

El botín

¡Éxito! El agente Andrade da las gracias a Lynn y a los otros miembros del grupo Vigilancia de Vecindario Menlo. Se dice que "El crimen no paga". Pero en este caso, ¡el anti-crimen paga bien!

AGENTE: **Primero,** quiero extenderles mis sinceras gracias y felicidades por el trabajo que está haciendo este grupo. Ustedes son nuestros ojos y orejas en la comunidad. Lynn, venga aquí conmigo, por favor. Tengo una sorpresa para usted.

LYNN: ¿Para mí?

AGENTE: Bueno, para usted y para los vecinos. No sé si ustedes lo saben, pero Lynn acaba de ayudarnos a romper uno de los grupos más peligrosos del crimen en esta ciudad.

GRUPO: (aplauso)

AGENTE: Durante los últimos tres años, son responsables por **millones de dólares** en robos de joyas, autos y otras cosas. Con una sola llamada telefónica, Lynn, usted nos proporcionó al líder. El grupo 88-Crime quiere ofrecerle la recompensa de $1.000,00 **(mil dólares)** por ayudar a este grupo a revitalizar el vecindario.

GRUPO: (mucho aplauso y silbatos) *(whistles).*

AGENTE: Y Lynn, la Joyería Ithil quiere demostrar su gratitud, también. En el auto robado había un botín de joyas robadas por valor de más de $350.781 **(trescientos cincuenta mil setecientos ochenta y un dólares)**. El presidente de la compañía quiere darle personalmente una recompensa de $200,00 **(doscientos dólares)** y este collar de oro y diamantes por valor de $860,00 **(ochocientos sesenta dólares)**.

LYNN: ¡Dios mío! No sé qué decir… sólo, ¡mil—no, millones de gracias a usted, agente!

C. ¿Comprende usted?   Estas oraciones son incorrectas. Corríjalas según la información en el diálogo.

1.   Lynn le da una recompensa al agente Andrade.

2.   Lynn acaba de romper un grupo de criminales con un solo tiro de una pistola.

3.   La Vigilancia Vecindaria Menlo va a recibir mil dólares para revitalizar el barrio.

4.   La joyería le da a Lynn un Rolex para decir "gracias".

D. Las joyas.   Identifique las siguientes prendas y joyas.

1. _____    **3.** _____    **5.** _____

2. _____   **4.** _____

E. 88-Crime.   Lea la siguiente descripción de 88-Crime y después indique si las declaraciones son **Ciertas (C)** o **Falsas (F).**

¿Qué es 88-Crime?

Es un programa del condado diseñado para ayudar a la policía y a otras agencias a solucionar crímenes. Esto se logra proporcionando al público una manera de telefonear un "soplo" o aviso confidencial anónimamente. La persona que haga esto recibirá una recompensa por la información que resulte en la detención y el procesamiento del criminal.

¿Cómo funciona 88-Crime?

Alguien llama al 88-Crime y sin dar su nombre ni ningún otro dato personal, ofrece información acerca de un crimen: dónde encontrar a una persona a quien las autoridades buscan; información acerca de bienes robados; o datos sobre un crimen que aún no se ha cometido. La persona que llama recibe un número de código y mantiene su anonimato. Hasta enero de 2003, 88-Crime tiene a su crédito:

- 3.673 detenciones por delitos y crímenes
- 3.647 casos definitivamente resueltos
- El decomiso *(seizure)* de más de cincuenta y ocho millones de dólares de narcóticos
- La recuperación de más de catorce millones de dólares de propiedad robada

(Courtesy 88-Crime, Tucson, AZ.)

1. _____ 88-Crime ofrece recompensas a los agentes de policía que resuelven crímenes.

2. _____ 88-Crime necesita todos los datos personales de la persona que llama.

3. _____ Al fin de enero de 2003, 88-Crime tiene trece mil seiscientas setenta y tres detenciones a su crédito.

4. _____ Recuperaron más de $14.000,00 en propiedad robada.

Estructuras   _Numbers: De cien a millones; los números ordinales_

❋ Use the following numbers to count from 100–1000.

100	**cien**	500	**quinientos**
101	**ciento uno**	600	**seiscientos**
102	**ciento dos**	700	**setecientos**
200	**doscientos**	800	**ochocientos**
300	**trescientos**	900	**novecientos**
400	**cuatrocientos**	1000	**mil**

❋ Use **cien** to say _one hundred_ exactly and if a larger number such as **mil** or **millones** follows **(cien mil)**, but use **ciento** in 101-199 **(ciento uno, ciento dos…, ciento noventa y nueve)**. Never use the word **un** before **cien** or **ciento** or **mil**. Although **cien** is used before both masculine and feminine nouns, multiples of one hundred (200, 300, etc.) agree in gender with the nouns they modify.

trescient**os** dólares
trescient**as** pulseras

❋ Most Hispanic countries use a period (**.**) to designate numbers in the thousands and a comma (**,**) to designate decimal points.

Spanish: **1.543** (English **1,543**)   Mil quinientos cuarenta y tres
Spanish: **1,5** (English **1.5**)   Uno con cinco _or_ uno coma cinco

❋ The word for _thousand_ is **mil. Mil** is not pluralized when counting.

1.543	**mil** quinientos cuarenta y tres
2.002	**dos mil dos**
7.033	**siete mil** treinta y tres

❋ When expressing the year, use **mil.**

2005	**dos mil cinco**
1999	**mil novecientos noventa y nueve**

❋ When counting in the millions, use **un millón, dos millones, tres millones,** etc. Use **de** before a noun that directly follows **millón** or **millones.** If another number is between the word **millón** or **millones** and the noun, omit the **de.**

un millón de dólares   **un millón trescientos mil** dólares

Los números ordinales

* To express numerical order in Spanish, use ordinal numbers.

★ **primer/o/a/os/as**	*first*	**sexto/a/os/as**	*sixth*
segundo/a/os/as	*second*	**séptimo/a/os/as**	*seventh*
★ **tercer/o/a/os/as**	*third*	**octavo/a/os/as**	*eighth*
cuarto/a/os/as	*fourth*	**noveno/a/os/as**	*ninth*
quinto/a/os/as	*fifth*	**décimo/a/os/as**	*tenth*

* The ordinal numbers have masculine and feminine forms, depending on the noun that follows them.
* Drop the **–o** of **primero** and **tercero** before masculine singular nouns.

el prime**r** sospechoso	*the first (male) suspect*
la prime**ra** sospechosa	*the first (female) suspect*
el terce**r** hombre	*the third man*
la terce**ra** mujer	*the third woman*

Para practicar

A. La sala de evidencia.   *Una vez al año, los agentes hacen inventario en la sala de evidencia y la sala de propiedad recuperada. Escriba el número de artículos que hay, según las siguientes indicaciones.*

MODELO: 200 collares de oro
   Hay doscientos collares de oro.

1. 100 anillos de platino *(platinum)*
2. 541 cámaras digitales
3. 428 autos
4. 1.000 relojes Rolex
5. 201 computadoras
6. 755 impresoras
7. 33 pulseras de rubíes y zafiros
8. 101 pulseras de diamantes
9. 999 collares con pendientes o placas
10. 2.223 navajas adornadas

B. La calculadora del botín.   *Un ladrón famoso por los crímenes perfectos lleva su botín a su alcahuete preferido, pero ése no ofrece bastante dinero. Nuestro ladrón decide intentar a venderlo en la subasta ebay. Escriba el número de la oferta ganadora para cada pieza.*

MODELO: un collar de oro /$322
   un collar de oro: trescientos veintidós dólares

1. un anillo de diamantes/$1.955,00
2. una pulsera y rubíes/$522,03
3. una navaja con adornos de oro/$799,00
4. dos relojes Rolex/$25.000,95
5. un anillo de plata *(silver)*/$100,00
6. un Cadillac Escalade/$35.638,00
7. cinco pares de aretes/$99,00

C. ¡La rueda de presos! Los primeros diez sospechosos aparecen en una rueda de presos para que Lynn los identifique. Póngalos en orden de aparición *(appearance)*.

MODELO: 1. Patricia Ramírez.
La primera sospechosa es Patricia Ramírez.

1.	Roberto González	**6.**	Eduardo Gallego
2.	Mariana Rivera	**7.**	Consuelo Bermúdez
3.	Héctor Gómez	**8.**	Alicia Cabrera
4.	Daniel Russo	**9.**	Jorge Vega
5.	Jaime Fernández	**10.**	Evita Pérez

Vocabulario Módulo 1

Sustantivos

la acera	sidewalk	**el/la merodeador/a**	prowler
el águila (f.)	eagle	**el monitoreo**	monitoring
la alerta	alert	**el odio**	hatred
la amistad	friendship	**el orgullo**	pride
el basurero	trash can	**la patrulla**	patrol
el boletín	bulletin	**el/la ratero/a**	petty thief,
el candado	lock		pickpocket
el carro	car	**el respeto**	respect
la cerradura	lock	**el sonido**	sound
el complejo	complex	**la sugerencia**	suggestion
la comunidad	community	**el tema**	theme
la falta	lack	**el triunfo**	triumph
el farol	streetlight	**el/la vecino/a**	neighbor
el/la gobernador/a	governor	**el vehículo**	vehicle
la grabación	recording	**la ventaja**	advantage

Verbos

acabar de + inf.	*to have just*	**entrenar**	*to train*
aprender	*to learn*	**impedir (i)**	*to impede*
armar	*to arm*	**molestar**	*to bother*
asistir	*to attend*	**olvidarse de**	*to forget*
bloquear	*to block*	**rastrear**	*to track, trace*
cooperar	*to cooperate*	**recuperar**	*to get back*
devolver (ue)	*to return something*	**suponer (g)**	*to suppose*
		tolerar	*to tolerate*
encargarse de	*to take charge of*	**vigilar**	*to watch*

Adjetivos

ausente	*absent*	**infrarrojo/a**	*infrared*
comunitario/a	*community*	**mismo/a**	*same*
corriente	*current*	**racial**	*racial*
estacionado/a	*parked*	**seguro/a**	*secure, safe*
forénsico/a	*forensic*	**unido/a**	*united*
hecho/a	*done, made*	**vecinal**	*neighborhood*

Otras expresiones

a pie	*on foot*	**ayer**	*yesterday*
anoche	*last night*	**en patines**	*on skates*
anteayer	*day before yesterday*	**valer la pena**	*to be worthwhile*

Módulo 2

Sustantivos

el alcahuete	*fence*	**la joyería**	*jewelry store*
el anillo	*ring*	**el maltrato**	*mistreatment*
el arete	*earring*	**la paz**	*peace*
el/la asesino/a	*assassin*	**la piedra**	*stone*
los bienes	*goods*	**la prenda**	*item*
el botín	*loot, haul*	**la propiedad**	*property*
la casa de empeño	*pawn shop*	**la pulsera**	*bracelet*
el código	*code*	**la recompensa**	*reward*
el condado	*county*	**el rubí**	*ruby*
el cuchillo	*knife*	**la sorpresa**	*surprise*
el dedo	*finger*	**la subasta**	*auction*
el diamante	*diamond*	**el valor**	*value*
la esmeralda	*emerald*	**la venta**	*sale*
el éxito	*success*	**el zafiro**	*sapphire*
la impresora	*printer*		

Verbos

arrancar	*to start (motor)*	**registrar**	*to search*
gustar	*to like*	**romper**	*to break, tear*
parar	*to stop*		

Adjetivos

anónimo/a	*anonymous*	**resuelto/a**	*resolved*
precioso/a	*precious*	**suave**	*soft, smooth*
proporcionado/a	*provided*	**varios/as**	*various, several*

Otras expresiones

chingado★	*fuck*	**¡Saque las manos!**	*Show your hands!*
¡De rodillas!	*On your knees!*	**Separe los pies.**	*Spread your legs.*
despacio	*slow*	**Suéltela.**	*Drop it.*
¡Felicidades!	*Congratulations!*	**Tire las llaves acá.**	*Throw the keys here.*
llamar por respaldo	*to call for backup*		
¡Manos arriba!	*Hands up!*	**Voltéese.**	*Turn around.*
¡Manos en la espalda!	*Hands behind your back!*		

Síntesis

A escuchar

Escuche este boletín de radio y entonces indique si las siguientes declaraciones son **Ciertas (C)** o **Falsas (F)**.

1. _____ La policía de la ciudad busca al ladrón responsable de unos robos residenciales.

2. _____ Es responsable por más de cien robos.

3. _____ El valor de los artículos recuperados es de más o menos dos cientos mil dólares.

4. _____ La policía tiene joyas de valor y equipo de computadoras.

5. _____ Para identificar la propiedad, la víctima tiene que llamar a la policía por teléfono.

A conversar

Hablen de lo bueno que hacen los grupos de Vigilancia vecinal. ¿Qué tipos de crímenes reportan? ¿Cómo ayudan a la policía?

MODELO: *Llaman a la policía si ven algo sospechoso.*

A leer

Every ethnic community establishes its "zone"—a social environment with places to shop, dine, visit... The many Puerto Ricans in New York find the Nuyorican Poets Café THEIR spot to touch bases with fellow Puerto Ricans and to connect with one another for a shared heritage.

The Nuyorican Poets Café, el sitio de encuentro de la comunidad conocido como "la meca de la palabra hablada", celebra tres décadas de servir como foco de poetas, dramaturgos y artistas. Empezó a iniciativa de un grupo de poetas en busca de un medio para explorar la identidad de los puertorriqueños nacidos en Nueva York. Así crearon un foro abierto al que recurrían los artistas semanalmente a esperar su turno para alzar la voz y expresar sus ideas con un ritmo y lenguaje desafiante y no-conformista.

¿Comprende usted?   La jerga del barrio local es sumamente importante para la policía, y cada área tiene su propia mezcla de *Spanglish* y de regionalismos nacionales. ¿Conoce usted algunas palabras de SU vecindario? En clase, escriban algunas en la pizarra y digan su significado.

A escribir

Escriba una lista de diez cosas que se roban comúnmente. Luego, en grupos de cuatro, pongan la lista en orden de las más mencionadas.

MODELO: *los televisores*

Algo más

Ventana cultural

El machismo

¿Quién es más macho?

1. Está en un restaurante con una mujer bonita. Entra otra mujer MUY bonita.
   - ❑ a. Usted la mira.
   - ❑ b. Usted escucha lo que dice la mujer con quien está.

2. Usted, su esposa y familia acaban de terminar una cena del Día de acción de gracias *(Thanksgiving)* y...
   - ❑ a. usted lleva unos platos a la cocina y ayuda a limpiar.
   - ❑ b. usted invita a sus amigos a tomar unas cervezas y mirar el partido de fútbol americano.

3. Está en la fiesta de Navidad *(Christmas)* de la compañía y una mujer bonita está coqueteando *(flirting)* con usted. Su mujer no está.
   - ❑ a. Decide decirle que es muy bonita.
   - ❑ b. Decide decirle que está casado.

4. Una mujer de 20 años es:
   - ❑ a. una mujer.
   - ❑ b. una chica.

5. Usted está con unos amigos jugando al básquetbol unos días después de una cita inicial con una mujer. Sus amigos quieren saber los detalles.
   - ❑ a. Les dice que quieren verse otra vez.
   - ❑ b. Les dice que sus poderes sexuales eran mágicos.

6. Está en el apartamento de una mujer conocida. Usted quiere una relación sexual. Ella dice "No". ¿Qué quiere decir eso?
   - ❑ a. "Te quiero mucho".
   - ❑ b. "No".

7. Está en un restaurante con una mujer que conoce por varios meses. Ella dice que quiere ser su amiga, nada más.
   - ❑ a. Usted la lleva a casa y le dice "Adiós".
   - ❑ b. Piensa que pueden ser amigos y no enamorados.

8. Usted y unos amigos están afuera trabajando en sus carros y una chica bonita con poca ropa pasa por allí. ¿Qué hacen?
   - ❑ a. Dicen "Hola" y eso es todo.
   - ❑ b. Dicen "Te queremos, chica. Ven acá." y mueven el cuerpo con un ritmo sensual.

9. Está con su novia y otros hombres la miran. Usted...
   - ❑ a. les da el mal de ojo *(evil eye)*.
   - ❑ b. le dice a su novia que es su culpa *(fault)* por la ropa que lleva.

10. Después de dos años de matrimonio, su mujer da a luz a un hijo *(gives birth to a son)*. Un día usted está solo con él y es necesario un cambio de pañales *(diaper change)*. Usted...
    - ❑ a. cambia el pañal.
    - ❑ b. no nota la necesidad.

En mis propias palabras. ¿Cómo contestaría usted *(how would you answer)* las preguntas de la encuesta? ¿Cuáles son las características de un hombre macho en SU opinión? ¿Todavía existe el machismo?

A buscar

LoJack está en muchos de los países hispanohablantes. Busque su publicidad en Internet. Empiece con www.grupodetector.com.

A conocer: Tnte. Margarita Moris Rivera

La Teniente Margarita Moris Rivera era la policía destacada del mes en Puerto Rico. Ella es Directora y Coordinadora de la División de delitos sexuales, maltrato a menores y violencia doméstica. Fue premiada por su desempeño y alto sentido del deber. Contribuye a la Policía de Puerto Rico para que mantenga la excelencia de servicio a la ciudadanía.

LECCIÓN 8

La violencia doméstica

Módulo 1
- Me golpea, me viola, me amenaza... pero me ama
- Describing daily routines: *Los verbos reflexivos*
- Nos apoyamos
- More on reflexive verbs: *Los verbos recíprocos*

Módulo 2
- El abuso de ancianos
- Expressing knowledge and familiarity: **Saber** *y* **conocer**
- Me acosa
- Receiving the action of a verb: *El objeto directo*

Síntesis
- A escuchar
- A conversar
- A leer
- A escribir

Algo más
- Ventana cultural: La diversidad entre hispanoamericanos
- A buscar
- A conocer: Carlos Álvarez, Director de la Policía de Miami-Dade

Módulo I

Me golpea, me viola, me amenaza... pero me ama

Handwritten margin notes (left):
dormirse – go to sleep
despertarse – wake up
acostarse – to get in bed
levantarse – to get up

cepillarse – brush hair
peinarse – comb hair
ducharse – shower
usar el hilo dental

Handwritten margin notes (right):
ahorcar – strangle
pelear – to fight
ahogar – drown

La rutina doméstica — despertarse, levantarse, lavarse, peinarse, vestirse, quitarse la ropa, acostarse

La violencia doméstica — ahogar, discutir, golpear, amenazar, violar

A. ¿Cómo se dice?   ¿Para qué parte de la rutina diaria se usan estos productos famosos?

I. Jabón Irish Spring — *lavarse*

2. Productos para el pelo Vidal Sassoon — *peinarse*

3. Ropa de Calvin Klein — *vestirse o quitarse la ropa*

4. Camas de Sealy Posturepedic — _____

B. Acciones.   Escriba el infinitivo del verbo que corresponda a cada una de estas definiciones.

I. La acción de usar las manos o puños *(fists)* para pegarle a una persona
golpear

2. Intentar causar la muerte de una persona poniéndole las manos en el cuello
ahorcar

3. La acción de forzar a una víctima a hacer actos sexuales contra su voluntad
violar

4. Las palabras o acciones que una persona enojada *(angry)* usa para indicar que una víctima va a estar en peligro _____ *amenazar*

¿Por qué lo hace?

Los agentes de patrulla están en la casa de Amanda y su esposo después de una noche violenta. El esposo, Jesús, está esposado, saliendo con los agentes. Amanda cuenta su historia.

AGENTE: ¿Esta violencia es normal?

AMANDA: No, claro que no. Sólo ocurre a veces. Cuando mi esposo esté cansado o borracho o frustrado. Yo intento ser buena esposa pero... no sé. Mire, todas las mañanas **me despierto** a las cuatro para limpiar la casa antes de salir para el trabajo. A veces no **me peino** porque no quiero hacer ruido y despertar a mi esposo—**se pone furioso.** Él **se preocupa** mucho ahora que no tiene empleo, y no **se levanta** hasta las diez u once de la mañana.

AGENTE: ¿Qué hace él mientras usted trabaja?

AMANDA: Dice que busca trabajo, pero no lo sé. Muchos días **no se baña** ni **se viste.** Cuando yo regreso del trabajo está en pijama a las cinco de la tarde. Si la cena no está preparada y en la mesa casi inmediatamente, **se pone** más furioso. Entonces, discutimos y él **me amenaza** o **me golpea.** Yo quiero ser buena esposa, pero no sé cómo...

AGENTE: Amanda, usted está en peligro con este hombre. Recomiendo que obtenga una orden de protección.

AMANDA: ¡Ay, no, Agente! Él de verás me ama... promete que ésta es la última vez. Él realmente me ama...

C. ¿Comprende usted?   Conteste las preguntas según la información del diálogo.

1. ¿Por qué está la policía en casa de Amanda?
2. ¿Dónde está su esposo?
3. ¿A qué hora se despierta Amanda? ¿Por qué?
4. ¿Qué hace su esposo durante el día?
5. ¿Qué pasa si la cena no está preparada inmediatamente?

D. Mandatos.   Estos mandatos se usan para varias posiciones físicas que el preso debe asumir. Estúdielos y entonces dé el mandato necesario para el resultado indicado.

* ¡Siéntese!   Sit down!   * ¡Levántese!   Get up!
* ¡Acuéstese!   Lie down!   * ¡Despiértese!   Wake up!

1. _Despiértese_ El preso está dormido y usted necesita su atención.

2. _Levántese_ Una persona entra en su oficina y usted le indica una silla.

3. _siéntese_ Una persona está en la silla y usted la quiere de pie *(standing/upright).*

4. _acuéstese_ Usted quiere que el preso se tumbe boca abajo para que no se escape.

Estructuras — *Describing daily routines: Los verbos reflexivos*

* Reflexive verbs express actions that people do *to* or *for* themselves.

* Reflexive verbs are preceded by reflexive pronouns. The pronoun **se** attached to the end of the infinitive indicates that the verb is reflexive (bañar**se**). **Se** is modified to match or to *reflect* the same person as the subject.

Reflexive   **Non-reflexive**

Yo me quito la ropa   Él me quita la ropa

bañarse *to bathe (oneself)*

yo	**me**	baño	*I bathe (myself)*
tú	**te**	bañas	*you bathe (yourself)*
usted/él/ella	**se**	baña	*you, he, she bathe(s) (yourself, himself, herself)*
nosotros	**nos**	bañamos	*we bathe ourselves*
ustedes/ellos/ellas	**se**	bañan	*you/they bathe (yourselves/themselves)*

* Reflexive verbs can be used to describe changes in state of mind.

El esposo **se pone** furioso si no hay cena.   *The husband gets furious if there is no dinner.*

* When a reflexive verb is used as an *infinitive*, a *present participle* **(–ando** or **–iendo)**, or *an affirmative command*, the reflexive pronoun that matches the subject may be attached to the end.

Yo quiero bañar**me** antes de **acostarme.**   *I want to bathe before I go to bed.*
Amanda está bañándo**se** ahora.   *Amanda is taking a bath now.*
Amanda, cálmese.   *Amanda, calm down.*

* Other reflexive verbs are:

acostarse (ue)	*to go to bed*	**llevarse mal**	*to not get along*
calmarse	*to calm down*	**ponerse** + adj.	*to become or to put on*
cuidarse	*to take care of oneself*	**preocuparse**	*to worry*
despertarse (ie)	*to wake up*	**quedarse**	*to stay*
dormirse (ue)	*to fall asleep*	**quitarse**	*to take off*
enojarse	*to get angry*	**sentarse (ie)**	*to sit down*
levantarse	*to get up*	**sentirse (ie)**	*to feel*
llevarse bien	*to get along well*	**vestirse (i)**	*to get dressed*

¡OJO!

When attaching the pronoun to a present participle, remember to put an accent on the vowel before the **-ndo** ending. When attaching the pronoun to an affirmative command, the accent goes over the third vowel from the right—after the new syllable (the pronoun at the end) is added.

Para practicar

A. El agente. El agente describe la rutina de su familia cuando él regresa a casa después de trabajar. Llene el espacio con el pronombre reflexivo correcto.

1. Yo regreso a la casa a las seis de la tarde y _____ lavo las manos y la cara.

2. Después de comer, mis hijos _____ quitan la ropa y _____ bañan.

3. Nosotros pasamos una hora juntos mirando la tele o leyendo y después mis hijos _____ acuestan.

4. Mi esposa y yo _____ acostamos a las once.

5. Antes de dormir, yo _____ pongo triste pensando en las víctimas de la violencia doméstica.

B. La rutina de Amanda. Ahora, Amanda le describe al agente la rutina de su casa. Complete las oraciones con el pronombre indicado si es una actividad reflexiva. Pero, ¡OJO! no todas las actividades son reflexivas. Si la actividad no es reflexiva, escriba la letra "x" en el espacio para la respuesta.

MODELO: A las seis y media yo _____ despierto y después yo _____ despierto a mi esposo.
A las seis yo __**me**__ *despierto, y después yo* __x__ *despierto a mi esposo.*

1. A las siete Jesús y yo _____ bañamos y después _____ vestimos.

2. Yo _____ visto con ropa conservadora, porque si no, Jesús me acusa de ser "puta".

3. Si el desayuno no está en la mesa rápidamente, Jesús _____ pone furioso.

4. Yo _____ pongo nerviosa si la comida está fría.

5. Cuando yo salgo para el trabajo, Jesús _____ acuesta otra vez porque está cansado.

C. Consecuencias de la violencia en casa. Estas víctimas quieren explicarles a sus esposos cómo se sienten. Forme oraciones completas para ayudarlas.

MODELO: A veces yo/ponerse nerviosa cuando regreso a casa.

A veces yo me pongo nerviosa cuando regreso a casa.

1. Nosotras/despertarse a las tres de la mañana por el miedo.
2. A veces yo tengo tantos moretones *(bruises)* que no puedo/levantarse.
3. Susana y Carlota/ponerse tristes pensando en la victimización de sus hijos.
4. Tú lloras mucho mucho mientras tú/bañarse.
5. Cuando él/despertarse está furioso.

Módulo I

Nos apoyamos

el maltratador

El Refugio: Albergue para mujeres maltratadas

la maltratada

los moretones

¡Es culpa mía! Lo siento...

Refugio ELEM Ayuda Emocional Legal Económica Médica

la consejera

el ojo morado

el grupo de apoyo

A. ¿Cómo se dice? Empareje las siguientes palabras con un sinónimo.

1. <u>d</u> maltratador   **a.** responsabilidad por algo negativo

2. <u>d</u> maltratado   **b.** persona que ofrece ayuda psicológica

3. <u>b</u> consejero   **c.** refugio

4. <u>c</u> albergue   **d.** víctima

5. <u>a</u> culpa   **d.** agresor

B. Acciones. Explique estos conceptos en sus propias palabras, en español. Use la memoria y la imaginación, pero ¡no use diccionario!

[handwritten: bruises and black eyes]

1. moretones y ojos morados
2. amenazar
3. albergue
4. apoyar *[handwritten: support]*
5. maltratador

La representante de Víctima-Testigo

Ana María es una ex-víctima de la violencia doméstica y ahora es parte del programa Víctima-Testigo de la ciudad. La casa de Amanda es muy peligrosa y Ana María le habla de las opciones.

ANA MARÍA: Amanda, claro que no quiere ir a un albergue—nadie *quiere* ir. Pero hay que comprender que su esposo es peligroso; sobre todo ahora con sus amenazas de muerte si hay cargos criminales.

AMANDA: ¡Ay! Él no habla en serio. Me ama... **nos amamos.** Siempre **nos amenazamos,** pero no **nos dañamos.** Estas amenazas son culpa del alcohol. No quiero abandonar a mi esposo cuando más me necesita. Yo no puedo vivir sola... no tengo dinero, ni familia. Soy inmigrante nueva. Ni tengo amigos...

ANA MARÍA: Por eso recomiendo el albergue donde yo trabajo. Es un refugio para mujeres como usted y yo. Es un lugar seguro y secreto donde hay esperanza de una nueva vida sin violencia.

AMANDA: ¿Cómo?

ANA MARÍA: Tenemos ayuda económica, médica y legal. Pero es mucho más que eso. En el albergue hay mujeres exactamente como nosotras: víctimas del abuso y la violencia. Allí, **nos comprendemos.** Somos una familia—**nos aceptamos** y **nos apoyamos** emocionalmente. **Nos escuchamos** los sueños y **nos motivamos.** Y más importante, **nos respetamos.**

AMANDA: **Pero** mi esposo y yo... **nos amamos.**

ANA MARÍA: Ánimo, Amanda. En realidad, aquí en la casa con él, ustedes **no se aman—se pelean... se maltratan,** pero no **se respetan.** Basta ya. Traiga unas cosas personales y los documentos importantes. Después del hospital, a la nueva vida.

C. ¿Comprende usted? Indique si las siguientes declaraciones son ciertas **(C)** o falsas **(F).** Si son falsas, corríjalas.

1. _____ Ana María no comprende la profundidad del dolor emocional de Amanda.

2. _____ Amanda tiene mucho entusiasmo para ir al albergue.

3. _____ Es evidente que el esposo quiere mucho a Amanda.

4. _____ En el refugio las residentes se maltratan.

5. _____ Amanda necesita llevar sus documentos importantes al albergue.

D. Víctimas.   Lea estas definiciones de "víctima" y "víctima derivada" según el estado de Arizona después indique si las descripciones indican Víctimas **(V)** o Víctimas Derivadas **(VD).**

VÍCTIMA

"Víctima" significa una persona que sufre una lesión física, aflicción mental extrema, o muerte como resultado directo de cualquiera de los siguientes:

a. Conducta criminalmente perjudicial;

b. Un acto de terrorismo internacional;

c. Un esfuerzo de buena fe de una persona para prevenir una conducta criminalmente perjudicial; o

d. Un esfuerzo de buena fe de una persona para aprehender a una persona sospechosa de participar en una conducta criminalmente perjudicial o un acto de terrorismo internacional.

VÍCTIMA DERIVADA

"Víctima derivada" signifíca:

a. La esposa, hijo, padre, padrastro, hijastro, hermanos carnales, o tutor de una víctima que murió como resultado de una conducta criminalmente perjudicial o acto de terrorismo internacional e incluye al hijo nacido después de la muerte de la víctima.

b. Un persona que viva en el hogar de una víctima que falleció como resultado de una conducta criminalmente perjudicial.

c. Un miembro de la familia de la víctima que fue testigo de la conducta criminalmente perjudicial.

d. Una persona que no sea miembro de la familia que fue testigo de un delito violento.

e. Una persona cuya asistencia sociopsicológica y cuidado para salud mental o cuya presencia durante la asistencia sociopsicológica y cuidado para salud mental de la víctima se requiere para que el tratamiento de la víctima tenga éxito.

1. V   VD   Un miembro de la familia de la víctima que fue testigo

2. V   VD   Una persona muerta como resultado del terrorismo internacional

3. V   VD   Los hijos de una persona muerta como resultado de terrorismo

4. V   VD   Una persona importante para el tratamiento de una persona traumatizada por el crimen

Courtesy of the ACJC in Arizona.

Estructuras   *More on reflexive verbs: Los verbos recíprocos*

※ Reciprocal verbs are conjugated in the same way as reflexive verbs. They are used to express that two or more people are doing something *to* or *for* each other.

Nosotros siempre **nos** ayudamos.	*We always help each other.*
Amanda y Jesús **se** quieren mucho.	*Amanda and Jesús love each other a lot.*
Los miembros del grupo saben apoyar**se** a cada paso.	*The members of the group know how to support one another at each step.*

* Many verbs, not usually used as reflexive verbs, can be made reciprocal by using the appropriate reflexive pronoun: **se** or **nos.**

Los consejeros **se consultan** cada día.	*The counselors consult each other every day.*
Nosotros **nos** damos ánimo.	*We give each other encouragement.*

Para practicar

A. Acciones mutuas.   Indique las acciones recíprocas de las siguientes personas.

MODELO: Los esposos/mirarse
               Los esposos se miran.

1. Los amantes/besarse *(kiss)* mucho. *Los amantes se besan mucho*
2. Los consejeros/consultarse antes de reunir el grupo. *Los consejeros se consultarse antes de reunir el grupo*
3. Tú y yo/comprenderse bien. *Tú y yo nos comprendemos bien.*
4. El abogado y el acusado/hablarse todos los días. *El abogado y el acusado se hablan todos los días*
5. Nosotros/ayudarse siempre. *Nosotros nos ayudamos siempres*

B. ¿Quiénes son?   Escriba el nombre de algunas personas famosas o conocidas para completar estas ideas.

MODELO: Nos queremos mucho.
               Mis padres y yo nos queremos mucho.

1. Se enojan con frecuencia.   **4.** No se hablan nunca.
2. Se divorcian.   **5.** Nos ayudamos mucho.
3. Nos vemos todos los días.

C. Un drama de familia.   Use los siguientes verbos para describir el noviazgo *(courtship)* de Amanda y Jesús. Después de terminar, escríbalo otra vez en la forma **nosotros.**

MODELO: verse por primera vez
               Amanda y Jesús se ven por primera vez. (Nosotros nos vemos por primera vez.)

1. mirarse los ojos   **6.** enamorarse
2. hablarse   **7.** casarse
3. no poder separarse   **8.** pelearse
4. pedirse los números de teléfono   **9.** amenazarse
5. abrazarse con pasión   **10.** divorciarse

Módulo 2

El abuso de ancianos

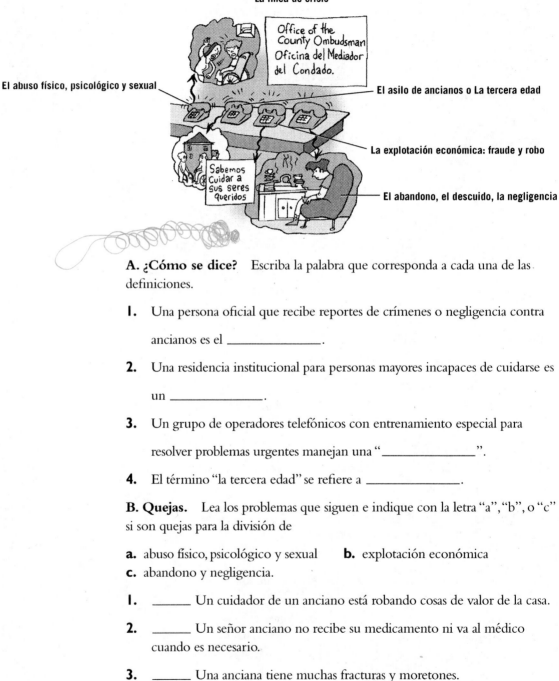

La línea de crisis

Office of the County Ombudsman
Oficina del Mediador del Condado.

El abuso físico, psicológico y sexual

El asilo de ancianos o La tercera edad

La explotación económica: fraude y robo

Sabemos Cuidar a sus seres queridos

El abandono, el descuido, la negligencia

A. ¿Cómo se dice?   Escriba la palabra que corresponda a cada una de las definiciones.

1.   Una persona oficial que recibe reportes de crímenes o negligencia contra ancianos es el _____.

2.   Una residencia institucional para personas mayores incapaces de cuidarse es un _____.

3.   Un grupo de operadores telefónicos con entrenamiento especial para resolver problemas urgentes manejan una "_____".

4.   El término "la tercera edad" se refiere a _____.

B. Quejas.   Lea los problemas que siguen e indique con la letra "a", "b", o "c" si son quejas para la división de

a. abuso físico, psicológico y sexual   **b.** explotación económica
c. abandono y negligencia.

1.   _____ Un cuidador de un anciano está robando cosas de valor de la casa.

2.   _____ Un señor anciano no recibe su medicamento ni va al médico cuando es necesario.

3.   _____ Una anciana tiene muchas fracturas y moretones.

¡La línea de crisis!

Los operadores de la línea de crisis del Ombudsman/Mediador del condado reciben cada día más llamadas sobre el abuso de los ancianos. Aquí hay algunas historias:

1. ¿Su hija es ladrona?

OPERADORA: Línea de Crisis. ¿En qué puedo servirle?

ANCIANA: Mi hija apareció esta mañana para bañarse y comer algo. Ella acaba de salir y yo acabo de notar que mi cartera con todo el dinero de mi cheque de Seguro Social no está.

OPERADORA: ¿Dónde vive su hija?

ANCIANA: No lo **sé.** Es drogadicta. Creo que vive en la calle.

2. La violencia

OPERADORA: Línea de Crisis. ¿En qué puedo servirle?

VOZ: *(angustiada)* Hay gritos y golpes en el apartamento vecino. Creo que hay una pelea enorme.

OPERADORA: ¿Quiénes viven allí?

VOZ: Es una familia muy simpática. Yo los **conozco** bien. Hay dos padres con tres hijos adolescentes y la mamá anciana del señor. La pobre sufre de demencia o Alzheimer's o algo y está cada día más loca. Yo **sé** que los niños están en la escuela y la señora está trabajando. Sólo el señor y su mamá están en casa ahora.

3. El asilo de ancianos

OPERADORA: Línea de Crisis. ¿En qué puedo servirle?

VOZ: ¿Estas llamadas son anónimas, ¿verdad? Nadie puede **saber** que yo llamo....Yo trabajo en un asilo para ancianos que ustedes **conocen** bien. Yo **sé** que hay mucho fraude con Medicare. Cobran al estado por medicamentos y servicios que los pacientes no reciben. Si ellos **saben** que yo hablo con ustedes, voy a perder mi trabajo. Y posiblemente ellos van a castigar *(punish)* a mis pacientes. Yo **conozco** muy bien a los dueños.

4. La negligencia y el descuido

OPERADORA: Línea de Crisis. ¿En qué puedo servirle?

VOZ: Quiero reportar la negligencia y el descuido que sufro en este asilo. No me prestan atención. No me dan comida. Yo pago mucho por el cuidado y yo **sé** mis derechos.

OPERADORA: (ella **reconoce** la voz): Señor Rojas, ¿es usted?

VOZ: ¿Usted me **conoce?** Sí, soy yo. Son las once de la mañana, y todavía no me traen el desayuno. Tengo hambre...no me prestan atención. No **sé** qué hacer.

OPERADORA: Pobrecito. Señor Rojas...creo que usted está un poco desorientado. No son las once de la mañana. Son las once de la noche. Duérmase. En unas horas van a traer el desayuno. No se preocupe. Buenas noches.

C. ¿Comprende usted?   Ponga el número de la historia que está reflejada en estas oraciones.

1. _____ Una empleada llama para reportar abusos financieros por los dueños del asilo.

2. _____ Una madre informa que después de la visita de su hija, ya no tiene dinero.

3. _____ Un señor llama otra vez para decir que no recibe buen tratamiento en el asilo.

4. _____ La persona que llama oye gritos y golpes del apartamento vecino.

D. Guía para prevenir y denunciar el abuso de ancianos.   Los abusos más comunes de ancianos son: abuso físico y emocional, abuso financiero y abuso en instituciones de cuidados a largo plazo. Lea el índice de temas de la guía y hable con un compañero de ejemplos específicos que quizás se encuentren en la guía.

MODELO: _El abuso emocional puede ser de aislar a un anciano y no incluirlo en actividades familiares._

Índice

Capítulo 1: Abuso de ancianos
Parte A: Abuso físico y emocional
¿Qué es el abuso físico y emocional de ancianos?
Cómo reconocer las señales de advertencia

Parte B: Abuso financiero de ancianos
¿Qué es el abuso financiero de ancianos?
Cómo reconocer las señales de advertencia
Fraude de ventas por teléfono
Robo de identidad
Estafas de mejoramiento de la vivienda
Peligros de la planificación de la herencia

Parte C: Abuso de ancianos en instituciones de cuidados a largo plazo
¿Qué son los cuidados a largo plazo?
Cómo elegir una institución de cuidados a largo plazo
Cómo reconocer las señales de advertencia
Declaración de derechos de los residentes

Esta guía fue preparada por la Dirección de Fraude de Medi-Cal y Abuso de Ancianos y por el Centro de Prevención del Crimen y la Violencia del Departamento de Justicia de California, junto con AARP. (Inclusion of this material in no way represents an endorsement of this textbook.)

Estructuras   *Expressing knowledge and familiarity: Saber y conocer*

❋ Spanish has two verbs to express different aspects of the English verb *to know.*

saber			
yo	**sé**	nosotros/as	**sabemos**
tú	**sabes**		
usted/él/ella	**sabe**	ustedes/ellos/ellas	**saben**

❋ Use **saber** to say that someone knows information or facts. When followed by an infinitive, **saber** means *to know how to do something.*

Yo **sé** el número de teléfono de la línea de crisis.

I know the crisis hotline phone number.

Muchos hijos no **saben** cuidar a los ancianos.

Many children don't know how to care for aging parents.

conocer			
yo	**conozco**	nosotros/as	**conocemos**
tú	**conoces**		
usted/él/ella	**conoce**	ustedes/ellos/ellas	**conocen**

❋ Use **conocer** to indicate that someone is personally *acquainted with* or *familiar with* a person or a place.

El mediador ya **conoce** muy bien a este señor.

The Ombudsman is familiar with the man.

Yo **conozco** un excelente asilo para ancianos.

I know an excellent nursing home.

Para practicar

A. ¿Quién sabe hacer...?   Use el verbo **saber** y uno de estos expertos para indicar quién sabe resolver estos problemas.

MODELO: ayudar con problemas emocionales
*Los psicólogos **saben** ayudar con problemas emocionales.*

a. un psicólogo   **b.** los médicos   **c.** un agente de seguros   **d.** la policía
e. mi hermana y yo

1.   recetar *(prescribe)* los medicamentos
2.   investigar el fraude
3.   preparar las comidas favoritas de nuestra madre
4.   organizar las finanzas para pagar el asilo o el hospital
5.   aliviar la frustración de los cuidadores

B. ¿Conoce usted a...?   Una amiga con una madre que sufre física y mentalmente en su vejez quiere recomendaciones de expertos o lugares que usted u otras personas conocen *personalmente.*

MODELO: ¿Conoce usted a un mediador para ancianos?
Sí, conozco al Ombudsman del Condado. o No, no conozco a nadie.

1.   ¿Conoce usted un buen asilo para mi mamá?
2.   ¿Conocen ustedes a una enfermera *(nurse)* para ayudarme?
3.   ¿Conoce a un buen médico especialista en gerontología?
4.   ¿Conoce usted alguna organización que apoye a los cuidadores de ancianos?
5.   ¿Conoce usted a investigadores contra el fraude?

C. ¿Saber o conocer?   Usted es operador de una línea de crisis para ancianos. Complete las preguntas que usted necesita hacer a los que llaman con la forma **usted** de **saber** o **conocer.**

1.   ¿_____ usted el número de teléfono para llamar en caso de emergencia médica?

2.   ¿_____ usted preparar las medicinas?

3.   ¿_____ usted al médico, el Dr. Sánchez?

4.   ¿_____ usted el Asilo Tercera Edad?

5.   ¿_____ usted llegar al hospital?

6.   ¿_____ usted bañar al paciente?

Módulo 2

Me *acosa*

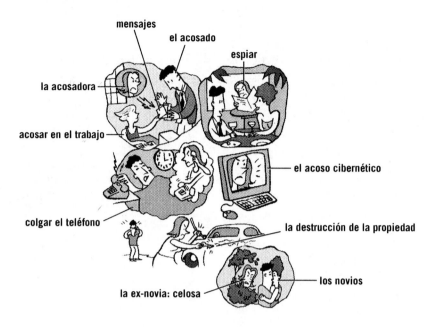

mensajes

el acosado

espiar

la acosadora

acosar en el trabajo

el acoso cibernético

colgar el teléfono

la destrucción de la propiedad

los novios

la ex-novia: celosa

A. ¿Cómo se dice?   Escriba la palabra que corresponda a cada una de las definiciones.

1. Perseguir, espiar y acosar a una persona son formas de _____.

2. Si una persona furiosa arruina las cosas de otra persona, es una infracción o

delito de _____.

3. Cuando una persona ve a su novio/a o ex-novio/a con *otra persona* a veces

está _____.

4. Usar computadoras para difamar o molestar a otra persona es el

_____.

5. Una persona que es víctima de un acosador es un _____.

B. Acciones. Use sus propias palabras para explicar estas acciones en español. Algunos de los verbos están en el dibujo. Otros están en la memoria.

I. colgar el teléfono   **3.** acechar

2. espiar   **4.** amenazar

¡No me amenaces!

Marisa es la nueva novia de Manuel. Ellos dos son víctimas del delito de acoso. La acosadora: la "ex" de Manuel, Rosa. Los acosados: Marisa y Manuel. La policía recomienda que ellos mantengan una documentación de los incidentes en un diario. Aquí hay un segmento del diario.

El 3 de agosto

Acabo de llegar del trabajo y hay tres llamadas de Rosa en el contestador automático. Dos llamadas son para Manuel, y la otra es para mí. Dice que es culpa mía que Manuel **la** abandone.

El 8 de agosto

Manuel está furioso. Está recibiendo—en el trabajo—una serie de fotos eróticas de Rosa. Cada foto tiene una nota provocativa que promete "una noche inolvidable"—como antes. ¿Por qué no acepta Rosa que él no **la** quiere?

El 10 de agosto

No sé qué hacer. Rosa no **nos** deja en paz. **Nos** llama a las dos o tres de la mañana y cuelga el teléfono. **Nos** espía en los restaurantes y en el cine. ¡No podemos escapar!

El 4 de septiembre

Por casi tres semanas, ¡no **nos** molesta Rosa! Y ahora, de repente, Manuel llama para decirme que ella está esperándo**lo** después del trabajo. **Lo** invita a tomar una copa en el bar antes de ir a casa. Cuando Manuel dice que no, ella empieza a amenazar**lo**. Ella dice: "Si yo no puedo tener**te**, nadie puede tener**te**." Ella está loca y nosotros tenemos miedo.

El 5 de septiembre

¡Gracias a Dios! Rosa está en la cárcel. Un vecino **la** observó entrando en nuestra casa y llamó a la policía. Parece que ella sí quiere matar**nos**. La policía ahora tiene en evidencia muchos explosivos que ella quería poner en nuestra casa.

C. ¿Comprende usted? Conteste las preguntas según la información del diálogo.

I. ¿Por qué está celosa Rosa?

2. ¿Dónde encuentra Manuel las fotos eróticas?

3. ¿Qué hace Rosa cuando Manuel no acepta su invitación de tomar una copa?

4. ¿Quién observa a Rosa entrando en la casa?

5. ¿Qué va a usar Rosa para matarlos?

D. Las peleas de gallos—crueldad de animales. Escriba tres opiniones suyas en cuanto a por qué se debe protestar contra actividades como estas peleas. Compare sus ideas con las de un compañero.

MODELO: *Los animales se matan por una diversión del hombre—¡qué barbaridad!*

Los diputados del sheriff del condado asaltaron una pelea de gallos y arrestaron a 20 hombres el sábado pasado en un huerto de limones al este del condado. Encontraron más de 100 gallos muertos y varios heridos, con navajas atadas a las patas.

Muchos corrieron al llegar los policías; había un área cerrada donde se peleaban los gallos. La ley prohíbe tales peleas y las actividades de mirarlas y apostar por los resultados. Los gallos usan las navajas y sus picos durante la pelea. También encontraron un estimulante que se usa para animarlos. Había más de 50 gallos vivos en jaulas que los diputados piensan matar. Se busca a los organizadores. Algunos de los detenidos dicen que en México tales peleas son legales y que el gobierno sólo quiere imponer impuestos para ganar dinero.

Estructuras   *Receiving the action of a verb: El objeto directo*

* Direct objects are people or things that are acted on by the subject of a sentence or question. The following sentences have their direct objects highlighted in bold. Human direct objects have an **a** preceding them.

Rosa acosa **a Manuel.**　　　*Rosa stalks Manuel.*
Marisa llama **a la policía.**　*Marisa calls the police.*
Rosa manda **fotos eróticas.**　*Rosa sends erotic photos.*

* The following pronouns will replace nouns that function as direct objects.

Direct object pronouns			
me	me	**nos**	(us)
te	you (familiar, singular)		
lo	him, it, you (for., sing., m.)	**los**	them, you (pl., m.)
la	her, it, you (for., sing., f.)	**las**	them, you (pl., f.)

* In Spanish, direct object pronouns are placed before (precede) a conjugated verb.

Rosa quiere a Manuel.　　　*Rosa loves Manuel.*
Rosa **lo** quiere.　　　　　*Rosa loves him.*
El policía busca **evidencia.**　*The officer looks for evidence.*
El policía **la** busca.　　　*The officer looks for it.*
¿El agente conoce **a las víctimas?**　*Does the agent know the victims?*
Sí, el agente **nos** conoce.　*Yes, the agent knows us well.*

* If an infinitive follows the conjugated verb and shares the same subject, the pronoun may be placed before the conjugated verb, or it may be added to the end of an infinitive.

Voy a llamar **a la policía.**	→	**La** voy a llamar.
		Voy a llamar**la.**
Necesito documentar **los incidentes.**	→	**Los** necesito documentar.
		Necesito documentar**los.**

* In the present progressive, the direct object pronoun may be placed before the conjugation of the verb **estar** or it may be added to the end of the participle ending in **–ndo.** When attaching the pronoun to the end participle form, remember to add an accent to the second to the last syllable of the *original participle.*

Estoy examinando **la evidencia.**	→	La estoy examinando.
		Estoy examin**á**ndo**la.**
Estamos buscando **al sospechoso.**	→	**Lo** estamos buscando.
		Estamos busc**á**ndo**lo.**

* When using direct object pronouns with command forms of the verb, the pronoun is *always* attached to the end of an affirmative command, and *is always* placed before a negative command. When attaching the pronoun to the end of the command, remember to place an accent on the second to last syllable of the *original command form.*

¿Llamo **al agente** ahora?	→	Sí, ll**á**me**lo** inmediatamente.
		No, no **lo** llame ahora.

Para practicar

A. La recepcionista.   Usted es una víctima de acoso por una persona desconocida *(unknown)*. El agente quiere saber si usted recibe las siguientes cosas del acosador. Contéstele lógicamente con un pronombre.

MODELO: AGENTE: ¿Recibe *llamadas telefónicas?*
USTED: *Sí, las recibo.*

1. ¿Recibe *amenazas?*
2. ¿Recibe *fotos eróticas?*
3. ¿Recibe *regalos (gifts)?*

4. ¿Recibe *invitaciones?*
5. ¿Recibe *dinero?*

B. El agente necesita ayuda.   El investigador del acoso necesita la ayuda de otros agentes y operadores. Quiere saber si todo está funcionando bien. Dígale que usted y los otros miembros del equipo están haciendo lo que pide.

MODELO: Llamar a las víctimas para confirmar la cita.
Estamos llamándolas ahora. o *Las estamos llamando ahora.*

1. preparar las órdenes de protección
2. buscar evidencia en el sitio del crimen
3. investigar las amenazas
4. sacar fotos de la escena
5. estudiar las pistas *(clues)*
6. entrevistar al sospechado

C. La emergencia.   Parece que el acosador está entrando en la casa de su ex-novia. Ella tiene miedo y le llama a usted, su vecino. Use mandatos para confirmar lo que ella necesita hacer—o no hacer.

MODELO: ¿Llamo a la policía?
Llámela inmediatamente.

1. ¿Abro las ventanas?
2. ¿Busco mi pistola?
3. ¿Invito a mi ex-novio a tomar una cerveza?
4. ¿Limpio la casa?
5. ¿Preparo una comida?
6. ¿Me escondo *(hide myself)* en el sótano?

Vocabulario Módulo 1

Sustantivos

el abandono	*abandonment*	**el fraude**	*fraud*
el albergue	*shelter*	**el grupo**	*group*
el apoyo	*support*	**la guía**	*guide*
el asilo	*asylum*	**el/la inmigrante**	*immigrant*
el cargo	*charge*	**el/la maltratador/a**	*abuser*
la cena	*dinner*	**el moretón**	*bruise*
la comida	*food, meal*	**la negligencia**	*neglect*
el/la consejero/a	*counselor*	**el ojo morado**	*black eye*
la crisis	*crisis*	**la puta★**	*whore*
la culpa	*fault, blame*	**el refugio**	*refuge*
el derecho	*right*	**la señal**	*signal*
el empleo	*job*	**el ser**	*being*
la esperanza	*hope*	**la tercera edad**	*retirement years*
el esfuerzo	*effort*	**la vez**	*time, occasion*
la fe	*faith*	**la vivienda**	*housing*

Verbos

abandonar	to abandon	llevarse bien/	to get along well,
ahogar	to drown, choke	mal con	not well with
amar	to love	obtener (g) (ie)	to obtain
amenazar	to threaten	ocurrir	to occur
bañarse	to bathe	pegar	to strike
calmarse	to calm down	peinarse	to comb one's
casarse	to get married		hair
despertarse (ie)	to wake up	quedarse	to stay, remain
elegir (i)	to choose, elect	reconocer (zc)	to recognize
enojarse	to get angry	sentarse (ie)	to sit down
golpear	to hit	sentirse (ie)	to feel
intentar	to attempt	vestirse (i)	to get dressed
lavarse	to wash	violar	to rape
levantarse	to get up		

Adjetivos

anciano/a	elderly	doméstico/a	domestic
borracho/a	drunk	frustrado/a	frustrated
conservador/a	conservative	furioso/a	furious
descuidado/a	neglected	maltratado/a	abused

Otras expresiones

a largo plazo	long-term	basta	enough
¡Ánimo!	Courage! Go for it!	de veras	really

Módulo 2

Sustantivos

el/la acosador/a	stalker	el explosivo	explosive
el acoso	stalking	el gallo	rooster
la ascendencia	ancestry	el gasto	expense
el bolsillo	pocket	el hogar	home
el cheque	check	el impuesto	tax
el/la comandante	commander	la jaula	cage
el contestador automático	answering machine	el lenguaje	language
la crueldad	cruelty	el/la mediador/a	mediator
el/la diputado/a	deputy	el medicamento	medication
la diversidad	diversity	el/la novio/a	sweetheart
el encarcelamiento	imprisonment	la orden	order
las estadísticas	statistics	la pista	clue, track
		la población	population

el poder	power	**la solicitud**	application
el porcentaje	percentage	**el sufrimiento**	suffering
la protección	protection	**el tamaño**	size
la reclamación	claim	**la tasa**	rate
la salud	health		

Verbos

acechar	to stalk	**denunciar**	to denounce
acosar	to stalk	**difamar**	to defame, libel
aparecer (zc)	to appear	**espiar**	to spy
apostar (ue)	to bet	**firmar**	to sign
arruinar	to ruin	**perseguir (i)**	to pursue
cobrar	to charge	**protestar**	to protest

Adjetivos

celoso/a	jealous	**inolvidable**	unforgettable
erótico/a	erotic	**provocativo/a**	provocative

Otras expresiones

en cuanto a	regarding	**tomar una copa**	to have a drink
fuera	outside		

Síntesis

A escuchar

Escuche las siguientes preguntas y después escriba una respuesta con oraciones completas.

1. _____

2. _____

3. _____

4. _____

5. _____

A conversar

La violencia doméstica es un problema enorme. A veces una mujer no se queja del abuso porque acepta su destino con una resignación de "Si Dios quiere". Hable con compañeros de las causas y efectos de tal tratamiento.

MODELO: *Una mujer se siente sin valor y sin remedio.*

A leer

Un delito puede dejar un impacto devastador y duradero en la vida de las víctimas. Si usted ha sido víctima de un delito, puede ser que su comunidad cuente con la ayuda necesaria.

El estado de Arizona proporciona ayuda financiera a las víctimas a través del Programa de Compensación para Víctimas. Puede hacer una solicitud para pedir ayuda financiera por los gastos en los que incurrió de su bolsillo como resultado directo del delito.

La Compensación para Víctimas le ayudará a pagar:

- Gastos médicos
- Gastos de consultas de orientación para salud mental
- Gastos funerarios
- Pérdida de salarios

La Junta no puede considerar reclamaciones por:

- Pérdida o daños a la propiedad
- Dolor y sufrimiento
- Gastos que beneficiarían al ofensor
- Una persona que esté cumpliendo una sentencia de encarcelamiento

Reprinted with the permission of the Arizona Criminal Justice Commission

¿Comprende Ud.?   Si las siguientes declaraciones son ciertas, escriba una **"C"**; si son falsas, escriba una **"F"** y haga las correcciones necesarias.

1. _____ Un delito puede dejar un impacto negativo en la víctima por mucho tiempo.

2. _____ Este programa no ofrece dinero para ayudar a la víctima.

3. _____ Es posible recibir ayuda financiera por gastos médicos y psicológicos.

4. _____ Una persona en la cárcel también puede hacer una solicitud.

A escribir

Usted es una víctima de un crimen y decide llenar la solicitud para pedir ayuda. Aquí tiene el formulario—complételo.

```
┌─────────────────────────────────────────────────────────────────────┐
│ Regresar por correo a:        Estado de Arizona      Fecha en que se   │
│                          Comisión de justicia penal de  recibió:_____  │
│                                 Arizona              Revisada          │
│                          Programa de compensación para  Por:_____    │
│                          víctimas de un acto criminal                  │
│                                                      Reclamación CVC No.│
└─────────────────────────────────────────────────────────────────────┘
```

✔ **Favor de llenar la solicitud lo más completamente posible y firmarla**

PARTE I: Información de la víctima

Apellido   Nombre   Segundo Nombre

Dirección   Sexo: £ Masculino
                                                            £ Femenino

Ciudad   Estado   Código postal

Fecha de nacimiento   Teléfono particular   Teléfono de trabajo
                              (   )   (   )
Número de seguro social

PARTE II: Información acerca del acto criminal

Tipo de acto:

£ Agresión sexual   £ Abuso   £ Robo   £ Secuestro
£ Homicidio   £ Acoso   £ Terrorismo £ DUI (manejar intoxicado por alcohol
                                                o drogas)

Fecha del acto: Agencia policial a la que se reportó:

Nombre del detective: Ubicación del acto:

Reprinted with the permission of the Arizona Criminal Justice Commission

Algo más

Ventana cultural

La diversidad entre hispanoamericanos

1. Edad: La población hispanoamericana es menor que la población estadounidense en general. La edad promedia es de 26,4 años en comparación a 34,9 años para la población en general.

2. Tamaño del hogar: El hogar típico consiste en 3,5 personas, casi una persona más en cada casa latina que en otros hogares, con un promedio de 2,6 personas.

3. Tasa de nacimiento: Hay más nacimientos en las familias latinas—104,8 por 1.000 mientras que hay sólo 65,4 en otras familias.

4. Poder económico adquisitivo: Los hispanoamericanos gastan $383 mil millones de dólares en compras.

5. Hogares en las ciudades: Casi 88% de los latinoamericanos viven en zonas metropolitanas, el grupo urbano más grande. Algunas estadísticas son impresionantes en cuanto al porcentaje de la población en estas ciudades: El Paso, 74%; San Antonio, 52%; Fresno, 41%; Seattle-Tacoma, 40%; Los Angeles, 38%; Albuquerque, 38%.

6. Lenguaje: El uso del español es la auto-identificación más mencionada. De la población latina en total, 56% hablan español en casa, 18% de esas personas son nacidas en Estados Unidos y 78% nacidas fuera de Estados Unidos. De los nacidos aquí, 35% dicen que son bilingües y 47% dicen que hablan inglés.

En mis propias palabras.   ¿Cuál es su reacción a los hispanoamericanos de aquí—son todos iguales o tienen personalidades diferentes individualmente y como parte de su ascendencia nacional?

A buscar

En Internet busque datos de los inmigrantes de una nación latina en Estados Unidos. Trate de saber el número de personas que hay, dónde se concentran, qué trabajos hacen y más. ¿Qué características en común tiene el grupo?

A conocer: Carlos Álvarez, Director de la Policía de Miami-Dade

En 1997, Carlos Álvarez fue nombrado Director de la Policía de Miami-Dade (MDPD). Entró al departamento en 1976 y recibió el puesto de Comandante en 1985. Cuatro años después se instaló como Jefe de la división de operaciones y en 1992 llegó a ser Director asistente.

Tiene un título de Florida International University y se graduó de la Academia nacional del FBI. Es un nativo de Cuba que llegó a Estados Unidos con su familia a los ocho años. Es el padre de tres hijos.

LECCIÓN 9

Delitos

Módulo 1
- Pregunte a la policía
- Expressing hope or desire: *Introducción breve al subjuntivo*
- La prostitución
- Giving advice or suggestions: *More on the subjunctive (Más sobre el subjuntivo)*

Módulo 2
- Los juegos de azar
- Giving recommendations: *El subjuntivo con expresiones impersonales*
- Delitos de fraude: *La identidad falsa*
- Expressing emotion and doubt: *El subjuntivo con expresiones de emoción y duda*

Síntesis
- A escuchar
- A conversar
- A leer
- A escribir

Algo más
- Ventana cultural: El poder del crimen organizado—los cárteles
- A buscar
- A conocer: Manuel Covarrubias

Módulo 1

Pregunte a la Policía

Para el policía **Para el acusado**

un casco balístico

el paralizador Taser

el chaleco antibalas

el bastón

las esposas

aparecer en la Corte ante el juez

la ficha policial

tomar las huellas digitales

sacar la foto

poner una fianza

esperar en la celda

A. ¿Cómo se dice? Escriba la palabra que corresponda a cada una de las definiciones.

1. La ropa protectiva para el cuerpo de un policía es un _____.

2. La protección que se pone en la cabeza contra los tiros es un

_____.

3. El _____ es un "palo" que se usa para golpear a los presos violentos.

4. Un aparato electrónico que inmoviliza a una persona violenta es un

_____.

5. El dinero que sirve de promesa para que un acusado vuelva a la corte es una

_____.

B. Sinónimos. Cada uno de estos cuatro grupos de palabras tiene verbos que son equivalentes o sinónimos. ¿Puede reconocer qué grupo de verbos es el mejor para completar cada una de las siguientes ideas? Ponga el número del grupo más lógico en el espacio.

1. recomendar, sugerir, insistir en   **3.** pedir, rogar
2. tener miedo, temer   **4.** no creer, dudar

MODELO: El policía _____ que la persona curiosa pida un simulacro del crimen y no se meta en actividades criminales.

Grupo 1

1. La mamá preocupada _____ que su hijo de 14 años tome alcohol y drogas.

2. El policía _____ que el delincuente esté diciendo la verdad.

3. La mamá _____ a su hijo que no salga con amigos delincuentes.

4. El juez _____ que la madre se comunique con los maestros de su hijo y le busque ayuda.

¡Quiero estar arrestada!

El Internet es una maravilla para los investigadores de cualquier tópico. Ahora, hay varios sitios web donde los agentes de policía pueden "charlar" informalmente e intercambiar información profesional y donde las personas curiosas pueden hacer preguntas directa—y anónimamente—a los expertos. "Preguntealpolicía.info" es uno de los sitios más populares. Aquí hay una de las preguntas más sorprendentes y las reacciones y sugerencias de la policía.

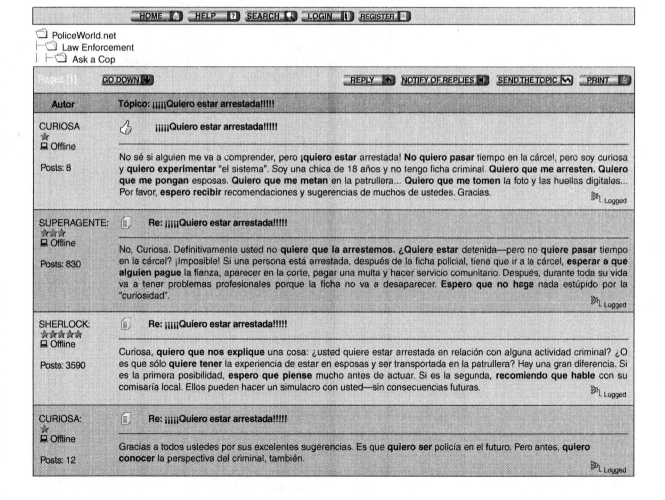

HOME	HELP ❓ SEARCH 🔍 LOGIN 🔓 REGISTER 📋

PoliceWorld.net
└ Law Enforcement
  └ Ask a Cop

Pages [1] GO DOWN ▼   REPLY ↩ NOTIFY OF REPLIES ◀ SEND THE TOPIC ⟲ PRINT 🖨

Autor	Tópico: ¡¡¡¡¡Quiero estar arrestada!!!!!
CURIOSA ★ 🖥 Offline Posts: 8	👍 **¡¡¡¡¡Quiero estar arrestada!!!!!** No sé si alguien me va a comprender, pero **¡quiero estar** arrestada! **No quiero pasar** tiempo en la cárcel, pero soy curiosa y **quiero experimentar** "el sistema". Soy una chica de 18 años y no tengo ficha criminal. **Quiero que me arresten. Quiero que me pongan** esposas. **Quiero que me metan** en la patrullera... **Quiero que me tomen** la foto y las huellas digitales... Por favor, **espero recibir** recomendaciones y sugerencias de muchos de ustedes. Gracias. Logged
SUPERAGENTE: ★★★ 🖥 Offline Posts: 830	📄 **Re: ¡¡¡¡¡Quiero estar arrestada!!!!!** No, Curiosa. Definitivamente usted no **quiere que la arrestemos.** ¿**Quiere estar** detenida—pero no **quiere pasar** tiempo en la cárcel? ¡Imposible! Si una persona está arrestada, después de la ficha policial, tiene que ir a la cárcel, **esperar a que alguien pague** la fianza, aparecer en la corte, pagar una multa y hacer servicio comunitario. Después, durante toda su vida va a tener problemas profesionales porque la ficha no va a desaparecer. **Espero que no haga** nada estúpido por la "curiosidad". Logged
SHERLOCK: ★★★★★ 🖥 Offline Posts: 3590	📄 **Re: ¡¡¡¡¡Quiero estar arrestada!!!!!** Curiosa, **quiero que nos explique** una cosa: ¿usted quiere estar arrestada en relación con alguna actividad criminal? ¿O es que sólo **quiere tener** la experiencia de estar en esposas y ser transportada en la patrullera? Hay una gran diferencia. Si es la primera posibilidad, **espero que piense** mucho antes de actuar. Si es la segunda, **recomiendo que hable** con su comisaría local. Ellos pueden hacer un simulacro con usted—sin consecuencias futuras. Logged
CURIOSA: ★ 🖥 Offline Posts: 12	📄 **Re: ¡¡¡¡¡Quiero estar arrestada!!!!!** Gracias a todos ustedes por sus excelentes sugerencias. Es que **quiero ser** policía en el futuro. Pero antes, **quiero conocer** la perspectiva del criminal, también. Logged

C. ¿Comprende usted?   Conteste las siguientes preguntas basadas en el diálogo.

1.   ¿Cómo se comunica "Curiosa" con los agentes de policía?
2.   ¿Qué quiere hacer "Curiosa"?
3.   ¿Qué no quiere hacer "Curiosa"?
4.   ¿Cuál es la recomendación de Sherlock?

D. Seguridad personal de los niños.   Lea la información sobre secuestros infantiles y termine la actividad.

LOS RIESGOS PARA SUS HIJOS

hechos y estadísticas de secuestros infantiles

- Los niños de todas las edades y razas están expuestos a los secuestros.

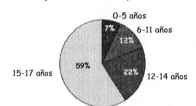

Secuestros de niños por una persona que no es un familiar, por edad

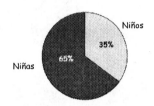

Secuestros de niños por una persona que no es un familiar, por sexo

- En 1999, hubo aproximadamente 58.200 "secuestros por parte de personas que no eran familiares del niño o de la niña". 99% de estos niños regresaron a casa. Solamente 115 de estos fueron secuestros serios y peligrosos.
  — Casi 60% de estos niños fueron devueltos sanos y salvos.

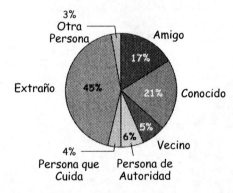

Identidad del secuestrador que no es un familiar

1.   ¿Cuál es el porcentaje de secuestros de niños hechos por personas que no son familiares, en el grupo de jóvenes de 15 a 17 años?
2.   ¿Se secuestra a más niños o a más niñas?
3.   En 1999, ¿cuántos secuestros serios y peligrosos hubo? ¿Y cuál fue el número total?
4.   ¿Hay más secuestros hechos por extraños o por personas conocidas?

Estructuras

Expressing hope or desire:
Introducción breve al subjuntivo

* In Lección 5 you learned about using command forms to tell people what you would like to see happen. This is the first phase of a grammatical concept called *the subjunctive mood*.
* All of the other verb forms you have learned so far are in *the indicative mood*. The indicative mood is generally used to describe what the speaker assumes to be true.
* The subjunctive mood is used to indicate that the speaker does *not* consider the statement to be a fact.
* Verbs in the subjunctive mood are used in the *subordinate clause* (usually the second clause of a sentence) when the *main clause* (usually the first clause of a sentence) expresses a suggestion, wish, doubt, emotion or attitude.

Indicative: La policía **arresta** a los criminales. (What *is...*)
Subjunctive: Curiosa **quiere que** el policía la **arreste.**
                     (What she *wants,* but may or may not be.)

* The formal command forms you previously learned and verbs in the subjunctive mood are derived by using the present tense **yo** form of the verb and changing the final vowel of **-ar** verbs to **-e** and the final vowels of **-er** and **-ir** verbs to **-a.**

	hablar	comer	vivir
Command	hable	coma	viva
que yo	hable	coma	viva
que tú	hables	comas	vivas
que él/ella/Ud.	hable	coma	viva
que nosotros/as	hablemos	comamos	vivamos
que Uds./ellos/ellas	hablen	coman	vivan

	ir	dar	estar	ser	saber
Command	vaya	dé	esté	sea	sepa
que yo	vaya	dé	esté	sea	sepa
que tú	vayas	des	estés	seas	sepas
que él/ella/Ud.	vaya	dé	esté	sea	sepa
que nosotros/as	vayamos	demos	estemos	seamos	sepamos
que Uds./ellos/ellas	vayan	den	estén	sean	sepan

* As with formal commands, verbs ending in:

–zar	become	**–ce**	empie**ce** usted
–gar	become	**–gue**	pa**gue** usted
–car	become	**–que**	bus**que** usted

* An **e** in the stem of the **nosotros** form of stem-changing **–ir** verbs changes to **i** and an **o** changes to **u** in the subjunctive. Note that this change occurs only with stem-changing **–ir** verbs, and not with **–ar** and **–er** verbs.

INFINITIVE		SUBJUNCTIVE
-ar	cerrar	**cierre, cierres, cierre,** cerremos, **cierren**
-er	volver	**vuelva, vuelvas, vuelva,** volvamos, **vuelvan**
but ¡OJO!		
-ir	sentir	sienta, sientas, sienta, **sintamos,** sientan
	dormir	duerma, duermas, duerma, **durmamos,** duerman

* The subjunctive of **hay** is **haya**.
* When there is only one subject that wants, desires, hopes, or prefers to do something, the verb is followed by an infinitive.

El policía quiere **ayudar.** *The policeman wants to help.*
Usted necesita **tener** cuidado. *You need to be careful.*

* When *one* subject wants, desires, hopes, prefers, etc. that a *second* subject do something, the two clauses are joined by **que** and the subjunctive is used in the second clause.

Yo espero **que el policía venga.** *I hope that the police come.*
El juez prefiere **que yo hable** con *The judge wants me to talk to*
un psicólogo. *a psychologist.*

Para practicar

A. ¿Mi hijo o yo?   Usted es un policía y el padre de un adolescente. Lea la siguiente lista de actividades e indique si usted prefiere hacerlas o si prefiere que su hijo las haga.

MODELO: trabajar contra el crimen.
Yo prefiero trabajar contra el crimen.
ir a la escuela
Yo prefiero que mi hijo vaya a la escuela.

1. tener una pistola
2. estudiar mucho
3. llevar un chaleco antibalas

4. dejar de tomar drogas

5. no salir por la noche si tiene clases el próximo día

6. estar en control de la casa

B. ¿El agente o los criminales? ¿El agente quiere que los criminales hagan las siguientes actividades? o ¿los criminales quieren que el agente las haga?

MODELO: creerse las mentiras
     Los criminales quieren que el agente se crea las mentiras.

1. aceptar responsabilidad por sus acciones

2. admitir su culpa

3. leer los Derechos Miranda

4. quitar las esposas

5. no usar el bastón

6. no luchar contra las esposas

C. El preso.   Usted es policía y tiene que arrestar a un joven nervioso. Haga una lista de cinco actividades que usted quiere que haga.

MODELO: *Quiero que ponga las manos en el carro.*

1.
2.
3.
4.
5.

Módulo I

La prostitución

En la calle

la Acusación Formal:
la instrucción de cargos en la corte

La Redada "Sting"

el pepe

la puta/ la ramera

el Proxeneta/ el Chulo

el abogado

A. ¿Cómo se dice?   Conteste las preguntas según la información del dibujo.

I. Una persona que ofrece actos sexuales a cambio de dinero es una

_____ y _____.

2. Dos palabras que indican que una persona que trafica en la prostitución

pero no participa en los actos sexuales son _____ y

_____.

3. Una _____ y _____ o "sting" por los agentes

secretos normalmente resulta en la detención de prostitutas o sus clientes.

4. Otro nombre callejero *(slang)* para un cliente de una prostituta es

_____.

5. Un negocio *(business)* de masaje que muchas veces en realidad es un burdel

(brothel) es un _____.

B. Más sinónimos.   Estudie estos grupos de sinónimos y escriba en cada
espacio la letra del grupo que mejor complete la idea. Después, complete la
oración con la forma correcta de cada verbo.

a. admitir = confesar
b. insistir en = exigir
c. recomendar = sugerir = aconsejar
d. proclamar la inocencia = declararse no culpable

MODELO: El chulo _____ que trabaja en el proxenetismo de
mujeres y niños.
a. admite, confiesa

I. El juez _____ la prostituta se someta a exámenes de salud.

2. Los abogados _____ que su cliente confiese su culpa.

3. La prostituta no quiere _____ que tiene un problema con las

sustancias controladas.

4. Durante la Acusación formal *(arraignment)* muchos presos _____.

La redada

En una redada o "sting", la policía arresta a un gran número de prostitutas, proxenetas y también clientes. Todos van a pagar las consecuencias de sus actividades. Para las prostitutas, unos exámenes de salud, y si resultan culpables, un programa de intervención completa. Para los clientes, "Escuela para los Pepes" ¡obligatoria!

El Pepe y su abogado:

PEPE: Tengo miedo. ¿Qué voy a hacer? Yo no quiero ir a la cárcel. ¡Y mi esposa me va a matar!

ABOGADO: Yo **sugiero** que usted **se declare** culpable durante la audiencia de la acusación formal y **recomiendo** que **demuestre** remordimiento. La pena mínima es su participación en "John's School—Escuela para los Pepes".

CLIENTE: ¡Me parece muy fácil!

ABOGADO: No es tan fácil: Ellos son muy exigentes *(demanding)*.

Exigen:

* que usted **se presente** a las clases cada sábado y domingo a las 6:45 de la mañana en punto y que no **salga** antes de las 3:30 de la tarde—sin excepción.
* que usted **pague** los exámenes de salud de las enfermedades de transmisión sexual.
* que usted **participe** activamente en todos los seminarios y clases sobre el impacto de la prostitución en las vecindades y en las familias, en la salud y otros campos.
* que usted **haga** un número determinado de horas de servicio a la comunidad.

Prohíben:

* que usted **salga** de la ciudad durante esta época.
* que usted **pierda** ni un momento de las clases.
* que usted **tenga** problemas con la policía durante la época de la condena condicional preventiva *(probation)*.

C. ¿Comprende usted?   Conteste las preguntas según la información del diálogo.

1. ¿Por qué tiene miedo el cliente?
2. ¿Qué recomienda el abogado que declare el cliente?
3. ¿Cuál es la pena mínima?
4. ¿Cree usted que esta pena mínima es difícil?

D. Programa de intervención para prostitutas. En Memphis, Tennessee se ofrece un programa de intervención para prostitutas con clases para avanzar en su vida. Después de leer la información, prepare un resumen de tres o más oraciones detallando lo positivo. Consulte con un compañero luego.

MODELO: *Es bueno que tengan una clase de preparación para entrevistas de empleo.*

Al llegar a la cárcel, a cada prostituta se le hacen pruebas de enfermedades sexuales y sobre el uso de drogas. Después de la sentencia, tienen clases semanales sobre:

- Autoestima
- SODA *(Stop, Observe, Decide, Act)*
- Habilidades para la vida
- Violencia doméstica
- Abuso sexual
- Enfermedades sexuales (VIH, SIDA, hepatitis)
- Abuso de sustancias ilegales
- Preparación para entrevistas de empleo
- Clases académicas para obtener el GED
- Colocación en puestos de empleo

Estructuras

Giving advice or suggestions:
More on the subjunctive:
(Más sobre el subjuntivo)

✳ When the following verbs are used in the first clause of a sentence and followed by **que,** the subjunctive form of the verb is always used.

aconsejar	*to advise*	**desear**	*to desire/wish*	**esperar**	*to hope/expect*
exigir (j)	*to demand*	**insistir en**	*to insist on*	**pedir (i)**	*to ask for/request*
permitir	*to permit*	**preferir (ie)**	*to prefer*	**prohibir**	*to prohibit*
recomendar (ie)	*to recommend*	**sugerir (ie)**	*to suggest*	**querer (ie)**	*to want*

Su abogado **exige** que usted **coopere.**

Your lawyer demands that you cooperate.

La ley **prohíbe** que los menores de edad **tomen** alcohol.

The law prohibits minors from drinking alcohol.

✳ Remember, if there is only one subject and no **que,** the infinitive form is used.

Yo **prefiero ir** a la cárcel

I prefer to go to jail.

Ellos **esperan participar** en la Escuela de Pepes.

They hope to participate in the John's School.

Para practicar

A. La Escuela para los Pepes.   Usted es el director de un centro de intervención para las prostitutas y para los clientes de prostitutas.

Decida si usted **permite, prohíbe,** o **insiste en que** los participantes hagan las siguientes actividades.

MODELO: usar palabras obscenas
> *Prohíbo que las prostitutas y los clientes usen palabras obscenas.*

1.   llamar por teléfono celular durante la instrucción
2.   fumar marihuana en las clases
3.   tomar medicina para las enfermedades de transmisión sexual
5.   respetar a los instructores
6.   salir a la calle para comer

B. La intervención.   Usted, un abogado, y su cliente están arreglando su participación en la "Escuela para los Pepes". Usted habla por teléfono con el director del programa para hacer los arreglos y ahora tiene que explicárselos a su cliente. Use: **sugerir que** o **insistir en que.**

MODELO: Su cliente puede empezar el programa en dos semanas.
> *El director sugiere que usted empiece el programa en dos semanas.*

1.   Su cliente puede visitar el programa un día antes.
2   Su cliente tiene que llegar a las 6 en punto de la mañana.
3.   Su cliente puede traer algo para comer.
4.   Su cliente tiene que cumplir 50 horas de servicio a la comunidad.
5.   Su cliente tiene que pagar los exámenes de salud.

C. El instructor.   Usted, un agente de policía, es instructor hoy en la Escuela para los Pepes. Haga una lista de cinco cosas que usted sugiere que hagan—o no hagan—los participantes durante la clase.

MODELO: *Yo sugiero que no duerman en mi clase.*

Módulo 2

Los juegos de azar

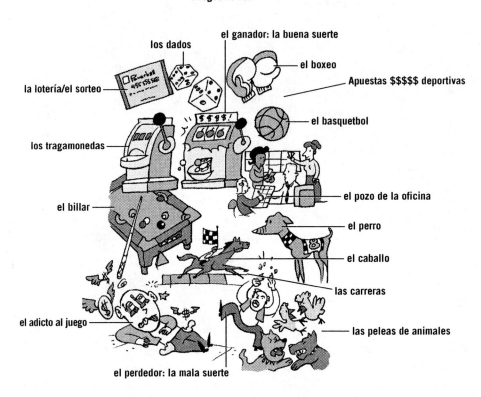

Juegos de azar

A. **¿Cómo se dice?** Escriba la palabra que corresponda a cada una de las definiciones.

1. Un juego de _____ depende totalmente de la suerte.

2. Una persona que tiene buena suerte y recibe el premio mayor o el gordo *(jackpot)* es un _____.

3. Una persona que tiene mala suerte y no gana nada es un

   _____.

4. Una _____ es una cantidad de dinero que "pone" un jugador con la esperanza de ganar aún más si su selección sale triunfante.

5. Una persona que quiere dejar de jugarse el dinero pero no puede es un

   _____.

B. Acciones.   Seleccione usted el verbo más lógico de esta lista para completar las ideas siguientes y escriba la forma correcta de cada uno.

jugar, apostar, perder, ganar

MODELO: El joven va a jugarse su último dólar con la esperanza de

_____ el dinero para pagar el alquiler.

ganar

I.   A mí me gustan mucho las carreras de caballos. Voy a _____ 50 dólares en la tercera carrera de Belmont.

2.   Este amuleto siempre me trae buena suerte; no puedo _____.

3.   Creo que esta noche la buena fortuna está conmigo. Voy a

_____ a los dados con un grupo de amigos.

4.   Me tocó el Jackpot en el tragamonedas: ¡voy a _____ mucho dinero!

El grupo de apoyo

Hay programas de 12 pasos para muchas de las adicciones que nos atormentan. Un grupo que gana popularidad rápidamente es el Grupo de Jugadores Anónimos.

MARCELA: Hola. Me llamo Marcela y soy adicta a los casinos—al principio el bingo, después los tragamonedas ¡Qué maravilla! Una vez, ¡gané un jackpot de $1.300,00! Pero pronto, después de perderlo todo la misma noche, no podía dejar de jugar. Cada noche vuelvo porque sé que es mi día de suerte. **Es común que pierda** todo el dinero para el alquiler y la comida. Estoy aquí porque sé que tengo un problema. **¡Ojalá que yo triunfe** sobre mi adicción!

TIMOTEO: Me llamo Tim. Estoy aquí porque tengo que estar aquí según la ley. No tengo problemas como ustedes. Puedo controlar mi deseo de apostar. Sólo juego a los dados los fines de semana. Estoy bien durante la semana. A veces participo en un juego de póker en vez de atender a mis estudios pero no es gran cosa. Mis papás están enojados porque por las noches, si no puedo dormir, frecuento los "cibercasinos" en mi computadora. (¡Tengo una tarjeta de crédito robada!) A veces pierdo, a veces gano. El juez dice que yo tengo un problema y que estoy en un estado de negación *(denial)* pero no es verdad. Yo estoy en control. **Es ridículo que yo esté** aquí y **es probable que no regrese** más a este grupo.

PABLO: Hola. Soy Pablo. En mi pueblo en Guatemala, es común que los hombres se reúnan por las noches para apostar en las peleas de gallos. Son horas agradables y emocionantes que pasamos allí. Es nuestra tradición. No comprendo por qué es ilegal en este país. **Es triste que esta tradición no se celebre** aquí.

C. ¿Comprende usted?   Conteste las preguntas según la información del diálogo.

I. ¿Cuál es el juego preferido de Marcela? ¿Por qué está en el grupo terapéutico?

2. ¿Tiene un problema Timoteo? ¿Qué cree usted?

3. ¿Cuál es la opinión de Pablo de las peleas de gallos?

4. ¿Cómo es posible que jóvenes como Tim tengan acceso a tantas oportunidades de apostar en juegos?

5. ¿Hay alguien en el grupo en un estado de negación? ¿Quién?

D. Cómo jugar a MegaMILLONES.   Se puede jugar legalmente o no, por medio de su corredor de apuestas. Aquí tiene información sobre cómo jugar "correctamente". Escriba las respuestas correctas al terminar.

Cómo Jugar a MegaMILLONES

Ahora hay 9 formas de ganar

- Obtenga una papeleta de juego de una tienda participante.
- Seleccione la forma de pago que usted preferiría si ganara el Premio Gordo. Puede elegir 26 pagos anuales o el valor en efectivo para que la cantidad entera se pague toda de una vez; se calcula que es un 40%–50% del Premio Gordo anunciado.
- Elija 5 números, de 1 a 47.
- Ahora elija su MEGA número, de 1 a 27.
- En cualquier jugada, puede marcar "Jugada Rápida" para elegir los 5 números solamente, o el MEGA número solamente, o ambos.
- Para jugar los mismos números en sorteos consecutivos, marque "Jugadas Futuras".
- Presente su papeleta de juego al vendedor, junto con $1 por cada jugada por sorteo.
- Asegúrese de verificar la información.
- Ahora vea el próximo sorteo de MegaMILLONES.
- Para reclamar un premio, debe presentar su boleto.

I. Hay que comprar una _____ de juego.

2. Se escogen _____ números y _____ de MEGA.

3. Si no quiere seleccionar números, puede marcar _____.

4. Cada jugada cuesta _____ dólar.

5. Si gana mucho dinero, el premio se llama _____.

6. Es posible recibir su dinero en _____ pagos anuales o todo a la vez, que es _____.

Estructuras   *Giving recommendations: El subjuntivo con expresiones impersonales*

* In addition to using the subjunctive to express desire for something to happen, it is also used after these expressions to make a subjective comment on the action that follows them.

Es bueno/malo/mejor que...	**Es preferible que...**
Es común que...	**Es raro que...**
Es increíble que...	**Es ridículo que...**
Es lógico que...	**Es triste que...**
Es importante que...	**Es una lástima que...**
Es necesario que...	**Es urgente que...**
Es normal que...	**Ojalá que...**

Es triste que mis padres sufran por mí.	*It is sad that parents should suffer because of me.*
Es ridículo que yo esté aquí.	*It is ridiculous for me to be here.*
Es una lástima que Tim no comprenda su problema.	*It is a shame that Tim does not understand his problem.*

* Impersonal expressions may be followed by an infinitive if they refer to generalizations. If they refer to specific people's actions, use the subjunctive.

Es mejor evitar los casinos en primer lugar.	*It is best to avoid casinos in the first place.*
Es mejor que tú evites a los amigos jugadores.	*It is best for you to avoid your friends who are "players."*

Para practicar

A. Las reglas.   Es la primera noche que Alejandro está en el Grupo de Jugadores Anónimos. Usted es su primer amigo. Explíquele a Alejandro que debe seguir las siguientes reglas del programa de 12 pasos.

MODELO: Es importante **asistir** a todas las reuniones.
          *Es importante que usted **asista** a todas las reuniones.*

1. Es bueno hablar en el grupo.
2. Está prohibido tomar alcohol o drogas.
3. Es importante escuchar las historias de otros jugadores problemáticos.
4. Está prohibido entrar en casino.
5. Es preferible llamarme si tiene ganas de apostar.
6. Es bueno conocer a los compañeros.
7. Es urgente ir a un consejero.

B. Alejandro no está cómodo.   La primera noche que una persona está en un nuevo lugar es natural que sienta emociones confusas. Aconséjele usted respondiendo a sus ideas con una de las expresiones impersonales.

Es normal que	**Es importante que**	**Es lógico que**
Es preferible que	**Es malo que**	**Es urgente que**
Es imposible que	**Es ridículo que**	**Es una lástima que**

MODELO: No quiero escuchar a estas personas.
Alejandro, es mejor que escuche a estas personas.

1.   No quiero participar en el grupo hoy.
2.   No quiero ir a la cárcel.
3.   Estoy muy triste y solo *(lonely)* esta noche.
4.   Quiero comprar lotería.
5.   Tengo mucho miedo.

C. ¡Imaginación!   Imagine que está aconsejando a un/a estudiante de la secundaria que admite que es adicto/a a los juegos. Escriba cinco recomendaciones positivas *(es bueno o importante o necesario… que…)* y cinco recomendaciones negativas *(es malo o ridículo o estúpido… que…)*

MODELO: *Es urgente que hables con tus padres.*

Módulo 2

Delitos de fraude: La identidad falsa

Delitos de engaño
La identificación falsa: clonación/reproducción y alteración

Formas de identificación

el permiso de residente

el pasaporte

el acta/la partida de nacimiento

el permiso para manejar

la tarjeta de Seguro Social

El robo de la identidad

la tarjeta de crédito

reproducción electrónica; la clonación electrónica

Falsificar la identificación

la alteración *(chalking)*

El lavado de cheques

A. ¿Cómo se dice?   Escriba la palabra que corresponda a cada una de las definiciones.

1. _____ es un documento que debe verificar y documentar quién es una persona.

2. Dos técnicas para falsificar la identificación son la _____ y la

   _____.

3. El _____ _____ _____ es una manera de robar cheques y cambiar la cantidad de dinero y el destinatario *(payee)* casi sin detección.

4. Un _____ _____ _____ es una manera de usar el buen nombre y el buen crédito de una persona inocente.

B. Formas de identificación.   Escriba la palabra que corresponda a cada una de las definiciones.

1. Un documento oficial del gobierno que certifica la ciudadanía *(citizenship)*

   de una nación es un _____.

2. Los _____ _____ _____ (las tarjetas verdes) verifican que un inmigrante tiene el derecho de vivir en este país.

3. El/La _____ _____ _____ da los datos importantes de una persona como la fecha y el lugar de su nacimiento.

4. Un número de _____ _____ es la identificación de la actividad económica que tiene una persona que trabaja en EE. UU.

La clonación de la identificación

Carolina, 20 años, es una estudiante con honores en una universidad conocida. Como muchos estudiantes de su edad, le gusta mucho entrar en los clubes con la identificación falsa. ¡Todos sus amigos lo hacen! Después de estar arrestada en una redada policial, ella ahora paga las consecuencias: una multa y la libertad condicional por un plazo de dos años. Para cumplir con las 50 horas de servicio a la comunidad, Carolina habla con un grupo de jóvenes sobre las consecuencias de sus actividades.

CAROLINA:	¿Cuántos de ustedes tienen identificación falsa?
ESTUDIANTE 1:	¡Todos la tenemos! Es casi obligatorio para nosotros. Para entrar en los bailes, los clubes, los casinos... para comprar una cerveza de vez en cuando.
CAROLINA:	**No me sorprende que** todos la **tengan.** Es tan fácil de conseguir. Pero **dudo que comprendan** las consecuencias de usar la identificación falsa—sobre todo en la época del terrorismo.
ESTUDIANTE 2:	Pues, en realidad ¿qué problema causamos con tomar un poco de cerveza y bailar en un club? La ley es demasiado severa con nosotros.
CAROLINA:	¡Esta fue mi actitud precisamente—antes de estar arrestada! Ahora no estoy tan segura. El bar donde nos arrestó la policía ahora tiene que pagar una multa enorme y **creo que van a perder** su permiso para servir alcohol. Yo ahora tengo una ficha policial y **dudo que sea** posible para mí tener una carrera como policía o abogada.
ESTUDIANTE:	¿Por qué?
CAROLINA:	Es un delito. Y, también hay consecuencias civiles. Acabo de recibir una noticia de audiencia—el dueño del bar presenta una acción civil contra nosotros para demandar los daños económicos de su negocio. **¡Pide que cada estudiante** le **pague** $25.000!
ESTUDIANTE:	No puede ser legal esto...
CAROLINA:	**Yo les prometo** que **es** legal—mucho más legal que lo que hicimos nosotros.

C. ¿Comprende usted?   Conteste las preguntas según la información del diálogo.

1.   ¿Por qué fue detenida Carolina?
2.   ¿Cuáles son las consecuencias criminales de sus actividades?
3.   ¿Por qué quieren los jóvenes tener identificación falsa?
4.   ¿Qué consecuencia civil hay para Carolina y sus amigos?

D. La falsificación de documentos.   Esta historia es verdadera, pero con los nombres cambiados para proteger a los inocentes. ¿El castigo debe ser tan severo? Compare su opinión con la de un compañero.

MODELO: *Hay miles (¿millones?) de personas en la misma situación. ¿Vamos a poder controlar a todas?*

La racha de arrestos en Nebraska tiene algo en común: carecer de un documento válido

Armando García-Martínez acaba de cumplir 18 años en la cárcel del Condado de Beaver. Allí ha estado detenido desde el 12 de diciembre. "Armando vino a Estados Unidos con una ilusión: la de tener una casa, de tener su propio carro", dijo uno de sus amigos. "Armando sabía que tenía que trabajar para que su ilusión se hiciera realidad". Ahora, es posible que pase siete años preso por haber sido acusado de falsificar documentos y de manejar ebrio *(DUI)*.

Marisol Echeverría, madre de

Pedro de 6 años, fue arrestada por manejar sin licencia de conducir. Espera una audiencia de deportación en la cárcel del Condado de Lincoln. Mientras su futuro se decide, sus amigos están cuidando a su hijo que es un ciudadano estadounidense.

Marisol y Armando son dos de los tantos inmigrantes indocumentados que han sido arrestados después del 11 de septiembre. En el suroeste de Nebraska, han arrestado a más de 500 personas por usar documentación falsa para obtener una licencia de conducir. Todas estas personas fueron acusadas de falsificación.

Estructuras

Expressing emotion and doubt: El subjuntivo con expresiones de emoción y duda

* The subjunctive can be used to express the way someone feels about what someone else is doing or about what is happening to someone else. Here are some common verbs of emotion that are commonly followed by the subjunctive.

me (te, le...) gusta que	**me (te, le...) molesta que...**
me (te, le...) encanta que	**me (te, le...) sorprende que...**
alegrarse de que...	**sentir que...**
estar contento/a de que...	**temer que...**
estar triste de que...	**tener miedo de que...**

Me alegro de que dejes de fumar.   *I'm happy that you are stopping smoking.*

Siento que los médicos **tengan** tantos problemas con los seguros.   *I'm sorry that doctors have so many problems with insurance.*

¿Le gusta a tu pareja que **fumes** mota?   *Does your partner like you smoking dope?*

No, pero **me molesta que se queje.**   *No, but it bothers me that s/he complains.*

* The subjunctive is also used to question the truth about something. It is used after verbs and expressions of doubt or uncertainty.

VERBS		EXPRESSIONS OF DOUBT
dudar que...	⇒	es dudoso que...
no creer que...	⇒	es posible/imposible que...
no estar seguro/a de que...	⇒	es probable/improbable que...
no es cierto que...	⇒	no es verdad que...

Dudo que Ud. tenga 21 años. *I doubt that you are 21 years old.*
Es posible que tengan *It's possible that they have false ID.*
identificación falsa.

* Since **creer que, estar seguro de que, es cierto que,** and **es verdad que** indicate that the speaker considers his or her assumptions to be true, they take the indicative in affirmative statements. When these verbs and expressions are used negatively, doubt is implied and the verb is in the subjunctive.

Creo que ella **miente.** *I believe she's lying.*
No creo que él **tome** alcohol. *I don't believe he drinks alcohol.*

* When these expressions are used in a question, they take the indicative if the speaker is merely seeking information, but use the subjunctive if the speaker is expressing doubt as to the answer.

—¿**Es verdad que** él **es** la víctima? *Is it true he is the victim?*
—Sí, **creo que es** la víctima. *Yes, I think he's the victim.*
—¿**Crees que sea él** criminal? *Do you think he's a criminal?*
—No, **no creo que sea él** criminal. *No, I don't think he's a criminal.*

* Use **quizás** or **tal vez** to say *maybe, perhaps.* The subjunctive is used after these expressions, unless the speaker feels quite sure that the assertion is true.

Quizás el documento **sea** falso. *Perhaps the document is false.*
(The speaker has some doubt.)
El documento es falso, quizás. *Perhaps the document is false.*
(The speaker thinks it is true.)

Para practicar

A. Las noticias del acusado. Usted es víctima del robo de identidad y acaba de saber que el criminal está en la cárcel. Diga la reacción que tiene ante esta serie de noticias, usando frases de esta lista:

> **Me alegro de que... Siento que... Me sorprende que...**

MODELO: El criminal está en ia cárcel.
Me alegro de que esté en la cárcel.

I. Va a salir de la cárcel mañana.
2. Tiene un buen abogado.
3. Sólo va a recibir una multa.
4. Otras víctimas van a presentar demandas civiles.
5. Yo no voy a perder mi dinero.
6. Una víctima vieja sufre mucho.

B. Los agentes. Los agentes de policía se consultan sobre un caso difícil de identificación falsa. Cada uno tiene una opinión diferente. Complete las ideas de los agentes usando la forma del verbo indicado en el subjuntivo o el indicativo.

MODELO: Dudo que el documento _____ (ser) falso.
Dudo que el documento sea falso.

I. Es verdad que el señuelo _____ (usar) varias identidades.

2. Dudo que el acusado _____ (ser) terrorista.

3. Es posible que _____ (ir) a la cárcel.

4. No dudo que _____ (tener) problemas civiles también.

5. Quizás _____ (llegar) su abogado pronto.

6. Es obvio que él no _____ (sentir) mucha culpa por sus delitos.

7. Dudamos que su familia lo _____ (saber).

8. Me molesta que no _____ (salir) de la cárcel con una fianza.

C. ¿Conoce usted a un menor de edad con identificación falsa? Si conoce usted a algún menor de edad que usa identificación falsa, tiene que ayudarlo. Escríbale una carta diciendo por qué usted no quiere que use la identificación para comprar alcohol y tabaco o entrar en bares o casinos. Use expresiones como: *yo creo que… , es importante que…, yo dudo que…, no es bueno que…*, etc.

MODELO: *Es importante que no compre tabaco porque es malo para la salud.*

Vocabulario Módulo I

Sustantivos

la acusación	*accusation*	**el chaleco antibalas**	*bullet-proof vest*
la autoestima	*self esteem*	**el chulo★**	*pimp*
el bastón	*night stick*	**la colocación**	*placement*
el casco balístico	*helmet*	**la enfermedad**	*illness*
la celda	*cell*	**la fianza**	*bail bond*

la habilidad	ability	la prueba	test
el hecho	fact	el/la psicólogo/a	psychologist
el masaje	massage	el puesto	position
el paralizador Taser	Taser stun gun	la ramera★	whore
la pena	penalty	la raza	race
el pepe★	john	la redada	sting
la promesa	promise	el remordimiento	remorse
la prostituta	prostitute	el riesgo	risk
el proxeneta	pimp	el tiro	shot

Verbos

aconsejar	to advise	exigir (j)	to require
admitir	to admit	luchar	to fight
confesar (ie)	to confess	permitir	to permit
cumplir	to fulfill	prohibir	to prohibit
desear	to desire	rogar (ue)	to beg
dudar	to doubt	sugerir (ie)	to suggest

Adjetivos

culpable	guilty	inocente	innocent
curioso/a	curious	salvo/a	unharmed
extraño/a	strange	sano/a	healthy
falso/a	false	sorprendente	surprising

Módulo 2

Sustantivos

el acta (f.)	certificate	el/la ganador/a	winner
la actitud	attitude	el gesto	gesture
el/la adicto/a	addict	la identidad	identity
el/la alcalde/sa	mayor	el juego	game
el alquiler	rent	el lavado	laundering
la apuesta	bet	la libertad	
el azar	chance	condicional	parole
el basquetbol	basketball	la lotería	lottery
el billar	pool	la maravilla	marvel
el boxeo	boxing	el nivel	level
el caballo	horse	el pago	payment
la carrera	race	la partida	game
el cártel	cartel	el partido	game, match
el/la ciudadano/a	citizen	el pasaporte	passport
la clonación	cloning	el/la perdedor/a	loser
el crédito	credit	el plazo	term
los dados	dice	el pozo	well, pool
el engaño	deceit	el premio	prize

la regla	rule	**la tarjeta**	card
el señuelo	decoy	**el tragamonedas**	slot machine
el sorteo	drawing	**la vestimenta**	clothes
la suerte	luck		

Verbos

atormentar	to torment	**fusilar**	to shoot
carecer (zc)	to lack	**prometer**	to promise
castigar	to punish	**reclamar**	to claim
falsificar	to falsify		

Adjetivos

ambos/as	both	**poderoso/a**	powerful
callado/a	quiet	**propio/a**	own
común	common	**ridículo/a**	ridiculous
deportivo/a	sporting	**suroeste**	southwest
justo/a	fair		

Otras expresiones

¡Carajo!★	Crap!	**Seguro Social**	Social Security
en efectivo	cash	**sobre todo**	above all
Es una lástima.	It's a shame.		
Ojalá	I hope, May Allah grant		

Síntesis

A escuchar

Escuche esta conversación entre una prostituta y un "pepe". Después, indique si la prostituta **(1)** o el pepe **(2)** dice las siguientes cosas.

1. _____ "¿Quiere una cita?"

2. _____ "No es una redada, ¿verdad?"

3. _____ "$100".

4. _____ "Sugiero que mantenga silencio".

5. _____ "¡Carajo!"

A conversar

La prostitución es la profesión más vieja, dicen. Hable con sus compañeros de si debe ser ilegal o no.

MODELO: _No creo que sea ilegal porque el cliente compra un servicio ofrecido voluntariamente._

A leer

Centro de detención para menores
Reglas básicas para obedecer

Se espera que usted obedezca todas la reglas. Al seguir las reglas, usted recibe privilegios. De no hacerlo, los pierde.

1. Necesitamos que obedezca las instrucciones que reciba del personal, verbales o escritas.

2. Comunicación: Hable con el personal respetuosamente—Señor, Señora o Señorita y su apellido. No hable con ningún menor castigado en su cuarto *(room restriction)*. No use insultos, comentarios raciales, gestos sexuales o pandilleros. No pase mensajes a nadie.

3. Vestimenta: Las camisetas deben usarse todo el tiempo. Los pantalones deben quedarle bien *(fit well)*. No se quite la pulsera de identificación.

4. Movimiento en grupo: Cuando se le indique ponerse en línea, hágalo callada y prontamente. No deje su grupo sin permiso.

5. Cuartos: Usted es responsable de cómo se encuentre su cuarto. No se permite que cubra la ventanilla. Solamente 3 libros a la vez—esto incluye periódicos y revistas, más una Biblia.

6. Fumar y contrabando: Fumar o cualquier otro contrabando está prohibido.

7. Escaparse: No intente escaparse.

¿Comprende usted?   Si las siguientes declaraciones son ciertas, escriba una **"C"**; si son falsas, escriba una **"F"** y haga las correcciones necesarias.

1. _____ Es importante seguir las instrucciones del personal.

2. _____ Hay uniforme para todos los menores.

3. _____ Es necesario moverse con su grupo.

4. _____ Se puede fumar en este centro.

A escribir

Escriba una lista de crímenes relacionados con identificación falsa. Compare su lista con la de un compañero.

MODELO: *cheques robados o falsificados, tarjetas "verdes" falsas*

Algo más

Ventana cultural: El poder del crimen organizado—los cárteles

domingo, 3 de julio, 1994

Asesinos colombianos matan al futbolista

Andrés Escobar fue asesinado a los 27 años por haber metido un gol sin querer a favor de Estados Unidos en un partido de Copa Mundial *(World Cup)*. Lo mataron al salir de una discoteca a las 3:30 de la mañana en Medellín, 150 millas al norte de Bogotá. Se sospecha que el grupo de hombres, que lo fusilaron 12 veces, le echó la culpa por eliminar al equipo colombiano de la competencia.

Se cree que los cárteles de drogas perdieron millones de dólares en apuestas con la esperanza del éxito del equipo. "Es increíble que haya llegado al nivel de los atletas", dijo el alcalde de Medellín, Luis Ramos Botero. Parece que la violencia de los cárteles de drogas surge de nuevo—hay rumores de una pelea entre el cártel de Medellín y el de Cali—los traficantes de cocaína más poderosos del mundo.

En mis propias palabras.   ¿Dónde ve usted la influencia de grupos como la mafia italiana o la mafia mexicana en Estados Unidos? ¿Qué controlan? ¿Cómo operan? ¿Es importante la lealtad *(loyalty)*? ¿La familia? ¿Cuáles son sus conexiones? ¿Son como pandillas poderosas a nivel nacional, internacional?

A buscar

El robo de identidad es un problema enorme. Escriba "robo de identidad" en su motor de búsqueda y mire los resultados.

A conocer: Manuel Covarrubias

Manuel Covarrubias es el segundo juez latino en el condado de Ventura, California. Fue nombrado a la Corte Superior por el ex-gobernador Gray Davis. Covarrubias dice que es un gran logro personal para él. Es el presidente pasado de la Mexican-American Bar Association; recibió su título de derecho de Loyola Law School. El alcalde de la comunidad, Manuel Lopez, dice que es importante que los jueces reflejen la etnicidad del pueblo; el primer juez latino, nombrado hace más de 20 años, fue Art Gutiérrez. Covarrubias es voluntario en programas escolares para enseñarles a los inmigrantes lo más básico del sistema de tribunales.

LECCIÓN 10

El crimen

Módulo I
- La escena del crimen
- Discussing past activities: *Introducción al pretérito*
- La investigación
- More on the preterite: *Verbos irregulares*

Módulo 2
- El defensor público
- Relating past activities: *Verbos en* **–ir** *con cambios en el pretérito*
- El fiscal
- More past activities: *Usos del pretérito*

Síntesis
- A escuchar
- A conversar
- A leer
- A escribir

Algo más
- Ventana cultural: El poder de los latinos
- A buscar
- A conocer: Richard T. García

Módulo I

La escena del crimen

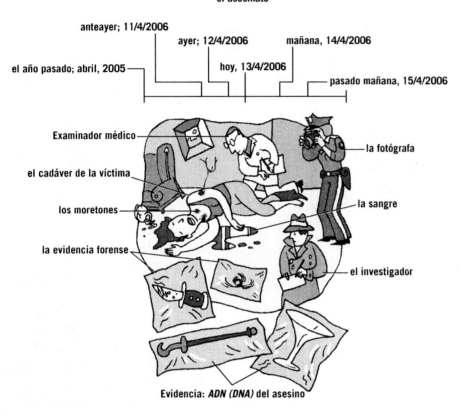

el asesinato

anteayer; 11/4/2006

ayer; 12/4/2006

mañana, 14/4/2006

el año pasado; abril, 2005

hoy, 13/4/2006

pasado mañana, 15/4/2006

Examinador médico

la fotógrafa

el cadáver de la víctima

los moretones

la sangre

la evidencia forense

el investigador

Evidencia: *ADN (DNA)* del asesino

A. ¿Cómo se dice?   Escriba la palabra que corresponda a cada una de las definiciones.

1.   La división investigadora que determina oficialmente la hora y la causa de la muerte es el _____ _____.

2.   El _____ es la materia genética que ayuda a identificar a las víctimas y a los criminales.

3.   La evidencia _____ ahora se analiza en un laboratorio electrónico.

4.   Una persona que comete un asesinato es un _____.

5.   El cuerpo de una persona muerta a veces se llama un _____.

B. ¿Pasado o futuro? Siga las pistas *(clues)* temporales en la oración para escoger el verbo correcto—futuro o pasado. ¡OJO! Se explica el pasado (pretérito) de los verbos en la sección de gramática de este módulo.

1. El asesinato _____ocurrió_____ **anteayer.** (va a ocurrir/ocurrió)

2. Los resultados forenses _____van a llegar_____ **mañana.** (van a llegar/llegaron)

3. **La semana pasada,** la víctima _____habló_____ con el sospechoso por teléfono. (va a hablar/habló)

4. **Ayer,** el examinador médico _____ la muerte un suicidio. (va a declarar/declaró)

5. **Pasado mañana** los testigos _____ (van a identificar/identificaron) al asesino de una rueda de presos.

En la escena del crimen

911 recibió una llamada anónima de un crimen—posiblemente un homicidio—en un apartamento de la ciudad. ¿Quién es la víctima? ¿Cómo la asesinaron? ¿Con qué motivo la asesinaron? Y más importante, ¿quién o quiénes son los asesinos? ¡Sólo la evidencia en la escena del crimen lo puede revelar!

INVESTIGADOR: ¿Qué **pasó?** ¿Quién es la víctima?

OFICIAL: Es un homicidio brutal. El examinador médico está con el cuerpo ahora, pero todavía no **identificaron** a la señorita. El conserje *(superintendent)* del edificio dice que ella no **vivió** aquí nunca y que él no la conoce. El residente de este apartamento **salió** de vacaciones la semana pasada y no va a regresar por tres semanas.

INVESTIGADOR: ¿Usted no **tocó** nada?

OFICIAL: Claro que no **toqué** nada. Cuando **llegué, dejé** la puerta abierta y **empecé** a hacer un dibujo *(sketch)* de la escena. Aquí lo tiene. ¡La pobre—tan joven!

INVESTIGADOR: Gracias, Oficial. *(al examinador médico)* Hola, Mario. ¿Qué tenemos?

EXAMINADOR MÉDICO: Es una señorita entre 20 y 25 años de edad, posiblemente latina, con indicaciones de una muerte muy violenta. No **determiné** todavía la causa precisa de la muerte ni **identifiqué** a la víctima, pero parece que la **estrangularon** y la **golpearon.** No sé si la **asaltaron** sexualmente. Parece que ella **tomó** champaña y **comió** caviar inmediatamente antes de morir. Vamos a hacer las pruebas forenses en el laboratorio. Con suerte vamos a encontrar ADN. Ya **terminé** aquí. ¡Qué triste!

C. ¿Comprende usted?   Conteste las preguntas según la información del diálogo.

1. ¿Quién es la víctima?
2. ¿Dónde está el residente del apartamento?
3. ¿Cómo murió la víctima?
4. ¿Qué comió ella?
5. ¿Qué pruebas va a hacer el examinador médico?

D. Permiso de entrada y registro.   Es posible darle permiso a la policía para entrar y registrar su casa si cree que no tiene nada que esconder o si cree que ya escondió todo tan bien que no lo van a encontrar. Llene el formulario con los detalles de un caso fingido *(invented)* y luego compare su caso con el de un/a compañero/a.

Permiso de entrada y registro

Número de reporte: _____

Yo, _____, teniendo custodia legal o control o autoridad o posesión personal de las propiedades localizadas en y descritas como:

_____

_____

_____

concedo autoridad total e incondicional al Departamento del Sherifato del Condado de Madison para entrar en esas propiedades para realizar la búsqueda de:

_____

_____

_____

y para realizar cualquier investigación relacionada con cualquier asunto de la ley, criminal o civil. Yo concedo este consentimiento libremente, con entendimiento e inteligencia, consciente de que los miembros del departamento tendrán acceso libre y sin restricciones a las propiedades, hasta que la presente investigación esté completa.

Firma: _____   Fecha: _____   Hora: _____

Oficial/Testigo: _____ Nº. de

Insignia/I.D. _____

Estructuras

Discussing past activities: Introducción al pretérito

* To tell what you did at a specific moment in the past, use the preterite tense.
* The regular forms of **-ar, -er,** and **-ir** verbs follow. Note that the **nosotros/as** forms of **-ar** and **-ir** verbs are the same in the present and preterite tenses.

	hablar	comer	vivir
yo	habl**é**	com**í**	viv**í**
tú	habl**aste**	com**iste**	viv**iste**
él/ella/Ud.	habl**ó**	com**ió**	viv**ió**
nosotros/as	habl**amos**	com**imos**	viv**imos**
ellos/ellas/Uds.	habl**aron**	com**ieron**	viv**ieron**

—¿Ya **habló** con el examinador médico?   *Did you already talk to the ME?*
—Sí, ya **hablé** con él.   *Yes, I already talked to him.*
—¿Cuándo **comió** usted?   *When did you eat?*
—Yo **comí** hace una hora.   *I ate an hour ago.*
—¿**Vivieron** las víctimas aquí?   *Did the victims live here?*
—Sí, **vivimos** todos aquí.   *Yes, we all lived here.*

* **Cambios ortográficos:** In the preterite, **-ar** verbs ending in **-car, -gar,** and **-zar** have spelling changes in the **yo** form.

buscar	→	**busqué,** buscaste, buscó, buscamos, buscaron
investigar	→	**investigué,** investigaste, investigó, investigamos, investigaron
empezar	→	**empecé,** empezaste, empezó, empezamos, empezaron

* There are no stem changes in the preterite for **-ar** or **-er** verbs.
* The verb **dar** uses **-er** endings in the preterite.

    dar → **di, diste, dio, dimos, dieron**

* In the preterite tense, infinitives ending in **-er** or **-ir** whose stems end in a vowel will follow the spelling rule that says that an unaccented **i** will change to a **y** when it appears between two vowels:

leer	→	leí, leíste, **leyó,** leímos, **leyeron**
oír	→	oí, oíste, **oyó,** oímos, **oyeron**

* **Hace** + a time expression + **que** + a verb in the preterite tells *how long ago* something happened.

Hace dos semanas que hablé   *I spoke to the victim two weeks ago.*
con la víctima.
Hace un año que Pablo salió   *Pablo got out of jail a year ago.*
de la cárcel.

▨ Omit **que** when starting the sentence with the verb rather than the time expression.

Hablé con ellos **hace una semana**.   *I spoke to them a week ago.*
Pablo entró a la cárcel **hace dos años**.   *Pablo entered jail two years ago.*

Para practicar

A. El/La estudiante de criminología.   Usted es un/a estudiante de criminología y tiene que repetir las acciones del investigador-profesor. Explique qué pasó ayer.

MODELO: El investigador examinó la evidencia.
Yo examiné la evidencia.

1. El investigador leyó el reporte forense.
2. El investigador habló con la familia de la víctima.
3. El investigador escribió unas notas.
4. El investigador investigó la escena del crimen.
5. El investigador empezó una investigación.
6. El investigador buscó los resultados de las pruebas en el laboratorio.
7. El investigador leyó los resultados forenses.

B. ¿Cuándo?   El investigador con quien usted trabaja tiene una lista de instrucciones para sus empleados. Explíquele que cada persona ya terminó su tarea.

MODELO: María tiene que revelar las fotos de la escena del crimen. *María…*
María ya reveló las fotos de la escena del crimen.

1. Usted tiene que buscar más evidencia en la escena del crimen. *Yo…*
2. El examinador médico tiene que preparar el reporte forense. *El examinador médico…*
3. Los investigadores tienen que localizar a los testigos. *Ellos…*
4. Usted tiene que interrogar a los testigos. *Yo…*
5. Ustedes tienen que escribir los reportes para el comandante. *Nosotros…*

▮▮ **C. ¿Cuánto tiempo hace que…?**   Conteste las siguientes preguntas indicando la última vez que hizo *(did)* estas actividades. Después, hágale las mismas preguntas a un/a compañero/a.

MODELO: ¿Cuánto tiempo hace que usted… investigar un crimen?
Hace dos días que investigué un crimen. Y usted, ¿cuánto tiempo hace que investigó un crimen?

1. consultar con el examinador médico de su ciudad?
2. buscar la identidad de una víctima?
3. llamar al 911?
4. usar su arma?
5. estudiar español?

Módulo I

La investigación

la orden de registro

la basura

el detective

la orden de arresto

está angustiado

la entrevista de los testigos   el interrogatorio del sospechoso

A. ¿Cómo se dice?   Escriba la palabra que corresponda a cada una de las definiciones.

I. Para abrir una puerta cerrada muchas veces se usa una_____.

2. Un _____ sigue todas las pistas e información para resolver un crimen.

3. Una orden de _____ permite que la policía detenga a un sospechoso.

4. Una orden de _____ permite que la policía entre en un sitio para buscar evidencia.

5. Cuando una cosa ya no es útil, la ponemos en la _____.

B. ¿Sabe usted?   En sus propias palabras, escriba una definición de las siguientes palabras o frases o úselas en una oración que demuestre su comprensión.

I. el interrogatorio   **2.** la entrevista   **3.** estar angustiado

Las interrogaciones

Las pruebas forenses del homicidio revelaron mucho sobre la mujer asesinada en el apartamento. Supieron su identidad, su profesión y su residencia actual. Siguiendo estas pistas, los investigadores empezaron a entrevistar e interrogar a los amigos y colegas de la víctima. Ahora están en el apartamento de la víctima hablando con su compañera de cuarto.

1. Entrevista con la compañera de apartamento: Carmen

INVESTIGADOR: ¿Reconoce usted a la persona en esta foto?

CARMEN: (gritando) ¡Ay, no! Es Paulina. ¿Qué pasó? ¿Dónde está? Necesito verla.

INVESTIGADOR: Sentimos decírselo, pero Paulina **fue** víctima de un homicidio. Está muerta. ¿Podemos hacerle unas preguntas?

CARMEN: (silencio angustiado)

INVESTIGADOR: ¿Cuándo **fue** la última vez que vio a Paulina?

CARMEN: Ayer por la mañana salimos juntas para el trabajo.

INVESTIGADOR: ¿Dónde **estuvo** anoche entre las ocho y las diez?

CARMEN: Aquí en el apartamento. Paulina y yo **hicimos** planes para celebrar su nuevo trabajo en Puerto Rico, pero ella no **vino** a la fiesta. Empecé a preocuparme un poco cuando ella tampoco regresó a casa anoche.

INVESTIGADOR: ¿Qué **hizo** entonces?

CARMEN: Primero llamé a su novio, pero él no **estuvo** con ella ayer. Entonces me dormí. **Quise** llamar a la policía, pero decidí esperar unas horas más.

INVESTIGADOR: ¿Podemos revisar la casa y sus posesiones?

CARMEN: ¿No necesitan una orden de registro?

INVESTIGADOR: No. Con su permiso... (momentos después) Carmen, usted está arrestada por el homicidio de Paulina. Tiene el derecho de mantener silencio.

2. En la comisaría

COMANDANTE: ¿Cómo **supieron** ustedes que fue Carmen?

INVESTIGADOR: **Supimos** que Carmen nos mintió cuando vimos el recibo del caviar y la champaña en la basura... y la llave del apartamento del amigo (su novio) que salió de vacaciones—a Puerto Rico.

COMANDANTE: ¿Y su motivo?

INVESTIGADOR: Celos. Paulina quiso empezar su nueva vida en Puerto Rico con el novio de Carmen.

C. ¿Comprende usted? Conteste las preguntas según la información del diálogo.

1. ¿Cómo se llama la víctima del homicidio?
2. ¿Quién es Carmen?
3. ¿Dónde estuvo Carmen anoche?
4. ¿Quién no vino a la fiesta?
5. ¿Cómo supo el investigador que Carmen no dijo la verdad?

D. La seguridad de las pistolas. La seguridad en el uso de pistolas es la ley. Los que poseen armas de fuego deben tener conocimientos básicos del funcionamiento de su pistola y tener plena conciencia de la responsabilidad de poseerla. ¿Usted puede pasar el examen para recibir su certificado? A ver...

Tome la prueba

1. Una práctica segura al manejar una pistola es apoyar el dedo en la parte de afuera del guardamonte *(trigger guard)* o en el lado de la pistola hasta estar listo para disparar.   C ☐   F ☐

2. Para conocer su blanco *(target)*, necesita saber que si la bala no da en el blanco o pasa completamente por el blanco puede dar contra una persona o un objeto.   C ☐   F ☐

3. Beber alcohol al manejar armas de fuego no es peligroso si el nivel de alcohol en la sangre permanece bajo el límite legal.   C ☐   F ☐

4. ¿Cuál de los puntos de seguridad debe recordar al manejar una pistola?   a b c d ☐☐☐☐
      a. Nunca dispare una pistola para celebrar.
      b. No dispare al agua ni contra superficies planas o duras.
      c. Use protección para los oídos y los ojos al disparar una pistola.
      d. Todos.

5. Una regla de seguridad es mantener la pistola apuntada hacia: a b c d ☐☐☐☐
      a. al norte.
      b. en la dirección menos peligrosa.
      c. hacia arriba.
      d. hacia abajo.

6. Otra regla es saber hacer esto correctamente: a b c d ☐☐☐☐
      a. Corregir un malfuncionamiento.
      b. Operar su pistola.
      c. Cargar su pistola.
      d. Limpiar su pistola.

Respuestas: 1. Cierto, 2. Cierto, 3. Falso, 4. D, 5. B, 6. B

Estructuras   *More on the preterite: Verbos irregulares*

※ In the preterite tense, the following verbs have irregular stems and irregular endings. The endings for all of these verbs are the same. **(-e, -iste, -o, -imos, -ieron).**

Infinitive	Stem	Conjugation
venir	**vin**	vine, viniste, vino, vinimos, vinieron
saber	**sup**	supe, supiste, supo, supimos, supieron
poner	**pus**	puse, pusiste, puso, pusimos, pusieron
poder	**pud**	pude, pudiste, pudo, pudimos, pudieron
querer	**quis**	quise, quisiste, quiso, quisimos, quisieron
hacer	**hic***	hice, hiciste, hizo*, hicimos, hicieron
tener	**tuv**	tuve, tuviste, tuvo, tuvimos, tuvieron
estar	**estuv**	estuve, estuviste, estuvo, estuvimos

*¡OJO! Note that only the third person singular form of **hacer** replaces the **-c** with a **-z** to preserve the pronunciation.

Ayer **supe** que Paulina fue asesinada.	*Yesterday I found out Paulina was murdered.*
No **pudimos** hablar con el investigador.	*We could not talk to the investigator.*
Hicieron muchas pruebas forenses.	*They did many forensic tests.*

* The preterite forms of the verbs **ir** and **ser** are also irregular. Note that they have identical conjugations and the meaning must be derived from the context.

ir/ser   fui, fuiste, fue, fuimos, fueron

—¿Quién **fue** el sospechoso?	*Who was the suspect?*
—**Fue** Gerardo Gómez.	*It was Gerardo Gómez.*
—¿Adónde **fue** el investigador?	*Where did the detective go?*
—**Fue** a hablar con el examinador médico.	*He went to talk to the medical examiner.*

Para practicar

A. ¿Qué hizo?   Usted pide una lista de las actividades del sospechoso que acaba de interrogar. Ponga estos verbos en el pretérito (forma "yo") para saber exactamente lo que hizo ayer.

MODELO: ir al trabajo
             Yo fui al trabajo.

1. querer almorzar con un amigo
2. no poder hablar con él
3. saber que mi amigo salió con mi novia
4. ponerme celoso
5. ir al apartamento de mi amigo para esperarlos
6. estar en el apartamento cuando ellos llegaron
7. no hacer nada

B. Evidencia forense.   Use el tiempo pretérito para describir lo que hizo el equipo del examinador médico para establecer la identidad de la víctima.

MODELO: examinar el contenido del estómago
Examinaron el contenido del estómago.

Ellos...

1. hacer varios estudios de la sangre
2. poner los datos en la computadora
3. hacer pruebas de ADN rápidamente

4. no poder establecer la identidad de la víctima
5. querer hacer una autopsía
6. saber la causa de la muerte

C. ¿Y usted?   Escriba una lista de las primeras cinco cosas que usted hizo la última vez que investigó un delito o un crimen. Después, compare su lista con la de un/a compañero/a.

MODELO: *Primero, identifiqué a la víctima.*

Módulo 2

El defensor público

El sistema jurídico: inocente hasta demostrar su culpabilidad

Fianza de $50,000 o a la cárcel

el soborno — la jueza — el fiscal — el defensor — el acusado

inocente: tiene una coartada *(alibi)* sólida

La acusación formal

A. ¿Cómo se dice?   Escriba la palabra que corresponda a cada una de las definiciones.

1. El abogado que defiende a un acusado es un _____.

2. La confirmación de que un sospechoso es inocente por estar en un sitio diferente al crimen es un _____.

3. Si un criminal le ofrece dinero u otro incentivo a un oficial para evitar su detención, comete el delito de _____.

4. El dinero que paga un acusado para mantenerse libre mientras espera su juicio es una _____.

B. Relaciones. Con un poco de lógica, se puede comprender la relación entre muchos términos legales en inglés y español. Estudie los siguientes términos y dé su equivalente en inglés.

1. el abogado defensor   **4.** la duda razonable

2. el historial criminal   **5.** los cargos criminales

3. la causa probable

La defensa

Después de su detención por el homicidio de Paulina, su mejor amiga y compañera de casa, Carmen, tiene la primera reunión con su abogado defensor, proporcionado por la corte. El abogado tomó las siguientes notas durante su encuentro inicial.

Reunión Con Carmen Duarte   Cárcel Central   14 abril   8:15

Delito: acusada de homicidio

*Primero quise establecer su estado mental con unas preguntas inocentes; me **dijo** su nombre y dirección y su profesión. Le pregunté si necesitaba algo y me **pidió** las fotos de su novio de su escritorio. Le **dije** que tal vez en unos días. Entonces **seguí** con unas preguntas de prueba: ¿Comprende los cargos en su contra?*

***Repitió** varias veces que sí—que mató a su amiga. También **dijo** que no recuerda el cargo adicional de intentar sobornar a un oficial policial. Le pregunté si ésta es la primera vez que está encarcelada y me **dijo** que sí—es la primera vez que tiene problemas legales.*

***Mintió.** Leí su historial criminal y tiene antecedentes de violencia: **Sirvió** treinta días encarcelada en Puerto Rico por asaltar a la novia de su "ex". En ese momento **preferí** no confrontarla con la verdad. Después me habló un poco de su novio y su mejor amiga y de que no **durmió** nada pensando en ellos. Por fin le expliqué el proceso de la acusación formal donde va a declararse culpable o inocente y muy francamente me **dijo** que es culpable. De eso, no hay duda. No tengo que establecer "duda razonable" ni comprobar su culpa. Sólo tengo que comprobar su inestabilidad mental.*

C. ¿Comprende usted?   Conteste las preguntas según la información del diálogo.

1. ¿Comprende Carmen los cargos?
2. Además *(Apart from)* del cargo de homicidio, ¿qué otro cargo tiene?
3. ¿Cómo sabe el defensor que mintió?
4. ¿Por qué no durmió Carmen?
5. ¿Qué quiere comprobar el defensor?

D. Francotirador de 16 años.   Arrestaron a un joven por el asesinato de un agente de CHP. Después de leer un poco de esta tragedia, hable con su compañero/a de otros incidentes de francotiradores. ¿Cuál es su motivo?

MODELO: *Lee Boyd Malvo tenía solamente 17 años en 2002 cuando él y John Allen Muhammad asesinaron a varias personas en el área de Washington, D.C. No entiendo por qué lo hicieron.*

Joven arrestado por asesinar a un oficial de CHP
22 abril, 2004

La policía hoy arrestó a un joven de 16 años como el sospechoso del asesinato de un oficial de la Patrulla de Carretera de California. Thomas Steiner, de 35 años, recibió tres disparos al salir de dar testimonio en la corte relacionado con multas de tráfico. Estaba en uniforme, con su pistola y todo su equipo de seguridad, según Art Acevedo, jefe de CHP.

"Hemos perdido a uno de nuestra familia", dijo el jefe de patrulla Mike Brown. La esposa de Steiner y sus padres estaban a su lado en el momento de su fallecimiento. Deja a un hijo de 3 años y un hijastro de 13 años.

"Un cobarde despreciable *(despicable)* lo asesinó a sangre fría, sólo para impresionar a sus compañeros de pandilla", dijo el comisario Helmick. Steiner fue el 201 oficial de CHP que murió estando de servicio en los 75 años de historia de la agencia. El gobernador Schwarzenegger participó, con cientos de policías, en su servicio funerario.

Estructuras   *Relating past activities: Verbos en -ir con cambios en el pretérito*

- The **-ar** and **-er** verbs that have stem changes in the present tense do not have them in the preterite. Use the regular infinitive stem to form the preterite.

El defensor **empezó** una conversación.   *The defense attorney started a conversation.*

La acusada **entendió** los cargos.   *The accused understood the charges.*

* Only **–ir** verbs have stem changes in the preterite tense. In stem-changing **–ir** verbs, **e** becomes **i** and **o** becomes **u** only in the third person (**él, ella, usted, ellos, ellas, ustedes**) preterite forms.

pedir → pedí, pediste, p**i**dió, pedimos, p**i**dieron
dormir → dormí, dormiste, d**u**rmió, dormimos, d**u**rmieron

Yo **pedí** su historial criminal.	*I asked for her "rap sheet."*
El guardaespaldas **pidió** agua.	*The bodyguard asked for water.*
Yo no **dormí** en la cárcel.	*I did not sleep in the jail.*
Carmen no **durmió** bien la primera noche.	*Carmen did not sleep well the first night.*

* Additional verbs that follow this pattern are:

e → i   servir, repetir, preferir, seguir, mentir, elegir, sentir
o → u   morir

* Verbs ending in **–cir** have a spelling change to **j.** Note that **decir** changes **e → i** in the stem. The verb **traer** also has this change to **j.** Use the following endings with these verbs.

–e, –iste, –o, –imos, –eron

traducir *(to translate)*	traduje, tradujiste, tradujo, tradujimos, tradujeron
decir *(to say or tell)*	dije, dijiste, dijo, dijimos, dijeron
traer *(to bring)*	traje, trajiste, trajo, trajimos, trajeron

* Additional verbs that follow this pattern are:

conducir *(to drive)* and **producir** *(to produce)*

Para practicar

A. En la cárcel.   Estoy en la cárcel esperando mi acusación formal. Diga usted si "yo" (el/la acusado/a) hice las siguientes cosas o si los miembros de la guardia las hicieron anoche. ¡OJO! Hay verbos de todo tipo aquí, no sólo los de arriba.

MODELO: tomar las huellas digitales
Los miembros de la guardia tomaron mis huellas digitales.

1. dormir por ocho horas
2. servir una comida terrible
3. pedir una llamada telefónica
4. preparar mis récords
5. investigar el historial criminal
6. seguir las instrucciones del investigador
7. pedir un defensor público para ayudarme
8. seguir las instrucciones de la policía

B. En el trabajo. Pregúntele a un/a compañero/a si hizo estas cosas en el trabajo. ¡OJO! Hay verbos de todo tipo aquí, no sólo los de arriba.

MODELO: decirles mentiras a los sospechosos
¿Les dijiste mentiras a los sospechosos?
No, no les dije mentiras a los sospechosos.

1. traducir por una víctima que no habla inglés
2. traer fotos de su familia a la oficina
3. conducir una patrullera
4. servir café a los miembros de la rueda de presos
5. leerles la Declaración de Derechos Miranda a los acusados
6. estar en el trabajo por más de 15 horas en un día
7. ponerle las esposas a una víctima

C. Un buen defensor. Con un/a compañero/a, invente a un defensor excelente y después escriba 5 cosas que hizo por uno de sus clientes.

MODELO: *Raúl es un defensor excelente. Estuvo tres horas con un cliente angustiado.*

Módulo 2

El fiscal

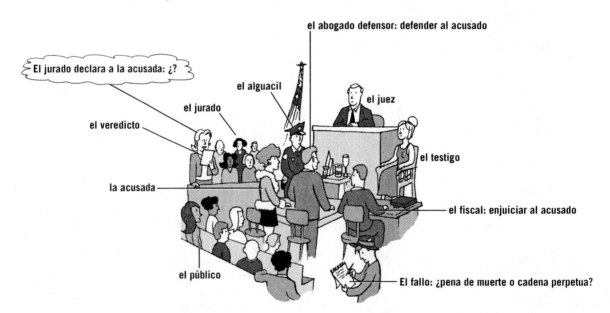

El jurado declara a la acusada: ¿?

el veredicto

el jurado

el alguacil

el abogado defensor: defender al acusado

el juez

el testigo

la acusada

el fiscal: enjuiciar al acusado

el público

El fallo: ¿pena de muerte o cadena perpetua?

A. ¿Cómo se dice? Escriba la palabra que corresponda a cada una de las definiciones.

1. El _____ es un abogado del estado que busca la condena de la acusada.

2. El _____ es el oficial encargado del proceso del juicio.

3. El grupo de doce personas que escucha la evidencia y determina la culpabilidad de un acusado es el _____.

4. El _____ es el proceso general en la corte que intenta determinar la culpabilidad o la inocencia de un acusado.

5. El presidente del jurado presenta el _____ de "culpable o inocente" al juez sobre cada uno de los cargos oficiales.

B. Más relaciones. Con un poco de lógica, se puede comprender la relación entre muchos términos legales en inglés y español. Estudie los siguientes términos y dé su equivalente en inglés.

1. duda razonable   **4.** pena capital
2. cadena perpetua   **5.** apelar la decisión
3. pena de muerte

El juicio

---

12 de mayo

Asesina "Caviar": ¡Culpable!

Chicago

El juicio de la "Asesina Caviar" **concluyó** ayer con un veredicto de "culpable". Los abogados defensores de Carmen Contreras, 22, **afirmaron** que la muerte de Paulina Prado, 23, **fue** accidental, pero los fiscales **presentaron** evidencia indicando un acto premeditado.

Según el fiscal, Paulina, la mejor amiga y compañera de cuarto de la acusada, **recibió** una promoción de empleo para encabezar la oficina de Puerto Rico. Ese mismo día, Raúl Gómez, colega de las amigas y novio de Carmen, **salió** de vacaciones a San Juan y **dejó** con Carmen la llave de su apartamento. Cuando Carmen **supo** que Paulina y Raúl **hicieron** planes de matrimonio y de una vida nueva en el Caribe, **se puso** furiosa. Entonces **hizo** un plan para matar a su amiga y rival. **Arregló** una celebración, **compró** champaña y caviar e **invitó** a Paulina a una fiesta en el apartamento de Raúl. Allí, **simuló** un asalto sexual y un robo y **plantó** evidencia que **implicó** a su novio. No obstante, *(however)* Raúl declaró su amor por la acusada y la **visitó** en la cárcel tres veces.

El jurado en el caso **deliberó** por menos de una hora antes de volver con el veredicto de culpable. Al escuchar el veredicto, la acusada no **demostró** ninguna emoción, pero su defensor **dijo** enfáticamente que va a apelar la decisión. El juez va a dictar el fallo en junio.

C. ¿Comprende usted?   Conteste las preguntas según la información del diálogo.

1. ¿Qué afirmaron los abogados defensores de Carmen?
2. ¿Qué probaron los fiscales?
3. ¿Por qué asesinó Carmen a Paulina?
4. ¿A quién quiso implicar Carmen?
5. ¿Qué va a hacer la defensa a causa del veredicto de culpable?

D. Guía de servicios del tribunal.   Se habla español en todas las oficinas del tribunal superior. A continuación vemos la guía de servicios—después de leer, evalúe los que se ofrecen y los que faltan, si los hay. Hable con su compañero/a para ver si sus opiniones coinciden.

MODELO: *Es muy práctico tener una guardería infantil.*

Guía para la comunidad sobre los programas y servicios del tribunal

Servicio de abogados
Hay un teléfono exclusivo para comunicarse con el servicio de referencia de la Asociación de abogados—una consulta de 30 minutos le cuesta $30.

Servicio de intérpretes
Hay servicios de interpretación para procedimientos jurídicos en 34 idiomas.

Folletos
Nuestros intérpretes tradujeron al español muchos documentos para uso en las salas del juzgado y folletos con información sobre los programas y servicios.

Centros de orientación legal
Información sobre diferentes asuntos legales: adopción, guardián público, cambio de nombre, reclamos menores, apelaciones, casos civiles, servicio de jurados, infracciones de tránsito, etc.

Escuela de información sobre los reglamentos de tránsito
Para borrar una infracción de tránsito de su expediente, puede asistir a clases una vez cada 18 meses.

Guardería infantil
Un servicio gratuito para padres de familia con necesidad de niñero al atender sus asuntos en el tribunal.

Servicio al público
En todos los mostradores *(counters)* hay tarjetas en español para dar su opinión del servicio que recibe. Nosotros valoramos su opinión.

Estructuras   *More past activities: Usos del pretérito*

Spanish, like English, has more than one tense to describe action in the past. Use the preterite tense to:

* Describe single events in the past that are considered complete.

Carmen **mató** a Paulina.	*Carmen murdered Paulina.*
El jurado **decidió** el veredicto.	*The jury decided the verdict.*

* Describe events that took place a specific number of times.

El novio la **visitó** en la cárcel **tres veces** esta semana.	*The boyfriend visited her in jail three times this week.*
Estuvo en la corte dos veces.	*He was in the courtroom twice.*

* Express the beginning or end of an action.

El juicio **empezó** en febrero y terminó ayer.	*The trial started in February and ended yesterday.*
El nuevo defensor **empezó** hace dos semanas.	*The new defense lawyer started two weeks ago.*

* Narrate a series of events.

Carmen **organizó** la fiesta, **compró** el caviar e **invitó** a la víctima.	*Carmen organized the party, bought the caviar, and invited the victim.*
Plantó la evidencia y **fue** a casa.	*She planted evidence and went home.*

* Describe mental or emotional reactions in the past.

Se enojó cuando supo la verdad.	*She got angry when she found out the truth.*
Se puso nervioso porque nadie contestó.	*He got nervous when no one answered the phone.*

Para practicar

A. El reportero.   Usted es un reportero que describe el juicio de Carmen. Use el pretérito para describir lo que pasó.

MODELO: Carmen/no demostrar ninguna emoción.
            Carmen no demostró ninguna emoción.

1. el juez/dar instrucciones al jurado
2. el alguacil/leer los cargos
3. el fiscal/presentar evidencia
4. el defensor/apelar el fallo
5. el jurado/escuchar los argumentos
6. el novio/venir a la corte

B. ¿Y usted?   Dígale a su jefe lo que usted hizo esta mañana durante el juicio.

MODELO: tomar muchas notas
Tomé muchas notas.

1. observar a los miembros del jurado
2. revisar la historia de la acusada
3. sacar fotos de los testigos
4. hacer una cita con un informante
5. investigar el historial criminal de un testigo
6. organizar los apuntes, escribir el reporte y mandarlo al redactor *(editor)*

C. El juicio.   Usted y su compañero/a son reporteros de un periódico famoso. Hoy cubren un homicidio sensacional. Inventen un crimen o busquen un crimen en el periódico y escriban un reporte periodístico explicando punto por punto lo que pasó.

MODELO: ***Titular (Headline)****: Famoso deportista acusado de asesinar a su esposa*
Las autoridades hoy acusaron a O. J. Simpson del homicidio de su esposa Nicole…

Vocabulario Módulo I

Sustantivos

ADN	*DNA*	**el/la examinador/a**	*examiner*
el apartamento	*apartment*	**el/la fiscal**	*district attorney*
el asesinato	*murder*	**el formulario**	*form*
la autopsia	*autopsy*	**el/la fotógrafo/a**	*photographer*
la búsqueda	*search*	**el interrogatorio**	*interrogation*
el cadáver	*cadaver*	**la investigación**	*investigation*
la causa	*cause*	**el laboratorio**	*laboratory*
los celos	*jealousy*	**el motivo**	*motive*
la coartada	*alibi*	**la orden de arresto**	*arrest warrant*
el consentimiento	*consent*	**la orden de registro**	*search warrant*
la criminología	*criminology*	**el permiso**	*permission*
la culpabilidad	*guilt*	**el registro**	*search*
el/la defensor/a	*defense attorney*	**el sistema judicial**	*judicial system*
el/la detective	*detective*	**el soborno**	*bribe*
el dibujo	*sketch*	**el suicidio**	*suicide*

Verbos

analizar	*to analyze*	**demostrar (ue)**	*to demonstrate*
asesinar	*to murder*	**estrangular**	*to strangle*
cargar	*to charge, load (gun)*	**realizar**	*to carry out*
		revelar	*to develop, reveal*
dar	*to give*	**revisar**	*to check*

Adjetivos

actual	*current*	**médico/a**	*medical*
angustiado/a	*anguished*	**sólido/a**	*solid*
forense	*forensic*		

Otras expresiones

hoy	*today*	**pasado mañana**	*day after tomorrow*

Módulo 2

Sustantivos

la cadena perpetua	*life imprisonment*	**la inestabilidad**	*instability*
el cargador	*clip, magazine*	**la guardia**	*guard duty*
la condena	*sentence*	**la inocencia**	*innocence*
la custodia	*custody*	**el jurado**	*jury*
la defensa	*defense*	**la justicia**	*justice*
la duda	*doubt*	**la pena de muerte**	*death penalty*
la escopeta	*shotgun*	**la pulgada**	*inch*
el fallecimiento	*death, passing*	**el público**	*public*
el fallo	*ruling*	**el reporte**	*report*
el/la		**el resultado**	*result*
francotirador/a	*sniper*	**el rifle**	*rifle*
el/la		**el sitio**	*place*
guardaespaldas	*bodyguard*	**el veredicto**	*verdict*

Verbos

apelar	*to appeal*	**encabezar**	*to head up*
comprobar (ue)	*to prove*	**enjuiciar**	*to judge*
confrontar	*to confront*	**implicar**	*to implicate*
declarar	*to declare*	**interrogar**	*to interrogate*
deliberar	*to deliberate*	**investigar**	*to investigate*
dictar	*to pronounce, pass (sentence)*	**plantar**	*to plant*
		simular	*to simulate*

Adjetivos

desmontable	*removable*	**razonable**	*reasonable*
encarcelado/a	*jailed*	**semiautomático/a**	*semi-automatic*
fijo/a	*fixed (as in a set place or time)*	**siguiente**	*following*
		tranquilo/a	*calm*

Otras expresiones

no obstante	*not withstanding*

Síntesis

A escuchar

Escuche el diálogo entre un investigador y un sospechoso y después decida si las siguientes declaraciones son ciertas **(C)** o falsas **(F).**

1. _____ El sospechoso no conoce a la víctima.

2. _____ María Cristina es víctima de un asalto sexual.

3. _____ Ayer el sospechoso estuvo en el trabajo todo el día.

4. _____ El sospechoso supo información del crimen que no debía saber.

5. _____ El investigador arrestó al sospechoso.

A conversar

Al momento de escribir este libro, se escoge el jurado para la denuncia *(lawsuit)* contra Scott Peterson, acusado del homicidio de su mujer y su hijo (todavía sin nacer). ¿Cuál es su opinión del crimen—es él inocente o culpable? ¿Y se acuerda de los cargos contra O.J. Simpson? ¿Qué opina usted? Hable con compañeros para escuchar sus opiniones.

MODELO: *Si Peterson quiere terminar su matrimonio con Laci, no es necesario matarla.*

A leer

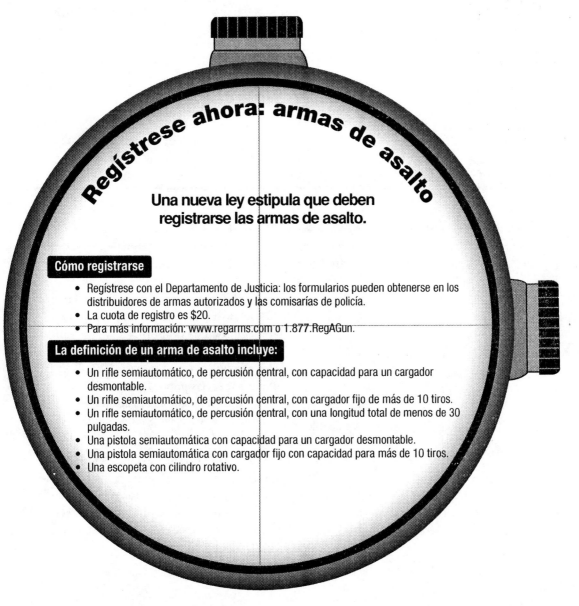

Regístrese ahora: armas de asalto

Una nueva ley estipula que deben registrarse las armas de asalto.

Cómo registrarse

- Regístrese con el Departamento de Justicia: los formularios pueden obtenerse en los distribuidores de armas autorizados y las comisarías de policía.
- La cuota de registro es $20.
- Para más información: www.regarms.com o 1.877.RegAGun.

La definición de un arma de asalto incluye:

- Un rifle semiautomático, de percusión central, con capacidad para un cargador desmontable.
- Un rifle semiautomático, de percusión central, con cargador fijo de más de 10 tiros.
- Un rifle semiautomático, de percusión central, con una longitud total de menos de 30 pulgadas.
- Una pistola semiautomática con capacidad para un cargador desmontable.
- Una pistola semiautomática con cargador fijo con capacidad para más de 10 tiros.
- Una escopeta con cilindro rotativo.

¿Comprende usted?   Si las siguientes declaraciones son ciertas, escriba una **"C"**; si son falsas, escriba una **"F"** y haga las correcciones necesarias.

1. _____ Es gratis registrar su arma de asalto.

2. _____ Un rifle semiautomático con cargador desmontable se debe registrar.

3. _____ Una pistola con cargador fijo de más de 10 tiros está exenta.

4. _____ Una escopeta con cilindro rotativo para cazar *(hunt)* no es parte de este programa.

A escribir

¿En qué se basa su decisión de estar a favor o en contra de armas de asalto? Escriba por lo menos tres razones para defender su posición.

MODELO: *Esta nación nos ofrece la libertad garantizada por la Constitución de poseer armas—por eso estoy a favor de las armas legales.*

Algo más

Ventana cultural: El poder de los latinos

El poder de los latinos...

Según el censo de 2000 (dos mil), hay más de 35.3 millones de hispanos en Estados Unidos y muchos de ellos hablan solamente español. El español es la segunda lengua de esta nación.

Para comunicarse con el público, colegas o familias, hay que hablar español. Se ve el impacto del español en los negocios, trabajando con los inmigrantes o con un nuevo ejecutivo de Colombia. Es imposible escaparse de la cultura popular en español—del chihuahua que "quiere Taco Bell" o de "la vida loca" de Ricky Martin. Las películas de Antonio Banderas y Jennifer López, así como la música de Marc Anthony, son las puertas a un mundo en español.

En las tiendas, las clínicas médicas y las escuelas se oye español por todas partes. Ahora es la lengua materna de 332 (trescientos treinta y dos) millones de personas. El español es tan importante que puede ayudarnos a obtener un trabajo—y muchas veces a recibir un salario más alto.

¿Ud. no está convencido todavía? Considere estos datos:
- Más de 3.3 millones de estudiantes en las escuelas secundarias estudian español.
- En empresas de California a Nueva York, muchos patrones pagan la matrícula para los empleados que estudian español.
- Varias agencias públicas del gobierno (government), la policía y los hospitales requieren que sus empleados estudien español.

Con un poco de español se puede hacer mucho. ¡Nuestro Presidente habla español! Y usted está en esta clase porque comprende que el mundo actual es un mundo en el que ayuda mucho saber español. ¡Adelante con el español!

En mis propias palabras. ¿Dónde ve usted la influencia de la población latina en Estados Unidos? Escriba sobre su papel *(role)* en el gobierno, en el campo político, en el mundo de los deportes, la música, las películas, la arquitectura, la comida...

A buscar

Busque datos de un crimen de mala fama en Internet en español, como los casos de O.J. Simpson, Jon Benet Ramsey, Scott Peterson, Kobe Bryant, Michael Jackson, Andrew Luster... No se olvide de que CNN tiene su sitio en español.

A conocer: Richard T. García

El nuevo jefe del FBI en Los Ángeles es el primer hispano en tener el puesto del director del departamento en el sur de California. Se encarga de la supervisión de 7 condados y 18 millones de personas; hay 1.100 empleados, de los cuales 670 son agentes. Sus casos incluyen: crimen organizado, tráfico de drogas y narcóticos. García trabajó antes en Puerto Rico, El Paso, Houston y Miami con el FBI; comenzó como policía en Dallas en 1975.

LECCIÓN 11

Tragedias

Módulo 1
- Pederastas sexuales
- Describing past situations: *El imperfecto*
- ¡Capturado!
- More on the imperfect: *Estados mentales, físicos y más*

Módulo 2
- La violación por acompañante: *¡El date-rape!*
- Narrating in the past: *El pretérito y el imperfecto*
- ¡Quería suicidarse!
- Contrasting past tenses: *El pretérito y el imperfecto*

Síntesis
- A escuchar
- A conversar
- A leer
- A escribir

Algo más
- Ventana cultural: La mordida
- A buscar
- A conocer: Anthony M. Chapa

Módulo I

Pederastas sexuales

el prófugo: Pederasta sexual de niños

la pornografía infantil

el niñero

A. ¿Cómo se dice?   Escriba la palabra que corresponda a cada una de las definiciones.

1.   Una criminal que escapa de la policía es un _Fugitive_.

2.   Una persona que cuida a los niños de otras personas es un(a)
el niñero.

3.   Un crimen sexual contra un menor perpetrado por un padre o hermano es
el _profugo_.

4.   Un agresor que comete actos sexuales violentos contra menores es un
pederastas.

5.   La venta de vídeos de _pornografia_ infantil es una industria que crece rápidamente por medio de Internet.

B. Relaciones.   Use la imaginación y la memoria para emparejar las frases en español con las frases in inglés.

1. ___C___ alias

2. ___d___ Registro de Agresores Sexuales

3. ___e___ libertad condicional

4. ___a___ libertad supervisada

5. ___b___ domicilio

a. supervised release

b. residence

c. alias

d. sex offender registry

e. probation

LOS PRÓFUGOS MÁS BUSCADOS POR LA POLICÍA

Acusado de: Violación de libertad supervisada; Delitos sexuales contra menores; Tentativa de secuestro de menores; Pornografía infantil

HERIBERTO ARREGUÍN CARRERAS

Aliases: Victor Carreras; Herb Arreguín; Salomón Victor

DESCRIPCIÓN

Pelo:	Negro	**Ojos:**	Verdes
Estatura:	6'0"	**Raza:**	Blanca
Peso:	200 libras		
Marcas notables:	Tatuaje de serpiente en la mano derecha; cicatriz en la cara.		
Último domicilio:	**Vivía** en 555 Avenida Maple, Trenton, New Jersey. No se conoce su residencia actual.		

Comentarios: Por no cumplir con el registro obligatorio como Delincuente Sexual, está en violación de su libertad supervisada. Se ha emitido una Orden de Arresto. No se sabe su domicilio actual ni el estado donde vive. Hay indicadores de que su agresión sexual contra menores aumenta. Es posible que se encuentre en México.

Modo de proceder: **Tenía** varias maneras de tentar a los niños a ir a su casa:

1. Con frecuencia **pasaba** horas en el parque hablando con las madres y los hijos para establecer confianza. Después de unos meses de relación, **ofrecía** sus servicios de niñero dando a la madre la oportunidad de salir de la casa sin niños.

2. Otras veces, **empezaba** conversaciones con niños que **esperaban** su transporte escolar. Les **ofrecía** regalos o dulces o abrazos paternales. Después de ganar la confianza de los niños, los **invitaba** a pasar el día con él en vez de ir a la escuela.

3. **Usaba** también numerosos pretextos: **decía** que su perro **estaba** perdido y que **necesitaba** ayuda para localizarlo o que la madre del niño **estaba** enferma y que él **iba** a llevar al niño a casa.

Hay evidencia de que una vez en su casa, los niños **eran** víctimas de toda clase de actos sexuales violentos incluyendo la sodomía y la violación. El agresor sexual entonces **grababa** a los niños en vídeo y **vendía** la pornografía en su sitio web.

RECOMPENSA

Se ofrece recompensa de un máximo de $10.000 por cualquier información que lleve directamente al arresto del sospechoso.

DEBE CONSIDERARSE ARMADO Y SUMAMENTE PELIGROSO

C. ¿Comprende usted? Conteste las preguntas según la información del fugitivo de la página anterior.

1. ¿Por qué busca la policía a Heriberto?

2. ¿Cuáles son los otros nombres que usa?

3. ¿Dónde vive ahora?

4. ¿Cuál era su última dirección conocida?

5. ¿Cuáles son tres de los delitos sexuales que cometía frecuentemente?

D. Encontrada por fin. El asesino acusado de la matanza de Dru Sjodin ya tenía récord como depredador sexual—sirvió 23 años en prisión por violar a dos mujeres e intentar violar a otra. Después de leer el artículo, hable con un/a compañero/a de soluciones posibles para evitar tales crímenes.

MODELO: *Lo mejor es no dejar salir de la prisión NUNCA a los pervertidos sexuales.*

MYNEWS.com

Search the Web and MYNEWS.com [   ] GO

| NEWS SUMMARY |
| US |
| INTERNATIONAL |
| MONEY |
| WEATHER |
| LOCAL NEWS |
| ENTERTAINMENT |
| SPORTS |
| POLITICS |
| HEALTH |
| TRAVEL |

Encontrada por fin

Cinco meses después de su rapto, se encuentra el cadáver de Dru Sjodin. Dru Sjodin, 22, desapareció el 22 de noviembre de 2003, al salir de su trabajo en Victoria's Secret en un centro comercial en Grand Forks, North Dakota. Hablaba por teléfono con su novio cuando se cortó la conexión.

Alfonso Rodríguez, 50, fue acusado de su secuestro el 1 de diciembre cuando las autoridades encontraron en su carro un cuchillo y sangre con ADN de Sjodin. Más tarde se encontró la funda *(sheath)* del cuchillo en el estacionamiento del centro. La funda se vendía en una tienda local, pero solamente con el tipo de cuchillo que se encontró en el carro de Rodríguez.

La búsqueda de Sjodin se interrumpió durante el invierno a causa del mal tiempo. Sus restos se localizaron en un barranco, el primer día que se reanudó *(restarted)* la búsqueda. Linda Walker, la madre de Dru, dijo: "Duele tanto". Su novio dijo: "Es la peor cosa que un ser humano puede imaginar".

Estructuras
Describing past situations: El imperfecto

* To talk about things that *used to be,* use the imperfect. While the preterite is used to describe the completed aspect of an event, the imperfect is used to indicate the habitual, repeated or ongoing nature of events or actions in the past.

* The formation of the imperfect tense is simple:

	tomar	**comer**	**vivir**
yo	tom**aba**	com**ía**	viv**ía**
tú	tom**abas**	com**ías**	viv**ías**
él/ella/Ud.	tom**aba**	com**ía**	viv**ía**
nosotros/as	tom**ábamos**	com**íamos**	viv**íamos**
ellos/ellas/Uds.	tom**aban**	com**ían**	viv**ían**

* The only three irregular verbs in the imperfect are:

	ir	ser	ver
yo	iba	era	veía
tú	ibas	eras	veías
él/ella/Ud.	iba	era	veía
nosotros/as	íbamos	éramos	veíamos
ellos/ellas/Uds.	iban	eran	veían

* The imperfect may be expressed in a variety of ways in English.

Habitual actions:

Él iba al parque cuando **quería** ver a los niños.	*He (often) went to the park when he wanted to see children.*
	He would go to the park when he wanted to see children.
	He used to go to the park when he wanted to see children.
El pederasta **vendía** pornografía infantil por la Web.	*The predator sold child pornography on the Web. (more than once)*
	The predator would sell child pornography on the Web. (more than once)
	The predator used to sell child pornography on the Web.

* Use the imperfect to express time and age in the past.

Yo **tenía** diez años entonces.	*I was ten years old then.*
Eran las tres de la tarde.	*It was three in the afternoon.*

* The imperfect tense of "hay" is **había** for both the singular and plural forms.

Había un sospechoso en el parque.	*There was a suspect in the park.*
Había varios sospechosos en el parque.	*There were several suspects in the park.*

Para practicar

A. Cuando era joven.   Indique si estas declaraciones eran verdad cuando usted era joven. Si no, corrija la oración.

MODELO: yo/ver pornografía en la televisión
Yo no veía pornografía en la televisión.

1.   nosotros/jugar en el parque Nosotros no jvegamos en l parque
2.   mis padres/permitir las drogas en la casa

3. Nosotros siempre/tener grafiti en la casa
4. yo/ir a la escuela en el transporte escolar
5. nosotros/ver programas de crimen en la televisión
6. Mis padres/protegerme de depredadores sexuales

B. Entonces y ahora. La tecnología es responsable por muchos cambios en el trabajo de los policía durante los últimos 100 años. Indique usted qué diferencias había en el pasado, en cuanto a estas descripciones de la policía de hoy.

MODELO: Hoy muchos policías llevan chalecos antibalas.
Antes, pocos policías llevaban chalecos antibalas.

1. Ahora pueden tomar las huellas digitales.
2. Ahora es fácil identificar a un sospechoso con pruebas forenses.
3. Ahora con cámaras de vídeo en la patrullera es posible ver la escena otra vez.
4. Ahora muchos agentes tienen Tasers.
5. Ahora muchas personas acosan a sus víctimas por Internet.
6. Ahora hay computadoras en las patrulleras.

C. ¿Y usted? Cuando era niño/a, ¿qué hacía usted cuando llegaba a casa después de la escuela? Haga una lista de cinco eventos o actividades que ocurrían en su casa. Después, compare su lista con la de un/a compañero/a para ver las diferentes costumbres que tenían.

MODELO: *Miraba la televisión y entonces hacía mi tarea.*

Módulo 1

¡Capturado!

la vecina alerta

el pederasta de niños

la reportera

la vocera de la policía

A. ¿Cómo se define?   Escriba una definición en español de estas palabras.

1. el reportero   **2.** el pervertido   **3.** capturado   **4.** la vocera

B. Acciones.   Escriba una oración original para cada verbo. ¡OJO! Se pueden conjugar.

1. tener miedo   **2.** acosar   **3.** esperar   **4.** preocuparse

¡Capturado!

*Muchas familias en el barrio Valle Dorado están un poco más tranquilas esta noche. Durante varias semanas, alguien **estaba** acosando a los niños allí. Ahora hay un arresto y la posible captura de uno de los prófugos más buscados de esta región. Sandy Rascón tiene los detalles.*

REPORTERA: Esta mañana, como todas las mañanas del año escolar, el grupo de amigos de Valle Dorado **esperaba** el autobús escolar. Pero esta mañana, no **era** como las otras. Los niños, entre los siete y ocho años de edad, **tenían** la compañía de un "nuevo amigo". Cuando confirmó que no **había** supervisión de adultos, Enrique David Pérez, 35, empezó a hablar con los estudiantes. Según uno de ellos, **"Estaba hablando** con nosotros de la escuela, y los deportes y... todo. María lo **conocía** del parque y **decía** que **era** un amigo de ella y su mamá. Nos **ofrecía** chocolates. **Parecía** muy simpático". Mientras Enrique Pérez hablaba con los niños, una vecina alerta que **trabajaba** en su patio reconoció el auto de nuestro Noticiero de ayer y llamó a la policía.

VECINA: Cuando vi el auto con los dragones, **sabía** que **era él**. ¡Yo **tenía** tanto miedo! No **quería** acercarme. Pero **estaba preocupada** por los niños—**sabía** que **era** peligroso. **Estaba** tan contenta cuando la policía llegó y lo capturó.

REPORTERA: La vocera de la policía expresó su agradecimiento a la vecina alerta y a la comunidad...

VOCERA: **Era** una situación peligrosísima. Todos **estábamos buscando** a este fugitivo durante más de seis semanas. Ya podemos dormir mejor esta noche.

C. ¿Comprende usted?   Conteste las preguntas según la información del diálogo.

1. ¿Dónde esperaban los niños?
2. ¿Quién era el "nuevo amigo"?
3. ¿Dónde estaba la vecina cuando lo vio?
4. ¿Por qué no tenían miedo del señor los niños?

D. Organigrama de un arresto.   La justicia criminal tiene una organización bien fija para proteger los derechos de todos. A continuación tiene los pasos en caso de una detención en la cual se toman las huellas digitales. ¿Sus prácticas son las mismas o diferentes? Compare esta información con la suya.

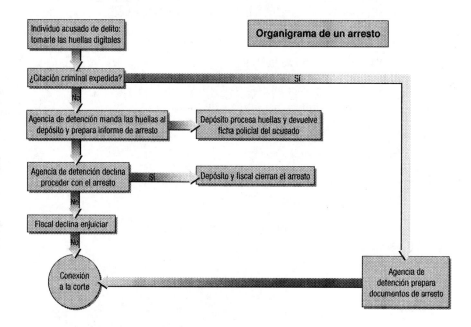

Estructuras   *More on the imperfect: Estados mentales, físicos y más*

* Use the imperfect to describe mental and physical states in the past.

Yo **tenía miedo** por los niños.	*I was frightened for the children.*
Yo **estaba contenta** cuando llegó la policía.	*I was happy when the police arrived.*

* The imperfect is used to indicate two activities in the past that were in progress at the same time. These two activities are often joined by **mientras** *(while).*

Mientras el hombre **hablaba** con los niños, la vecina **trabajaba** en su jardín.
While the man was talking to the children, the neighbor was working in her garden.
talking → while working

La vecina **prestaba** atención **mientras**   *The neighbor was paying attention while*
el reportero **describía** el vehículo.   *the reporter was describing the vehicle.*
paying attention → while describing

* Use the imperfect to indicate that an action in the past was interrupted by another event (often in the preterite) or was never completed.

El pederasta **iba** a secuestrar a la   *The predator was going to kidnap*
niña cuando llegó la policía.   *the girl when the police arrived.*
going to kidnap *(never completed)* → *(because)* the police arrived.

* In the imperfect, the verbs **conocer, saber, querer,** and **poder** have English equivalents with slightly different implications.

conocer—**Conocí** implies that you met someone.
   Conocía implies that you knew him.

saber—**Supe** implies that you found something out.
   Sabía implies that you knew it.

querer—**Quise** implies that you tried to do something.
   Quería implies that you wanted to.

poder—**Pude** implies that you managed to do something.
   Podía implies that you tried.

Para practicar

A. ¡Llegó la policía!   ¿Qué hacían estos criminales cuando llegó la policía?

MODELO: el ladrón
   El ladrón robaba una casa.

1. el asesino
2. el soplón
3. el camello
4. el pandillero
5. el pederasta

B. A la vez...   Diga qué más pasaba en el mismo *(same)* momento en que ocurrieron estas actividades.

MODELO: Mientras los niños esperaban el autobús, el pederasta...
   Mientras los niños esperaban el autobús, el pederasta los miraba.

1. Mientras la policía lo buscaba, el prófugo ...
2. Mientras los pandilleros pintaban grafiti, los vecinos...
3. Mientras los ladrones planeaban el robo, él soplón...
4. Mientras las prostitutas caminaban por la calle, los clientes...
5. Mientras un agente esposaba al criminal, el otro agente...

C. ¿Qué hacía usted? ¿Recuerda usted la última vez que capturó a un criminal? Describa las circunstancias y entonces describa cómo se sentía física y emocionalmente antes del arresto, durante el arresto y después.

MODELO: *Era un caso de ventas de drogas ilegales con unos hombres que eran peligrosos. Yo estaba preocupado antes del arresto. Durante el arresto me sentía mejor cuando los tenía en esposas. Después del arresto me sentía...*

Módulo 2

La violación por acompañante: ¡El date-rape!

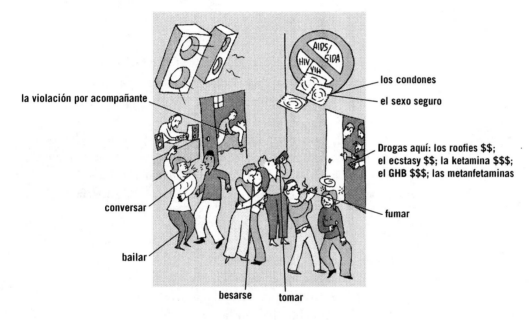

A. ¿Cómo se dice? Escriba la palabra que corresponda a cada una de las definiciones.

1. El asalto sexual por una persona conocida se llama _____.

2. Una de las drogas de "club" que facilita el sexo involuntario se llama los

_____.

3. Para practicar el sexo seguro, el hombre debe ponerse un _____.

4. Un resultado terrible del sexo sin protección puede ser la infección

_____.

5. El _____ es una de las enfermedades más problemáticas del mundo. Se asocia casi siempre con el sexo y las drogas.

B. Acciones.   Use usted la memoria para indicar el verbo que describe estas oraciones.

1.   En una fiesta, muchas personas mueven sus cuerpos al ritmo de la música.

_____.

2.   Cuando dos o más personas hablan: _____.

3.   Es la acción de inhalar y exhalar humo de cigarros o puros o marihuana o

_____.

4.   La acción de demostrar cariño *(affection)* con la boca: _____.

La violación por acompañante

Antecedentes

ELLA: Él **era** tan guapo...¡y su sonrisa **era** fabulosa! **Hablábamos** y **hablábamos** y **teníamos** tanto en común—**escuchábamos** la misma música, **estudiábamos** las mismas clases. Me **gustaba** mucho. **Quería** salir con él otra vez.

ÉL: Ella **era,** pero, ¡tan caliente! **Tenía** ese vestido sexy que **revelaba** todo su cuerpo tan fino. **Sabía** que **tenía** interés en mí por la manera en que me **sonreía** y me **tocaba** el brazo mientras **hablábamos. Parecía** tan abierta y contenta...Yo **tenía** unos vídeos en casa—ella **quería** verlos.

Acción

ELLA: Cuando me **invitó** a su casa para mirar el nuevo vídeo, **acepté. Llegamos** a su casa y **tomamos** vino...

ÉL: Y mientras **mirábamos** el vídeo, yo la **besé**... nos **besamos.** A ella le **gustaba.** Le **quité** el vestido porque **íbamos** a tener sexo...

ELLA: Cuando me **quitó** el vestido, le **dije** que ¡no!

ÉL: Para ayudarla a relajarse, **puse** un "roofie" en su vino.

ELLA: No sé qué **pasó** entonces. Me **sentí** muy rara. Cuando me **desperté, estaba** en su cama. Me **dijo** que **fue** el mejor sexo de su vida. **Empecé** a llorar. Me **bañé** y **fui** a la policía para reportar la violación por acompañante. Estoy tan mortificada. Hoy, **supe** que él **resultó** positivo de VIH *(HIV)*. Me atormenta esa noche....

ÉL: El sexo **fue** consensual—ella **vino** a mi casa. ¿Asalto sexual? ¡Ja!

C. ¿Comprende usted?   Conteste las preguntas según la información del diálogo.

1.   Según ella, ¿cómo era él al principio?
2.   Según él, ¿cómo era ella al principio?
3.   ¿Qué señales positivas daba ella?
4.   ¿Qué hicieron ellos en su casa?
5.   ¿Qué hizo él para hacerla relajarse?

D. ¡Culpable! Un jurado declaró culpable a Andrew Luster del crimen de violación por acompañante. ¿Cuáles eran sus motivaciones? Prepare sus ideas para compartir con la clase después de leer su historia.

MODELO: *Simplemente le fascinaba el control—la idea de PODER hacerlo.*

El Diario

Miércoles 20 de Marzo de 2004

Jurado declara culpable de violación al fugitivo Andrew Luster

El heredero de Max Factor, Andrew Luster, 39, fue declarado culpable de 86 cargos incluyendo violación, sodomía, posesión de drogas y armas y envenenamiento. Es posible que esté en prisión toda la vida.

Luster huyó *(fled)* durante su juicio—fue puesto en libertad después de pagar su fianza.

Lo capturaron en Puerto Vallarta. La evidencia en contra de él incluyó vídeos de él en actos sexuales con mujeres inconscientes por las drogas GHS *(gamma hydroxybutyrate)* y éxtasis. El fiscal dijo: "Estos vídeos son los más horrorosos y perturbadores que verán".

Estructuras   *Narrating in the past: El pretérito y el imperfecto*

* While the preterite and the imperfect are both aspects of the past tense, they are not interchangeable. Each gives a different message about time frames.
* The preterite is often used to describe an action that is "perfectly complete" within the sentence and captures an instant of time in the past, like a photograph.

Yo la **invité** a mi casa.	*I invited her to my house.*
Ella **aceptó** la invitación.	*She accepted the invitation.*

* The imperfect is often described in terms of a video camera. The focus is on the progression of action through time in the past, rather than on the completeness of the action.

In fact, use of the imperfect sometimes means that the action may have been abandoned before completion. (The action is *imperfectly* complete in the sentence.)

Yo **hablaba** con ella cuando llegó mi amigo.	*I was talking to her when my friend arrived.* *(action interrupted)*
Yo **tomaba** vino cuando perdí la consciencia.	*I was drinking wine when I passed out.* *(action interrupted)*

❋ Compare the following sentences and tell why the imperfect or preterite was used.

*Mientras ella **tomaba** el vino, yo **metí** un roofie.*
*Mientras **hablábamos, tomábamos** vino.*

Para practicar

A. ¿Por qué?   Explique las circunstancias que causaron estas acciones.

MODELO: Yo llamé al policía porque...
Yo llamé al policía porque mi compañero me asaltó.

1.   Yo quería salir con él porque...
2.   Yo quería salir con ella porque...
3.   Yo fui a su casa porque...
4.   Yo le quité el vestido porque...
5.   Yo estaba mortificada porque...

B. Ahora y entonces.   En el pasado, la sociedad y la investigación criminal eran muy diferentes de ahora. Diga si las siguientes personas normalmente hacían *(imperfecto)* o no hacían estas actividades hace 50 años. Entonces, diga si (probablemente) alguien hizo *(pretérito)* la actividad ayer o no.

MODELO: los investigadores/buscar evidencia ADN *(DNA)*
En el pasado, los investigadores no buscaban evidencia de ADN.
Ayer alguien buscó evidencia de ADN.

1.   los hombres/poner drogas sexuales en la bebida de sus compañeras
2.   la policía/usar computadoras para condenar a los criminales
3.   los jóvenes/ir a *raves*
4.   la policía/leer la Declaración Miranda
5.   los periodistas/reportar homicidios

C. En parejas.   Usted y su compañero/a son dos investigadores asociados con una unidad que se especializa en crímenes sexuales. Inventen una víctima interesante, los detalles de sus casos y lo que ustedes hicieron por ellos. Comparen a sus víctimas con las "víctimas" de otros investigadores en la clase.

MODELO: E1:   *Mi último caso era de una joven de 15 años que conoció a su novio por Internet y salió de su casa para ir a conocerlo en persona en Las Vegas.*
E2:   *¡Y el mío era de una prostituta que todavía trabajaba después de saber que tenía SIDA!*

Módulo 2

¡Quería suicidarse!

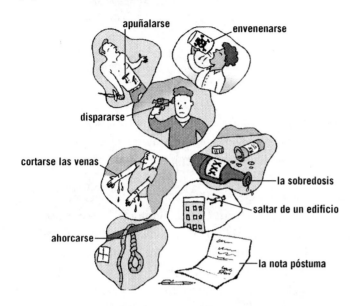

A. ¿Cómo se dice?   Escriba la palabra que corresponda a cada una de las definiciones.

1.   Meterse a la fuerza un cuchillo o una navaja en el corazón para matarse es

_____ .

2.   Para _____ un suicida necesita tomar muchas sustancias tóxicas.

3.   Perder la sangre del cuerpo al abrir las muñecas *(wrists)* es _____ .

4.   Tomar muchas píldoras y también alcohol resulta en una _____ .

B. Describa.   Escriba una definición de lo siguiente en sus propias palabras.

1.   el suicidio
2.   la violación por acompañante
3.   la nota póstuma

Quería suicidarme

Después de la violación violenta a manos de su "amigo", Cristina sufría física y emocionalmente. No dormía, revivía constantemente los momentos terribles, tenía miedo de salir de la casa... Un año después, cuando supo que su agresor sufría de SIDA, se puso tan deprimida que no pudo aguantar (stand) el dolor. Ésta es su historia, como la cuenta a una reportera:

CRISTINA: Yo **pensé:** "Si esta **iba** a ser mi vida, ya no la **quería"**. **Tomé** la decisión de suicidarme.

REPORTERA: ¿Qué **hizo?**

CRISTINA: No le **dije** nada a nadie. **Pasé** tiempo con mi familia y con mis amigos como si nada. **Usé** Internet para investigar suicidios sin dolor y **llamé** a mi médico. Le **dije** que **perdí** mis tranquilizantes, y me **dio** más.

REPORTERA: ¿Cuántas pastillas **tomó?**

CRISTINA: No lo sé... muchas... y mucho alcohol. **Tenía** miedo—mucho miedo. Pero primero **escribí** una nota de despedida a mi familia y a mis amigos y les **pedí** perdón; que no **era** su culpa. Entonces **escribí** un e-mail a una amiga que **conocí** en el "chat-room" del sitio web de suicidio. No sé cómo lo **hizo,** pero ella **estaba** preocupada cuando **leyó** mi nota y **se comunicó** con la policía. Ellos **investigaron** mi identidad y **llamaron** a la policía de mi ciudad. Un oficial **llegó** a mi casa, me **encontró,** y me **dio** primeros auxilios hasta que **vino** la ambulancia. A este policía —ahora un buen amigo—le debo mi vida. Y, gracias a él y su apoyo, es una vida que quiero mucho.

C. ¿Comprende usted?   Si las siguientes declaraciones son ciertas, escriba una **"C"**; si son falsas, escriba una **"F"** y haga las correcciones necesarias.

1. Cristina sufría mucho después del incidente con su "amigo".
2. Después de la violación, Cristina habló del incidente incesantemente.
3. Ella decidió ahorcarse cuando supo que el "amigo" sufría de SIDA.
4. Un policía la rescató.
5. Cristina no está contenta con su vida ahora.

D. Los padres pueden proteger a sus hijos en la "Web".   El Procurador General ofrece sugerencias para la seguridad de los niños en Internet. Piense en dos ideas más para ayudar a los padres y explíqueselas a sus compañeros.

MODELO: *Traficar con pornografía es ilegal—reporte los sitios a la policía.*

Los padres pueden proteger a sus hijos en la "Web"

* Ponga su computadora en un lugar central, como su sala, para facilitar la vigilancia de sus hijos cuando están en Internet.
* Use programas especiales para bloquear acceso a la pornografía.
* Conecte a sus hijos a Internet usted mismo y no deje que ellos sepan su contraseña *(password)*.
* Enseñe a sus hijos a no proveer ningún tipo de información personal sin su permiso.
* Tenga cuidado de las salas de charla donde los individuos tratan de arreglar una cita en persona con sus hijos. El Internet es un patio de recreo para los pedófilos.

Estructuras   *Contrasting past tenses: El pretérito y el imperfecto*

* When you tell a story in the past, you will often use both the preterite and the imperfect aspects of the past, even in the same sentence.
* Use the preterite to describe events that took place in sequence.

Tomé la decisión, **llamé** al médico y **escribí** una nota póstuma.

I made the decision, called the doctor and wrote a suicide note.

* Use the imperfect to set the scene, giving background information against which the action takes place.

Era un día normal. **Brillaba** el sol. **Hacía** calor. Yo **trabajaba** en mi oficina.

It was a normal day. The sun was shining. It was hot. I was working in my office.

* Note that in the preceding scene, nothing has happened. Only the stage has been set for the action to happen against.

De repente, un hombre **entró** en la comisaría. Me **gritó** muy agitadamente. Cuando **se calmó** me **explicó** que su amiga deprimida *(depressed)* **tomó** pastillas.

Suddenly, a man opened the door to the station. He shouted at me very nervously. When he calmed down, he explained that his depressed friend took pills.

* Remember that it is sometimes helpful to think of the imperfect as an activity or state that goes on through time, and the preterite as an action that is over and done with in an instant.

Para practicar

A. Caperucita Roja. Use la forma correcta del verbo en paréntesis en el pretérito o el imperfecto para terminar esta versión criminal de Caperucita Roja *(Little Red Riding Hood)*.

Érase una vez 1. _____ (haber) una muchacha que

2. _____ (ser) muy bonita y que 3. _____ (llamarse)

Caperucita Roja. Ella y su mamá 4. _____ (vivir) en una casa muy

vieja en el desierto. Todos los días, Caperucita Roja 5. _____

(caminar) por el desierto. Allí, ella 6. _____ (jugar) con los animales

y siempre 7. _____ (estar alerta) a la actividad criminal en su

barrio. Un día su mamá le 8. _____ (decir): "Caperucita Roja, hace

dos minutos yo 9. _____ (saber) que tu abuela

10. _____ (sufrir) un accidente de tráfico esta mañana. La policía la

11. _____ (mandar) al hospital y después a su casa en una

patrullera. Tú tienes que ir a su casa y llevarle las cosas que necesita. También, por

favor, quiero que le lleves esta sopa de pollo que yo le 12. _____

(hacer)". Caperucita Roja 13. _____ (ponerse) sus zapatos de tenis

Reebok y 14. _____ (ir) inmediatamente en dirección a la casa de

su abuela. En el camino, ella 15. _____ (ver) al criminal coyote que

seguramente 16. _____ (tener) planes malévolos. Ella, que no

17. _____ (saber) que sería peligroso hablarle, le

18. _____ (decir): "Voy a la casa de mi abuela para traerle estas

cosas que mi madre le 19. _____ (hacer)". Cuando Caperucita

Roja 20. _____ (llegar) a la casa de su abuela, ya había muchos

policías que 21. _____ (tener) al coyote en esposas. Él

22. _____ (estar) furioso. Mientras el coyote

23. _____ (entrar) por la ventana, el sistema de vigilancia

electrónica 24. _____ (llamar) a la policía. Ellos

25. _____ (responder) inmediatamente y 26. _____

(arrestar) al pobre coyote. Por ser su tercera condena por un delito mayor, va a

pasar el resto de su vida en la cárcel.

B. ¿Y usted?   Con cinco oraciones o menos, diga la acción principal de un cuento tradicional de niños, sin dar los nombres de los personajes. Después, sus compañeros deben identificar el cuento. ¡Es mejor si tiene tema criminal!

Vocabulario Módulo 1

Sustantivos

el agradecimiento	*gratitude*	**el/la pederasta**	*predator*
la captura	*capture*	**el/la pervertido/a**	*pervert*
el depósito	*depository*	**la pornografía**	*pornography*
el/la depredador/a	*predator*	**el/la prófugo/a**	*fugitive*
los dulces	*candy*	**el rapto**	*abduction*
el incesto	*incest*	**el regalo**	*gift*
el modo de	*modus operandi*	**el/la reportero/a**	*reporter*
proceder	*(m.o.)*	**la sodomía**	*sodomy*
el/la niñero/a	*babysitter*	**la tragedia**	*tragedy*
el noticiero	*news program*	**el/la vocero/a**	*spokesperson*
el organigrama	*organizational chart*		

Verbos

acercarse	*to approach*	**encontrar (ue)**	*to find*
aumentar	*to increase*	**grabar**	*to record*
confirmar	*to confirm*	**prestar atención**	*to pay attention*
doler (ue)	*to hurt, cause pain*	**tentar (ie)**	*to tempt*

Adjetivos

capturado/a	*captured*	**infantil**	*child*
escolar	*school*	**último/a**	*last*

Otras expresiones

a causa de	*on account of*	**en vez de**	*in place of*

Módulo 2

Sustantivos

el abuso	*abuse*	**el jurado**	
el/la acompañante	*companion*	**investigador**	*grand jury*
el/la agresor/a	*aggressor*	**el lío**	*hassle*
el condón	*condom*	**la metanfetamina**	*methamphetamine*
la confianza	*confidence*	**la mordida★**	*bribe*
la despedida	*farewell*	**la nota**	*note*
el/la heredero/a	*heir*	**el/la pedófilo/a**	*pedophile*

★ denotes slang

la píldora	pill		
el puro	cigar	el sueldo	salary
los restos	remains	el/la terapeuta	therapist
el sexo	sex	el tranquilizante	tranquilizer
SIDA	AIDS	la vena	vein
la sonrisa	smile	VIH	HIV

Verbos

abusar	to abuse	enfrentar	to face
aguantar	to endure, stand	envenenar	to poison
ahorcar	to hang	fascinar	to fascinate
almacenar	to store	relajarse	to relax
anular	to annul	saltar	to jump
apuñalar	to stab	sonreír (i)	to smile
bailar	to dance	suicidarse	to commit suicide
desmembrar (ie)	to dismember		

Adjetivos

caliente	hot	perturbador/a	disturbing
consensual	consensual	póstumo/a	posthumous
deprimido/a	depressed	raro/a	strange
exonerado/a	exonerated	seguro/a	safe
horroroso/a	horrendous	traslado/a	transferred
mortificado/a	mortified		

Otras expresiones

de repente	suddenly	en común	in common

Síntesis

A escuchar

Escuche el siguiente árticulo de CNN y decida si las declaraciones a continuación son ciertas (C) o falsas (F).

1. Un jurado declaró la inocencia de Michael Jackson.
2. Ésta es la primera vez que Jackson fue acusado de abusar de niños.
3. Los abogados de Jackson tienen miedo de que esta vez él no sea exonerado.
4. El fiscal de Santa Barbara dice que es muy probable que Jackson no vaya a la cárcel por la posibilidad de la libertad condicional.

A conversar

🚶🚶🚶 Un pedófilo, Edward Stokes, que admitió ante su terapeuta que abusó sexualmente de más de 200 víctimas fue liberado porque anularon su última convicción al no poder confrontar a su víctima en la corte. El joven se suicidó antes de su juicio.

¿Qué opina usted?

MODELO: *¡Ya lo dije—no dejarlos salir de la prisión nunca!*

A leer

Traslado al depósito de cadáveres: los cuerpos + los artefactos

Morgue: Almacenar los cuerpos hasta que se comience el trabajo

Artefactos	**Restos humanos**
Limpieza	Radiografía
Archivarlos y fotografiarlos	Fluoroscopio + Rayos X
Fotografiar las heridas y evidencia	Limpiar los restos
Identificación presunta *(alleged)*	Fotografiarlos
Copias para la unidad de identificación	Autopsia
	Descripción de los restos
	Causa de la muerte, heridas
	Examen antropológico: Edad, sexo, estatura
	Tomar muestras ADN
	Ropa
	Archivar

Resultados de la investigación:

¿Comprende usted? Llene los espacios en blanco según la información del artículo.

1. Con los artefactos, hay que _____ y _____.

2. Hay que limpiar los artefactos _____.

3. El examen antropológico es para determinar: _____, _____ y _____.

4. Es necesario tomar muestras _____ para finalizar la identificación.

5. La _____ en los restos forma parte de la evidencia.

A escribir

Cuál es el peor caso que experimentó en su carrera o que supo de las noticias? Escriba un resumen breve de un caso horroroso.

MODELO: *Lo que hizo Jeffrey Dahmer era inimaginable; luego supe de un hombre en Alemania que mató, desmembró y se comió a otro—¡dijo que éste se ofreció voluntario y que fue una muerte placentera (pleasant) para la víctima!*

Algo más

Ventana cultural: La mordida

En muchas naciones del mundo, aceptar un soborno o una mordida es tan normal que se espera. Hay varias razones, desde la corrupción con permiso oficial a los sueldos bajos de algunos puestos en el gobierno y el mundo de negocios. En Estados Unidos generalmente no se deja sobornar a las autoridades, pero siempre hay excepciones. La pregunta es: ¿Cuál va a ser su reacción si alguien le ofrece una mordida? Como vimos en la sección de peleas de animales, a veces las personas que vienen de otro país no saben ni entienden las reglas del sistema aquí y esperan que sean iguales las costumbres. Si tengo una licencia vencida *(expired)* y el policía me detiene por velocidad excesiva, ¿no se le puede dar una mordida y seguir mi camino? ¿Es otra infracción haber tratado de "comprar" mi inocencia?

En mis propias palabras. ¿Usted ofreció o le ofrecieron una mordida alguna vez? Describa la situación—¡puede ser imaginaria!

MODELO: *Pagué una mordida de $20 para no tener que ir a la comisaría en Ensenada, Baja California, la Nochebuena (Christmas Eve). Mi infracción era un cambio de sentido ilegal. Estaba contenta de no tener el lío y pensaba que era una ganga (bargain).*

A buscar

Usted necesita información de las agencias gubernamentales y no sabe dónde empezar. Escriba "Gobierno: Estados Unidos" en su motor de búsqueda y va a encontrar MUCHA información.

A conocer: Anthony M. Chapa

Anthony M. Chapa fue nombrado jefe de la oficina del Servicio Secreto en Los Ángeles. Su puesto es el más alto para un hispano en esta agencia. Está encargado de más de 100 agentes; sus responsabilidades incluyen: fraude de tarjetas de crédito y de computadora, servicios protectores, falsificación de identidad, dinero falso, instituciones financieras y transferencias electrónicas de dinero.

LECCIÓN 12

Repaso II

Lección 7: La policía y la comunidad—¡unidas!
- **Se** impersonal
- **Acabar de** + infinitivo
- **Gustar**
- De cien a millones; los números ordinales

Lección 8: La violencia doméstica
- Los verbos reflexivos
- Los verbos recíprocos
- **Saber** y **conocer**
- El objeto directo

Lección 9: Delitos
- Introducción breve al subjuntivo
- Más sobre el subjuntivo
- El subjuntivo con expresiones impersonales
- El subjuntivo con expresiones de emoción y duda

Lección 10: El crimen
- Introducción al pretérito
- Verbos irregulares
- Verbos en **–ir** con cambios en el pretérito
- Usos del pretérito

Lección 11: Tragedias
- El imperfecto
- Estados mentales, físicos y más
- El pretérito y el imperfecto
- El pretérito y el imperfecto

¿Recuerda a Lynn, la vecina del barrio Menlo que ayudaba mucho a la policía—y especialmente al oficial de su comunidad, el oficial Andrade? En este capítulo, los dos van a seguir trabajando juntos para establecer la paz y seguridad de la vecindad, y nosotros los vamos a ayudar.

Lección 7

La policía y la comunidad—¡unidas!

Módulo 1

A. Esto es un/una... Hoy hay una reunión para los vecinos del barrio Menlo. Mientras el oficial Andrade explica cómo luchar contra el crimen, usted tiene que explicarle a un vecino anciano para qué se usa cada cosa y si se vende en Home Depot.

MODELO: las alarmas de incendios

Se usan para indicar la presencia de humo en la casa. Se venden en Home Depot.

1. las llaves
2. los perros guardianes
3. el detector de movimiento
4. la cerradura
5. la policía

B. Los vecinos ideales. El oficial Andrade dice que los vecinos necesitan completar varias tareas para mejorar la seguridad del barrio. Dígale quién acaba de hacer cada recomendación.

MODELO: Ustedes necesitan limpiar el parque.

Nosotros acabamos de limpiar el parque.

1. Mateo tiene que buscar más basureros.
2. Marco tiene que ayudar a los vecinos viejos.
3. Ustedes tienen que instalar sistemas de seguridad.
4. Tú tienes que poner luces en la casa.
5. Alejandro y Justino tienen que vigilar a los niños.

C. ¿Qué se hace? Escriba una lista de cinco cosas que se hacen y cinco cosas que no se hacen para protegerse contra el crimen.

MODELO: *Se habla con los vecinos. No se dejan abiertas las puertas.*

D. Imaginación. Un cliente de una tienda grande compra un detector de movimiento, nuevas cerraduras (candados), un librito para números de teléfono, un sistema LoJack, y bolsas de plástico para la basura. Use la imaginación para identificar cinco cosas que acaban de ocurrir para llevar al cliente a la tienda con esta lista de productos. Compare su lista con la lista de un/a compañero/a.

MODELO: *Acaba de ocurrir un crimen en su barrio.*

Módulo 2

A. Los sospechosos inconformes. Usted trabaja hoy con un grupo de nuevos reclutas *(recruits)*. Explíqueles cuándo deben gritar lo siguiente.

MODELO: ¡Necesito apoyo!
Si un agente está en peligro, y quiere la ayuda de otros agentes.

1. ¡Manos arriba! **3.** ¡Suéltelo!
2. ¡Voltéese! **4.** ¡Separe los pies!

B. Gustos. Indique qué les gusta hacer a las siguientes personas para proteger sus casas y a sus vecinos. Escoja la actividad indicada de la lista.

MODELO: A las personas que viven cerca de la escuela
A las personas que viven cerca de la escuela, les gusta vigilar a los niños.

1. A nosotros, los jugadores de básquetbol | **a.** estar alerta por si pasa algo aquí
2. A mí, porque paso mucho tiempo en casa | **b.** los sistemas de monitoreo
3. A mí, como no estoy mucho en casa | **c.** tener el parque limpio y libre de drogas
4. Al oficial de la comunidad | **d.** encontrar un barrio sin vigilancia
5. A los criminales | **e.** tener vecinos cooperativos

C. El botín. Gracias a unos vecinos alertas, ustedes recuperaron un botín de joyas y otras cosas valiosas. Escriba (con ¡letras!) el número de artículos en el inventario.

MODELO: Hay 251 cámaras.
Hay doscientas cincuenta y una cámaras.

1. Hay 555 navajas.
2. Hay 100 computadoras.
3. Hay 2.763 personas que quieren reclamar estas cosas.
4. Hay $3.000.000 en efectivo *(cash)*.
5. Hay 70 relojes Rolex.

D. ¿Y usted?   A usted, ¿qué ejercicio le gusta hacer en su trabajo? Escriba una lista de tres actividades que a usted le gustan.

MODELO: *Me gusta escribir reportes de mis actividades.*

Lección 8

La violencia doméstica

Módulo I

A. Solamente hablo un poco de español.   Alejandro está trabajando como voluntario de Víctima-Testigo cuando una señora que tiene dificultad con el idioma le pide ayuda. Ponga la palabra o la frase en español que la cliente quiere describir.

MODELO: SEÑORA: Mi esposo es una persona violenta. Me grita, me golpea...
ALEJANDRO: *¿Es un maltratador?*

1.   Yo tengo marcas de los golpes por todo el cuerpo.

¿Usted tiene _____?

2.   Después de un golpe, no puedo abrir el ojo—está feo.

¿Usted tiene un _____ _____?

3.   Quiero escapar de mi casa. Mi amiga me habla de una casa especial para personas como yo.

¿Ella habla de un _____?

4.   Mi esposo siempre grita que me va a matar.

¿Él la _____?

B. La directora del albergue.   La directora de un albergue tiene una lista de productos que necesita comprar para sus clientes. Diga para qué van a usar estos productos.

MODELO: La señora Vargas quiere champú.
       Quiere lavarse el pelo.

1.   Los niños necesitan pasta dental *(toothpaste).*
2.   Mariana pide jabón *(soap).*
3.   Susana quiere pantalones y una blusa.
4.   Todos los residentes piden camas nuevas.
5.   Gloria y Susana necesitan un radio-reloj con despertador.

C. Sugerencias. La señora no sabe qué marcas debe comprar. Ayúdele y diga qué marcas usan las siguientes personas para las actividades del ejercicio B.

MODELO: Mis hermanos/productos de *Vidal Sassoon.*
Mis hermanos se peinan con productos de Vidal Sassoon.

1. Mi familia/*Crest*
2. Mi hermana/champú *Suave* y acondicionador *Pantene.*
3. Mi hermana/*Móssimo*
4. Nosotros/*Sealy Posturepedic*
5. Mi tío/con radio-reloj *SONY*

D. Buenos amigos. En el albergue, Susana y Mariana le explican a la directora por qué se llevan bien. Dicen que todo es a base del respeto mutuo y la cooperación. Use las siguientes acciones recíprocas para explicárselo al jefe y escriba dos acciones más.

MODELO: hablar con confianza
Nos hablamos con confianza.

1. consultar con preguntas   **3.** _____

2. ayudar con el trabajo   **4.** _____

Módulo 2

Buenos días. Esta mañana usted va a ser voluntario en la oficina del Mediador del Condado. Por favor, dirija estas llamadas a una de las secciones indicadas.

A. ¡Necesito ayuda! Usted trabaja hoy en la oficina del Mediador del Condado. Dígales a estos clientes cuál es la división que necesitan.

a. *el asilo de ancianos*   **b.** *servicios médicos*
c. *división de fraude*   **d.** *servicios para cuidadores*

1. _____ Marisela: La medicina de mi mamá es tan cara que ella no puede comprar lo que necesita en la farmacia.

2. _____ Celina: Estoy con mi mamá enferma las 24 horas al día. Me pongo irritada con cualquier cosa. No quiero ser así. No sé qué hacer.

3. _____ Joyce: Acabo de recibir un recibo del médico de mi mamá. Hay muchas medicinas y muchas pruebas que ella nunca recibió. Es posible que los dueños de su asilo hagan algo ilegal.

4. _____ Armando: Yo quiero cuidar a mi papá en casa, pero parece que él está cada día peor con su Alzheimer's y necesita cuidado profesional. ¿Qué puedo hacer?

B. El experto.   Cuando usted es voluntario en una agencia gubernamental, todo el mundo cree que usted es un experto en todo. Termine estas preguntas de los clientes con la forma correcta de **saber** o **conocer**.

MODELO: ¿_____ usted un buen asilo para ancianos? Quiero visitarlo para ver si le gusta a mi mamá.
¿Conoce usted un buen asilo para ancianos?

1.   Yo no _____ cambiar un pañal de adulto *(adult diaper)*. ¿Puede usted hacer una demostración?

2.   Yo busco a un buen gerontólogo para mis papás. ¿_____ usted a un buen doctor cerca de aquí?

3.   ¿_____ usted si hay un abogado pro bono para ancianos?

4.   ¿_____ usted el Hospital General? ¿Es bueno?

5.   ¿_____ usted si es peligroso darles bebidas alcohólicas a los ancianos?

C. Los acosadores.   Usted ayuda a investigar la querella *(lawsuit)* de una víctima de un acosador. Conteste con pronombres las preguntas que ella le hace.

MODELO: ¿Investigan ustedes amenazas?
Sí, las investigamos.

1.   ¿Entrevistan a los sospechosos?
2.   ¿Sacan fotos de la casa?
3.   ¿Facilitan órdenes de protección?
4.   ¿Tienen vigilancia para mi casa?
5.   ¿Escuchan mis llamadas telefónicas?

D. Otra vez los expertos.   Conteste estas preguntas de la víctima con un mandato formal y un pronombre.

MODELO: ¿Contesto el teléfono por la noche?
No lo conteste.

1.   ¿Llamo a una amiga para acompañarme?
2.   ¿Mantengo un archivo con todos los incidentes?
3.   ¿Compro una pistola?
4.   ¿Registro una querella formal?
5.   ¿Le doy mi nuevo número de teléfono a mi ex-novio?

Lección 9

Delitos

Módulo 1

A. El policía bien vestido. Hoy usted está trabajando en el departamento de equipos de seguridad para la policía. Identifique lo que estos agentes describen.

MODELO: El palo que se usa para defenderse de presos violentos
Es un bastón.

1. Cuando necesito sujetar las manos de un preso, necesito éstas.
2. Es posible que el caso que investigamos hoy se ponga violento. Necesito protección para el cuerpo en caso de un tiroteo.
3. Esta noche hay un campeonato *(championship game)* de básquetbol universitario. Si el equipo de nuestra universidad gana, sin duda habrá motines *(riots)*. Debemos tener el aparato electrónico que inmoviliza a los sujetos.
4. Hay una pareja de francotiradores que aterrorizan la ciudad. Si estoy de patrulla esta noche, quiero protegerme la cabeza y la cara.

B. El preso joven. Después del trabajo hoy, el oficial Andrade va a hablar con el hijo de un amigo que tiene problemas con la ley y está en la cárcel. Ahora le pide consejos a Andrade. Llene el espacio con el subjuntivo del verbo indicado.

1. Yo te recomiendo que _____ (admitir) la culpabilidad.

2. Te sugiero que _____ (hablar) con tu abogado.

3. Quiero que _____ (decir) los nombres de los cómplices.

4. Espero que _____ (saber) tú que soy tu amigo y que quiero ayudarte.

5. Insisto en que _____ (ser) honesto con tus padres.

C. El sexo en la calle. En sus propias palabras, escriba una definición de cada frase, o úsela en una oración.

1. el pepe   3. la redada
2. la puta   4. el chulo

Módulo 2

A. Los juegos del azar. Como agente secreto en un casino, usted busca juegos legales e ilegales. ¿Puede usted emparejar el juego con su definición y luego indicar si es legal o ilegal en su ciudad?

I. _____ el tragamonedas

a. competencia para ver el animal más veloz

2. _____ las peleas de gallos o la perrera

b. juego electrónico

3. _____ los dados

c. combate hasta la muerte entre animales

4. _____ las carreras de caballos

d. el tirador espera sacar 7 u 11

B. Formas de identificación. *Ahora hay muchos delitos de identidad falsa. Está en una clase de reconocimiento de identificación falsa y usted tiene muchas observaciones y recomendaciones para los participantes.*

MODELO: Es común que los adolescentes _____ (tener) identificación falsificada.
Es común que los adolescentes tengan identificación falsificada.

I. Es una lástima que _____ (haber) tantas víctimas inocentes del robo de identidad.

2. Es importante que _____ (verificar) ustedes la forma de identificación.

3. Es preferible que los bares _____ (usar) verificación electrónica.

5. Es urgente que usted _____ (buscar) a un policía si un cliente tiene identificación falsa.

6. Es evidente que ustedes _____ (ser) unas personas responsables.

C. En el club. *Muchos oficiales quieren ganar dinero extra, y trabajan en varios campos de la seguridad. Esta noche hay una fiesta grande en un club y el oficial Andrade está en la puerta.*

MODELO: La ley exige que ustedes _____ (tener) 21 años para entrar.
La ley exige que ustedes tengan 21 años para entrar.

I. La ley prohíbe que nosotros les _____ (vender) alcohol.

2. Insisto en que ustedes me _____ (enseñar) su identificación oficial.

3. Temo que esta tarjeta de identificación _____ (ser) falsificada.

4. Les sugiero que _____ (irse) inmediatamente.

5. Espero que ustedes _____ (comprender) los peligros del alcohol.

D. La adolescencia.   Usted y su amigo/a quieren comprar cerveza en una tienda, pero sólo tienen 16 años. Formulen un plan de acción para poder comprar la cerveza.

MODELO: E1:   *Quiero que tú compres una identificación falsa.*

Lección 10

El crimen

Módulo 1

A. El jefe viejo.   Su jefe del trabajo tiene tendencia de olvidar las palabras que busca. Llene el espacio con la palabra que él quiere decir.

MODELO: La evidencia está en la oficina de los <u>doctores que determinan la hora y la causa de la muerte.</u>
                ¿El examinador médico? ¿El forense?

1.   El <u>cuerpo muerto</u> revela todos los secretos de la muerte.
2.   Van a hacer unas pruebas en <u>el material genético</u> para verificar la identificación.
3.   La víctima perdió <u>mucho fluido vital rojo</u> por la profundidad de las heridas.
4   El examinador médico ya identificó a <u>la persona que cometió el asesinato.</u>
5.   En el depósito de cadáveres, los examinadores médicos hacen toda clase de pruebas en la evidencia <u>orgánica y material que se encontró en la escena del crimen y en el mismo cuerpo.</u>

B. La investigación.   Hoy el oficial Andrade investigó un nuevo homicidio y tiene una lista de actividades importantes que tiene que completar para la investigación. Transforme su lista de quehaceres al pretérito (forma "yo") para demostrar que todo está hecho. La lista:

MODELO: *Buscar* evidencia importante
                Busqué evidencia importante.

1.   *Ver y examinar* la escena del crimen
2.   *Entregar* la evidencia al laboratorio
3.   *Escribir* notas en un cuadernito *(notebook)*
4.   *Empezar* a entrevistar a los testigos
5.   *Sacar* fotos de la escena
6.   *Llamar* a la familia de la víctima

C. ¿Un robo?   Usted y el oficial Andrade investigaron un robo en la farmacia esta mañana, y entrevistaron a los dos empleados que estuvieron allí cuando ocurrió el crimen. Convierta este Informe de Incidente—que ahora está en el presente—al pretérito.

MODELO: *Venimos a la farmacia a las siete.*
Vinimos a la farmacia a las siete.

1. Algo *hace* ruido.

2. No *podemos* ver nada al principio.

3. Entonces *vemos* a dos personas cerca del gabinete de seguridad con las sustancias controladas.

4. *Quiero* ir a llamar a la policía y Alejandro *quiere* observar a los ladrones *(robbers)*.

5. Le *digo* al policía que *tenemos* un problema en la farmacia.

6. Ustedes *llegan* rápidamente y les *ponen* esposas a los criminales.

7. V*amos* con ustedes para hacer esta declaración.

D. Una emergencia. Describa (o invente) una emergencia en la que participó usted. Use el pretérito para decirnos 1) el problema 2) lo que usted hizo y 3) el resultado.

MODELO: *Yo descubrí un cadáver en la calle. Yo llamé al 911 y le expliqué el problema al operador. Entonces la policía llegó e investigó el crimen y arrestaron a los asesinos.*

Módulo 2

A. El proceso legal: la defensa. Usted y el oficial Andrade acaban de arrestar a un sospechoso joven y nervioso. Él no comprende lo que le va a pasar ahora. Explíquele estos términos del proceso penal.

MODELO: El defensor público
Si usted no puede pagar a un abogado para su representación legal, el defensor público le puede representar en las audiencias.

1. el soborno   **3.** el procurador
2. la fianza   **4.** la coartada

B. ¿El defensor o el acusado? Usted es un abogado que defiende a una persona detenida. Diga quién hizo lo siguiente anoche—usted o el acusado.

MODELO: preparar la defensa
Yo preparé la defensa.

1. dormir en la cárcel

2. traer los papeles legales

3. pedir un vaso de agua y más comida

4. despertarse con mucho miedo

5. declararse culpable o no culpable ante el juez

6. preparar la defensa para el cliente

7. seguir las instrucciones de los guardias en la cárcel

8. ir a comer en un restaurante antes de la audiencia

C. ¿Qué hizo el acusado ayer?   La madre del acusado quiere saber lo que hizo su hijo ayer en la cárcel. Usando estos verbos, escriba un reporte de las actividades:

dormir, mirar, comer, pedir, decir, hablar, consultar, levantarse, hacer ejercicio, estar

MODELO: *Miró la televisión por una hora.*

Lección 11

Tragedias

Módulo 1

A. Crímenes contra niños.   Hoy usted es voluntario con el grupo de 88-CRIME y cuando contesta el teléfono, un informante anónimo quiere darle información. Llene el espacio con la palabra que quiere decir.

MODELO: Yo quiero hablar con el _____ (persona encargada de la agencia).
director

1.   Acabo de ver un póster de uno de los _____ (persona que huye *(flees)* de la policía) más buscados.

2.   La información es sobre un _____ sexual de niños (pedófilo en serie).

3.   Tengo pruebas de que su computadora está llena de _____ (material sexual explícito con niños).

4.   ¿Su modo de proceder? Siempre ofrece sus servicios de _____ (persona que cuida a los chicos) para que la madre pueda tener tiempo libre.

5.   Tiene varios _____ (nombres diferentes que usa para escapar de la identificación).

B. Busca y captura.   ¡El informante que llama con el "tip" anónimo es un héroe! Gracias a su llamada, la policía capturó al depredador peligroso. Aquí está la historia de su día de ayer. Llene el espacio con el tiempo **imperfecto** del verbo.

Ayer, yo no 1. _____ (tener) mucha energía. Luego, mientras

2. _____ (trabajar), 3. _____ (sentirme) mal. Me

acosté temprano para mirar la televisión. Casi 4. _____ (estar)

dormido cuando empezó el programa: **America's Most Wanted:** Los Más

Buscados de América. Me 5._____ (interesar) el tema del progra-

ma: un pervertido que abusa sexualmente de los niños. El sujeto

6. _____ (llamarse) Rubén Jiménez, pero también

7. _____ (usar) muchos alias. La foto que mostraron

8. _____ (ser) vieja, pero no 9. _____ (haber)

ninguna duda. Yo 10. _____ (estar) muy nervioso cuando

reconocí al prófugo. El narrador del programa 12. _____ (hablar)

de mi nuevo vecino. Llamé inmediatamente al número de teléfono en la

pan talla para decirles que en este momento, el prófugo 13. _____

(encontrarse) en casa. Llegó la policía en 5 minutos.

C. ¡Sorprendidos! Estos oficiales de policía sorprendieron a los siguientes
criminales mientras cometían crímenes. Use la imaginación para describir—en
el tiempo imperfecto—lo que hacían los criminales cuando la policía entró.

MODELO: el pervertido sexual
El pervertido sexual miraba pornografía infantil.

1. el asesino   **4.** el ladrón de autos
2. el ratero   **5.** el ladrón de identidades
3. el narcotraficante

Módulo 2

A. La violación por acompañante. Muchos asaltos sexuales entre
conocidos son el resultado de la pérdida de control por las drogas o el alcohol.
Las consecuencias también pueden ser severas. Identifique estas **posibles** causas
y consecuencias de la violación.

MODELO: demostrarse cariño *(affection)* tocando labios con otra persona
besarse

1. una droga de club que facilita el sexo involuntario
2. una infección que muchas veces aparece antes del SIDA
3. una cosa a veces de látex que es importante en el "sexo seguro"
4. el asalto sexual entre personas que se conocen

B. ¿Qué pensaba el joven?   A veces los criminales no piensan antes de actuar. Lea esta historia triste de un criminal sin sesos *(brains)* y llene el espacio con la forma correcta del imperfecto o el pretérito para saber lo que le pasó.

1. _____ (ser) las tres de la mañana y un estudiante universitario

2. _____ (regresar) a su residencia estudiantil después de una fiesta

¡excelente! Él 3. _____ (estar) _____ más que un

poco borracho y no 4. _____ (manejar) bien su coche. También

5. _____ (estar) frustrado porque no 6. _____

(poder) encontrar un espacio para estacionar su carro. De repente,

7. _____ (ver) un sólo espacio y 8. _____ (llegar) allí

en el mismo instante que otro estudiante que 9. _____ (entrar) en

el espacio. Nuestro amigo 10. _____ (ponerse) tan furioso que

11. _____ (abrir) la puerta del otro coche y

12. _____ (empezar) a asaltar al otro chofer. Un testigo, horrori-

zado, 13. _____ (llamar) a la policía que 14. _____

(llegar) rápidamente. Mientras el estudiante borracho 15. _____

(luchar) con el oficial, una bolsa grande de cocaína 16. _____

(salir) de sus pantalones. El policía lo 17. _____ (detener) por

manejar bajo la influencia del alcohol, asalto y posesión de drogas.

C. ¿Y usted?   ¿Recuerda una vez cuando arrestó a un criminal estúpido? Narre, por favor, lo que pasó.

Spanish-English Glossary

* denotes slang

a causa de *on account of* 11
a la derecha *to the right* 3
a la izquierda *to the left* 3
a largo plazo *long-term* 8
a pie *on foot* 7
a sus órdenes *at your service; may I help you?* PC
a veces *at times* 3
abajo *down* 3
abandonar *to abandon* 8
el abandono *abandonment* 8
abierto/a *open* 3
el/la abogado/a *lawyer* 1
abrazar *to embrace* 8
el abrazo *hug* 3
abril *April* PC
abrir *to open* 4
el/la abuelo/a *grandparent* 3
aburrido/a *bored* 2
abusar *to abuse* 11
el abuso *abuse* 11
acá *here* 5
acabar de + inf. *to have just* 7
acechar *to stalk* 8
la acera *sidewalk* 7
acercarse *to approach* 11
el/la acompañante *companion* 11
aconsejar *to advise* 9
el/la acosador/a *stalker* 8
acosar *to stalk* 8
el acoso *stalking* 8
acostarse (ue) *to go to bed* 4
el acta (f.) *certificate* 9
la actitud *attitude* 9
actual *current* 10
la acusación *accusation* 9
el/la acusado/a *accused* 4
además *besides* 2
adentro *inside* 5
el/la adicto/a *addict* 9
adiós *good-bye* PC
admitir *to admit* 9
ADN *DNA* 10
¿Adónde? *Where to?* 2
la advertencia *warning* 2
afilado/a *sharpened* 3
afuera *outside* 5
agacharse *to crouch down* 5
el/la agente *officer, agent* PC

agosto *August* PC
el agradecimiento *gratitude* 11
el/la agresor/a *aggressor* 11
el agua (f.) *water* 2
aguantar *to endure, stand* 11
el águila (f.) *eagle* 7
ahogar *to drown, choke* 8
ahora *now* 1
ahorcar *to hang* 11
ahorita *right now* 1
el aire *air* 5
al lado de *next to* 3
el alambre *wire* 4
el albergue *shelter* 8
el alcahuete *fence* 7
el/la alcalde/sa *mayor* 9
la alcoba *bedroom* 3
el alcohol *alcohol* 2
la alerta *alert* 7
algo *something* 1
el alguacil *sheriff, bailiff* 4
alguien *somebody* 5
algún/uno/a *some* 5
el aliento *breath* 2
allí *there* 2
almacenar *to store* 11
almorzar (ue) *to have lunch* 4
el alquiler *the rent* 9
alto *stop* 2
alto/a *tall* 1
el/la amante *lover* 8
amar *to love* 8
amarillo/a *yellow* 1
ambos/as *both* 9
la ambulancia *ambulance* 5
la amenaza *threat* 3
amenazar *to threaten* 8
la ametralladora *machine gun* 3
el/la amigo/a *friend* PC
la amistad *friendship* 7
analizar *to analyze* 10
anciano/a *elderly* 8
angustiado/a *anguished* 10
el anillo *ring* 7
¡Ánimo! *Courage! Go for it!* 8
el año *year* 2
anoche *last night* 7

anónimo/a *anonymous* 7
anteayer *day before yesterday* 7
antes *before* PC
antipático/a *unpleasant* 1
anular *to annul* 11
anunciar *to announce* 4
apagar *to put out* 5
Apague el motor. *Stop the motor.* 2
el aparato *apparatus* 5
aparecer (zc) *to appear* 8
el apartamento *apartment* 10
apelar *to appeal* 10
el apellido *last name* 1
el apodo *nickname* 1
apostar (ue) *to bet* 8
el apoyo *support* 8
aprehender *to apprehend* 8
aprender *to learn* 7
la apuesta *bet* 9
apuñalar *to stab* 11
aquí *here* 2
el árbol *tree* 1
el archivo *file* 12
el arete *earring* 7
el arma de fuego (f.) *firearm* 3
armar *to arm* 7
el armario *wardrobe* 5
arrancar *to start (motor)* 7
arrestar *to arrest* 4
arriba *up, above* 3
las arribas* *uppers* 4
arruinar *to ruin* 8
el asalto *assault* 2
la ascendencia *ancestry* 8
el ascensor *elevator* 5
asesinar *to murder* 10
el asesinato *murder* 10
el/la asesino/a *assassin* 7
asiático/a *Asian* 1
el asiento *seat* 2
el asilo *asylum* 8
el/la asistente *assistant* PC
asistir *to attend* 7
atacar *to attack* 3
atado/a *tied* 8
el atasco *jam (traffic)* 2
atormentar *to torment* 9

atrás *back* 2
la audiencia *hearing* 2
aumentar *to increase* 11
la ausencia *absence* 5
ausente *absent* 7
el auto(móvil) *automobile* 3
el autobús *bus* 1
la autoestima *self esteem* 9
la autopista *freeway* 2
la autopsia *autopsy* 10
el auxilio *help* 6
ayer *yesterday* 7
la ayuda *help* 2
el azar *chance* 9
azul *blue* 1

bailar *to dance* 11
Baje del carro. *Get out of the car.* 2
bajo/a *short (height)* 1
la bala *bullet* 3
la balanza *scale* 4
el balazo *bullet shot* 3
bañarse *to bathe* 8
la banca *bench* 2
el banco *bank* 1
el baño *bathroom* 3
la barricada *barricade* 5
el barrio *neighborhood* 1
el básquetbol *basketball* 9
basta *enough* 8
el bastón *cane, night stick* 1, 9
la basura *trash* 1
el basurero *trash can* 7
el baúl *trunk* 2
el/la bebé *baby* 3
beber *to drink* 2
besar *to kiss* 8
la biblioteca *library* 5
la bicicleta *bicycle* 1
bien *well* PC
los bienes *goods* 7
bienvenidos *welcome* PC
el bigote *moustache* 1
el billar *pool* 9
blanco/a *white* 1
bloquear *to block* 7
la blusa *blouse* 1
la boca *mouth* 2
la boca de incendios *fire hydrant* 2
la bocina *horn* 2
el boletín *bulletin* 7

la bolsa *purse, bag* 1
el bolsillo *pocket* 8
la bomba *fire truck, bomb* 5
el bombero *firefighter* 2
bonito/a *pretty* 1
borracho/a *drunk* 2
borrado/a *erased* 3
las botas *boots* 1
el botín *loot, haul* 7
el boxeo *boxing* 9
el brazo *arm* 1
buenas noches *good evening, good night* PC
buenas tardes *good afternoon* PC
buenos días *good morning* PC
buscar *to look for* 1
la búsqueda *search* 10

el caballo *horse* 9
el cabello *hair* 2
la cabeza *head* 1
la cabina *cab* 2
la cachucha *cap* 1
el cadáver *cadaver* 10
la cadena *chain* 1
la cadena perpetua *life imprisonment* 10
caer (ig) *to fall* 5
el café *coffee, café* 1
la caja *bed (of truck), box* 2
la cajuela *trunk* 2
los calcetines *socks* 1
el calendario *calendar* PC
la calidad *quality* 4
caliente *hot* 11
callado/a *quiet* 9
la calle *street* 1
el callejón *alley* 1
calmarse *to calm down* 8
calvo/a *bald* 1
la cama *bed* 3
la cámara *camera* 3
el cambio *change* 2
el camello* *drug dealer* 3
la camilla *stretcher* 5
caminar *to walk* 2
el camino *road* 2
el camión *truck* 1
la camioneta *station wagon, van* 1
la camisa *shirt* 1
la camiseta *T-shirt* 1
el candado *lock* 7

canoso/a *gray-haired* 1
cansado/a *tired* 2
el capó *hood* 2
la captura *capture* 11
capturado/a *captured* 11
la cara *face* 1
¡Carajo!* *Crap!* 9
la cárcel *jail* 4
carecer (zc) *to lack* 9
el cargador *clip, magazine* 10
cargar *to charge, load (gun)* 10
el cargo *charge* 8
la carrera *race* 9
la carretera *highway* 2
el carril *lane* 2
el carro *car* 7
el cártel *cartel* 9
la cartelera *billboard* 2
la cartera *wallet* 3
la casa *house* 1
la casa de empeño *pawn shop* 7
casarse *to get married* 8
el casco balístico *helmet* 9
el caso *case* 1
castaño/a *brown (hair, eyes)* 1
castigar *to punish* 9
la causa *cause* 10
Ceda el paso *Yield* 2
la celda *cell* 9
los celos *jealousy* 10
celoso/a *jealous* 8
la cena *dinner* 8
cerca de *near* 3
cerrado/a *closed* 2
la cerradura *lock* 7
cerrar (ie) *to close* 4
la cerveza *beer* 2
Chale.* *Nope.* 3
el chaleco antibalas *bullet-proof vest* 9
el/la chavo/a* *boy/girlfriend of gang member* 3
el cheque *check* 8
chico/a *small* 2
la chimenea *fireplace* 3
chingado* *fuck* 7
el chivo* *marihuana* 4
chocar *to crash* 2
el chofer *driver* 2
el/la cholo/a* *person of mixed race, gang member* 3
los chonis *underwear (boxers)* 1

el choque *crash* 2
el chulo* *pimp* 9
la cicatriz *scar* 1
el cielo raso *ceiling* 5
el cine *theater* 1
el cinturón de seguridad *seat belt* 2
la cita *appointment, date* 1
la ciudad *city* 1
el/la ciudadano/a *citizen* 9
claro (que sí/no) *of course (not)* 1
la clonación *cloning* 9
la coartada *alibi* 10
la cobija *blanket* 5
cobrar *to charge* 8
la coca* *cocaine* 4
el coche *car* 2
la cocina *kitchen* 3
el código *code* 7
el cofre *hood* 2
cojo/a *lame* 1
el/la colega *colleague* 2
colgar (ue) *to hang up* 5
la colocación *placement* 9
colocar *to place* 5
el/la comandante *commander* 8
el comedor *dining room* 3
comenzar (ie) *to begin* 4
comer *to eat* 1
cometer *to commit* 2
la comida *food, meal* 8
la comisaría *police station* 1
como *as* 4
¿Cómo está Ud.? *How are you? (formal)* PC
¿Cómo estás? *How are you? (familiar)* PC
¿Cómo se llama Ud.? *What is your name? (formal)* PC
¿Cómo te llamas? *What is your name? (familiar)* PC
¿Cómo? *How?* 1
la cómoda *dresser* 3
el/la compañero/a *companion* 3
el complejo *complex* 7
comprar *to buy* 4
comprobar (ue) *to prove* 10
la computadora *computer* 3
común *common* 9
la comunidad *community* 7
comunitario/a *community* 7

con permiso *excuse me* PC
el condado *county* 7
la condena *sentence* 10
el condón *condom* 11
conducir (zc) *to drive* 2
el/la conductor/a *driver* 2
la conexión *connection* 4
confesar (ie) *to confess* 9
la confianza *confidence* 11
confirmar *to confirm* 11
confrontar *to confront* 10
confundido/a *confused* 2
conocer (zc) *to know, be acquainted with* 1
consciente *conscious* 5
la consecuencia *consequence* 2
el/la consejero/a *counselor* 8
consensual *consensual* 11
el consentimiento *consent* 10
conservador/a *conservative* 8
contar (ue) *to count* 4
contento/a *content, happy* 2
el contestador automático *answering machine* 8
contestar *to answer* 2
contra *against* 5
conversar *to talk* 1
cooperar *to cooperate* 7
la corbata *tie* 1
el correo *mail* 1
correr *to run* 2
corriente *current* 7
cortar *to cut* 3
la corte *court* 4
corto/a *short (length)* 1
la cosa *thing* 3
el crédito *credit* 9
creer *to believe* 2
el crimen *crime* 1
el/la criminal *criminal* 3
la criminología *criminology* 10
la crisis *crisis* 8
el cruce *crossing* 2
la crueldad *cruelty* 8
¿Cuál es la fecha de hoy? *What's today's date?* PC
¿Cuál/es? *Which (one/s)?* 1
¿Cuándo? *When?* 1
¿Cuánto/a? *How much?* 1
¿Cuántos/as? *How many?* 1
el cuarto *room* 5

cubrir *to cover* 5
la cucaracha* *marihuana (cockroach)* 4
el cuchillo *knife* 7
el cuello *neck* 5
el cuerno del chivo* *AK-47* 3
el cuerpo *body* 1
el cuidado *care* 4
la culpa *fault, blame* 8
la culpabilidad *guilt* 10
culpable *guilty* 9
cumplir *to fulfill* 9
la cuota *fee* 2
curioso/a *curious* 9
la custodia *custody* 10

los dados *dice* 9
el daño *damage* 2
dar *to give* 10
dar vuelta *to turn around* 2
darse prisa *to hurry up* 2
de *of, from* 1
de acuerdo a *according to* 7
de nada *you're welcome* PC
de repente *suddenly* 11
¡De rodillas! *On your knees!* 7
de veras *really* 8
debajo de *under* 3
deber *to ought to, should* 5
decidir *to decide* 2
decir (i) (g) *to say, tell* 4
declarar *to declare* 10
dedicado *dedicated* PC
el dedo *finger* 7
defender (ie) *to defend* 3
la defensa *defense* 10
el/la defensor/a *defense attorney* 10
dejar *to leave (behind)* 4
delantero/a *front* 2
deliberar *to deliberate* 10
el delito *crime, felony* 4
demasiado *too much* 2
demoler (ue) *to demolish* 5
demostrar (ue) *to demonstrate* 10
dentro de *within* 5
denunciar *to denounce* 8
el departamento *department, apartment* 1
deportivo/a *sporting* 9
el depósito *depository* 11

el/la depredador/a *predator* 11

deprimido/a *depressed* 11

derecho *straight* 2

el derecho *right* 8

el derrumbe *collapse* 5

el desafío *challenge* 3

desamparado/a *homeless* 1

desaparecer (zc) *to disappear* 1

el desastre *disaster* 5

descansar *to rest* 2

el descapotable *convertible* 2

descompuesto/a *broken down* 2

desconocer (zc) *to be unknown* 7

Describa... *Describe...* 3

descuidado/a *neglected* 8

desear *to desire* 9

desesperado/a *desperate* 5

desinflado/a *uninflated, flat* 2

desmembrar (ie) *to dismember* 11

desmontable *removable* 10

despachar *to dispatch* 5

despacio *slow* 7

la despedida *farewell* 11

despertarse (ie) *to wake up* 8

después *after* 2

el desvío *detour* 2

el/la detective *detective* 10

el detector de metales *metal detector* 3

detenido/a *stopped* 2

detrás de *in back of* 3

devolver (ue) *to return something* 7

el diamante *diamond* 7

el dibujo *sketch* 10

diciembre *December* PC

dictar *to pronounce, pass (sentence)* 10

difamar *to defame, libel* 8

Dígame. *Tell me.* 3

el dinero *money* 1

¡Dios mío! *My God!* 3

el/la diputado/a *deputy* 8

la dirección *address* 1

dirigirse a *to direct oneself to* 7

discapacitado/a *disabled* 2

Disculpe. *Pardon me.* PC

discutir *to argue* 2

diseñar *to design* 7

el disparo *shot* 3

disponible *available* 4

el dispositivo *device* 7

la diversidad *diversity* 8

el divorcio *divorce* 3

Doble... *Turn...* 3

el documento *document* 2

doler (ue) *to hurt, cause pain* 11

el dolor *pain* 5

doméstico/a *domestic* 8

domingo *Sunday* PC

¿Dónde? *Where?* 1

dormir (ue) *to sleep* 3

el dormitorio *bedroom* 3

la droga *drug* 2

el/la drogadicto/a *drug addict* 3

la duda *doubt* 10

dudar *to doubt* 9

los dulces *candy* 11

duradero/a *lasting* 8

durante *during* 2

ebrio/a *drunk* 2

la edad *age* 1

el edificio *building* 1

el ejemplo *example* 4

él *he* PC

elegir (i) *to choose, elect* 8

el elevador *elevator* 5

ella *she* PC

ellos/as *they* PC

el embotellamiento *bottleneck* 2

la emergencia *emergency* 1

empezar (ie) *to begin* 4

el empleo *job* 8

en común *in common* 11

en contra de *against* 4

en cuanto a *regarding* 8

en efectivo *cash* 9

en este momento *at this moment* 2

en patines *on skates* 7

en punto *on the dot* 1

en realidad *in reality* 3

en vez de *in place of* 11

enamorarse *to fall in love* 8

encabezar *to head up* 10

encarcelado/a *jailed* 10

el encarcelamiento *imprisonment* 8

encargarse de *to take charge of* 7

encima de *on top of, above* 3

encontrar (ue) *to find* 11

encubierto/a *undercover* 3

el/la enemigo/a *enemy* 3

enero *January* PC

la enfermedad *illness* 9

el/la enfermero/a *nurse* 2

enfermo/a *sick* 2

enfrentar *to face* 11

enfrente de *in front of* 3

el engaño *deceit* 9

enjuiciar *to judge* 10

enojarse *to get angry* 8

enseñar *to show, teach* 3

entender (ie) *to understand* 3

entonces *then* 3

la entrada *entry* 3

entrar *to enter* 1

entre *between* 3

entregar *to hand over* 5

entrenar *to train* 7

la entrevista *interview* 1

envenenar *to poison* 11

el equipo *team, equipment* 1

el equipo electrónico *home theater* 3

erótico/a *erotic* 8

Es que... *It's just that...* 2

es un placer *it's a pleasure* PC

Es una lástima. *It's a shame.* 9

la escalera *stairs* 3

escapar *to escape* 2

la escena *scene* 3

escoger *to choose* 5

escolar *school* 11

esconder *to hide* 5

escondido/a *hidden* 3

la escopeta *shotgun* 10

escribir *to write* 1

el escritorio *desk* 5

escuchar *to listen (to)* 1

la escuela *school* 2

ese* *dude* 3

el esfuerzo *effort* 8

la esmeralda *emerald* 7

la espalda *back* 3

el espejo *mirror* 3

el (espejo) retrovisor *rearview mirror* 2

la esperanza *hope* 8

esperar *to wait for, to hope* 2
espiar *to spy* 8
las esposas *handcuffs* 3
el/la esposo/a *husband, wife* 2
la esquina *corner* 5
la estación *station* 1
estacionado/a *parked* 7
el estacionamiento *parking* 2
las estadísticas *statistics* 8
el estado *state* 1
la estafa *deception, rip-off* 8
estallar *to explode* 5
estar *to be* 2
la estatura *stature* 1
el estéreo *stereo* 1
la estofa* *stash* 4
estrangular *to strangle* 10
la estrella *star* 2
estremecer *to tremble* 5
el/la estudiante *student* 4
evacuar *to evacuate* 5
la evidencia *evidence* 3
evitar *to avoid* 5
el/la examinador/a *examiner* 10
examinar *to examine* 2
el exceso *excess* 2
exigir (j) *to require* 9
el éxito *success* 7
exonerado/a *exonerated* 11
el expediente *file, dossier* 10
el explosivo *explosive* 8
extraño/a *strange* 9

la falda *skirt* 1
fallecer (zc) *to pass away* 8
el fallecimiento *death, passing* 10
el fallo *ruling* 10
falsificar *to falsify* 9
falso/a *false* 9
la falta *misdemeanor, lack* 4, 7
familiar *family-related* 3
la farlopa* *cocaine* 4
el faro *headlight* 2
el farol *streetlight* 7
fascinar *to fascinate* 11
la fe *faith* 8
febrero *February* PC
la fecha *date* 1
¡Felicidades! *Congratulations!* 7
la feria *change* 3
el ferrocarril *railroad* 2

la fianza *bail bond* 9
la ficha policial *police record* 4
el fierro* *gun* 3
la fiesta *party* 1
la figura *figure* 3
fijo/a *fixed* 10
el filero *knife* 3
firmar *to sign* 8
el/la fiscal *district attorney* 10
flaco/a *skinny* 1
forense *forensic* 10
forénsico/a *forensic* 7
el formulario *form* 10
la foto(grafía) *photograph* 4
el/la fotógrafo/a *photographer* 10
la fractura *fracture* 5
el/la francotirador/a *sniper* 10
el fraude *fraud* 8
los frenos *brakes* 2
frente a *facing* 5
el frío *cold* 2
frustrado/a *frustrated* 8
el fuego *fire* 5
fuera *outside* 8
fuerte *strong* 1
el/la fugitivo/a *fugitive* 3
fumar *to smoke* 2
furioso/a *furious* 8
fusilar *to shoot* 9

el gallo *rooster* 8
el/la ganador/a *winner* 9
la ganga* *gang* 3
el garaje *garage* 3
la gasolina *gasoline* 5
el gasto *expense* 8
el gato/a *cat* 4
el gesto *gesture* 9
el gimnasio *gym* 5
el/la gobernador/a *governor* 7
golpear *to hit* 8
la goma *tire* 2
gordo/a *fat* 1
la gorra *cap* 1
la grabación *recording* 7
grabar *to record* 11
gracias *thank you* PC
el grafiti *graffiti* 3
la granada *grenade* 3
grande *big* 1

gratis *free (of charge)* 4
gratuito/a *free of charge* 7
la gravedad *gravity* 10
gris *gray* 1
gritar *to shout* 5
la grúa *tow truck* 2
el grupo *group* 8
guapo/a *handsome* 1
el/la guardaespaldas *bodyguard* 10
el guardafango *fender* 2
la guardia *guard duty* 10
güero/a *blond* 1
la guerra *war* 3
la guía *guide* 8
gustar *to like* 7

la habilidad *ability* 9
la habitación *room* 5
hablar *to talk, speak* 2
Hábleme. *Talk to me.* 3
hacer *to do, make* 2
el hambre (f.) *hunger* 2
hasta luego *see you later* PC
hay *there is, are* 1
el hecho *fact* 9
hecho/a *done, made* 7
la hemorragia *hemorrhage* 5
el/la heredero/a *heir* 11
la herencia *inheritance* 8
la herida *wound* 5
herido/a *wounded* 2
el/la hermanastro/a *stepbrother/sister* 3
el hermano carnal *blood brother* 8
el/la hermano/a *brother/sister* 3
la herramienta *tool* 2
el/la hijastro/a *stepchild* 3
el/la hijo/a *son/daughter* 3
el hogar *home* 8
hola *hello, hi* PC
el hombre *man* 1
el hombro *shoulder* 1
el homicidio *murder* 4
la hora *hour* 1
horroroso/a *horrendous* 11
el hospital *hospital* 5
hoy *today* 10
la huella digital *fingerprint* 4
el huerto *orchard* 8
el hueso *bone* 5
el humo *smoke* 4

el hurto   *larceny, burglary*   4

la identidad   *identity*   9
la identificación   *identification*   3
la iglesia   *church*   2
igualmente   *likewise*   PC
impedir (i)   *to impede*   7
implicar   *to implicate*   10
la impresora   *printer*   7
el impuesto   *tax*   8
el incendio   *fire*   4
el incesto   *incest*   11
incluir (y)   *to include*   8
la indicación   *direction*   2
indio/a   *Indian*   1
la inestabilidad   *instability*   10
infantil   *child-like*   11
inflamable   *flammable*   5
la infracción   *violation*   2
infrarrojo/a   *infrared*   7
inmediatamente   *immediately*   1
el/la inmigrante   *immigrant*   8
la inocencia   *innocence*   10
inocente   *innocent*   9
inolvidable   *unforgettable*   8
insistir (en)   *to insist (on)*   2
instalar   *to install*   2
insultar   *to insult*   3
intentar   *to attempt*   8
el intermitente   *turn signal*   2
interrogar   *to interrogate*   10
el interrogatorio   *interrogation*   10
intoxicado/a   *intoxicated*   2
la investigación   *investigation*   10
investigar   *to investigate*   10
invisible   *invisible*   3
ir   *to go*   2
el jardín   *garden, yard*   3

la jaula   *cage*   8
la jefatura   *headquarters*   1
el/la jefe/a   *boss, chief*   3
la jerga   *slang*   4
joven   *young*   1
la joya   *jewel*   3
la joyería   *jewelry store*   7
el juego   *game*   9
jueves   *Thursday*   PC
el/la juez/a   *judge*   2
el/la jugador/a   *player*   3

jugar (ue)   *to play*   4
el juicio   *judgment*   2
julio   *July*   PC
junio   *June*   PC
juntos/as   *together*   2
el jurado   *jury*   10
el jurado investigador   *grand jury*   11
la justicia   *justice*   10
justo/a   *fair*   9

el laboratorio   *laboratory*   10
lacio/a   *straight*   1
el ladrillo   *brick*   5
el/la ladrón/ona   *thief*   3
la lana*   *money (wool)*   3
largo/a   *long*   1
lastimado/a   *injured*   2
el lavado   *laundering*   9
lavarse   *to wash*   8
leer   *to read*   1
lejos de   *far from*   3
el lenguaje   *language*   8
el lente protector   *goggles*   6
los lentes   *glasses*   1
el letrero   *sign*   5
levantarse   *to get up*   8
la libertad condicional   *parole*   9
la libra   *pound*   1
la licencia   *license*   2
el limpiaparabrisas   *windshield wiper*   2
limpiar   *to clean*   2
la limpieza   *cleaning*   5
la línea   *line*   2
el lío   *hassle*   11
liso/a   *straight (hair)*   1
la llama   *flame*   5
llamar   *to call*   2
llamar por respaldo   *to call for backup*   7
la llanta   *tire*   2
la llanta de repuesto   *spare tire*   2
la llave   *key*   5
llegar   *to arrive*   1
llevar   *to wear, to carry*   1
llevarse bien/mal con   *to get along well, not well with*   8
llorar   *to cry*   3
la lluvia   *rain*   5
Lo siento   *I'm sorry*   PC
loco/a   *crazy*   3

lograr   *to succeed*   7
la lotería   *lottery*   9
luchar   *to fight*   9
el lugar   *place*   3
lunes   *Monday*   PC
la luz   *light*   2

el machete   *big knife*   3
la madrastra   *stepmother*   3
la madre   *mother*   PC
el/la maestro/a   *teacher*   3
mal   *not well*   PC
el maletero   *trunk*   2
maltratado/a   *abused*   8
el/la maltratador/a   *abuser*   8
el maltrato   *mistreatment*   7
la mañana   *morning*   1
mañana   *tomorrow*   1
mandar   *to send*   1
¿Mande?   *Excuse me?*   PC
manejar   *to drive*   2
la manguera   *hose*   5
la mano   *hand*   1
¡Manos arriba!   *Hands up!*   7
¡Manos en la espalda!   *Hands behind your back!*   7
la máquina   *machine*   4
la maravilla   *marvel*   9
la marca   *brand, make*   2
marcar   *to dial*   5
la marcha   *gear*   2
martes   *Tuesday*   PC
marzo   *March*   PC
más   *more*   1
más o menos   *more or less*   PC
el masaje   *massage*   9
matar   *to kill*   3
mayo   *May*   PC
mayor   *older, greater*   4
Me llamo...   *My name is...*   PC
el/la mediador/a   *mediator*   8
mediano/a   *medium*   1
la medianoche   *midnight*   1
las medias   *panty hose*   1
el medicamento   *medication*   8
médico/a   *medical*   10
el mediodía   *noon*   1
medir (i)   *to measure*   4
mejor   *better*   4
el mejoramiento   *improvement*   8
menor   *younger, minor*   2
menos   *less*   4

el mensaje *message* 5

mentir (ie) *to lie* 4

la mercancía *merchandise* 4

el/la merodeador/a *prowler* 7

la mesa *table* 5

la metanfetamina *methamphe-tamine* 11

meterse *to get involved with* 3

mi *my* 4

el miedo *fear* 2

el/la miembro *member* 3

mientras *while* 3

miércoles *Wednesday* PC

la migra* *INS* 3

mirar *to look at, watch* 1

mismo/a *same* 7

el modo de proceder *modus operandi (m.o.)* 11

molestar *to bother* 7

el monitoreo *monitoring* 7

el monte *the mountain* 7

la mordida* *bribe* 11

moreno/a *brown haired, (or brown skinned)* 1

el moretón *bruise* 8

morir (ue) *to die* 3

mortificado/a *mortified* 11

la mota* *marihuana* 3

el motín *riot* 12

el motivo *motive* 10

la moto(cicleta) *motorcycle* 2

mover (ue) *to move* 5

el movimiento *movement* 1

el/la muchacho/a *boy/girl* PC

la muchedumbre *crowd* 5

mucho gusto *pleased/nice to meet you* PC

los muebles *furniture* 5

la muerte *death* 2

muerto/a *dead* 5

la mujer *woman* 1

la (mujer) policía *police officer* 1

la multa *ticket, fine* 1

muy *very* PC

el nacimiento *birth* 1

nada *nothing* 4

nadie *nobody* 5

el narcotraficante *drug traffick-er* 3

la nariz *nose* 1

la navaja* *switchblade* 3

necesitar *to need* 2

la negligencia *neglect* 8

el negocio *business* 4

negro/a *black* 1

el neumático *tire* 2

el/la nieto/a *grandchild* 3

la nieve *snow* 5

la nieve* *cocaine (snow)* 4

el/la niñero/a *babysitter* 11

ningún/a *none* 5

el nivel *level* 9

no hay de qué *you're welcome* PC

no obstante *not withstanding* 10

el nombre *name* 1

nosotros/as *we* PC

la nota *note* 11

las noticias *news* 1

el noticiero *news program* 11

noviembre *November* PC

el/la novio/a *sweetheart* 8

nuestro/a *our* 4

nunca *never* 5

observar *to observe* 2

obtener (g) (ie) *to obtain* 8

octubre *October* PC

ocultar *to hide* 7

ocupado/a *busy* 2

ocurrir *to occur* 8

el odio *hatred* 7

oír (ig) (y) *to hear* 3

Ojalá *I hope, May Allah grant* 9

el ojo *eye* 1

el ojo morado *black eye* 8

oler (ue) *to smell* 5

el olor *smell* 5

olvidarse de *to forget* 7

la orden *order* 8

la orden de arresto *arrest warrant* 10

la orden de registro *search warrant* 10

la oreja *ear* 1

el organigrama *organizational chart* 11

el orgullo *pride* 7

el oro *gold* 1

Oye. *Hey.* 3

el padrastro *stepfather* 3

el padre *father* 3

el pago *payment* 9

la palabra *word* 7

el palo *stick* 9

la pandilla *gang* 3

el/la pandillero/a *gang member* 3

el pánico *panic* 5

los pantalones *pants* 1

las pantuflas *slippers* 1

el pañuelo *handkerchief* 3

el papel *paper* 2

el parabrisas *windshield* 2

el parachoques *bumper* 2

la parada *stop (bus)* 2

el paralizador Taser *Taser stun gun* 9

el/la paramédico *paramedic* 5

parar *to stop* 7

Pare el carro. *Stop the car* 2

parecer (zc) *to seem* 3

la pared *wall* 3

el parque *park* 2

el parquímetro *parking meter* 1

la partida *game* 9

el partido *game, match* 9

pasado mañana *day after tomorrow* 10

el/la pasajero/a *passenger* 2

el pasaporte *passport* 9

pasar *to pass, spend (time)* 4

el paseo *drive* 2

el pasillo *hall* 5

la pastilla *pill* 5

la pata *leg, paw, foot (animal)* 8

la patrulla *patrol* 7

la patrullera *patrol car* 1

la paz *peace* 7

el peaje *toll* 2

el/la peatón/ona *pedestrian* 2

el pecho *chest* 5

el/la pederasta *predator* 11

pedir (i) *to ask for, order* 4

el/la pedófilo/a *pedophile* 11

pegar *to strike* 8

peinarse *to comb one's hair* 8

la pelea *fight* 3

el peligro *danger* 2

peligroso/a *dangerous* 1

pelirrojo/a *red-headed* 1

el pelo *hair* 1

pelón/ona *bald* 1

el pelotero* *drug dealer* 3

peludo/a *hairy* 1

la pena *penalty* 9

la pena de muerte *death penalty* 10

pensar (ie) *to think, plan* 4

peor *worse* 4

las pepas* *uppers* 4

el pepe* *john* 9

pequeño/a *small* 1

el/la perdedor/a *loser* 9

perder (ie) *to lose* 4

perdido/a *lost* 2

perdón *pardon me* PC

el periódico *newspaper* 2

permanecer (zc) *to remain* 5

el permiso *permission* 10

permitir *to permit* 9

pero *but* 2

el/la perro/a *dog* 1

perseguir (i) *to pursue* 8

la persona *person* 1

perturbador/a *disturbing* 11

el/la pervertido/a *pervert* 11

pesado/a *heavy* 7

pesar *to weigh* 4

el peso *weight* 1

el pico *beak* 8

el pie *foot* 1

la piedad *mercy* 7

la piedra *stone* 7

la pierna *leg* 1

la píldora *pill* 11

pillar* *to score (drugs)* 4

pinchado/a (ponchado/a*) *punctured* 2

el piso *floor* 5

la pista *clue, track* 8

la pistola *pistol* 3

la placa *badge, license plate* 2

la planificación *planning* 8

la planta baja *ground floor* 3

plantar *to plant* 10

la plata* *money (silver)* 3

la playera *T-shirt* 1

el plazo *term* 9

la pluma *pen* 2

la población *population* 8

pobre *poor* 1

el/la pobrecito/a *poor thing* 5

el poder *power* 8

poder (ue) *to be able, can* 4

poderoso/a *powerful* 9

el/la (mujer) policía *police officer* 1

la policía *police department* 1

el polvo de ángel *angel dust* 3

poner (g) *to put, place* 3

Ponga... *Put...* 3

por favor *please* PC

¿Por qué? *Why?* 1

el porcentaje *percentage* 8

la pornografía *pornography* 11

porque *because* 1

el portero *doorman* 1

póstumo/a *posthumous* 11

el pozo *well, pool* 9

el precio *price* 4

precioso/a *precious* 7

la pregunta *question* 3

premeditado/a *premeditated* 4

el premio *prize* 9

la prenda *item* 7

prender *to turn on* 5

preocupado/a *worried* 2

preparar *to prepare* 2

la presión *pressure* 5

el/la preso/a *prisoner* 4

prestar atención *to pay attention* 11

previo/a *previous* 4

primero *first* 3

los primeros auxilios *first aid* 5

la prisa *hurry* 2

el/la prisionero/a *prisoner* 3

el problema *problem* 2

el procurador general *attorney general* 10

producir (zc) *to produce* 3

el/la prófugo/a *fugitive* 11

profundo/a *deep* 5

prohibir *to prohibit* 9

promedio/a *average* 7

la promesa *promise* 9

prometer *to promise* 9

pronto *soon* 3

la propiedad *property* 7

propio/a *own* 9

proporcionado/a *provided* 7

el propósito *proposition* 4

la prostituta *prostitute* 9

la protección *protection* 8

proteger *to protect* 5

protestar *to protest* 8

provocativo/a *provocative* 8

el proxeneta *pimp* 9

próximo/a *next* 5

la prueba *test* 9

el/la psicólogo/a *psychologist* 9

el público *public* 10

la puerta *door* 1

pues *well* 3

el puesto *position* 9

la pulgada *inch* 10

la pulsera *bracelet* 7

el pulso *pulse* 5

el puñal *dagger* 3

el puro *cigar* 11

la puta* *whore* 8

que *that, than* 4

¿Qué día es hoy? *What day is today?* PC

¿Qué fecha es hoy? *What's today's date?* PC

¿Qué hubo?* *What happened?* 3

¿Qué onda?* *What's up?* 3

¿Qué? *What?* 1

quedarse *to stay, remain* 8

la queja *complaint* 5

quemado/a* *burned, wasted* 4

la quemadura *burn* 5

la querella *lawsuit* 12

querer (ie) *to want* 4

querido/a *dear* 3

¿Quién/es? *Who?* 1

Quítese... *Remove...* 2

quizás *maybe* 3

racial *racial* 7

radicar* *to hang out* 3

la ramera* *whore* 9

el rapto *abduction* 11

raro/a *strange* 11

rastrear *to track, trace* 7

la rata* *stool pigeon* 3

la ratería *shoplifting, theft* 4

el/la ratero/a *petty thief, pickpocket* 7

la raza *race* 9

la razón *reason* 2

razonable *reasonable* 10

realizar *to carry out* 10

el recado *message* 10

la recámara *bedroom* 3

recibir *to receive* 2
la reclamación *claim* 8
reclamar *to claim* 9
recomendar (ie) *to recommend* 3
la recompensa *reward* 7
reconocer (zc) *to recognize* 8
recordar (ue) *to remember* 1
recto/a *straight* 2
recuperar *to get back* 7
la redada *sting* 9
el refugio *refuge* 8
el regalo *gift* 11
registrar *to search* 4
el registro *registration, search* 2, 10
la regla *rule* 9
regresar *to return* 1
regular *so-so* PC
relajarse *to relax* 11
el reloj *watch, clock* 1
remolcar *to tow* 2
el remordimiento *remorse* 9
repetir (i) *to repeat* 4
el reporte *report* 10
el/la reportero/a *reporter* 11
rescatar *to rescue* 5
el rescate *rescue* 5
el respeto *respect* 7
la respiración *breathing* 5
respirar *to breathe* 5
los restos *remains* 11
la resucitación cardiopulmonar *CPR* 5
resuelto/a *resolved* 7
el resultado *result* 10
la reunión *meeting* 1
revelar *to develop, reveal* 10
revisar *to check* 10
rico/a *rich* 1
ridículo/a *ridiculous* 9
el riesgo *risk* 9
el rifle *rifle* 10
el/la rival *rival* 3
rizado/a *curly* 1
el robo *robbery* 4
rogar (ue) *to beg* 9
rojo/a *red* 1
romper *to break, tear* 7
la ropa *clothing* 1
roto/a *broken, torn* 1
el rubí *ruby* 7
rubio/a *blond* 1

la rueda *wheel* 2
el ruido *noise* 3
la rutina *routine* 4

sábado *Saturday* PC
saber *to know* 3
sacar *to take (out)* 4
la sacudida *shaking* 5
sacudir *to shake* 5
la sala *living room* 3
la salida *exit* 2
salir (g) *to leave, go out* 1
saltar *to jump* 11
la salud *health* 8
salvar *to save* 5
salvo/a *unharmed* 9
las sandalias *sandals* 1
la sangre *blood* 5
sano/a *healthy* 9
¡Saque las manos! *Show your hands!* 7
el/la sargento *sergeant* 4
el/la secretario/a *secretary* PC
secreto/a *secret* 3
el secuestro *kidnapping* 4
la sed *thirst* 2
seguir (i) *to continue, follow* 4
la seguridad *security* 3
el seguro *insurance* 2
Seguro Social *Social Security* 9
seguro/a *secure, safe* 7
el semáforo *stoplight* 2
la semana *week* PC
semiautomático/a *semi-automatic* 10
la seña *sign, signal* 3
la señal *signal* 8
sentarse (ie) *to sit down* 8
sentido único *one way* 2
sentirse (ie) *to feel* 8
el señuelo *decoy* 9
Separe los pies. *Spread your legs.* 7
septiembre *September* PC
ser *to be* 1
el ser *being* 8
serio/a *serious* 2
servir (i) *to serve* 4
el sexo *sex* 11
sí *yes* 1
SIDA *AIDS* 11
siempre *always* 2

Siga derecho. *Straight ahead.* 3
siguiente *following* 10
Silencio. *Be quiet.* 3
la silla *chair* 3
Simón.* *Sure.* 3
el simulacro *drill* 6
simular *to simulate* 10
la sirena *siren* 2
el sistema de seguridad *security system* 3
el sistema judicial *judicial system* 10
el sitio *place* 10
el soborno *bribe* 10
sobre todo *above all* 9
la sobredosis *overdose* 4
sobrio/a *sober* 2
¡Socorro! *Help!* 5
la sodomía *sodomy* 11
solamente *only* 2
solar *sun* 2
la solicitud *application* 8
sólido/a *solid* 10
sólo *only* 2
el sombrero *hat* 1
el sonido *sound* 7
sonreír (i) *to smile* 11
la sonrisa *smile* 11
el/la soplón/soplona *whistle blower* 3
sorprendente *surprising* 9
la sorpresa *surprise* 7
el sorteo *drawing* 9
sospechar *to suspect* 5
el/la sospechoso/a *suspect* 1
el sótano *basement* 3
soy *I am* PC
su *his, her, your, their* 4
suave *soft, smooth* 7
Suba al carro. *Get in the car.* 2
la subasta *auction* 7
subir *to go up, climb* 3
sucio/a *dirty* 2
la sudadera *sweatshirt* 1
el sueldo *salary* 11
Suelte... *Drop...* 3
Suéltela. *Drop it.* 7
el sueño *sleep, dream* 2
la suerte *luck* 9
el suéter *sweater* 1
el sufrimiento *suffering* 8
sufrir *to suffer* 2

la sugerencia suggestion 7
sugerir (ie) to suggest 9
suicidarse to commit suicide 11
el suicidio suicide 10
sujetarse to hold on to something 5
la supervivencia survival 5
suponer (g) to suppose 7
suroeste southwest 9

el tacón heel 1
tal such 8
tal vez perhaps 1
el tamaño size 8
también too, also 2
tampoco neither 5
tan as 4
tanto/a as much 4
tantos/as as many 4
la tarde afternoon 1
la tarjeta card 9
la tasa rate 8
el tatuaje tattoo 1
el techo roof, ceiling 2
el tema theme 7
temer to fear 2
la temperatura temperature 5
tener (ie) (g) to have 4
el/la teniente lieutenant 6
tentar (ie) to tempt 11
el/la terapeuta therapist 11
la tercera edad retirement years 8
terminar to end, finish 3
el terremoto earthquake 5
el territorio territory 3
el testigo witness 1
la tienda store 1
la tierra earth 5
el tiquete* ticket 2
el tirador shooter 5
Tire las llaves acá. Throw the keys here. 7
el tiro shot 9
el tiroteo shooting 4
el tiroteo en marcha drive-by shooting 3
la toalla towel 5

tocar to play (music), to touch 1
todavía yet, still 3
todo all 1
el todo-terreno SUV 2
tolerar to tolerate 7
tomar to take, drink 2
tomar una copa to have a drink 8
el trabajo work 1
traducir (zc) to translate 3
traer (ig) to bring 3
el tráfico traffic 1
el tragamonedas slot machine 9
la tragedia tragedy 11
el traje suit 1
el tranquilizante tranquilizer 11
tranquilo/a calm 10
el tránsito traffic 1
traslado/a transfer 11
triste sad 2
el triunfo triumph 7
la troca/el troque* truck 2
tu your (familiar) 4
tú you (familiar) PC
tumbarse to lie down 8
la ubicación location 7

último/a last 11
un poquito a little bit 2
unido/a united 7
el uniforme uniform 3
usted you (formal) PC
ustedes you (plural) PC
útil useful 5

valer la pena to be worthwhile 7
el valor value 7
los vaqueros jeans 1
varios/as various, several 7
el vato* homeboy 3
Vaya a... Go to... 3
vecinal neighborhood 7
el/la vecino/a neighbor 7
el vehículo vehicle 7
la velocidad speed 2
la vena vein 11

vencer to expire 2
el/la vendedor/a salesperson 3
vender to sell 2
Venga. Come. 2
venir (ie) (g) to come 4
la venta sale 7
la ventaja advantage 7
la ventana window 3
ver to see 1
¿Verdad? True? Right? 1
verdadero/a true 3
verde green 1
el veredicto verdict 10
la vesda marihuana 4
el vestido dress 1
la vestimenta clothes 9
vestirse (i) to get dressed 8
la vez time, occasion 8
la víctima victim 1
la vida life 3
el vidrio glass 5
viejo/a old 1
el viento wind 5
viernes Friday PC
la vigilancia surveillance 3
vigilar to watch 7
VIH HIV 11
la violación sexual rape 4
violar to rape 8
violento/a violent 2
visitar to visit 2
la vivienda housing 8
vivir to live 2
el/la vocero/a spokesperson 11
el volante steering wheel 2
volar (ue) to fly 5
Voltéese. Turn around. 7
volver (ue) to return 4
la voz voice 5

ya already 4
la yerba* marihuana (grass) 4
la yesca* marihuana 4
yo I PC

el zacate* grass 4
el zafiro sapphire 7
el zapato shoe 1

English-Spanish Glossary

a little bit *un poquito* 2
to abandon *abandonar* 8
abandonment *el abandono* 8
abduction *el rapto* 11
ability *la habilidad* 9
above all *sobre todo* 9
absence *la ausencia* 5
absent *ausente* 7
abuse *el abuso* 11
to abuse *abusar* 11
abused *maltratado/a* 8
abuser *el/la maltratador/a* 8
according to *de acuerdo a* 7
accusation *la acusación* 9
accused *el/la acusado/a* 4
addict *el/la adicto/a* 9
address *la dirección* 1
to admit *admitir* 9
advantage *la ventaja* 7
to advise *aconsejar* 9
after *después* 2
afternoon *la tarde* 1
against *en contra de, contra* 4, 5
age *la edad* 1
agent *el/la agente* 1
aggressor *el/la agresor/a* 11
AIDS *SIDA* 11
air *el aire* 5
AK-47 *el cuerno del chivo** 3
alcohol *el alcohol* 2
alert *la alerta* 7
alibi *la coartada* 10
all *todo* 1
alley *el callejón* 1
already *ya* 4
always *siempre* 2
ambulance *la ambulancia* 5
to analyze *analizar* 10
ancestry *la ascendencia* 8
angel dust *el polvo de ángel* 3
anguished *angustiado/a* 10
to announce *anunciar* 4
to annul *anular* 11
anonymous *anónimo/a* 7
to answer *contestar* 2
answering machine *el contestador automático* 8
apartment *el apartamento* 10

apparatus *el aparato* 5
to appeal *apelar* 10
to appear *aparecer (zc)* 8
application *la solicitud* 8
appointment, date *la cita* 1
to apprehend *aprehender* 8
to approach *acercarse* 11
April *abril* PC
to argue *discutir* 2
arm *el brazo* 1
to arm *armar* 7
to arrest *arrestar* 4
arrest warrant *la orden de arresto* 10
to arrive *llegar* 1
as *tan* 4
as, like *como* 4
as many *tantos/as* 4
as much *tanto/a* 4
Asian *asiático/a* 1
to ask for, order *pedir (i)* 4
assassin *el/la asesino/a* 7
assault *el asalto* 2
assistant *el/la asistente* PC
asylum *el asilo* 8
at this moment *en este momento* 2
at times *a veces* 3
at your service; may I help you? *a sus órdenes* PC
to attack *atacar* 3
to attempt *intentar* 8
to attend *asistir* 7
attitude *la actitud* 9
attorney general *el procurador general* 11
auction *la subasta* 7
August *agosto* PC
automobile *el auto(móvil)* 3
autopsy *la autopsia* 10
available *disponible* 4
average *promedio/a* 7
to avoid *evitar* 5

baby *el/la bebé* 3
babysitter *el/la niñero/a* 11
back *atrás* 2
back *la espalda* 3
badge, license plate *la placa* 2

bail bond *la fianza* 9
bald *calvo/a, pelón/ona* 1
bank *el banco* 1
barricade *la barricada* 5
basement *el sótano* 3
basketball *el básquetbol* 9
to bathe *bañarse* 8
bathroom *el baño* 3
to be *ser, estar* 1, 2
to be able, can *poder (ue)* 4
Be quiet. *Silencio.* 3
to be unknown *desconocer (zc)* 7
to be worthwhile *valer la pena* 7
beak *el pico* 8
because *porque* 1
bed *la cama* 3
bed (of truck), box *la caja* 2
bedroom *el dormitorio, la recámara, la alcoba* 3
beer *la cerveza* 2
before *antes* PC
to beg *rogar (ue)* 9
to begin *empezar (ie), comenzar (ie)* 4
being *el ser* 8
to believe *creer* 2
bench *la banca* 2
besides *además* 2
to bet *apostar (ue)* 8
bet *la apuesta* 9
better *mejor* 4
between *entre* 3
bicycle *la bicicleta* 1
big *grande* 1
big knife *el machete* 3
billboard *la cartelera* 2
birth *el nacimiento* 1
black *negro/a* 1
black eye *el ojo morado* 8
blanket *la cobija* 5
to block *bloquear* 7
blond *rubio/a, güero/a* 1
blood *la sangre* 5
blood brother *el hermano carnal* 8
blouse *la blusa* 1
blue *azul* 1
body *el cuerpo* 1

bodyguard *el/la guardaespaldas* 10

bomb *la bomba* 5

bone *el hueso* 5

boots *las botas* 1

bored *aburrido/a* 2

boss, chief *el/la jefe/a* 3

both *ambos/as* 9

to bother *molestar* 7

bottleneck *embotellamiento* 2

boxing *el boxeo* 9

boy/girl *el/la muchacho/a* PC

boy/girlfriend of gang member *el/la chavo/a** 3

bracelet *la pulsera* 7

brakes *los frenos* 2

brand, make *la marca* 2

to break, tear *romper* 7

breath *el aliento* 2

to breathe *respirar* 5

breathing *la respiración* 5

bribe *el soborno, la mordida** 10, 11

brick *el ladrillo* 5

to bring *traer (ig)* 3

broken down *descompuesto/a* 2

broken, torn *roto/a* 1

brother/sister *el/la hermano/a* 3

brown (hair, eyes) *castaño/a* 1

brown haired, (or brown skinned) *moreno/a* 1

bruise *el moretón* 8

building *el edificio* 1

bullet *la bala* 3

bulletin *el boletín* 7

bullet shot *el balazo* 3

bullet-proof vest *el chaleco antibalas* 9

bumper *el parachoques* 2

burn *la quemadura* 5

burned, wasted *quemado/a** 4

bus *el autobús* 1

business *el negocio* 4

busy *ocupado/a* 2

but *pero* 2

to buy *comprar* 4

cab *la cabina* 2

cadaver *el cadáver* 10

cage *la jaula* 8

calendar *el calendario* PC

to call *llamar* 2

to call for backup *llamar por respaldo* 7

calm *tranquilo/a* 10

to calm down *calmarse* 8

camera *la cámara* 3

candy *los dulces* 11

cane *el bastón* 1

cap *la gorra, la cachucha* 1

capture *la captura* 11

captured *capturado/a* 11

car *el carro, el coche* 2, 7

card *la tarjeta* 9

care *el cuidado* 4

to carry out *realizar* 10

cartel *el cártel* 9

case *el caso* 1

cash *en efectivo* 9

cat *el/la gato/a* 4

cause *la causa* 10

ceiling *el cielo raso* 5

cell *la celda* 9

certificate *el acta (f.)* 9

chain *la cadena* 1

chair *la silla* 3

challenge *el desafío* 3

chance *el azar* 9

change *el cambio, la feria* 2, 3

charge *el cargo* 8

to charge (money) *cobrar* 8

to charge, load (gun) *cargar* 10

check *el cheque* 8

to check *revisar* 10

chest *el pecho* 5

child *infantil* 11

to choose *escoger* 5

to choose, elect *elegir (i)* 8

church *la iglesia* 2

cigar *el puro* 11

citizen *el/la ciudadano/a* 9

city *la ciudad* 1

claim *la reclamación* 8

to claim *reclamar* 9

to clean *limpiar* 2

cleaning *la limpieza* 5

clip, magazine *el cargador* 10

cloning *la clonación* 9

to close *cerrar (ie)* 4

closed *cerrado/a* 2

clothes *la vestimenta* 9

clothing *la ropa* 1

clue, track *la pista* 8

cocaine *la coca*, la farlopa** 4

cocaine (snow) *la nieve** 4

code *el código* 7

coffee, café *el café* 1

cold *el frío* 2

collapse *el derrumbe* 5

colleague *el/la colega* 2

to comb one's hair *peinarse* 8

to come *venir (ie) (g)* 4

Come. *Venga.* 2

commander *el comandante* 8

to commit *cometer* 2

to commit suicide *suicidarse* 11

common *común* 9

community *comunitario/a* 7

community *la comunidad* 7

companion *el/la compañero/a, el/la acompañante* 3, 11

complaint *la queja* 5

complex *el complejo* 7

computer *la computadora* 3

condom *el condón* 11

to confess *confesar (ie)* 9

confidence *la confianza* 11

to confirm *confirmar* 11

to confront *confrontar* 10

confused *confundido/a* 2

Congratulations! *¡Felicidades!* 7

connection *la conexión* 4

conscious *consciente* 5

consensual *consensual* 11

consent *el consentimiento* 10

consequence *la consecuencia* 2

conservative *conservador/a* 8

content, happy *contento/a* 2

to continue, follow *seguir (i)* 4

convertible *el descapotable* 2

to cooperate *cooperar* 7

corner *la esquina* 5

counselor *el/la consejero/a* 8

to count *contar (ue)* 4

county *el condado* 7

Courage! Go for it! *¡Ánimo!* 8

court *la corte* 4

to cover *cubrir* 5
CPR *la resucitación cardiopulmonar* 5
Crap! *¡Carajo!** 9
crash *el choque* 2
to crash *chocar* 2
crazy *loco/a* 3
credit *el crédito* 9
crime *el crimen* 1
crime, felony *el delito* 4
criminal *el/la criminal* 3
criminology *la criminología* 10
crisis *la crisis* 8
crossing *el cruce* 2
to crouch down *agacharse* 5
crowd *la muchedumbre* 5
cruelty *la crueldad* 8
to cry *llorar* 3
curious *curioso/a* 9
curly *rizado/a* 1
current *corriente* 7
current *actual* 10
custody *la custodia* 10
to cut *cortar* 3

dagger *el puñal* 3
damage *el daño* 2
to dance *bailar* 11
danger *el peligro* 2
dangerous *peligroso/a* 1
date *la fecha* 1
day after tomorrow *pasado mañana* 10
day before yesterday *anteayer* 7
dead *muerto/a* 5
dealer *el pelotero** 4
dear *querido/a* 3
death *la muerte* 2
death penalty *la pena de muerte* 10
death, passing *el fallecimiento* 10
deceit *el engaño* 9
December *diciembre* PC
deception, rip-off *la estafa* 8
to decide *decidir* 2
to declare *declarar* 10
decoy *el señuelo* 9
dedicated *dedicado* PC
deep *profundo/a* 5
to defame, libel *difamar* 8

to defend *defender (ie)* 3
defense *la defensa* 10
defense attorney *el/la defensor/a* 10
to deliberate *deliberar* 10
to demolish *demoler (ue)* 5
to demonstrate *demostrar (ue)* 10
to denounce *denunciar* 8
department, apartment *el departamento* 1
depository *el depósito* 11
depressed *deprimido/a* 11
deputy *el/la diputado/a* 8
Describe... *Describa...* 3
to design *diseñar* 7
to desire *desear* 9
desk *el escritorio* 5
desperate *desesperado/a* 5
detective *el/la detective* 10
detour *el desvío* 2
to develop, reveal *revelar* 10
device *el dispositivo* 7
to dial *marcar* 5
diamond *el diamante* 7
dice *los dados* 9
to die *morir (ue)* 3
dining room *el comedor* 3
dinner *la cena* 8
to direct oneself to *dirigirse a* 7
direction *la indicación* 2
dirty *sucio/a* 2
disabled *discapacitado/a* 2
to disappear *desaparecer (zc)* 1
disaster *el desastre* 5
to dismember *desmembrar (ie)* 11
to dispatch *despachar* 5
district attorney *el/la fiscal* 10
disturbing *perturbador/a* 11
diversity *la diversidad* 8
divorce *el divorcio* 3
DNA *ADN* 10
to do, make *hacer* 2
document *el documento* 2
dog *el/la perro/a* 1
domestic *doméstico/a* 8
done, made *hecho/a* 7
door *la puerta* 1
doorman *el portero* 1

to doubt *dudar* 9
doubt *la duda* 10
down *abajo* 3
drawing *el sorteo* 9
dress *el vestido* 1
dresser *la cómoda* 3
drill *el simulacro* 6
to drink *beber* 2
drive *el paseo* 2
to drive *manejar, conducir (zc)* 2
drive-by shooting *el tiroteo en marcha* 3
driver *el chofer* 2
driver *el/la conductor/a* 2
Drop it. *Suéltela.* 7
Drop... *Suelte...* 3
to drown, choke *ahogar* 8
drug *la droga* 2
drug addict *el/la drogadicto/a* 3
drug dealer *el camello**, *el pelotero* 3
drug trafficker *el narcotraficante* 3
drunk *borracho/a, ebrio/a* 2
dude *ese** 3
during *durante* 2

eagle *el águila (f.)* 7
ear *la oreja* 1
earring *el arete* 7
earth *la tierra* 5
earthquake *el terremoto* 5
to eat *comer* 1
effort *el esfuerzo* 8
elderly *anciano/a* 8
elevator *el ascensor* 5
elevator *el elevador* 5
to embrace *abrazar* 8
emerald *la esmeralda* 7
emergency *la emergencia* 1
to end, finish *terminar* 3
to endure, stand *aguantar* 11
enemy *el/la enemigo/a* 3
enough *basta* 8
to enter *entrar* 1
entry *la entrada* 3
erased *borrado/a* 3
erotic *erótico/a* 8
to escape *escapar* 2
to evacuate *evacuar* 5
evidence *la evidencia* 3

to examine   *examinar*   2

examiner   *el/la examinador/a*
10

example   *el ejemplo*   4

excess   *el exceso*   2

excuse me   *con permiso*   PC

Excuse me?   *¿Mande?*   PC

exit   *la salida*   2

exonerated   *exonerado/a*   11

expense   *el gasto*   8

to expire   *vencer*   2

to explode   *estallar*   5

explosive   *el explosivo*   8

eye   *el ojo*   1

face   *la cara*   1

to face   *enfrentar*   11

facing   *frente a*   5

fact   *el hecho*   9

fair   *justo/a*   9

faith   *la fe*   8

to fall   *caer (ig)*   5

to fall in love   *enamorarse*   8

false   *falso/a*   9

to falsify   *falsificar*   9

family related   *familiar*   3

far from   *lejos de*   3

farewell   *la despedida*   11

to fascinate   *fascinar*   11

fat   *gordo/a*   1

father   *el padre*   3

fault, blame   *la culpa*   8

fear   *el miedo*   2

to fear   *temer*   2

February   *febrero*   PC

fee   *la cuota*   2

to feel   *sentirse (ie)*   8

fence   *el alcahuete*   7

fender   *el guardafango*   2

fight   *la pelea*   3

to fight   *luchar*   9

figure   *la figura*   3

file   *el archivo*   12

file, dossier   *el expediente*   10

to find   *encontrar (ue)*   11

finger   *el dedo*   7

fingerprint   *la huella digital*   4

fire   *el incendio, el fuego*   4, 5

fire hydrant   *la boca de incendios*   2

fire truck   *la bomba*   5

firearm   *el arma de fuego (f.)*
3

firefighter   *el bombero*   2

fireplace   *la chimenea*   3

first   *primero*   3

first aid   *los primeros auxilios*
5

fixed   *fijo/a*   10

flame   *la llama*   5

flammable   *inflamable*   5

floor   *el piso*   5

to fly   *volar (ue)*   5

following   *siguiente*   10

food, meal   *la comida*   8

foot   *el pie*   1

forensic   *forénsico/a*   7

forensic   *forense*   10

to forget   *olvidarse de*   7

form   *el formulario*   10

fracture   *la fractura*   5

fraud   *el fraude*   8

free (of charge)   *gratis, gratu-
ito/a*   4, 7

freeway   *la autopista*   2

Friday   *viernes*   PC

friend   *el/la amigo/a*   PC

friendship   *la amistad*   7

front   *delantero/a*   2

frustrated   *frustrado/a*   8

fuck   *chingado**   7

fugitive   *el/la fugitivo/a, el prófu-
go/a*   3, 11

to fulfill   *cumplir*   9

furious   *furioso/a*   8

furniture   *los muebles*   5

game   *el juego, la partida*   9

game, match   *el partido*   9

gang   *la pandilla, la ganga**   3

gang member   *el/la pandillero/a*
3

garage   *el garaje*   3

garden, yard   *el jardín*   3

gasoline   *la gasolina*   5

gear   *la marcha*   2

gesture   *el gesto*   9

to get along well, not well with
llevarse bien/mal con   8

to get angry   *enojarse*   8

to get back   *recuperar*   7

to get dressed   *vestirse (i)*   8

Get in the car.   *Suba al carro.*
2

to get involved with   *meterse*
3

to get married   *casarse*   8

Get out of the car.   *Baje del
carro.*   2

to get up   *levantarse*   8

gift   *el regalo*   11

to give   *dar*   10

glass   *el vidrio*   5

glasses   *los lentes*   1

to go   *ir*   2

to go to bed   *acostarse (ue)*   4

Go to...   *Vaya a...*   3

to go up, climb   *subir*   3

goggles   *el lente protector*   6

gold   *el oro*   1

good afternoon   *buenas tardes*
PC

good evening, good night   *buenas noches*   PC

good morning   *buenos días*
PC

good-bye   *adiós*   PC

goods   *los bienes*   7

governor   *el/la gobernador/a*
7

graffiti   *el grafiti*   3

grand jury   *el jurado investigador*
11

grandchild   *el/la nieto/a*   3

grandparent   *el/la abuelo/a*   3

grass   *el zacate**   4

gratitude   *el agradecimiento*
11

gravity   *la gravedad*   10

gray   *gris*   1

gray haired   *canoso/a*   1

green   *verde*   1

grenade   *la granada*   3

ground floor   *la planta baja*   3

group   *el grupo*   8

guard duty   *la guardia*   10

guide   *la guía*   8

guilt   *la culpabilidad*   10

guilty   *culpable*   9

gun   *el fierro**   3

gym   *el gimnasio*   5

hair   *el pelo, el cabello*   1, 2

hairy   *peludo/a*   1

hall   *el pasillo*   5

hand   *la mano*   1

to hand over   *entregar*   5

handcuffs   *las esposas*   3

handkerchief   *el pañuelo*   3

Hands behind your back!
  ¡Manos en la espalda! 7
Hands up! *¡Manos arriba!* 7
handsome *guapo/a* 1
to hang *ahorcar* 11
to hang out *radicar** 3
to hang up *colgar (ue)* 5
hassle *el lío* 11
hat *el sombrero* 1
hatred *el odio* 7
to have *tener (ie) (g)* 4
to have a drink *tomar una copa* 8
to have just *acabar de + inf.* 7
to have lunch *almorzar (ue)* 4
he *él* PC
head *la cabeza* 1
to head up *encabezar* 10
headlight *el faro* 2
headquarters *la jefatura* 1
health *la salud* 8
healthy *sano/a* 9
to hear *oír (ig) (y)* 3
hearing *la audiencia* 2
heavy *pesado/a* 7
heel *el tacón* 1
heir *el/la heredero/a* 11
hello, hi *hola* PC
helmet *el casco balístico* 9
help *la ayuda, el auxilio* 2, 6
Help! *¡Socorro!* 5
hemorrhage *la hemorragia* 5
here *aquí, acá* 2, 5
Hey. *Oye.* 3
hidden *escondido/a* 3
to hide *esconder, ocultar* 5, 7
highway *la carretera* 2
his, her, your, their *su* 4
to hit *golpear* 8
HIV *VIH* 11
to hold on to something *sujetarse* 5
home *el hogar* 8
home theater *el equipo electrónico* 3
homeboy *el vato** 3
homeless *desamparado/a* 1
hood *el capó, el cofre* 2
hope *la esperanza* 8
horn *la bocina* 2
horrendous *horroroso/a* 11

horse *el caballo* 9
hose *la manguera* 5
hospital *el hospital* 5
hot *caliente* 11
hour *la hora* 1
house *la casa* 1
housing *la vivienda* 8
How are you? (familiar)
  ¿Cómo estás? PC
How are you? (formal) *¿Cómo está Ud.?* PC
How many? *¿Cuántos/as?* 1
How much? *¿Cuánto/a?* 1
How? *¿Cómo?* 1
hug *el abrazo* 3
hunger *el hambre (f.)* 2
hurry *la prisa* 2
to hurry up *darse prisa* 2
to hurt, cause pain *doler (ue)* 11
husband, wife *el/la esposo/a* 2

I *yo* PC
I am *soy* PC
I hope, May Allah grant *Ojalá* 9
identification *la identificación* 3
identity *la identidad* 9
illness *la enfermedad* 9
I'm sorry *Lo siento* PC
immediately *inmediatamente* 1
immigrant *el/la inmigrante* 8
to impede *impedir (i)* 7
to implicate *implicar* 10
imprisonment *el encarcelamiento* 8
improvement *el mejoramiento* 8
in back of *detrás de* 3
in common *en común* 11
in front of *enfrente de* 3
in place of *en vez de* 11
in reality *en realidad* 3
incest *el incesto* 11
inch *la pulgada* 10
to include *incluir (y)* 8
to increase *aumentar* 11
Indian *indio/a* 1
infrared *infrarrojo/a* 7
inheritance *la herencia* 8
injured *lastimado/a* 2

innocence *la inocencia* 10
innocent *inocente* 9
INS *la migra** 3
inside *adentro* 5
to insist (on) *insistir (en)* 2
instability *la inestabilidad* 10
to install *instalar* 2
to insult *insultar* 3
insurance *el seguro* 2
to interrogate *interrogar* 10
interrogation *el interrogatorio* 10
interview *la entrevista* 1
intoxicated *intoxicado/a* 2
to investigate *investigar* 10
investigation *la investigación* 10
invisible *invisible* 3
It's a pleasure. *Es un placer.* PC
It's a shame. *Es una lástima.* 9
It's just that... *Es que...* 2
item *la prenda* 7

jail *la cárcel* 4
jailed *encarcelado/a* 10
jam (traffic) *el atasco* 2
January *enero* PC
jealous *celoso/a* 8
jealousy *los celos* 10
jeans *los vaqueros* 1
jewel *la joya* 3
jewelry store *la joyería* 7
job *el empleo* 8
john *el pepe** 9
judge *el/la juez/a* 2
to judge *enjuiciar* 10
judgement *el juicio* 2
judicial system *el sistema judicial* 10
July *julio* PC
jump *saltar* 11
June *junio* PC
jury *el jurado* 10
justice *la justicia* 10

key *la llave* 5
kidnapping *el secuestro* 4
to kill *matar* 3
to kiss *besar* 8
kitchen *la cocina* 3
knife *el cuchillo, el filero* 7, 3

to know   *saber*   3
to know, be acquainted with
   conocer (zc)   I

laboratory   *el laboratorio*   10
lack   *la falta*   7
to lack   *carecer (zc)*   9
lame   *cojo/a*   I
lane   *el carril*   2
language   *el lenguaje*   8
larceny, burglary   *el hurto*   4
last   *último/a*   I I
last name   *el apellido*   I
last night   *anoche*   7
lasting   *duradero/a*   8
laundering   *el lavado*   9
lawsuit   *la querella*   12
lawyer   *el/la abogado/a*   I
to learn   *aprender*   7
to leave (behind)   *dejar*   4
to leave, go out   *salir (g)*   I
leg   *la pierna*   I
leg, paw, foot (animal)   *la pata*
   8
less   *menos*   4
level   *el nivel*   9
library   *la biblioteca*   5
license   *la licencia*   2
to lie   *mentir (ie)*   4
to lie down   *tumbarse*   8
lieutenant   *el/la teniente*   6
life   *la vida*   3
life imprisonment   *la cadena
   perpetua*   10
light   *la luz*   2
to like   *gustar*   7
likewise   *igualmente*   PC
line   *la línea*   2
to listen (to)   *escuchar*   I
to live   *vivir*   2
living room   *la sala*   3
location   *la ubicación*   7
lock   *la cerradura, el candado*
   7
long   *largo/a*   I
long-term   *a largo plazo*   8
to look at, watch   *mirar*   I
to look for   *buscar*   I
loot, haul   *el botín*   7
to lose   *perder (ie)*   4
loser   *el/la perdedor/a*   9
lost   *perdido/a*   2
lottery   *la lotería*   9

to love   *amar*   8
lover   *el/la amante*   8
luck   *la suerte*   9

machine   *la máquina*   4
machine gun   *la ametralladora*
   3
mail   *el correo*   I
man   *el hombre*   I
March   *marzo*   PC
marihuana   *la mota*, el chivo*,
   la yesca, la vesda*   3, 4
marihuana (cockroach)   *la
   cucaracha**   4
marihuana (grass)   *la yerba**
   4
marvel   *la maravilla*   9
massage   *el masaje*   9
May   *mayo*   PC
maybe   *quizás*   3
mayor   *el/la alcalde/sa*   9
to measure   *medir (i)*   4
mediator   *el/la mediador/a*   8
medical   *médico/a*   10
medication   *el medicamento*   8
medium   *mediano/a*   I
meeting   *la reunión*   I
member   *el/la miembro*   3
merchandise   *la mercancía*   4
mercy   *la piedad*   7
message   *el mensaje, el recado*
   5, 10
metal detector   *el detector de
   metales*   3
methamphetamine   *la metanfetamina*   I I
midnight   *la medianoche*   I
mirror   *el espejo*   3
misdemeanor   *la falta*   4
mistreatment   *el maltrato*   7
modus operandi (m.o.)   *el
   modo de proceder*   I I
Monday   *lunes*   PC
money   *el dinero*   I
money (silver)   *la plata**   3
money (wool)   *la lana**   3
monitoring   *el monitoreo*   7
more   *más*   I
more or less   *más o menos*
   PC
morning   *la mañana*   I
mortified   *mortificado/a*   I I
mother   *la madre*   PC

motive   *el motivo*   10
motorcycle   *la moto(cicleta)*   2
mountain   *el monte*   7
moustache   *el bigote*   I
mouth   *la boca*   2
to move   *mover (ue)*   5
movement   *el movimiento*   I
murder   *el homicidio, el asesinato*   4, 10
to murder   *asesinar*   10
my   *mi*   4
My God!   *¡Dios mío!*   3
My name is...   *Me llamo...*   PC

name   *el nombre*   I
near   *cerca de*   3
neck   *el cuello*   5
to need   *necesitar*   2
neglect   *la negligencia*   8
neglected   *descuidado/a*   8
neighbor   *el/la vecino/a*   7
neighborhood   *el barrio*   I
neighborhood   *vecinal*   7
neither   *tampoco*   5
never   *nunca*   5
news   *las noticias*   I
news program   *el noticiero*
   I I
newspaper   *el periódico*   2
next   *próximo/a*   5
next to   *al lado de*   3
nickname   *el apodo, el
   sobrenombre*   I
night stick   *el bastón*   9
nobody   *nadie*   5
noise   *el ruido*   3
none   *ningún/una/a*   5
noon   *el mediodía*   I
nose   *la nariz*   I
not well   *mal*   PC
not withstanding   *no obstante*
   10
note   *la nota*   I I
nothing   *nada*   4
notice   *el aviso*   2
November   *noviembre*   PC
now   *ahora*   I
nurse   *el/la enfermero/a*   2

to observe   *observar*   2
to obtain   *obtener (g) (ie)*   8
to occur   *ocurrir*   8
October   *octubre*   PC

of course (not)   *claro (que sí/no)*   1
of, from   *de*   1
officer   *el/la oficial*   PC
old   *viejo/a*   1
older, greater   *mayor*   4
on account of   *a causa de*   11
on foot   *a pie*   7
on skates   *en patines*   7
on the dot   *en punto*   1
on top of, above   *encima de*   3
On your knees!   *¡De rodillas!*   7
one way   *sentido único*   2
only   *sólo, solamente*   2
open   *abierto/a*   3
to open   *abrir*   4
orchard   *el huerto*   8
order   *la orden*   8
organizational chart   *el organigrama*   11
to ought to, should   *deber*   5
our   *nuestro/a*   4
outside   *afuera, fuera*   5, 8
overdose   *la sobredosis*   4
own   *propio/a*   9

pain   *el dolor*   5
panic   *el pánico*   5
pants   *los pantalones*   1
panty hose   *las medias*   1
paper   *el papel*   2
paramedic   *el/la paramédico*   5
pardon me   *perdón, disculpe*   PC
park   *el parque*   2
parked   *estacionado/a*   7
parking   *el estacionamiento*   2
parking meter   *el parquímetro*   1
parole   *la libertad condicional*   9
party   *la fiesta*   1
to pass away   *fallecer (zc)*   8
to pass, spend (time)   *pasar*   4
passenger   *el/la pasajero/a*   2
passport   *el pasaporte*   9
patrol   *la patrulla*   7
patrol car   *la patrullera*   1
pawn shop   *la casa de empeño*   7
to pay attention   *prestar atención*   11

payment   *el pago*   9
peace   *la paz*   7
pedestrian   *el/la peatón/ona*   2
pedophile   *el/la pedófilo/a*   11
pen   *la pluma*   2
penalty   *la pena*   9
percentage   *el porcentaje*   8
perhaps   *tal vez*   1
permission   *el permiso*   10
to permit   *permitir*   9
person   *la persona*   1
person of mixed race   *el/la cholo/a**   3
pervert   *el/la pervertido/a*   11
petty thief, pickpocket   *el/la ratero/a*   7
photograph   *la foto(grafía)*   4
photographer   *el/la fotógrafo/a*   10
pill   *la pastilla, la píldora*   5, 11
pimp   *el chulo*, el proxeneta*   9
pistol   *la pistola*   3
place   *el lugar, el sitio*   3, 10
to place   *colocar*   5
placement   *la colocación*   9
planning   *la planificación*   8
to plant   *plantar*   10
to play (games, sports)   *jugar (ue)*   4
to play (music), to touch   *tocar*   1
player   *el/la jugador/a*   3
please   *por favor*   PC
pleased/nice to meet you   *mucho gusto*   PC
pocket   *el bolsillo*   8
to poison   *envenenar*   11
police department   *la policía*   1
police officer   *el/la (mujer) policía*   1
police record   *la ficha policial*   4
police station   *la comisaría*   1
pool   *el billar*   9
poor   *pobre*   1
poor thing   *el/la pobrecito/a*   5
population   *la población*   8
pornography   *la pornografía*   11
position   *el puesto*   9
posthumous   *póstumo/a*   11
pound   *la libra*   1

power   *el poder*   8
powerful   *poderoso/a*   9
precious   *precioso/a*   7
predator   *el/la pederasta, el/la depredador/a*   11
premeditated   *premeditado/a*   4
to prepare   *preparar*   2
pressure   *la presión*   5
pretty   *bonito/a*   1
previous   *previo/a*   4
price   *el precio*   4
pride   *el orgullo*   7
printer   *la impresora*   7
prisoner   *el/la prisionero/a, el/la preso/a*   3, 4
prize   *el premio*   9
problem   *el problema*   2
to produce   *producir (zc)*   3
to prohibit   *prohibir*   9
to promise   *prometer*   9
promise   *la promesa*   9
to pronounce, pass (sentence)   *dictar*   10
property   *la propiedad*   7
proposition   *el propósito*   4
to prostitute   *la prostituta*   9
protect   *proteger*   5
protection   *la protección*   8
to protest   *protestar*   8
to prove   *comprobar (ue)*   10
provided   *proporcionado/a*   7
provocative   *provocativo/a*   8
prowler   *el/la merodeador/a*   7
psychologist   *el/la psicólogo/a*   9
public   *el público*   10
pulse   *el pulso*   5
punctured   *pinchado/a (ponchado/a*)*   2
to punish   *castigar*   9
purse, bag   *la bolsa*   1
to pursue   *perseguir (i)*   8
to put out   *apagar*   5
to put, place   *poner (g)*   3
Put...   *Ponga...*   3

quality   *la calidad*   4
question   *la pregunta*   3
quiet   *callado/a*   9

race   *la carrera*   9
race (ethnicity)   *la raza*   9

racial   *racial*   7
railroad   *el ferrocarril*   2
rain   *la lluvia*   5
rape   *la violación sexual*   4
to rape   *violar*   8
rate   *la tasa*   8
to read   *leer*   1
really   *de veras*   8
rearview mirror   *el (espejo)*
   retrovisor   2
reason   *la razón*   2
reasonable   *razonable*   10
to receive   *recibir*   2
to recognize   *reconocer (zc)*   8
to recommend   *recomendar (ie)*
   3
to record   *grabar*   11
recording   *la grabación*   7
red   *rojo/a*   1
red-headed   *pelirrojo/a*   1
refuge   *el refugio*   8
regarding   *en cuanto a*   8
registration   *el registro*   2
to relax   *relajarse*   11
to remain   *permanecer (zc)*   5
remains   *los restos*   11
to remember   *recordar (ue)*   1
remorse   *el remordimiento*   9
removable   *desmontable*   10
Remove...   *Quítese...*   2
rent   *el alquiler*   9
to repeat   *repetir (i)*   4
report   *el reporte*   10
reporter   *el/la reportero/a*   11
to require   *exigir (j)*   9
rescue   *el rescate*   5
to rescue   *rescatar*   5
resolved   *resuelto/a*   7
respect   *el respeto*   7
to rest   *descansar*   2
result   *el resultado*   10
retirement years   *la tercera*
   edad   8
to return   *regresar, volver (ue)*
   1, 4
to return something   *devolver*
   (ue)   7
reward   *la recompensa*   7
rich   *rico/a*   1
ridiculous   *ridículo/a*   9
rifle   *el rifle*   10
right   *el derecho*   8
right now   *ahorita*   1

ring   *el anillo*   7
riot   *el motín*   12
risk   *el riesgo*   9
rival   *el/la rival*   3
road   *el camino*   2
robbery   *el robo*   4
roof, ceiling   *el techo*   2
room   *el cuarto, la habitación*
   5
rooster   *el gallo*   8
routine   *la rutina*   4
ruby   *el rubí*   7
to ruin   *arruinar*   8
rule   *la regla*   9
ruling   *el fallo*   10
to run   *correr*   2

sad   *triste*   2
safe   *seguro/a*   11
salary   *el sueldo*   11
sale   *la venta*   7
salesperson   *el/la vendedor/a*
   3
same   *mismo/a*   7
sandals   *las sandalias*   1
sapphire   *el zafiro*   7
sargeant   *el/la sargento*   4
Saturday   *sábado*   PC
to save   *salvar*   5
to say, tell   *decir (i) (g)*   4
scale   *la balanza*   4
scar   *la cicatriz*   1
scene   *la escena*   3
school   *la escuela*   2
school   *escolar*   11
to score (drugs)   *pillar**   4
to search   *registrar*   4
search   *la búsqueda, el registro*
   10
search warrant   *la orden de reg-*
   istro   10
seat   *el asiento*   2
seat belt   *el cinturón de seguri-*
   dad   2
secret   *secreto/a*   3
secretary   *el/la secretario/a*   PC
secure, safe   *seguro/a*   7
security   *la seguridad*   3
security system   *el sistema de*
   seguridad   3
to see   *ver*   1
see you later   *hasta luego*   PC
to seem   *parecer (zc)*   3

self esteem   *la autoestima*   9
to sell   *vender*   2
semi-automatic   *semiautomáti-*
   co/a   10
to send   *mandar*   1
sentence   *la condena*   10
September   *septiembre*   PC
serious   *serio/a*   2
to serve   *servir (i)*   4
sex   *el sexo*   11
to shake   *sacudir*   5
shaking   *la sacudida*   5
sharpened   *afilado/a*   3
she   *ella*   PC
shelter   *el albergue*   8
sheriff, bailiff   *el alguacil*   4
shirt   *la camisa*   1
shoe   *el zapato*   1
to shoot   *fusilar*   9
shooter   *el tirador*   5
shooting   *el tiroteo*   4
shoplifting, theft   *la ratería*   4
short (height)   *bajo/a*   1
short (length)   *corto/a*   1
shot   *el disparo, el tiro*   3, 9
shotgun   *la escopeta*   10
shoulder   *el hombro*   1
to shout   *gritar*   5
Show your hands!   *¡Saque las*
   manos!   7
to show, teach   *enseñar*   3
sick   *enfermo/a*   2
sidewalk   *la acera*   7
sign   *el letrero*   5
to sign   *firmar*   8
sign, signal   *la seña*   3
signal   *la señal*   8
to simulate   *simular*   10
siren   *la sirena*   2
to sit down   *sentarse (ie)*   8
size   *el tamaño*   8
sketch   *el dibujo*   10
skinny   *flaco/a*   1
skirt   *la falda*   1
slang   *la jerga*   4
to sleep   *dormir (ue)*   3
sleep, dream   *el sueño*   2
slippers   *las pantuflas*   1
slot machine   *el tragamonedas*
   9
slow   *despacio*   7
small   *pequeño/a, chico/a*   1, 2
smell   *el olor*   5

to smell *oler (ue)* 5

smile *la sonrisa* 11

to smile *sonreír (i)* 11

to smoke *fumar* 2

smoke *el humo* 4

sniper *el/la francotirador/a* 10

snow *la nieve* 5

sober *sobrio/a* 2

Social Security *Seguro Social* 9

socks *los calcetines* 1

sodomy *la sodomía* 11

soft, smooth *suave* 7

solid *sólido/a* 10

some *algún/uno/a* 5

somebody *alguien* 5

something *algo* 1

son/daughter *el/la hijo/a* 3

soon *pronto* 3

so-so *regular* PC

sound *el sonido* 7

southwest *suroeste* 9

spare tire *la llanta de repuesto* 2

speed *la velocidad* 2

spokesperson *el/la vocero/a* 11

sporting *deportivo/a* 9

Spread your legs. *Separe los pies.* 7

to spy *espiar* 8

to stab *apuñalar* 11

stairs *la escalera* 3

to stalk *acosar, acechar* 8

stalker *el/la acosador/a* 8

stalking *el acoso* 8

star *la estrella* 2

to start (motor) *arrancar* 7

stash *la estofa** 4

state *el estado* 1

station *la estación* 1

station wagon, van *la camioneta* 1

statistics *las estadísticas* 8

stature *la estatura* 1

to stay, remain *quedarse* 8

steering wheel *el volante* 2

stepbrother/sister *el/la hermanastro/a* 3

stepchild *el/la hijastro/a* 3

stepfather *el padrastro* 3

stepmother *la madrastra* 3

stereo *el estéreo* 1

stick *el palo* 9

sting *la redada* 9

stone *la piedra* 7

stool pigeon *la rata** 3

stop *alto* 2

to stop *parar* 7

stop (bus) *la parada* 2

Stop the car. *Pare el carro.* 2

Stop the motor. *Apague el motor.* 2

stoplight *el semáforo* 2

stopped *detenido/a* 2

store *la tienda* 1

to store *almacenar* 11

straight (hair) *lacio/a, liso/a* 1

straight *recto/a, derecho* 2

Straight ahead. *Siga derecho.* 3

strange *extraño/a, raro/a* 9, 11

to strangle *estrangular* 10

street *la calle* 1

streetlight *el farol* 7

stretcher *la camilla* 5

to strike *pegar* 8

strong *fuerte* 1

student *el/la estudiante* 4

to succeed *lograr* 7

success *el éxito* 7

such *tal* 8

suddenly *de repente* 11

to suffer *sufrir* 2

suffering *el sufrimiento* 8

to suggest *sugerir (ie)* 9

suggestion *la sugerencia* 7

suicide *el suicidio* 10

suit *el traje* 1

sun *solar* 2

Sunday *domingo* PC

support *el apoyo* 8

to suppose *suponer (g)* 7

Sure. *Simón.** 3

surprise *la sorpresa* 7

surprising *sorprendente* 9

surveillance *la vigilancia* 3

survival *la supervivencia* 5

suspect *el/la sospechoso/a* 1

to suspect *sospechar* 5

SUV *el todo-terreno* 2

sweater *el suéter* 1

sweatshirt *la sudadera* 1

sweetheart *el/la novio/a* 8

switchblade *la navaja** 3

table *la mesa* 5

to take (out) *sacar* 4

to take charge of *encargarse de* 7

to take, drink *tomar* 2

to talk *conversar* 1

Talk to me. *Hábleme.* 3

to talk, speak *hablar* 2

tall *alto/a* 1

Taser stun gun *el paralizador Taser* 9

tattoo *el tatuaje* 1

tax *el impuesto* 8

teacher *el/la maestro/a* 3

team *el equipo* 1

Tell me. *Dígame.* 3

temperature *la temperatura* 5

to tempt *tentar (ie)* 11

term *el plazo* 9

territory *el territorio* 3

test *la prueba* 9

thank you *gracias* PC

that, than *que* 4

to the left *a la izquierda* 3

to the right *a la derecha* 3

theater *el cine* 1

theme *el tema* 7

then *entonces* 3

therapist *el/la terapeuta* 11

there *allí* 2

there is, are *hay* 1

they *ellos/as* PC

thief *el/la ladrón/ona* 3

thing *la cosa* 3

to think, plan *pensar (ie)* 4

thirst *la sed* 2

threat *la amenaza* 3

to threaten *amenazar* 8

Throw the keys here. *Tire las llaves acá.* 7

Thursday *jueves* PC

ticket, fine *la multa (el tiquete*)* 1

tie *la corbata* 1

tied *atado/a* 8

time, occasion *la vez* 8

tire *la llanta, la goma, el neumático* 2

tired *cansado/a* 2

today *hoy* 10

together *juntos/as* 2

to tolerate *tolerar* 7

toll *el peaje* 2
tomorrow *mañana* 1
too much *demasiado* 2
too, also *también* 2
tool *la herramienta* 2
to torment *atormentar* 9
to tow *remolcar* 2
tow truck *la grúa* 2
towel *la toalla* 5
to track, trace *rastrear* 7
traffic *el tráfico, el tránsito* 1
tragedy *la tragedia* 11
to train *entrenar* 7
tranquilizer *el tranquilizante* 11
transferred *traslado/a* 11
to translate *traducir (zc)* 3
trash *la basura* 1
trash can *el basurero* 7
tree *el árbol* 1
to tremble *estremecer* 5
triumph *el triunfo* 7
truck *el camión, la troca/el troque* * 1, 2
true *verdadero/a* 3
True? Right? *¿Verdad?* 1
trunk *el maletero, la cajuela, el baúl* 2
T-shirt *la camiseta, la playera* 1
Tuesday *martes* PC
to turn around *dar vuelta* 2
Turn around. *Voltéese.* 7
to turn on *prender* 5
turn signal *el intermitente* 2
Turn... *Doble...* 3

under *debajo de* 3
undercover *encubierto/a* 3
to understand *entender (ie)* 3
underwear (boxers) *los chonis* 1
unforgettable *inolvidable* 8
unharmed *salvo/a* 9
uniform *el uniforme* 3
uninflated, flat *desinflado/a* 2
united *unido/a* 7
unpleasant *antipático/a* 1
up, above *arriba* 3

uppers *las arribas*, las pepas** 4
useful *útil* 5

value *el valor* 7
various, several *varios/as* 7
vehicle *el vehículo* 7
vein *la vena* 11
verdict *el veredicto* 10
very *muy* PC
victim *la víctima* 1
violation *la infracción* 2
violent *violento/a* 2
to visit *visitar* 2
voice *la voz* 5
to wait for, to hope *esperar* 2
to wake up *despertarse (ie)* 8
to walk *caminar* 2

wall *la pared* 3
wallet *la cartera* 3
to want *querer (ie)* 4
war *la guerra* 3
wardrobe *el armario* 5
warning *la advertencia* 2
to wash *lavarse* 8
to watch *vigilar* 7
watch, clock *el reloj* 1
water *el agua (f.)* 2
we *nosotros/as* PC
to wear, to carry *llevar* 1
Wednesday *miércoles* PC
week *la semana* PC
to weigh *pesar* 4
weight *el peso* 1
welcome *bienvenidos* PC
well *bien* PC
well *pues* 3
well, pool *el pozo* 9
What day is today? *¿Qué día es hoy?* PC
What is your name? (familiar) *¿Cómo te llamas?* PC
What is your name? (formal) *¿Cómo se llama Ud.?* PC
What? *¿Qué?* 1
What happened? *¿Qué hubo?* *¿Qué pasó?* 3
What's today's date? *¿Cuál es la fecha de hoy?* PC

What's today's date? *¿Qué fecha es hoy?* PC
What's up? *¿Qué onda?* * 3
wheel *la rueda* 2
When? *¿Cuándo?* 1
Where to? *¿Adónde?* 2
Where? *¿Dónde?* 1
Which (one/s)? *¿Cuál/es?* 1
while *mientras* 3
whistle blower *el/la soplón/soplona* 3
white *blanco/a* 1
Who? *¿Quién/es?* 1
whore *la puta*, la ramera** 8, 9
Why? *¿Por qué?* 1
wind *el viento* 5
window *la ventana* 3
windshield *el parabrisas* 2
windshield wiper *el limpia-parabrisas* 2
winner *el/la ganador/a* 9
wire *el alambre* 4
within *dentro de* 5
witness *el testigo* 1
woman *la mujer* 1
word *la palabra* 7
work *el trabajo* 1
worried *preocupado/a* 2
worse *peor* 4
wound *la herida* 5
wounded *herido/a* 2
to write *escribir* 1

year *el año* 2
yellow *amarillo/a* 1
yes *sí* 1
yesterday *ayer* 7
yet, still *todavía* 3
Yield *Ceda el paso* 2
you (familiar) *tú* PC
you (formal) *usted* PC
you (plural) *ustedes* PC
you're welcome *de nada* PC
you're welcome *no hay de qué* PC
young *joven* 1
younger *menor* 2
your (familiar) *tu* 4

Index

a
  personal, 170
abuse
  elder abuse, 200
  sexual abuse, 265, 273
el abuso
  de ancianos, 200
  de niños, 265, 269
  sexual, 273
acabar de + infinitivo, 174
accidents, 127
los accidentes, 127
el acoso, 205
adjectives
  agreement of, 26
  placement of, 26
  plural of, 26
  possessive, 105
  with **estar,** 66
  with **ser,** 25
alphabet, 4
articles
  definite, 30
  indefinite, 30
automobiles
  car parts, 46, 54
  car security and theft, 171, 173
los automóviles
  las partes, 46, 54
  la seguridad y el robo, 171, 173
el barrio, 17, 75
booking, 112
-cer and **-cir**
  present indicative, 92
  preterite indicative, 253
el calendario
  los días, 8
  los meses, 10
  la fecha, 11
la carretera, 46
la casa
  house vocabulary, 75
commands, 52
community policing, 167
comparisons, 114, 120
conocer,
  present indicative, 92
  vs. **saber,** 92
courtesy expressions, 13
dates (calendar), 11
date rape, 273

days of the week, 8
el defensor público, 250
los desastres, 137
direct objects, 207
disasters, 137
domestic violence, 192, 196
las drogas, 102-104
  en la calle, 102-104
drug traffic, 102-104
las emergencias, 127, 132, 137, 142
emergencies, 127, 132, 137, 142
equipment for law enforcement, 216
el equipo para la policía, 216
estar
  formal commands, 135
  present indicative, 65
  present subjunctive, 219
  preterite indicative, 249
  vs. **ser,** 82
  with adjectives, 66
  with present progressive, 78
la evidencia forense, 241
el examinador médico, 241
la familia, 80
  family vocabulary, 80
la ficha policial, 112
fire, 142
el fiscal, 250
forensic evidence, 241
gambling, 226
las gangas, 80, 85
gangs, 80, 85
graffiti, 85
el grafiti, 85
greetings, 3
gustar, 178
hacer
  formal commands, 130
  present indicative, 92
  preterite indicative, 249
  to indicate "ago", 174
hay 7
  imperfect indicative, 267
  in narration, 275
  irregular verbs, 268
  regular verbs, 267
  uses of, 271
  vs. preterite, 279
homicide, 242

el homicidio, 242
los incendios, 142
indirect object, 178
interrogative words, 36
introductions, 3
ir,
  formal command, 135
  imperfect indicative, 267
  ir a + infinitive to express the future, 88
  present subjunctive, 219
  preterite indicative, 88
jewelry types, 180
las joyas, 180
los juegos ilegales, 226
jugar,
  present indicative, 110
medical examiner, 241
months, 10
los narcotraficantes, 102-104
negative expressions, 140
Neighborhood Watch, 167
numbers
  cardinal, 4-7
  0-100, 4-7
  101-millions, 183
  ordinal, 184
oír
  present indicative, 92
  preterite indicative, 244
las pandillas, 80, 85
pedir,
  present indicative, 110
  preterite indicative, 253
personal **a,** 170
personal information, 19
poder
  present indicative, 110
  preterite indicative, 249
la policía de la comunidad, 167
poner
  present indicative, 92
  preterite indicative, 249
por qué, 36
preferir
  present indicative, 110
  preterite indicative, 253
present indicative tense,
  of **-ar** verbs, 55
  of **-er, -ir** verbs, 60

of **e** → **i** stem-changing verbs, 110
of **e** → **ie** stem-changing verbs, 110
of **o** → **ue** stem-changing verbs, 110
of **u** → **ue** stem-changing verbs, 110
present participle
  formation of, 78
  irregular form, 78
present progressive, 78
preterite indicative,
  in narration, 257
  irregular verbs, 249, 253
  special meanings of, 272
  spelling changes, 244
  stem-changing verbs, 253
  vs. imperfect, 279
pronouns
  direct object, 207
  indirect object, 178
  reflexive, 194
  subject, 12
  with commands, 135
prosecutor, 250
la prostitución, 221
prostitution, 221
public defender, 250
qué, 36
querer
  present indicative, 110
  preterite indicative, 249
questions, 36
reciprocal, 198

reflexive verbs
  constructions, 194
  pronouns, 194
  verbs, 194
saber
  formal command, 135
  present indicative, 92
  present subjunctive, 219
  preterite indicative, 249
  vs. **conocer,** 92
salir
  present indicative, 92
los saludos, 3
se
  impersonal, 170
  passive voice, 170
  reflexive pronoun, 194
security, 167
la seguridad
  en la vecindad, 167
  en la casa, 75
ser
  formal command, 135
  imperfect indicative, 268
  present indicative, 25
  present subjunctive, 219
  preterite indicative, 249
  vs. **estar,** 82
  with adjectives, 25
stalking, 205
stem-changing verbs
  present indicative, 110
  preterite indicative, 249
subjunctive
  expressions with, 224–234
  general concept, 219

present tense of irregular verbs, 219
present tense of regular verbs, 219
suicide, 277
el suicidio, 277
superlatives, 120
surveillance, 75, 167
tener
  idiomatic expressions with, 66
  present indicative, 66
  preterite indicative, 249
tener que + infinitive, 66
los testigos, 22, 24, 26
traer
  present indicative, 92
  preterite indicative, 253
traffic tickets, 46, 52, 53, 57, 62
el tráfico y las infracciones, 46, 52, 53, 57, 62
venir
  present indicative, 92
  preterite indicative, 253
ver
  present indicative, 60
  witness descriptions, 22, 24, 26
la vigilancia, 75
la vigilancia vecindaria, 167
la violación (por acompañante), 273
la violencia doméstica, 192, 196

In your time in the Marines,